75 Readings

An Anthology

75 Readings

An Anthology

Seventh Edition

McGraw-Hill College

Boston   Burr Ridge, IL   Dubuque, IA   Madison, WI   New York
San Francisco   St. Louis   Bangkok   Bogotá   Caracas   Lisbon
London   Madrid   Mexico City   Milan   New Delhi   Seoul
Singapore   Sydney   Taipei   Toronto

McGraw-Hill College

A Division of The McGraw-Hill Companies

75 Readings: An Anthology

This book is printed on acid-free paper.

1 2 3 4 5 7 8 9 0 DOC/DOC 9 3 2 1 0 9 8

ISBN 0-07-092067-2

Editorial director: *Philip Butcher*
Sponsoring editor: *Tim Julet*
Editorial assistant: *Alan Joyce*
Marketing manager: *Lesley Denton*
Senior project manager: *Jean Lou Hess*
Production associate: *Debra R. Benson*
Cover designer: *James E. Shaw*
Supplement coordinator: *Becky Szura*
Compositor: *Carlisle Composition, Ltd.*
Typeface: *10/12 Palatino*
Printer: *R. R. Donnelley & Sons Company*

Library of Congress Cataloging–in–Publication Data

75 readings : an anthology / [edited by Santi Buscemi , Charlotte
    Smith]. --7th ed.
        p.   cm.
    Includes index.
    ISBN 0-07-092067-2
    1. College readers.   2. English language--Rhetoric.   I. Buscemi,
Santi V.   II. Smith, Charlotte.
PE1417.A13   1999   98-26943
808'.0427--dc21

http://www.mhhe.com

About the Authors

SANTI BUSCEMI teaches reading and writing and chairs the English Department at Middlesex County College in Edison, New Jersey.

CHARLOTTE SMITH teaches English composition and technical writing at Adirondack Community College in Queensbury, New York.

v

Preface

75 Readings: An Anthology is designed to introduce students to a range of traditional and contemporary essays, as well as to topical pieces by international and ethnically diverse writers. The primary aim of the book is to expose students to a variety of rhetorical strategies, writing styles, and topics, while retaining maximum flexibility for the instructor. As with earlier editions, we have sought essays that provide good structural models for rhetorical techniques and that raise complex questions about current and enduring issues. Thus, the essays need not be used merely to illustrate form. Because there is no pedagogical apparatus in the text itself to direct such use (apparatus is provided in an instructor's manual), *75 Readings* can be used with a variety of teaching approaches.

The seventh edition includes ten new readings. This time, we decided to pay greatest attention to Chapter 10, which has been re-named Argument and Persuasion and which contains selections of both of these types of writing listed under appropriate sub-headings. New in this chapter are Mike Wallace's "The Press Needs a National Monitor," with a response by Don Hewitt; Debra Dickerson's "Who Shot Johnny?"; Richard Rodriguez's "Bilingual Education: Outdated and Unrealistic"; and Ann N. Martin's "Food Pets Die For." Also new in this chapter is "Next Time You Are Sick, You'd Better Go To The Vet . . . ," one of the few selections with group authorship ever to have appeared in *75 Readings*.

Other new selections include James Weldon Johnson's "Travelling South" and Naton Leslie's "Don't Get Comfortable" (Chapter 1); Donald Hall's "Four Types of Reading" (Chapter 5); and Annie Dillard's "Fecundity" (Chapter 6).

An instructor's manual, prepared by Santi V. Buscemi of Middlesex County College, Edison, New Jersey, and Charlotte Smith of Adirondack Community College, Queensbury, New York, provides brief author biographies, discussion questions, and journal and paper assignments for each essay in the anthology.

Acknowledgments

Special thanks are due to those instructors who reviewed the anthology and offered their suggestions for the seventh edition: Jan Agard, Muskegon Community College; Marge Bartelt, Edison Community College; Richard Fabrizio, Pace University; Jerome Garger, Lane Community College; Judy Hawkins, Crafton Hills College; Pamela Laskin, City College of New York; Robert Perrin, Indiana State University; Terry Scambray, Fresno City College; Grant Strickland, Monroe County Community College; Mary Tyler, Muskegon Community College; and Kathy White, Pima Community College.

In addition, we wish to thank Tim Julet and Alan Joyce of McGraw-Hill.

Santi V. Buscemi
Charlotte Smith

Contents

Chapter 3
PROCESS   93

Chapter 4
DEFINITION   131

Power & Politics —
Description
of place

Chapter 8
CAUSE AND EFFECT   279

Chapter 9 *likeness*
ANALOGY   321

Chapter 10
ARGUMENT AND PERSUASION   353

Argument

Persuasion

Thematic
Contents

Growing Up, Growing Old

Power and Politics

The Media and the Arts

Science and Technology

Health and Medicine

Use and Abuse of Language

Chapter

Narration

A Hanging

George Orwell

It was in Burma, a sodden morning of the rains. A sickly light, like   1
yellow tinfoil, was slanting over the high walls into the jail yard.
We were waiting outside the condemned cells, a row of sheds
fronted with double bars, like small animal cages. Each cell measured about ten feet by ten and was quite bare within except for a
plank bed and a pot of drinking water. In some of them brown
silent men were squatting at the inner bars, with their blankets
draped round them. These were the condemned men, due to be
hanged within the next week or two.

One prisoner had been brought out of his cell. He was a   2
Hindu, a puny wisp of a man, with a shaven head and vague liquid eyes. He had a thick, sprouting moustache, absurdly too big
for his body, rather like the moustache of a comic man in the
films. Six tall Indian warders were guarding him and getting
him ready for the gallows. Two of them stood by with rifles
and fixed bayonets, while the others handcuffed him, passed a
chain through his handcuffs and fixed it to their belts, and
lashed his arms tight to his sides. They crowded very close
about him, with their hands always on him in a careful, caress-
ing grip, as though all the while feeling him to make sure he was
there. It was like men handling a fish which is still alive and may
jump back into the water. But he stood quite unresisting, yielding his arms limply to the ropes, as though he hardly noticed
what was happening.

3   Eight o'clock struck and a bugle call, desolately thin in the wet air, floated from the distant barracks. The superintendent of the jail, who was standing apart from the rest of us, moodily prodding the gravel with his stick, raised his head at the sound. He was an army doctor, with a grey toothbrush moustache and a gruff voice. "For God's sake hurry up, Francis," he said irritably. "The man ought to have been dead by this time. Aren't you ready yet?"

4   Francis, the head jailer, a fat Dravidian in a white drill suit and gold spectacles, waved his black hand. "Yes sir, yes sir," he bubbled. "All iss satisfactorily prepared. The hangman iss waiting. We shall proceed."

5   "Well, quick march, then. The prisoners can't get their breakfast till this job's over."

6   We set out for the gallows. Two warders marched on either side of the prisoner, with their rifles at the slope; two others marched close against him, gripping him by arm and shoulder, as though at once pushing and supporting him. The rest of us, magistrates and the like, followed behind. Suddenly, when we had gone ten yards, the procession stopped short without any order or warning. A dreadful thing had happened—a dog, come goodness knows whence, had appeared in the yard. It came bounding among us with a loud volley of barks, and leapt round us wagging its whole body, wild with glee at finding so many human beings together. It was a large woolly dog, half Airedale, half pariah. For a moment it pranced round us, and then, before anyone could stop it, it had made a dash for the prisoner, and jumping up tried to lick his face. Everyone stood aghast, too taken aback even to grab at the dog.

7   "Who let that bloody brute in here?" said the superintendent angrily. "Catch it, someone!"

8   A warder, detached from the escort, charged clumsily after the dog, but it danced and gambolled just out of his reach, taking everything as part of the game. A young Eurasian jailer picked up a handful of gravel and tried to stone the dog away, but it dodged the stones and came after us again. Its yaps echoed from the jail walls. The prisoner, in the grasp of the two warders, looked on incuriously, as though this was another for-

African + white ✓

mality of the hanging. It was several minutes before someone managed to catch the dog. Then we put my handkerchief through its collar and moved off once more, with the dog still straining and whimpering.

It was about forty yards to the gallows. I watched the bare brown back of the prisoner marching in front of me. He walked clumsily with his bound arms, but quite steadily, with that bobbing gait of the Indian who never straightens his knees. At each step his muscles slid neatly into place, the lock of hair on his scalp danced up and down, his feet printed themselves on the wet gravel. And once, in spite of the men who gripped him by each shoulder, he stepped slightly aside to avoid a puddle on the path.

still have a purpose

It is curious, but till that moment I had never realised what it means to destroy a healthy, conscious man. When I saw the prisoner step aside to avoid the puddle, I saw the mystery, the unspeakable wrongness, of cutting a life short when it is in full tide. This man was not dying, he was alive just as we were alive. All the organs of his body were working—bowels digesting food, skin renewing itself, nails growing, tissues forming—all toiling away in solemn foolery. His nails would still be growing when he stood on the drop, when he was falling through the air with a tenth of a second to live. His eyes saw the yellow gravel and the grey walls, and his brain still remembered, foresaw, reasoned—reasoned even about puddles. He and we were a party of men walking together, seeing, hearing, feeling, understanding the same world; and in two minutes, with a sudden snap, one of us would be gone—one mind less, one world less.

The gallows stood in a small yard, separate from the main grounds of the prison, and overgrown with tall prickly weeds. It was a brick erection like three sides of a shed, with planking on top, and above that two beams and a crossbar with the rope dangling. The hangman, a grey-haired convict in the white uniform of the prison, was waiting beside his machine. He greeted us with a servile crouch as we entered. At a word from Francis the two warders, gripping the prisoner more closely than ever, half led, half pushed him to the gallows and helped him clumsily up the ladder. Then the hangman climbed up and fixed the rope round the prisoner's neck.

instigate

12   We stood waiting, five yards away. The warders had formed in a rough circle round the gallows. And then, when the noose was fixed, the prisoner began crying out on his god. It was a high, re-iterated cry of "Ram! Ram! Ram! Ram!", not urgent and fearful like a prayer or a cry for help, but steady, rhythmical, almost like the tolling of a bell. The dog answered the sound with a whine. The hangman, still standing on the gallows, produced a small cotton bag like a flour bag and drew it down over the prisoner's face. But the sound, muffled by the cloth, still persisted, over and over again: "Ram! Ram! Ram! Ram! Ram!"

13   The hangman climbed down and stood ready, holding the lever. Minutes seemed to pass. The steady, muffled crying from the prisoner went on and on, "Ram! Ram! Ram!" never faltering for an instant. The superintendent, his head on his chest, was slowly poking the ground with his stick; perhaps he was counting the cries, allowing the prisoner a fixed number—fifty, perhaps, or a hundred. Everyone had changed colour. The Indians had gone grey like bad coffee, and one or two of the bayonets were wavering. We looked at the lashed, hooded man on the drop, and listened to his cries— each cry another second of life; the same thought was in all our minds: oh, kill him quickly, get it over, stop that abominable noise!

14   Suddenly the superintendent made up his mind. Throwing up his head he made a swift motion with his stick. "Chalo!" he shouted almost fiercely.

let's go

15   There was a clanking noise, and then dead silence. The prisoner had vanished, and the rope was twisting on itself. I let go of the dog, and it galloped immediately to the back of the gallows; but when it got there it stopped short, barked, and then retreated into a corner of the yard, where it stood among the weeds, looking timorously out at us. We went round the gallows to inspect the prisoner's body. He was dangling with his toes pointed straight downwards, very slowly revolving, as dead as a stone.

16   The superintendent reached out with his stick and poked the bare body; it oscillated slightly. "*He's* all right," said the superintendent. He backed out from under the gallows, and blew out a deep breath. The moody look had gone out of his face quite suddenly. He glanced at his wrist-watch. "Eight minutes past eight. Well, that's all for this morning, thank God."

The warders unfixed bayonets and marched away. The dog, 17
sobered and conscious of having misbehaved itself, slipped after
them. We walked out of the gallows yard, past the condemned cells
with their waiting prisoners, into the big central yard of the prison.
The convicts, under the command of warders armed with lathis,
were already receiving their breakfast. They squatted in long rows,
each man holding a tin pannikin, while two warders with buckets
marched round ladling out rice; it seemed quite a homely, jolly
scene, after the hanging. An enormous relief had come upon us
now that the job was done. One felt an impulse to sing, to break
into a run, to snigger. All at once everyone began chattering gaily.

The Eurasian boy walking beside me nodded towards the 18
way we had come, with a knowing smile: "Do you know, sir, our
friend (he meant the dead man), when he heard his appeal had
been dismissed, he pissed on the floor of his cell. From fright.
Kindly take one of my cigarettes, sir. Do you not admire my new
silver case, sir? From the boxwallah, two rupees eight annas.
Classy European style."   ~~owner of a box (possession)~~

Several people laughed—at what, nobody seemed certain. 19

Francis was walking by the superintendent, talking garru- 20
lously: "Well, sir, all has passed off with the utmost satisfactori-
ness. It wass all finished—flick! like that. It iss not always so—oah,
no! I have known cases where the doctor wass obliged to go beneath the gallows and pull the prisoner's legs to ensure decease.
Most disagreeable!"

"Wriggling about, eh? That's bad," said the superintendent. 21

"Ach, sir, it iss worse when they become refractory! One man, 22
I recall, clung to the bars of hiss cage when we went to take him
out. You will scarcely credit, sir, that it took six warders to dislodge
him, three pulling at each leg. We reasoned with him. 'My dear fellow,' we said, 'think of all the pain and trouble you are causing to
us!' But no, he would not listen! Ach, he wass very troublesome!"

I found that I was laughing quite loudly. Everyone was laugh- 23
ing. Even the superintendent grinned in a tolerant way. "You'd
better all come out and have a drink," he said quite genially. "I've
got a bottle of whisky in the car. We could do with it."

We went through the big double gates of the prison, into the 24
road. "Pulling at his legs!" exclaimed a Burmese magistrate

"lathee" = stick

that's funny story

suddenly, and burst into a loud chuckling. We all began laughing again. At that moment Francis's <u>anecdote</u> seemed extraordinarily funny. We all had a drink together, native and European alike, quite amicably. The dead man was a hundred yards away.

1931

Salvation

Langston Hughes

1   I was saved from sin when I was going on thirteen. But not really saved. It happened like this. There was a big revival at my Auntie Reed's church. Every night for weeks there had been much preaching, singing, praying, and shouting, and some very hard-ened sinners had been brought to Christ, and the membership of the church had grown by leaps and bounds. Then just before the revival ended, they held a special meeting for children, "to bring the young lambs to the fold." My aunt spoke of it for days ahead. That night I was escorted to the front row and placed on the mourners' bench with all the other young sinners, who had not yet been brought to Jesus.

2   My aunt told me that when you were saved you saw a light, and something happened to you inside! And Jesus came into your life! And God was with you from then on! She said you could see and hear and feel Jesus in your soul. I believed her. I had heard a great many old people say the same thing and it seemed to me they ought to know. So I sat there calmly in the hot, crowded church, waiting for Jesus to come to me.

3   The preacher preached a wonderful rhythmical sermon, all moans and shouts and lonely cries and dire pictures of hell, and then he sang a song about the ninety and nine safe in the fold, but one lit-tle lamb was left out in the cold. Then he said: "Won't you come? Won't you come to Jesus? Young lambs, won't you come?" And he held out his arms to all us young sinners there on the mourners'

bench. And the little girls cried. And some of them jumped up and went to Jesus right away. But most of us just sat there.

A great many old people came and knelt around us and 4 prayed, old women with jet-black faces and braided hair, old men with work-gnarled hands. And the church sang a song about the lower lights are burning, some poor sinners to be saved. And the whole building rocked with prayer and song.

Still I kept waiting to *see* Jesus. 5

Finally all the young people had gone to the altar and were 6 saved, but one boy and me. He was a rounder's son named Westley. Westley and I were surrounded by sisters and deacons praying. It was very hot in the church, and getting late now. Finally Westley said to me in a whisper: "God damn! I'm tired o' sitting here. Let's get up and be saved." So he got up and was saved.

Then I was left all alone on the mourners' bench. My aunt 7 came and knelt at my knees and cried, while prayers and songs swirled all around me in the little church. The whole congregation prayed for me alone, in a mighty wail of moans and voices. And I kept waiting serenely for Jesus, waiting, waiting—but he didn't come. I wanted to see him, but nothing happened to me. Nothing! I wanted something to happen to me, but nothing happened.

I heard the songs and the minister saying: "Why don't you 8 come? My dear child, why don't you come to Jesus? Jesus is waiting for you. He wants you. Why don't you come? Sister Reed, what is this child's name?"

"Langston," my aunt sobbed. 9

"Langston, why don't you come? Why don't you come and be 10 saved? Oh, Lamb of God! Why don't you come?"

Now it was really getting late. I began to be ashamed of my- 11 self, holding everything up so long. I began to wonder what God thought about Westley, who certainly hadn't seen Jesus either, but who was now sitting proudly on the platform, swinging his knickerbockered legs and grinning down at me, surrounded by deacons and old women on their knees praying. God had not struck Westley dead for taking his name in vain or for lying in the temple. So I decided that maybe to save further trouble, I'd better lie, too, and say that Jesus had come, and get up and be saved.

So I got up. 12

13   Suddenly the whole room broke into a sea of shouting, as they saw me rise. Waves of rejoicing swept the place. Women leaped in the air. My aunt threw her arms around me. The minister took me by the hand and led me to the platform.

14   When things quieted down, in a hushed silence, punctuated by a few ecstatic "Amens," all the new young lambs were blessed in the name of God. Then joyous singing filled the room.

15   That night, for the last time in my life but one—for I was a big boy twelve years old—I cried. I cried, in bed alone, and couldn't stop. I buried my head under the quilts, but my aunt heard me. She woke up and told my uncle I was crying because the Holy Ghost had come into my life, and because I had seen Jesus. But I was really crying because I couldn't bear to tell her that I had lied, that I had deceived everybody in the church, that I hadn't seen Jesus, and that now I didn't believe there was a Jesus any more, since he didn't come to help me.

1940

Grandmother's Victory

Maya Angelou

1   "Thou shall not be dirty" and "Thou shall not be impudent" were the two commandments of Grandmother Henderson upon which hung our total salvation.

2   Each night in the bitterest winter we were forced to wash faces, arms, necks, legs, and feet before going to bed. She used to add, with a smirk that unprofane people can't control when venturing into profanity, "and wash as far as possible, then wash possible."

3   We would go to the well and wash in the ice-cold, clear water, grease our legs with the equally cold stiff Vaseline, then tiptoe into

the house. We wiped the dust from our toes and settled down for schoolwork, cornbread, clabbered milk, prayers, and bed, always in that order. Momma was famous for pulling the quilts off after we had fallen asleep to examine our feet. If they weren't clean enough for her, she took the switch (she kept one behind the bedroom door for emergencies) and woke up the offender with a few aptly placed burning reminders.

The area around the well at night was dark and slick, and boys 4 told about how snakes love water, so that anyone who had to draw water at night and then stand there alone and wash knew that moccasins and rattlers, puff adders, and boa constrictors were winding their way to the well and would arrive just as the person washing got soap in her eyes. But Momma convinced us that not only was cleanliness next to Godliness, dirtiness was the inventor of misery.

The impudent child was detested by God and a shame to its 5 parents and could bring destruction to its house and line. All adults had to be addressed as Mister, Missus, Miss, Auntie, Cousin, Unk, Uncle, Buhbah, Sister, Brother, and a thousand other appellations indicating familial relationship and the lowliness of the addressor.

Everyone I knew respected these customary laws, except for 6 the powhitetrash children.

Some families of powhitetrash lived on Momma's farm land 7 behind the school. Sometimes a gaggle of them came to the Store, filling the whole room, chasing out the air, and even changing the well-known scents. The children crawled over the shelves and into the potato and onion bins, twanging all the time in their sharp voices like cigar-box guitars. They took liberties in my Store that I would never dare. Since Momma told us that the less you say to whitefolks (or even powhitetrash) the better, Bailey and I would stand, solemn, quiet, in the displaced air. But if one of the playful apparitions got close to us, I pinched it. Partly out of angry frustration and partly because I didn't believe in its flesh reality.

They called my uncle by his first name and ordered him 8 around the Store. He, to my crying shame, obeyed them in his limping dip-straight-dip fashion.

My grandmother, too, followed their orders, except that she 9 didn't seem to be servile because she anticipated their needs.

10   "Here's sugar, Miz Potter, and here's baking powder. You didn't buy soda last month, you'll probably be needing some."

11   Momma always directed her statements to the adults, but sometimes, Oh painful sometimes, the grimy, snotty-nosed girls would answer her.

12   "Naw, Annie . . ."—to Momma? Who owned the land they lived on? Who forgot more than they would ever learn? If there was any justice in the world, God should strike them dumb at once!—"Just give us some extra sody crackers, and some more mackerel."

13   At least they never looked in her face, or I never caught them doing so. Nobody with a smidgen of training, not even the worst roustabout, would look right in a grown person's face. It meant the person was trying to take the words out before they were formed. The dirty little children didn't do that, but they threw their orders around the Store like lashes from a cat-o'-nine-tails.

14   When I was around ten years old, those scruffy children caused me the most painful and confusing experience I had ever had with my grandmother.

15   One summer morning, after I had swept the dirt yard of leaves, spearmint-gum wrappers and Vienna-sausage labels, I raked the yellow-red dirt, and made half-moons carefully, so that the design stood out clearly and mask-like. I put the rake behind the Store and came through the back of the house to find Grandmother on the front porch in her big, wide white apron. The apron was so stiff by virtue of the starch that it could have stood alone. Momma was admiring the yard, so I joined her. It truly looked like a flat redhead that had been raked with a big-toothed comb. Momma didn't say anything but I knew she liked it. She looked over toward the school principal's house and to the right at Mr. McElroy's. She was hoping one of those community pillars would see the design before the day's business wiped it out. Then she looked upward to the school. My head had swung with hers, so at just about the same time we saw a troop of powhitetrash kids marching over the hill and down by the side of the school.

16   I looked to Momma for direction. She did an excellent job of sagging from her waist down, but from the waist up she seemed to be pulling for the top of the oak tree across the road. Then she began to moan a hymn. Maybe not to moan, but the tune was so

slow and the meter so strange that she could have been moaning. She didn't look at me again. When the children reached halfway down the hill, halfway to the Store, she said without turning, "Sister, go on inside."

I wanted to beg her, "Momma, don't wait for them. Come on [17] inside with me. If they come in the Store, you go to the bedroom and let me wait on them. They only frighten me if you're around. Alone I know how to handle them." But of course I couldn't say anything, so I went in and stood behind the screen door.

Before the girls got to the porch I heard their laughter crackling [18] and popping like pine logs in a cooking stove. I suppose my lifelong paranoia was born in those cold, molasses-slow minutes. They came finally to stand on the ground in front of Momma. At first they pretended seriousness. Then one of them wrapped her right arm in the crook of her left, pushed out her mouth and started to hum. I realized that she was aping my grandmother. Another said, "Naw, Helen, you ain't standing like her. This here's it." Then she lifted her chest, folded her arms and mocked that strange carriage that was Annie Henderson. Another laughed, "Naw, you can't do it. Your mouth ain't pooched out enough. It's like this."

I thought about the rifle behind the door, but I knew I'd never [19] be able to hold it straight, and the .410, our sawed-off shotgun, which stayed loaded and was fired every New Year's night, was locked in the trunk and Uncle Willie had the key on his chain. Through the fly-specked screen door, I could see that the arms of Momma's apron jiggled from the vibrations of her humming. But her knees seemed to have locked as if they would never bend again.

She sang on. No louder than before, but no softer either. No [20] slower or faster.

The dirt of the girls' cotton dresses continued on their legs, [21] feet, arms, and faces to make them all of a piece. Their greasy uncolored hair hung down, uncombed, with a grim finality. I knelt to see them better, to remember them for all time. The tears that had slipped down my dress left unsurprising dark spots, and made the front yard blurry and even more unreal. The world had taken a deep breath and was having doubts about continuing to revolve.

The girls had tired of mocking Momma and turned to other [22] means of agitation. One crossed her eyes, stuck her thumbs in both

sides of her mouth and said, "Look here, Annie." Grandmother
hummed on and the apron strings trembled. I wanted to throw a
handful of black pepper in their faces, to throw lye on them, to
scream that they were dirty, scummy peckerwoods, but I knew I
was as clearly imprisoned behind the scene as the actors outside
were confined to their roles.

23   One of the smaller girls did a kind of puppet dance while her
fellow clowns laughed at her. But the tall one, who was almost a
woman, said something very quietly, which I couldn't hear. They
all moved backward from the porch, still watching Momma. For
an awful second I thought they were going to throw a rock at
Momma, who seemed (except for the apron strings) to have
turned into stone herself. But the big girl turned her back, bent
down and put her hands flat on the ground—she didn't pick up
anything. She simply shifted her weight and did a hand stand.

24   Her dirty bare feet and long legs went straight for the sky. Her
dress fell down around her shoulders, and she had on no drawers.
The slick pubic hair made a brown triangle where her legs came
together. She hung in the vacuum of that lifeless morning for only
a few seconds, then wavered and tumbled. The other girls clapped
her on the back and slapped their hands.

25   Momma changed her song to "Bread of Heaven, bread of
Heaven, feed me till I want no more."

26   I found that I was praying too. How long could Momma hold
out? What new indignity would they think of to subject her to?
Would I be able to stay out of it? What would Momma really like
me to do?

27   Then they were moving out of the yard, on their way to town.
They bobbed their heads and shook their slack behinds and
turned, one at a time:

28   "Bye, Annie."

29   "Bye, Annie."

30   "Bye, Annie."

31   Momma never turned her head or unfolded her arms, but she
stopped singing and said, " 'Bye, Miz Helen, 'bye, Miz Ruth, 'bye,
Miz Eloise."

32   I burst. A firecracker July-the-Fourth burst. How could
Momma call them Miz? The mean nasty things. Why couldn't she
have come inside the sweet, cool store when we saw them breast-

ing the hill? What did she prove? And then if they were dirty, mean, and impudent, why did Momma have to call them Miz?

She stood another whole song through and then opened the 33 screen door to look down on me crying in rage. She looked until I looked up. Her face was a brown moon that shone on me. She was beautiful. Something had happened out there, which I couldn't completely understand, but I could see that she was happy. Then she bent down and touched me as mothers of the church "lay hands on the sick and afflicted" and I quieted.

"Go wash your face, Sister." And she went behind the candy 34 counter and hummed, "Glory, glory, hallelujah, when I lay my burden down."

I threw the well water on my face and used the weekday 35 handkerchief to blow my nose. Whatever the contest had been out front, I knew Momma had won.

I took the rake back to the front yard. The smudged footprints 36 were easy to erase. I worked for a long time on my new design and laid the rake behind the wash pot. When I came back in the Store, I took Momma's hand and we both walked outside to look at the pattern.

It was a large heart with lots of hearts growing smaller inside, 37 and piercing from the outside rim to the smallest heart was an arrow. Momma said, "Sister, that's right pretty." Then she turned back to the Store and resumed, "Glory, glory, hallelujah, when I lay my burden down."

1970

No Name Woman

Maxine Hong Kingston

"You must not tell anyone," my mother said, "what I am about to 1 tell you. In China your father had a sister who killed herself. She jumped into the family well. We say that your father has all brothers because it is as if she had never been born.

2   "In 1924 just a few days after our village celebrated seventeen hurry-up weddings—to make sure that every young man who went 'out on the road' would responsibly come home—your father and his brothers and your grandfather and his brothers and your aunt's new husband sailed for America, the Gold Mountain. It was your grandfather's last trip. Those lucky enough to get contracts waved goodbye from the decks. They fed and guarded the stowaways and helped them off in Cuba, New York, Bali, Hawaii. 'We'll meet in California next year,' they said. All of them sent money home.

3   "I remember looking at your aunt one day when she and I were dressing; I had not noticed before that she had such a protruding melon of a stomach. But I did not think, 'She's pregnant,' until she began to look like other pregnant women, her shirt pulling and the white tops of her black pants showing. She could not have been pregnant, you see, because her husband had been gone for years. No one said anything. We did not discuss it. In early summer she was ready to have the child, long after the time when it could have been possible.

4   "The village had also been counting. On the night the baby was to be born the villagers raided our house. Some were crying. Like a great saw, teeth strung with lights, files of people walked zigzag across our land, tearing the rice. Their lanterns doubled in the disturbed black water, which drained away through the broken bunds. As the villagers closed in, we could see that some of them, probably men and women we knew well, wore white masks. The people with long hair hung it over their faces. Women with short hair made it stand up on end. Some had tied white bands around their foreheads, arms, and legs.

5   "At first they threw mud and rocks at the house. Then they threw eggs and began slaughtering our stock. We could hear the animals scream their deaths—the roosters, the pigs, a last great roar from the ox. Familiar wild heads flared in our night windows; the villagers encircled us. Some of the faces stopped to peer at us, their eyes rushing like searchlights. The hands flattened against the panes, framed heads, and left red prints.

6   "The villagers broke in the front and the back doors at the same time, even though we had not locked the doors against

them. Their knives dripped with the blood of our animals. They smeared blood on the doors and walls. One woman swung a chicken, whose throat she had slit, splattering blood in red arcs about her. We stood together in the middle of our house, in the family hall with the pictures and tables of the ancestors around us, and looked straight ahead.

"At that time the house had only two wings. When the men came back, we would build two more to enclose our courtyard and a third one to begin a second courtyard. The villagers pushed through both wings, even your grandparents' rooms, to find your aunt's, which was also mine until the men returned. From this room a new wing for one of the younger families would grow. They ripped up her clothes and shoes and broke her combs, grinding them underfoot. They tore her work from the loom. They scattered the cooking fire and rolled the new weaving in it. We could hear them in the kitchen breaking our bowls and banging the pots. They overturned the great waist-high earthenware jugs; duck eggs, pickled fruits, vegetables burst out and mixed in acrid torrents. The old woman from the next field swept a broom through the air and loosed the spirits-of-the-broom over our heads. 'Pig.' 'Ghost.' 'Pig,' they sobbed and scolded while they ruined our house.

"When they left, they took sugar and oranges to bless themselves. They cut pieces from the dead animals. Some of them took bowls that were not broken and clothes that were not torn. Afterward we swept up the rice and sewed it back up into sacks. But the smells from the spilled preserves lasted. Your aunt gave birth in the pigsty that night. The next morning when I went for the water, I found her and the baby plugging up the family well.

"Don't let your father know that I told you. He denies her. Now that you have started to menstruate, what happened to her could happen to you. Don't humiliate us. You wouldn't like to be forgotten as if you had never been born. The villagers are watchful."

Whenever she had to warn us about life, my mother told stories that ran like this one, a story to grow up on. She tested our strength to establish realities. Those in the emigrant generations who could not reassert brute survival died young and far from home. Those of us in the first American generations have had to figure out <u>how the invisible world</u> the emigrants built around our childhoods <u>fits in solid</u> America.

11   The emigrants confused the gods by <u>diverting their curses</u>, <u>misleading them with crooked streets and false names.</u> They must try to confuse their offspring as well, who, I suppose, threaten them in similar ways—always trying <u>to get things straight</u>, always trying <u>to name the unspeakable</u>. The Chinese I know <u>hide their names; sojourners take new names</u> when their lives change and guard their real names with silence.

12   Chinese-Americans, when you try to understand what things in you are Chinese, how do you separate what is <u>peculiar to child-hood</u>, to <u>poverty</u>, <u>insanities</u>, one family, your <u>mother who marked your growing with stories</u>, from what is Chinese? What is Chinese tradition and what is the movies?

13   If I want to learn what clothes my aunt wore, whether flashy or ordinary, I would have to begin, "Remember <u>Father's drowned-in-the-well sister</u>?" I cannot ask that. My mother has told me once and for all the useful parts. She will add nothing unless powered by Necessity, a <u>riverbank that guides her life</u>. She plants vegetable gardens rather than lawns; she carries the odd-shaped tomatoes home from the fields and <u>eats food left for the gods</u>.

14   Whenever we did frivolous things, we used up energy; we flew high kites. We children came up off the ground over the melting cones our parents brought home from work and the American movie on New Year's Day—*Oh, You Beautiful Doll* with Betty Grable one year, and *She Wore a Yellow Ribbon* with John Wayne another year. After the one carnival ride each, we paid in guilt; our tired father ~~counted his change~~ on the dark walk home.

15   <u>Adultery is extravagance.</u> Could people who hatch their own chicks and eat the embryos and the heads for delicacies and boil the feet in vinegar for party food, leaving only the gravel, eating even the gizzard lining—could such people engender a prodigal aunt? To be a woman, to have a daughter in starvation time was a waste enough. <u>My aunt</u> could not have been the lone romantic who <u>gave up everything for sex.</u> Women in the old China did not choose. Some man had commanded her to lie with him and be his

secret evil. I wonder whether he masked himself when he joined the raid on her family.

Perhaps she had encountered him in the fields or on the mountain where the daughters-in-law collected fuel. Or perhaps he first noticed her in the marketplace. He was not a stranger because the village housed no strangers. She had to have dealings with him other than sex. Perhaps he worked an adjoining field, or he sold her the cloth for the dress she sewed and wore. His demand must have surprised, then terrified her. She obeyed him; she always did as she was told.

When the family found a young man in the next village to be her husband, she had stood tractably beside the best rooster, his proxy, and promised before they met that she would be his forever. She was lucky that he was her age and she would be the first wife, an advantage secure now. The night she first saw him, he had sex with her. Then he left for America. She had almost forgotten what he looked like. When she tried to envision him, she only saw the black and white face in the group photograph the men had had taken before leaving.

The other man was not, after all, much different from her husband. They both gave orders: she followed. "If you tell your family, I'll beat you. I'll kill you. Be here again next week." No one talked sex, ever. And she might have separated the rapes from the rest of living if only she did not have to buy her oil from him or gather wood in the same forest. I want her fear to have lasted just as long as rape lasted so that the fear could have been contained. No drawn-out fear. But women at sex hazarded birth and hence lifetimes. The fear did not stop but permeated everywhere. She told the man, "I think I'm pregnant." He organized the raid against her.

On nights when my mother and father talked about their life back home, sometimes they mentioned an "outcast table" whose business they still seemed to be settling, their voices tight. In a commensal tradition, where food is precious, the powerful older people made wrongdoers eat alone. Instead of letting them start separate new lives like the Japanese, who could become samurais and geishas, the Chinese family, faces averted but eyes glowering sideways, hung on to the offenders and fed them leftovers. My *dual process — equal justice ends*

aunt must have lived in the same house as my parents and eaten at an outcast table. My mother spoke about the raid as if she had seen it, when she and my aunt, a daughter-in-law to a different household, should not have been living together at all. Daughters-in-law lived with their husbands' parents, not their own; a synonym for marriage in Chinese is "taking a daughter-in-law." Her husband's parents could have sold her, mortgaged her, stoned her. But they had sent her back to her own mother and father, a mysterious act hinting at disgraces not told me. Perhaps they had thrown her out to deflect the avengers.

20   She was the only daughter; her four brothers went with her father, husband, and uncles "out on the road" and for some years became western men. When the goods were divided among the family, three of the brothers took land, and the youngest, my father, chose an education. After my grandparents gave their daughter away to her husband's family, they had dispensed all the adventure and all the property. They expected her alone to keep the traditional ways, which her brothers, now among the barbarians, could fumble without detection. The heavy, deep-rooted women were to maintain the past against the flood, safe for returning. But the rare urge west had fixed upon our family, and so my aunt crossed boundaries not delineated in space.

21   The work of preservation demands that the feelings playing about in one's guts not be turned into action. Just watch their passing like cherry blossoms. But perhaps my aunt, my forerunner, caught in a slow life, let dreams grow and fade and after some months or years went toward what persisted. Fear at the enormities of the forbidden kept her desires delicate, wire and bone. She looked at a man because she liked the way the hair was tucked behind his ears, or she liked the question-mark line of a long torso curving at the shoulder and straight at the hip. For warm eyes or a soft voice or a slow walk—that's all—a few hairs, a line, a brightness, a sound, a pace, she gave up family. She offered us up for a charm that vanished with tiredness, a pigtail that didn't toss when the wind died. Why, the wrong lighting could erase the dearest thing about him.

22   It could very well have been, however, that my aunt did not take subtle enjoyment of her friend, but, a wild woman, kept rollicking company. Imagining her free with sex doesn't fit, though.

I don't know any women like that, or men either. Unless I see her life branching into mine, she gives me no ancestral help.

To sustain her being in love, she often worked at herself in the mirror, guessing at the colors and shapes that would interest him, changing them frequently in order to hit on the right combination. She wanted him to look back.

On a farm near the sea, a woman who tended her appearance reaped a reputation for eccentricity. All the married women blunt-cut their hair in flaps about their ears or pulled it back in tight buns. No nonsense. Neither style blew easily into heart-catching tangles. And at their weddings they displayed themselves in their long hair for the last time. "It brushed the backs of my knees," my mother tells me. "It was braided, and even so, it brushed the backs of my knees."

At the mirror my aunt combed individuality into her bob. A bun could have been contrived to escape into black streamers blowing in the wind or in quiet wisps about her face, but only the older women in our picture album wear buns. She brushed her hair back from her forehead, tucking the flaps behind her ears. She looped a piece of thread, knotted into a circle between her index fingers and thumbs, and ran the double strand across her forehead. When she closed her fingers as if she were making a pair of shadow geese bite, the string twisted together catching the little hairs. Then she pulled the thread away from her skin, ripping the hairs out neatly, her eyes watering from the needles of pain. Opening her fingers, she cleaned the thread, then rolled it along her hairline and the tops of her eyebrows. My mother did the same to me and my sisters and herself. I used to believe that the expression "caught by the short hairs" meant a captive held with a depilatory string. It especially hurt at the temples, but my mother said we were lucky we didn't have to have our feet bound when we were seven. Sisters used to sit on their beds and cry together, she said, as their mothers or their slaves removed the bandages for a few minutes each night and let the blood gush back into their veins. I hope that the man my aunt loved appreciated a smooth brow, that he wasn't just a tits-and-ass man.

Once my aunt found a freckle on her chin, at a spot that the almanac said predestined her for unhappiness. She dug it out with a hot needle and washed the wound with peroxide.

27   More attention to her looks than these pullings of hairs and pickings at spots would have caused gossip among the villagers. They owned work clothes and good clothes, and they wore good clothes for feasting the new seasons. But since a woman combing her hair hexes beginnings, my aunt rarely found an occasion to look her best. Women looked like great sea snails—the corded wood, babies, and laundry they carried were the whorls on their backs. The Chinese did not admire a bent back; goddesses and warriors stood straight. Still there must have been a marvelous freeing of beauty when a worker laid down her burden and stretched and arched.

28   Such commonplace loveliness, however, was not enough for my aunt. She dreamed of a lover for the fifteen days of New Year's, the time for families to exchange visits, money, and food. She plied her secret comb. And sure enough she cursed the year, the family, the village, and herself.

29   Even as her hair lured her imminent lover, many other men looked at her. Uncles, cousins, nephews, brothers would have looked, too, had they been home between journeys. Perhaps they had already been restraining their curiosity, and they left, fearful that their glances, like a field of nesting birds, might be startled and caught. Poverty hurt, and that was their first reason for leaving. But another, final reason for leaving the crowded house was the never-said.

30   She may have been unusually beloved, the precious only daughter, spoiled and mirror gazing because of the affection the family lavished on her. When her husband left, they welcomed the chance to take her back from the in-laws; she could live like the little daughter for just a while longer. There are stories that my grandfather was different from other people, "crazy ever since the little Jap bayoneted him in the head." He used to put his naked penis on the dinner table, laughing. And one day he brought home a baby girl, wrapped up inside his brown western-style greatcoat. He had traded one of his sons, probably my father, the youngest, for her. My grandmother made him trade back. When he finally got a daughter of his own, he doted on her. They must have all loved her, except perhaps my father, the only brother who never went back to China, having once been traded for a girl.

Brothers and sisters, newly men and women, had to efface 31
their sexual color and present plain miens. Disturbing hair and
eyes, a smile like no other, threatened the ideal of five generations
living under one roof. To focus blurs, people shouted face to face
and yelled from room to room. The immigrants I know have loud
voices, unmodulated to American tones even after years away
from the village where they called their friendships out across the
fields. I have not been able to stop my mother's screams in public
libraries or over telephones. Walking erect (knees straight, toes
pointed forward, not pigeon-toed, which is Chinese-feminine)
and speaking in an inaudible voice, I have tried to turn myself
American-feminine. Chinese communication was loud, public.
Only sick people had to whisper. But at the dinner table, where the
family members came nearest one another, no one could talk, not
the outcasts nor any eaters. Every word that falls from the mouth
is a coin lost. Silently they gave and accepted food with both
hands. A preoccupied child who took his bowl with one hand got
a sideways glare. A complete moment of total attention is due
everyone alike. Children and lovers have no singularity here, but
my aunt used a secret voice, a separate attentiveness.

She kept the man's name to herself throughout her labor and 32
dying; she did not accuse him that he be punished with her. To
save her inseminator's name she gave silent birth.

He may have been somebody in her own household, but in- 33
tercourse with a man outside the family would have been no less
abhorrent. All the village were kinsmen, and the titles shouted in
loud country voices never let kinship be forgotten. Any man
within visiting distance would have been neutralized as a lover—
"brother," "younger brother," "older brother"—one hundred and
fifteen relationship titles. Parents researched birth charts probably
not so much to assure good fortune as to circumvent incest in a
population that has but one hundred surnames. Everybody has
eight million relatives. How useless then sexual mannerisms, how
dangerous.

As if it came from an atavism deeper than fear, I used to add 34
"brother" silently to boys' names. It hexed the boys, who would or
would not ask me to dance, and made them less scary and as familiar and deserving of benevolence as girls.

35 But, of course, I hexed myself also—no dates. I should have stood up, both arms waving, and shouted out across libraries, "Hey, you! Love me back." I had no idea, though, how to make attraction selective, how to control its direction and magnitude. If I made myself American-pretty so that the five or six Chinese boys in the class fell in love with me, everyone else—the Caucasian, Negro, and Japanese boys—would too. Sisterliness, dignified and honorable, made much more sense.

36 Attraction eludes control so stubbornly that whole societies designed to organize relationships among people cannot keep order, not even when they bind people to one another from childhood and raise them together. Among the very poor and the wealthy, brothers married their adopted sisters, like doves. Our family allowed some romance, paying adult brides' prices and providing dowries so that their sons and daughters could marry strangers. Marriage promises to turn strangers into friendly relatives—a nation of siblings.

37 In the village structure, spirits shimmered among the live creatures, balanced and held in equilibrium by time and land. But one human being flaring up into violence could open up a black hole, a maelstrom that pulled in the sky. The frightened villagers, who depended on one another to maintain the real, went to my aunt to show her a personal, physical representation of the break she had made in the "roundness." Misallying couples snapped off the future, which was to be embodied in true offspring. The villagers punished her for acting as if she could have a private life, secret and apart from them.

38 If my aunt had betrayed the family at a time of large grain yields and peace, when many boys were born, and wings were being built on many houses, perhaps she might have escaped such severe punishment. But the men—hungry, greedy, tired of planting in dry soil—had been forced to leave the village in order to send food-money home. There were ghost plagues, bandit plagues, wars with the Japanese, floods. My Chinese brother and sister had died of an unknown sickness. Adultery, perhaps only a mistake during good times, became a crime when the village needed food.

39 The round moon cakes and round doorways, the round tables of graduated sizes that fit one roundness inside another, round

windows and rice bowls—these talismans had lost their power to warn this family of the law: A family must be whole, faithfully keeping the descent line by having sons to feed the old and the dead, who in turn look after the family. The villagers came to show my aunt and her lover-in-hiding a broken house. The villagers were speeding up the circling of events because she was too short-sighted to see that her infidelity had already harmed the village, that waves of consequences would return unpredictably, some-times in disguise, as now, to hurt her. This roundness had to be made coin-sized so that she would see its circumference: Punish her at the birth of her baby. Awaken her to the inexorable. People who refused fatalism because they could invent small resources insisted on culpability. Deny accidents and wrest fault from the stars.

After the villagers left, their lanterns now scattering in various 40 directions toward home, the family broke their silence and cursed her. "Aiaa, we're going to die. Death is coming. Death is coming. Look what you've done. You've killed us. Ghost! Dead ghost! Ghost! You've never been born." She ran out into the fields, far enough from the house so that she could no longer hear their voices, and pressed herself against the earth, her own land no more. When she felt the birth coming, she thought that she had been hurt. Her body seized together. "They've hurt me too much," she thought. "This is gall, and it will kill me." With forehead and knees against the earth, her body convulsed and then relaxed. She turned on her back, lay on the ground. The black well of sky and stars went out and out and out forever; her body and her com-plexity seemed to disappear. She was one of the stars, a bright dot in blackness, without home, without a companion, in eternal cold and silence. An agoraphobia rose in her, speeding higher and higher, bigger and bigger; she would not be able to contain it; there would be no end to fear.

Flayed, unprotected against space, she felt pain return, focus- 41 ing her body. This pain chilled her—a cold, steady kind of surface pain. Inside, spasmodically, the other pain, the pain of the child, heated her. For hours she lay on the ground, alternately body and space. Sometimes a vision of normal comfort obliterated reality: She saw the family in the evening gambling at the dinner table, the young people massaging their elders' backs. She saw them congratulating one another, high joy on the mornings the rice shoots came up. When these pictures burst, the stars drew yet further apart. Black space opened.

42   She got to her feet to fight better and remembered that old-fashioned women gave birth in their pigsties to fool the jealous, pain-dealing gods, who do not snatch piglets. Before the next spasms could stop her, she ran to the pigsty, each step a rushing out into emptiness. She climbed over the fence and knelt in the dirt. It was good to have a fence enclosing her, a tribal person alone.

43   Laboring, this woman who had carried her child as a foreign growth that sickened her every day, expelled it at last. She reached down to touch the hot, wet, moving mass, surely smaller than anything human, and could feel that it was human after all—fingers, toes, nails, nose. She pulled it up on to her belly, and it lay curled there, butt in the air, feet precisely tucked one under the other. She opened her loose shirt and buttoned the child inside. After resting, it squirmed and thrashed and she pushed it up to her breast. It turned its head this way and that until it found her nipple. There, it made little snuffling noises. She clenched her teeth at its preciousness, lovely as a young calf, a piglet, a little dog.

44   She may have gone to the pigsty as a last act of responsibility: She would protect this child as she had protected its father. It would look after her soul, leaving supplies on her grave. But how would this tiny child without family find her grave when there would be no marker for her anywhere, neither in the earth nor the family hall? No one would give her a family hall name. She had taken the child with her into the wastes. At its birth the two of them had felt the same raw pain of separation, a wound that only the family pressing tight could close. A child with no descent line would not soften her life but only trail after her, ghostlike, begging her to give it purpose. At dawn the villagers on their way to the fields would stand around the fence and look.

45   Full of milk, the little ghost slept. When it awoke, she hardened her breasts against the milk that crying loosens. Toward morning she picked up the baby and walked to the well.

46   Carrying the baby to the well shows loving. Otherwise abandon it. Turn its face into the mud. Mothers who love their children

take them along. It was probably a girl; there is some hope of for-
giveness for boys.

"Don't tell anyone you had an aunt. Your father does not   47
want to hear her name. She has never been born." I have believed
that sex was unspeakable and words so strong and fathers so
frail that "aunt" would do my father mysterious harm. I have
thought that my family, having settled among immigrants who
had also been their neighbors in the ancestral land, needed to
clean their name, and a wrong word would incite the kinspeople
even here. But there is more to this silence: They want me to participate in her punishment. And I have.

In the twenty years since I heard this story I have not asked for   48
details nor said my aunt's name; I do not know it. People who can
comfort the dead can also chase after them to hurt them further—
a reverse ancestor worship. The real punishment was not the raid
swiftly inflicted by the villagers, but the family's deliberately forgetting her. Her betrayal so maddened them, they saw to it that
she would suffer forever, even after death. Always hungry, always
needing, she would have to beg food from other ghosts, snatch
and steal it from those whose living descendants give them gifts.
She would have to fight the ghosts massed at crossroads for the
buns a few thoughtful citizens leave to decoy her away from village and home so that the ancestral spirits could feast unharassed.
At peace, they could act like gods, not ghosts, their descent lines
providing them with paper suits and dresses, spirit money, paper
houses, paper automobiles, chicken, meat, and rice into eternity—
essences delivered up in smoke and flames, steam and incense rising from each rice bowl. In an attempt to make the Chinese care
for people outside the family, Chairman Mao encourages us now
to give our paper replicas to the spirits of outstanding soldiers and
workers, no matter whose ancestors they may be. My aunt remains forever hungry. Goods are not distributed evenly among
the dead.

My aunt haunts me—her ghost drawn to me because now, af-   49
ter fifty years of neglect, I alone devote pages of paper to her,
though not origamied into houses and clothes. I do not think she

always means me well. I am telling on her, and she was a spite suicide, drowning herself in the drinking water. The Chinese are always very frightened of the drowned one, whose weeping ghost,
wet hair hanging and skin bloated, waits silently by the water to
pull down a substitute.

                                                                   1975

Travelling South*

James Weldon Johnson

1   The farther I got below Washington the more disappointed I became in the appearance of the country. I peered through the car
windows, looking in vain for the luxuriant semi-tropical scenery
which I had pictured in my mind. I did not find the grass so green,
nor the woods so beautiful, nor the flowers so plentiful, as they
were in Connecticut. Instead, the red earth partly covered by
tough, scrawny grass, the muddy straggling roads, the cottages of
unpainted pine boards, and the clay daubed huts imparted a
"burnt up" impression. Occasionally we ran through a little white
and green village that was like an oasis in a desert.

2   When I reached Atlanta my steadily increasing disappointment was not lessened. I found it a big, dull, red town. This dull red
color of that part of the South I was then seeing had much, I think,
to do with the extreme depression of my spirits—no public
squares, no fountains, dingy street-cars, and, with the exception of
three or four principal thoroughfares, unpaved streets. It was raining when I arrived and some of these unpaved streets were absolutely impassable. Wheels sank to the hubs in red mire, and I actually stood for an hour and watched four or five men work to save
a mule, which had stepped into a deep sink, from drowning, or,
rather, suffocating in the mud. The Atlanta of today is a new city.

*Editor's title.

On the train I had talked with one of the Pullman car porters, 3
a bright young fellow who was himself a student, and told him
that I was going to Atlanta to attend school. I had also asked him
to tell me where I might stop for a day or two until the University
opened. He said I might go with him to the place where he
stopped during his "layovers" in Atlanta. I gladly accepted his offer, and went with him along one of those muddy streets until we
came to a rather rickety looking frame house, which we entered.
The proprietor of the house was a big, fat, greasy looking brown-
skinned man. When I asked him if he could give me accommoda-
tion he wanted to know how long I would stay. I told him perhaps
two days, not more than three. In reply he said, "Oh, dat's all right
den," at the same time leading the way up a pair of creaky stairs.
I followed him and the porter to a room, the door of which the proprietor opened while continuing, it seemed, his remark, "Oh, dat's
all right den," by adding, "You kin sleep in dat cot in de corner der.
Fifty cents please." The porter interrupted by saying, "You needn't
collect from him now, he's got a trunk." This seemed to satisfy the
man, and he went down leaving me and my porter friend in the
room. I glanced around the apartment and saw that it contained a
double bed and two cots, two wash-stands, three chairs, and a
time-worn bureau with a looking glass that would have made
Adonis appear hideous. I looked at the cot in which I was to sleep
and suspected, not without good reasons, that I should not be the
first to use the sheets and pillowcase since they had last come from
the wash. When I thought of the clean, tidy, comfortable sur-
roundings in which I had been reared, a wave of homesickness
swept over me that made me feel faint. Had it not been for the
presence of my companion, and that I knew this much of his history—that he was not yet quite twenty, just three years older than
myself, and that he had been fighting his own way in the world,
earning his own living and providing for his own education since
he was fourteen—I should not have been able to stop the tears that
were welling up in my eyes.

I asked him why it was that the proprietor of the house 4
seemed unwilling to accommodate me for more than a couple of
days. He informed me that the man ran a lodging house especially
for Pullman porters, and as their stays in town were not longer

than one or two nights it would interfere with his arrangements to have anyone stay longer. He went on to say, "You see this room is fixed up to accommodate four men at a time. Well, by keeping a sort of table of trips, in and out, of the men, and working them like checkers, he can accommodate fifteen or sixteen in each week, and generally avoid having an empty bed. You happen to catch a bed that would have been empty for a couple of nights." I asked him where he was going to sleep. He answered, "I sleep in that other cot tonight; tomorrow night I go out." He went on to tell me that the man who kept the house did not serve meals, and that if I was hungry we would go out and get something to eat.

5   We went into the street, and in passing the railroad station I hired a wagon to take my trunk to my lodging place. We passed along until, finally, we turned into a street that stretched away, up and down hill, for a mile or two; and here I caught my first sight of colored people in large numbers. I had seen little squads around the railroad stations on my way south; but here I saw a street crowded with them. They filled the shops and thronged the sidewalks and lined the curb. I asked my companion if all the colored people in Atlanta lived in this street. He said they did not, and assured me that the ones I saw were of the lower class. I felt relieved, in spite of the size of the lower class. The unkempt appearance, the shambling, slouching gait and loud talk and laughter of these people aroused in me a feeling of almost repulsion. Only one thing about them awoke a feeling of interest; that was their dialect. I had read some Negro dialect and had heard snatches of it on my journey down from Washington; but here I heard it in all of its fullness and freedom. I was particularly struck by the way in which it was punctuated by such exclamatory phrases as "Lawd a mussy!" "G'wan man!" "Bless ma soul!" "Look heah chile!" These people talked and laughed without restraint. In fact, they talked straight from their lungs, and laughed from the pits of their stomachs. And this hearty laughter was often justified by the droll humor of some remark. I paused long enough to hear one man say to another, "W'at's de mattah wid you an' yo' fr'en' Sam?" And the other came back like a flash, "Ma fr'en? He ma fr'en? Man! I'd go to his funeral jes de same as I'd go to a minstrel show." I have since learned that this ability to laugh heartily is, in part, the salvation

of the American Negro; it does much to keep him from going the way of the Indian.

The business places of the street along which we were passing 6 consisted chiefly of low bars, cheap dry-goods and notion stores, barber shops, and fish and bread restaurants. We, at length, turned down a pair of stairs that led to a basement, and I found myself in an eating-house somewhat better than those I had seen in passing; but that did not mean much for its excellence. The place was smoky, the tables were covered with oil-cloth, the floor covered with sawdust, and from the kitchen came a rancid odor of fish fried over several times, which almost nauseated me. I asked my companion if this were the place where we were to eat. He informed me that it was the best place in town where a colored man could get a meal. I then wanted to know why somebody didn't open a place where respectable colored people who had money could be accommodated. He answered, "It wouldn't pay; all the respectable colored people eat at home, and the few who travel generally have friends in the towns to which they go, who entertain them." He added, " Of course, you could go in any place in the city; they wouldn't know you from white."

I sat down with the porter at one of the tables, but was not 7 hungry enough to eat with any relish what was put before me. The food was not badly cooked; but the iron knives and forks needed to be scrubbed, the plates and dishes and glasses needed to be washed and well dried. I minced over what I took on my plate while my companion ate. When we finished we paid the waiter twenty cents each and went out. We walked around until the lights of the city were lit. Then the porter said that he must get to bed and have some rest, as he had not had six hours' sleep since he left Jersey City. I went back to our lodging-house with him.

When I awoke in the morning there were, besides my new- 8 found friend, two other men in the room, asleep in the double bed. I got up and dressed myself very quietly, so as not to awake anyone. I then drew from under the pillow my precious roll of greenbacks, took out a ten dollar bill, and very softly unlocking my trunk, put the remainder, about three hundred dollars, in the inside pocket of a coat near the bottom; glad of the opportunity to put it unobserved in a place of safety. When I had carefully locked my trunk, I tiptoed toward the door with the intention of going out to look for a decent restaurant where I might get something fit to eat. As I was easing the door open, my porter friend said with a yawn, "Hello! You're going out?" I answered him, "Yes." "Oh!" he yawned again, "I guess I've had enough sleep; wait a minute, I'll go with you." For the instant his friendship bored and embarrassed me. I had visions of another meal in the greasy restaurant of the day before. He must have divined my thoughts; for he went on to say, " I know a woman across town who takes a few boarders; I think we can go over there and get a good breakfast." With a feeling of mingled fears and doubts regarding what the breakfast might be, I waited until he had dressed himself.

9   When I saw the neat appearance of the cottage we entered my fears vanished, and when I saw the woman who kept it my doubts followed the same course. Scrupulously clean, in a spotless white apron and colored head handkerchief, her round face beaming with motherly kindness, she was picturesquely beautiful. She impressed me as one broad expanse of happiness and good nature. In a few minutes she was addressing me as "chile" and "honey." She made me feel as though I should like to lay my head on her capacious bosom and go to sleep.

And the breakfast, simple as it was, I could not have had at any restaurant in Atlanta at any price. There was fried chicken, as it is fried only in the South, hominy boiled to the consistency where it could be eaten with a fork, and biscuits so light and flaky that a fellow with any appetite at all would have no difficulty in disposing of eight or ten. When I had finished I felt that I had experienced the realization of, at least, one of my dreams of Southern life.

10   During the meal we found out from our hostess, who had two boys in school, that Atlanta University opened on that very day. I had somehow mixed my dates. My friend the porter suggested that I go out to the university at once and offered to walk over and show me the way. We had to walk because, although the university was not more than twenty minutes distance from the center of the city, there were no street-cars running in that direction. My first sight of the school grounds made me feel that I was not far from home; here the red hills had been terraced and covered with

green grass; clean gravel walks, well shaded, lead up to the build-ings; indeed, it was a bit of New England transplanted. At the gate my companion said he would bid me goodby, because it was likely that he would not see me again before his car went out. He told me that he would make two more trips to Atlanta, and that he would come out and see me; that after his second trip he would leave the Pullman service for the winter and return to school in Nashville. We shook hands, I thanked him for all his kindness, and we said goodby.

I walked up to a group of students and made some inquiries. 11 They directed me to the president's office in the main building. The president gave me a cordial welcome; it was more than cor-dial; he talked to me, not as the official head of a college, but as though he were adopting me into what was his large family, to personally look after my general welfare as well as my education. He seemed especially pleased with the fact that I had come to them all the way from the North. He told me that I could have come to the school as soon as I had reached the city, and that I had better move my trunk out at once. I gladly promised him that I would do so. He then called a boy and directed him to take me to the matron, and to show me around afterwards. I found the ma-tron even more motherly than the president was fatherly. She had me to register, which was in effect to sign a pledge to abstain from the use of intoxicating beverages, tobacco, and profane language, while I was a student in the school. This act caused me no sacri-fice; as, up to that time, I was free from either habit. The boy who was with me then showed me about the grounds. I was especially interested in the industrial building.

The sounding of a bell, he told me, was the signal for the stu- 12 dents to gather in the general assembly hall, and he asked me if I would go. Of course I would. There were between three and four hundred students and perhaps all of the teachers gathered in the room. I noticed that several of the latter were colored. The presi-dent gave a talk addressed principally to new comers; but I scarcely heard what he said, I was so much occupied in looking at those around me. They were of all types and colors, the more in-telligent types predominating. The colors ranged from jet black to pure white, with light hair and eyes. Among the girls especially there were many so fair that it was difficult to believe that they had Negro blood in them. And, too, I could not help but notice that many of the girls, particularly those of the delicate brown shades, with black eyes and wavy dark hair, were decidedly pretty. Among the boys, many of the blackest were fine specimens of young manhood, tall, straight, and muscular, with magnificent heads; these were the kind of boys who developed into the patriarchal "uncles" of the old slave régime.

13   When I left the University it was with the determination to get my trunk, and move out to the school before night. I walked back across the city with a light step and a light heart. I felt perfectly satisfied with life for the first time since my mother's death. In passing the railroad station I hired a wagon and rode with the driver as far as my stopping place. I settled with my landlord and went upstairs to put away several articles I had left out. As soon as I opened my trunk a dart of suspicion shot through my heart; the arrangement of things did not look familiar. I began to dig down excitedly to the bottom till I reached the coat in which I had concealed my treasure. My money was gone! Every single bill of it. I knew it was useless to do so, but I searched through every other coat, every pair of trousers, every vest, and even into each pair of socks. When I had finished my fruitless search I sat down dazed and heartsick. I called the landlord up, and informed him of my loss; he comforted me by saying that I ought to have better sense than to keep money in a trunk, and that he was not responsible for his lodgers' personal effects. His cooling words brought me enough to my senses to cause me to look and see if anything else was missing. Several small articles were gone, among them a black and gray necktie of odd design upon which my heart was set; almost as much as the loss of my money, I felt the loss of my tie.

14   After thinking for awhile as best I could, I wisely decided to go at once back to the university and lay my troubles before the president. I rushed breathlessly back to the school. As I neared the grounds the thought came across me, would not my story sound fishy? Would it not place me in the position of an impostor or beggar? What right had I to worry these busy people with the results of my carelessness? If the money could not be recovered, and I

doubted that it could, what good would it do to tell them about it. The shame and embarrassment which the whole situation gave me caused me to stop at the gate. I paused, undecided, for a moment; then turned and slowly retraced my steps, and so changed the whole course of my life.

If the reader has never been in a strange city without money or friends, it is useless to try to describe what my feelings were; he could not understand. If he has been, it is equally useless, for he understands more than words could convey. When I reached my lodgings I found in the room one of the porters who had slept there the night before. When he heard what misfortune had befallen me he offered many words of sympathy and advice. He asked me how much money I had left, I told him that I had ten or twelve dollars in my pocket. He said, "That won't last you very long here, and you will hardly be able to find anything to do in Atlanta. I'll tell you what you do, go down to Jacksonville and you won't have any trouble to get a job in one of the big hotels there, or in St. Augustine." I thanked him, but intimated my doubts of being able to get to Jacksonville on the money I had. He reassured me by saying, "Oh, that's all right. You express your trunk on through, and I'll take you down in my closet." I thanked him again, not knowing then, what it was to travel in a Pullman porter's closet. He put me under a deeper debt of gratitude by lending me fifteen dollars, which he said I could pay back after I had secured work. His generosity brought tears to my eyes, and I concluded that, after all, there were some kind hearts in the world.

I now forgot my troubles in the hurry and excitement of getting my trunk off in time to catch the train, which went out at seven o'clock. I even forgot that I hadn't eaten anything since morning. We got a wagon—the porter went with me—and took my trunk to the express office. My new friend then told me to come to the station at about a quarter of seven, and walk straight to the car where I should see him standing, and not to lose my nerve. I found my rôle not so difficult to play as I thought it would be, because the train did not leave from the central station, but from a smaller one, where there were no gates and guards to pass. I followed directions, and the porter took me on his car, and

15

16

locked me in his closet. In a few minutes the train pulled out for Jacksonville.

17   I may live to be a hundred years old, but I shall never forget the agonies I suffered that night. I spent twelve hours doubled up in the porter's basket for soiled linen, not being able to straighten up on account of the shelves for clean linen just over my head. The air was hot and suffocating and the smell of damp towels and used linen was sickening. At each lurch of the car over the none too smooth track, I was bumped and bruised against the narrow walls of my narrow compartment. I became acutely conscious of the fact that I had not eaten for hours. Then nausea took possession of me, and at one time I had grave doubts about reaching my destination alive. If I had the trip to make again, I should prefer to walk.

1912

The Day the Fire Came

Virginia Bell Dabney

1   The last rain in these mountains this summer was about July 11. It is now the twenty-first day of August and it has not rained for one month and ten hot days. All of us who live here think some computer glitch has been made in weather deliveries and we are getting Arizona weather by mistake. Days that usually have a high of eighty degrees now reach into the parching nineties. Thunderheads rise in the west, look us over, and then go somewhere else to rain. Grass crackles underfoot, the birds quit singing after the sun is up. Many have packed it up and left; the indigo buntings are gone and the wood thrush has taken his flute to damper places.

2   I sit limply on the porch with a cold drink; the dog lies at my feet eyeing my glass. Finally I give him an ice cube and he crunches

it, licking up the tiny ice puddles. I give him another and he wants it, but not now, so he takes it over to a dusty bush and buries it. It is the first drink the bush has had in forty-two days.

3   A wind comes up in the afternoon, leaving the dogwoods limp and the poplars yellowing prematurely. There is a smell in the air that I remember from another time; it is of green leaves hot and burned in the sun. I keep watching the horizon and sniffing for any faint whiff of fire starting in the woods, made wary for all time by what happened when I was eleven.

4   On a Sunday in April 1930, my mother was pacing from the yard to our upstairs hallway window and then down again. She was watching a column of smoke rising beyond our woods to the west. I caught her nervousness and watched also, but without her added awareness that there had been very little rainfall during the winter and early spring. There were new leaves on the trees, but on the forest floor the old leaves were as dry and separate as cornflakes.

5   I heard Mother report to my sister Allison that the smoke seemed to be moving our way. Allison was in bed, feverish and coughing. She wanted to get up and help us, but my mother said, "Only if necessary," and started gathering possessions we could take with us if the fire came nearer. Allison was coughing more, the smoke was bothering her. Mother was dumping drawer contents into a box. I lugged down books I wanted to save and Mother told me, "There's no room in the car for those, Vallie."

6   Our neighbor Carl Stevens drove into the yard and my mother met him on the porch. There was a tense conversation. "Mrs. Bell, you and the girls better get out right quick. That fire is picking up fast. You all better come over to our house. It's got so much plowed land around it I think it will be safe."

7   "Allison is sick in bed," Mother told him. "You can take the girls and I can come behind you."

8   But she had hardly finished when I burst into tears. I grabbed her arm and said, "I won't go unless you go too!" I was sure she would be caught in the fire if we left first. Carl looked at my stricken face and said, "I'll just take Allison." He went into the bedroom with my mother, picked Allison up in her blankets, and carried her out to his car.

9   The wind picked up, smoke was blueing the air around us, and the smell of burning leaves stung our noses. My mother pulled her Model T near the porch and put a box with our silver, her photographs, and her handmade linens into the tiny trunk space. She had already put our suitcases on the running board. Now she hastily gathered up some new WearEver pots and pans packed in salesmen's suitcases and flung them on the bare sand of the tennis court. Burning ash was flying over us. "Get in," Mother yelled at me, and I did so only because she had her foot on the running board itself. She backed the car out, and as we fled through smoke growing thicker every minute, she leaned out of the window and called Mac, the dog. He came running. "Lean out and call him," she told me, and I did. He ran easily not far behind us; he had never followed the car before but understood this was a crisis.

10   I thought but didn't ask about the cows in the pasture and the chickens in the chicken houses. There were new chicks under the brooder, and I told myself that the brooder house was off by itself and maybe . . . .

11   At Carl's house my mother parked the car near their drive. We all ran toward the open field on the north side of the Stevenses' big house to watch the fire. I could see our house standing calmly among its oak trees. Behind it to the north the fire seemed to be going away, though the smoke was so thick it was hard to tell. We could see great rolling balls of fire in the treetops and I thought I could feel the heat on my face.

12   "If the wind just doesn't change . . . ," my mother said.

13   We stood there until I couldn't stand the tension and began to cry, but Mother said, "Hush, that only makes things worse," and I stopped, wanting to watch and at the same time afraid to see what would happen. The whole woods beyond our house, our orchard in its grassy clearing, were in flames. There was a crackling sound as branches broke and fell from trees like burning logs in a fireplace, showering sparks. Over our heads birds were flying from the fire. Our house stood peacefully silhouetted against the orange-and-black swirl of smoke and flame.

14   Suddenly I heard my mother say tightly. "The wind's shifted," and we watched as a great ball of fire, tumbling and rolling on the

wind, came toward our house. It caught first in the highest oak-tree branches, and they flared like torches. My mother turned away and said. "That's it." I stared long enough to see burning branches drop on our roof and the entire scene obliterated by smoke that had tongues of flames roaring through it.

My mother and I walked back to the Stevenses' back porch 15 and sat on the steps, she silent and her face white. After a while Carl came over and said, "It's not coming here. Your fields just burned over and it stopped at the road."

"The house gone?" she said, looking up. 16

"It's gone," he said. "All those trees dropped fire on it." 17

I can remember almost nothing else about the rest of that day. 18 My mother could not go back to our place because some of the old trees were still burning and the ground was still hot.

We had supper at the Stevenses' big table, and afterward Miss 19 Lou, Carl's wife, took me upstairs to a tiny room under sloping eaves and showed me a bed with a feather mattress. When I sank into it its billows rose around me. It was warm and cozy and I snuggled in deeply.

I was still asleep at faint daylight when Mother, unable to rest, 20 went to the kitchen and found Carl, Miss Lou, and Carl's mother fixing breakfast. They gave her coffee and a hot biscuit and then Carl went with her to look at the smoking ruins of our farm.

The barn was gone, the machine shed vanished, the wood- 21 shed and its attached room, where my mother kept her equipment for developing photographs, were ash heaps. One of the chicken houses was a mass of hot melted asphalt roofing over incinerated birds and twisted metal feeders. Another still stood, the new one set off by itself and built for the largest new brood of chickens, which were now gone with the brooder house.

My mother and Carl walked down the pasture hill, seeking 22 the cows they believed might have escaped. At the bottom, up to their knees in the stream, the devastated woods behind them, both of them stood, their udders distended with milk. Carl went back to his house to get milk buckets.

Neither Allison nor I was allowed to go back to view the ru- 23 ins. We stood with Miss Lou looking across the fields at the black skeletons of trees around the dark pile of rubble that had been our house. We stared numbly, trying to sort out what had happened.

24   My mother was walking from one pile of rubble to another, feeling, she said later, in a daze, when our neighbors the Woodfords drove up in their wagon. Their own house and buildings were safe but they had lost some good forest. Mrs. Woodford put her arm around Mother and said, "We've been praying for you and the girls. Now we want you all to come stay with us until things are straightened out. We'll be so glad to have you, you know."

25   Her earnest goodness touched my mother, but it was not her way to turn to others. "I'm not sure yet what I have to do," she said, "but it's wonderfully kind of you to offer." She laid a hand briefly on Mrs. Woodford's arm. "I just have to work things out."

26   Mother and Mrs. Woodford moved from ruin to ruin, picking up pieces of things, trying to identify them. One was a darkened dish with a garland of roses; looking at it in her neighbor's hand, Mother said, "Those were my best dessert bowls." She carried it around with her as they walked.

27   Before the day was half over, people from miles around were coming to find out what had happened to the Bells, to ask if they could help, and to wander about the stricken farmyard. Tom Walker came on foot and asked my mother what she was going to do now. "Ye ain't wantin' to stay here, are ye?"

28   "I don't have any other home, Mr. Walker."

29   He spat with no change of expression. "I tole my wife that's what ye'd say. Ye ain't no quitter, I tole her."

30   The Painters also urged my Mother to move in with them until she could decide what to do, but she thanked them with the same words she'd said to others. She did not say that she had already decided what to do; she was probably not ready to put it into words. When the others had gone, she asked Carl to come with her to look at the chicken house that had been untouched by fire. It still smelled of recently poured cement and new wood. As she opened the door she said, "You see this little room we set off for feed? I think I can stay in here while a place is fixed up for all of us."

31   "It's right small . . . ," Carl said doubtfully.

"But look, I could put a cot over there, and some kind of stove ₃₂ here. And a table and chair. That's all I need right now."

He shook his head. "You know you can stay with us. You'd be ₃₃ comfortable and real close by."

"But Carl, I need to be here. I'll have the dog, you know." ₃₄

That, of course, is how it was. I was sent to stay with my other ₃₅ sister, Daphne, so I could finish out the school year. Allison, still running a fever, was put to bed at the home of a friend who was a nurse. As she had already decided, Mother moved into the feed room of the chicken house, from which she directed and helped with the cleanup of all that was left of our house, barn, and sheds. She kept finding remnants of her life that she turned over and over: a solidified aluminum puddle on the tennis court where the pots and pans she'd tried to save had melted; the handles to her bread mixer and meat grinder, the wooden parts burned off, the machines twisted and useless; fragments of rose glass from the shattered hanging lamp in the living room.

Before they were hauled away, she touched the warped brass ₃₆ bedsteads, the broken shards of pitchers and basins, and the cracked, streaked pieces of my father's plate collection that had once shone from a plate rail in our new dining room.

Mother did not allow herself to sigh over these things for long; ₃₇ there was too much to do. One of the first things she did was to walk through deep ash in the ruined woods to see what was left. The young silver-green white pines were gone, and the hollies, once so thick, were unrecognizable. But the trunks of the large blackened oaks and maples still stood, two or three large barren branches left pointing upward. Walking behind my mother with an ax, our hired man, Solomon, cut a notch here and there in the charred bark; underneath there was solid, unburned wood.

"There's a lot of timber here good for building if we can get it ₃₈ out," my mother told Solomon. "Enough for all of us," she said thoughtfully. In her mind, a plan was already taking shape that would distract her from despair and keep her from always watching the skies and listening for rain.

1990

Don't Get Comfortable

Naton Leslie

1 This story is about a railroad detective named Charley Best. Best worked in the 1920s on the narrow-gauge lines between Pitts-burgh and the lumber and mining hill towns of northwestern Pennsylvania. My father tells this story and said his father told it to him, having known Best or known others who knew him. Or maybe my grandfather rode those rails to work in the camps; I know he worked for the railroad, lighting kerosene lamps on the bridge over the Allegheny River and during winter breaking ice from cables that hoisted lanterns high above the girders.

2 My father tells that story too, how when he was five years old his father would take him out at night when he made his rounds on the bridge over the Allegheny in Mahoning, Pennsylvania. His father would climb over the side, hanging on to the slick catwalk while he broke cables free after an ice storm. The night would be filled with frigid gusts, and the wind was particularly strong that high above the river. On the swaying iron bridge my grandfather ordered my father to "take a holt" of the side railing. He was never frightened during these trips because his father was so strong, sure-footed, and careful. It must have been like watching an ath-lete, my grandfather climbing catlike over the rail, hitting the ice-bound cables with steady blows from the ball-peen. He was a compact man, and every movement, every swing of the hammer, seemed to come from the center of his body.

3 This was 1934, and my grandfather was lucky to have this bit of a job, this small paycheck, in the mountains of Pennsylvania where no farm made it, where the mines had begun to play out. So, though the job was dangerous and hard, he did it, and because I remember my grandfather as a meticulous man, I'm sure he did it well. Why he took my father along is less clear, though my grandmother may have asked him to get him out of her hair for a while, not realizing the danger, or perhaps my grandfather as-sumed his son would have to do the job someday. He'd been

taught how to plant, to shoe horses, to make medicines, and to build outbuildings by his own father on the homestead farm. Perhaps my grandfather was teaching his son about the railroad.

Once, as my father tells it, a train crossed the bridge while they 4 were on it. It was a bitterly cold, moonless night, and the lanterns seemed to light only the barest arc of the old iron bridge. My grandfather was hanging from a side rail, breaking ice and edging a cable through the pulley, when the headlamp of the train broke the darkness. He hollered to my father to hop over the side of the bridge and hold on, to "get a purchase and don't let go no matter what." Then, as the train caused the bridge to quake and sway, my father felt his father's arm around him and his own weight release from his arms as his father held them both by one arm, sixty feet above the icy Allegheny. "Imagine," my father says when he tells the story, "a five-year-old boy and I wasn't even scared," though I wonder if he says that in tribute to his naive courage or in acknowledgment of trusting his father so utterly that fear never occurred to him.

I don't know where my grandfather heard of Charley Best. 5 The area was sparsely populated; it had been homesteaded in the mid-nineteenth century and remained wholly wilderness until the first oil well in the nation, the Drake Well, was drilled in Titusville. Those who worked in the lumber and mining camps, and later in oil fields and railroad yards, were all like Charley Best and my grandfather, raised on hardscrabble farms in the Allegheny Mountains, farms now part of the Allegheny National Forest, a mixed old-growth-second-growth wilderness replacing their hard-won clearings and plantings. They were coarse, often violent people for whom fighting was merely another kind of work. For Charley Best, his work became violence. Best had a fierce reputation, and my father, who used to see him at Walker's store in Mahoning, said he looked the part. The railroad detective bought cigars at Walker's, and even there he carried a sidearm, what my father thought was an enormous Colt. He was a big man, and my father also remembers his wide hat, the high leather boots with the pant cuffs tucked inside, and the huge chain stretched across his chest, Prince Albert style, upon which hung a nickel-plated railroad watch my father thought was as big as an alarm clock. Mostly, though, he remembers that handgun and a handlebar mustache Best had cultivated to curl around his wide face. My father poses as Best as he tells the story, striding the catwalks and tops of rail-cars, wind whipping his mustache back like flames. But it's the same picture he paints of his grandfather, Doc, one of the original homesteaders in Forest County. We have a photograph of him, published in a volume of local history, his reportedly immense size diminished by a team of oxen behind him, that same mustache flaring like horns.

6   My father heard a story about Doc at the funeral of one of his uncles, and in it his mustache and oxen are part of the scenery. Doc Leslie had taken cattle into Brookville, Pennsylvania, to sell. Later, while he was having a drink at the Sigel Hotel, one of the men from town said, "Aren't you scared traveling all the way back to Blue Jay Ridge with that much money on you, Doc?"

7   My father doesn't say what Doc said back—some grunt or mumble through his mustache—but later, on Blood Road in his oxcart, Doc was jumped by three men wearing bandannas, like the outlaws they had read about in dime novels.

8   It was only a joke. These were friends of Doc's, out only to put a scare in him, but when one of them said "Stick 'em up," Doc replied, "Stick 'em up, hell. There'll be feet up and shit flying," as he leaped from the cart, scattering the men with his bullwhip. When my father tells it, he pantomimes rolling up one sleeve to signify the fight, his eyes fierce and fixed. The story is frozen at that point: Doc poised for action, the flight of the men inevitable.

9   Part of Charley Best's story is arrested as well. Best patrolled the tops of railcars as they sped across the hills toward the coal fields. My father said those who hopped trains rode Charley's line only twice: the first time you were warned, and if you took Detective Best's warning with humility, you got where you wanted to go. But Best remembered, and the second time he caught you riding free, you were off.

10   "Off?" I once asked, interrupting my father for once as he told the story. His irritation was clear.

11   "Yeah, *off*," he said, his arms poised in the act of grabbing someone by the scruff of the neck and back of the trousers. I re-membered a postcard drawn by Wobbly leader Joe Hill, a comic

gravel
gravel

portrait of himself being booted from a train, and had less admiration for Best and more sympathy for the hoboes who just wanted a ride and ended up flying.

I could see them soaring, sprawling like skydivers over the empty air of the railroad cut, over the sixty-foot drop from the bridge in Mahoning. I've always been hesitant about heights—not actually frightened, only concerned and reluctant about climbing, a controllable vertigo. Not that I have suffered many spectacular falls. Once I fell off, or more accurately, ran off, the top of an extension ladder when a wasp landed on my nose. I simply turned around, stepped off the top of the ladder, and began to run, heading straight down to a gravel parking lot of the car dealership where I was working. I was pretty skinned up, landing on my forearms to protect my face from the gravel, and my coworker, a young biker named Rocky, said, "Man, did you crash 'n' burn!" Perhaps I got this timidity from my mother, who also shied from heights. I remember my father, mother, older sister, and myself climbing a fire tower in the Allegheny Mountains. My mother and I made it about halfway up when the open sides and the lack of a railing sent me back down. My father and sister made it to the top, and I watched from the ground as they laughed and climbed impossibly higher.

My sister trusted my wild and unpredictable father and would follow him, while my trust in him had limits. Probably he had learned not to fear heights from his father on that railroad bridge; he even took a job as a tree-topper for a lumber company and later as a lineman for the power company. When he was sixteen he got a job as a ground hand, or "ground squirrel," as they called the young boys who dragged limbs by the butt to the burn pile. He grew to love the work, part of the postwar rural electrification program, and when not piling brush he watched the men high in trees worrying off limbs with bow saws.

Finally he got his own climbing gear: long hooks like bayonets that strapped to his high-topped boots and a wide leather belt to wrap around tree trunks. He got so good he'd climb a tree, and eventually a utility pole, with only his hooks and hands on the trunk, using the belt only when he reached the top. He said he loved heights; on top of a tree on a mountain he said he could see

timidity
timidity

all of Forest County, see deer move in herds and bears trailing cubs on the ridge miles away. Working for the power company, my father climbed poles on wide rights of way cut across the mountains, high power lines carrying thousands of volts from transformer substations to light lamps in a farmhouse on remote Blue Jay Ridge.

15   But he fell. Twice. The first time, he says, they were putting up new lines on poles in residential Brookville. Poles were originally treated with creosote to prevent decay, a dark, oil-based coating that smelled vaguely of kerosene and urine, now outlawed in favor of a pressure treatment with brine. These were old poles, put up at the turn of the century during the first wave of utility construction, and that morning my father climbed the first one. He says he had just hooked on his belt and was looking up at the late autumn sky, a mix of clouds and high blue. He thought, "Those clouds sure are moving fast," and then he realized it was he who was moving, not the clouds, as the pole was falling, breaking off at the rotten base. He tells how he managed to take off his belt and scamper to the other side, riding the pole to the ground as it bent, then snapped.

16   The other time he fell was more dangerous, and more miraculous. He was at the top of a forty-five-foot pole, and according to the newspaper article from the *Oil City Derrick* his belt snapped and he pitched backward. My father says that after he felt the belt give he reached for the crossarm. His fingertips barely reached the glass insulators on his right, but he was unable to grasp them or the wooden beam, and he fell. He flipped backward twice in the air, landed on his feet, bounced, and fell on his side. He stood up, apparently unhurt, but when he tried to unbuckle his tool harness he found the fingers on his left hand would not work; he had broken his wrist in two places. Later he would develop severe back problems and would suffer years of pain, caused I'm sure by that jarring fall, though he never seemed to connect the two.

17   He doesn't tell either of those stories often. You don't tell stories that could have ended so finally. I heard him once admit to waking up in the middle of the night, years later, a dream of fingertips grazing the crossarm tearing him into sweaty wakefulness. And these stories are among the few illustrating a point or a

moral. My father would sometimes say, after telling one of these stories, that there's only one thing you need to know to do "high work": "Don't get comfortable." What he means goes beyond the commonplace "Keep your wits about you." It's the lesson I forgot when I ran off the top of that ladder—whenever doing anything high up, do it with the knowledge of where you are. I use this advice whenever I work on ladders or roofs—whenever I am moving about and stop thinking about being up high, I force myself to remember; I stop and say aloud, "Don't get comfortable."

Charley Best would not have told his own story either. Perhaps that's why others told the story for him. My father claims he grew mean and that his father did not like Best, not because he threw men off trains but because he shot a twelve-year-old boy in the back for stealing coal from the railyard at night. The boy, a homeless child the railroad workers called Hard Rock Pete, hung around the railyards, and the gandy dancers and switch operators often shared their lunches with him, casually adopting him. My grandfather said he was shy and weak, and they all assumed he slept in abandoned work shacks or boxcars in the yard. Best, my grandfather claimed, saw the boy at night, stooping over and pulling lumps of coal into a shirt hooped to make a sack. Best claimed at the investigation that he couldn't tell it was Hard Rock Pete—the boy was tall and wore bulky clothes that late fall evening, hiding his frail frame. When he stood up and lit a cigarette, Best saw him, and when the detective's menacing voice called out, the boy ran. That's when Charley Best shot him with the big Colt. [18]

But that's not the story of Charley Best my father often tells; that's another story, or actually part of the longer version of the story, because it shows how mean Best got afterward, how what happened changed him. I remember once my father was telling the story at my grandmother Harnish's house, a gathering of men in his mother-in-law's parlor listening, among them Sam, her second husband, who in the last year had been forced to sit on the couch with an oxygen tank beside him, alternately reaching for the hose and mask to give him the oxygen black lung denied him and bending over, panting with effort, to spit tobacco juice into a plastic bucket. [19]

20   My father began telling the story sitting down, but was standing by the time he began describing Best, the Harnish men listening closely though they had heard the story before, while I sat
watching the story being retold as I leaned forward in the straight-
backed chair moved into the room and parked near the television.
I had recently turned thirteen and was splitting my time between
the room where adult men sat, talking slowly, and the cousins outside exploring the forty-acre farm I had already mapped over the
years of visits. Sam's son Warren had finally finished a long-
winded story that made my father edgy and restless, and how he
had managed to get to the story of Charley Best I'm not sure, but
the story was well under way.

21   Best had been assigned jurisdiction, lacking any other police,
over several mining camps in northwestern Pennsylvania, and
was sent to arrest a miner in Chickasaw, near the New York border, who was accused of stealing. My father added that he probably only had stolen coal from the railyard, as everyone did in the
1930s. Warren interrupted briefly to tell how he and his brothers
stole coal from the Clarion yards, but my father skillfully steered
the conversation back to Best.

22   "Chickasaw was a rough mining camp, just up the river from
Mahoning, and Charley Best was sent there, where there was no
other law, to arrest that miner," he began again, and everyone
leaned comfortably back into the story, glad Warren had been
stopped. He explained how Best arrived in town, Colt revolver
displayed prominently, cigar under his ample mustache, and how
he walked over to the tavern, a slapped-up, long and low shed affair, where he assumed he would find the thief. The men inside sat
on rough stools, and the ceiling of plank was held up with twelve-
inch rough-cut beams. "One of them eyes Best, and Best figured
that was him and that he'd have to slug it out with the miner to
take him." My father's eyes grew narrow and menacing.

23   I'd heard this story many times and knew the men in the room
had heard it too; they were sitting through the telling as though it
were a ritual, a stage in their conversation they always reached,
and passed. But then an unexpected reaction from Sam drew their
attention from my father, who was perched on his knees at the end
of the story. Sam did not speak much in those last years because

speech was breath, and each breath was bought with larger portions of his strength. Yet there in the room filled with his sons and
the husbands of his daughters, he pushed out a hurried "Yes," and
quickly drawing on the oxygen as the heads of the men turned to
him, added, "I drove those miners to Chickasaw every day in an
old buckboard—they were usually drunk. A rough, wild bunch,"
he said, spitting a brown stream and reaching for the hose again.
"Yes, that's how it happened."

My father never worked in the mines, so was spared the black 24
lung from which Sam and so many others suffered, but he often
spoke of the mines as though he had worked there, as he had lived
among the miners, played with their children, fought with their
sons, and eventually drunk and laughed with them after work on
the power lines. In his father's day the miners began forming
unions, and these hardened men formed even harder coal-black
clumps of strikers. One of them, Piercy MacIntyre, was an orga-
nizer and therefore was even rougher than most. The bosses in
Chickasaw claimed he had been sent in from the outside, an agi-
tator, but some of the men said he came from around Blue Jay
Ridge, from a hill farm so far back "the owls carried knapsacks."

My father had met Piercy MacIntyre, but he knew his son 25
Jackie better. The miners said Piercy had been a boxer in France
during World War I, and whether true or not, he did teach his son
Jackie how to box. He'd take the boy, eight or nine years old, down
to Walker's store, and men would clear a makeshift ring in the corner, moving stock to form a rough square. Walker would then hold
the bets as Jackie's opponent, usually an older boy of twelve or so,
was announced. My father claims Jackie beat all comers, and my
father, younger by two or three years, always rooted for him as fer-
vently as he did for Joe Louis when his father would struggle to
pick up Louis's fights through the static on KDKA radio. He tells
how Louis knocked out Max Schmeling, the Nazi superman, so
quickly that once they got the station in, all they heard was the
count to ten.

Twenty-five years later, after my father had moved one hun- 26
dred miles away to work in the mills of Ohio, he ran into Jackie
MacIntyre at Republic Steel. He spoke to him, and though Jackie,
now John, didn't remember him as one of his youngest fans

among the dozens or more who had watched him fight as a kid, my father said they talked briefly of people they knew, even about Charley Best. My father said he was puzzled to see how the guys in the mill picked on him, and MacIntyre didn't seem to care. My father thought, "You guys don't know who you're dealing with."

27   Although my father had moved to the edge of the industrial Midwest, the mountains and forests remained home to him, and we went back every weekend to visit. And he hunted in Pennsylvania, not along the industrial riverbanks of Ohio. My father liked only two sports, boxing and hunting, and he tried to teach me both. I never caught on to boxing, partly because my father couldn't coach me while we sparred without beginning to fight in earnest, burying me in a flurry of open-palmed combinations and jabs. I liked the fluidity of the movements, the backpedaling, the duck-and-jab; however, I was not destined to be a boxer. I have a glass jaw, a nerve positioned in my face that makes a knockout a matter of one punch. My father found this fatal flaw one day while we sparred in the living room. One quick jab to my left jaw and I felt nothing—I saw pinpoints of light and awoke to my father shaking his head and saying, "The kid's got a glass jaw." As a boxer I was finished.

28   But hunting was another matter. Early on, my father declared I was a natural good shot, that I had a "good eye" that made up, I suppose, for my bad jaw. I could pick off pennies at twenty-five yards with a .22-caliber rifle, and after I got a shotgun, a 16-gauge, my father spent one long afternoon throwing clay pigeons, which I shot out of the air. He threw more than seventy, and I missed two. I enjoyed target shooting not only because I was good at it but because I did it without thinking. I simply knew when I was on target and then pulled the trigger. I guess it was instinct or something reflexive.

29   Yet, by age eighteen, I had pretty much lost interest in hunting. Animals made poor targets; they were hard to find, but when found, too big and easy. For a target shooter, walking all day for one shot at an easy target was not much of a thrill. I still went hunting with my father when in my teens, but I had no real enthusiasm for the sport, as he did. I tried to find it; I remember not eating one day, thinking that it would make me a keener hunter, but it only made me a hungry one. What I liked was the evening, getting

comfortable down at Archie's camp, near his stone fireplace, listening to hunting stories.

The last time I went hunting with my father I was eighteen. I [30] hadn't been deer hunting that last fall because the season fell during final exam week at college, and it was with some relief that I realized this would happen every year. However, I went hunting for turkey that spring. I think I liked turkey hunting most because the hunt occurred in midautumn and midspring, the two most beautiful times of the year to be in the forest. You also could go deeper into the woods because, unlike a deer, once a turkey was shot it was not hard to pull it out of the woods. Dragging a hundred pounds of deer carcass over several miles of rough terrain quickly dampened the thrill of the hunt.

It was a cold April in the mountains that year; patches of snow [31] still clung to rocks and roots in the forest, and springs remained frozen, even in the bright sunshine. My father led the way through the woods we hunted north of Brookville, stepping around the icy stones and fallen limbs with sure-footed grace and speed. Every hour or so we would stop and cradle our shotguns, and my father would bring out the wooden turkey call, a cedar box with a top that wagged loosely when shaken, chalk between box and lid giving off a decent gobble.

The turkey call was a new addition to our hunting gear. My fa- [32] ther had never gone in for gimmicks as a hunter, although he thought my aunt Clair's trick of rubbing apple cores on her boots to attract deer might account for her yearly success. However, in the over twenty-five years he had been hunting, he had never bagged a wild turkey. He was well known among the locals for regularly bringing out a deer. He'd have a deer within the first couple of hours of the opening day of the season and could be found down at Archie's camp or at the Sigel Hotel by early afternoon, telling how the deer, never a trophy buck but respectable, would have risen from his bed twenty-five yards from my father's stand at first light. But turkeys had always eluded him, so he bought the call and had been practicing for months, brief chirps and throaty gobbles rising from our basement ever since September.

That day we had walked farther into the woods than usual, [33] so far that we found ourselves on Windfall Ridge, or so it was called on my father's topo map. The ridge was steep and treeless, and the North Fork Creek ran noisily below. My father had noticed a stand of beech, and knowing turkeys like beechnuts, we had stopped to look for signs. Sure enough, my father found a large patch where turkeys had been scratching the winter-decayed leaves, a large flock probably discovered and broken up by other hunters earlier in the morning. The turkeys would still be in the area, scattered over Windfall, calling out to regroup. We stood and listened, but all I heard was the icy North Fork and a high wind in the trees.

34   So my father decided to try calling them in, making first a few hesitant chirps, then a long and short gobble that he'd heard was the turkey equivalent of "I'm over here."

35   And a turkey answered. The bird sounded like it was on the edge of the ridge, about fifty yards in front of us, but neither of us could see it. We walked cautiously toward the sound, my heart pounding for my father, hoping he'd at long last get a shot at the turkey. As we reached the ridge we split, my father wandering to the right of a tall pine growing in the fragile earth of the rim of the ridge, I to the left. The turkey flew out of the tree in a great bluster of wings. It flew left and was clearly my shot.

36   I snapped up my shotgun and found him quickly, flying high but in range. Then I thought about it. I wished the bird had flown right, to give my father the shot, wished it was not flying over the ice-filmed North Fork into which I would surely have to wade, waist high, to retrieve the bird. And I knew I did not want to kill the turkey; I had no need of it.

37   So I shot behind it, the bird's wings flapping comically faster after the sound echoed over the ridge. The turkey flew higher, out of range of another shot from me or my father, not landing until it reached the next ridge. I turned to look at my father, who said, "How'd you miss him?"

38   "Jerked the trigger, I think," I said, still looking over at the ridge where the bird had disappeared. "Or I choked; I don't know," I added.

39   "Hell, a good shot like you must have hit him," he said. "Maybe he went down with a few shot in him."

"Nah, he was too high up, out of range," I answered, not ₄₀
wanting to have to wade the creek anyway and hike the next ridge
looking for the bird.

But we did cross the creek, over the back of a windfallen tree, ₄₁
and after searching for the bird for a while decided we had had
our shot for the day and gave up. It was midafternoon, and it was
a long way back, and I, having slipped into the North Fork on the
return crossing, wearily tramped behind my father, one boot
sloshing with creek water.

By the time we arrived at the Sigel Hotel my father was con- ₄₂
vinced I had hit the gobbler but that, as he said, "death is invisible, while life can be seen." A slain animal is still, and the natural
camouflage is perfect. He believed we didn't find a dead turkey
because it blended in with the rocks and undergrowth.

At the Sigel hotel we sat at the long bar, adding our hunting ₄₃
outfits of red wool caps and canvas game vests to those of other
hunters gathered there. My father began telling the story of our
hunt to the man at his right elbow, and eventually to two or
three down the counter. "The boy here got a shot, and I know he
hit him—you should have seen the feathers fly! This kid is a
great wingshot," he continued, telling of my slaughter of clay
pigeons.

The other men answered his story with others, and through ₄₄
that, through the progress of stories to the next, he began telling
the story of Charley Best. "He walked into this bar, a smoky place
with a low ceiling supported by big, twelve-inch rough-cut post,"
he said, his hands surrounding one in the air, "rough like everything else in those camps."

Best looked around the smoky room, and when he spotted the ₄₅
man eyeing him he said, "You'd better finish that drink, because
you're coming with me. You're under arrest."

The man sat with his stool tipped backward against a post, ₄₆
and when Best approached he said, "Well, I guess you're going to
have to pull that big revolver, because I'm not going anywhere."
Best was standing over him, and my father was on his feet in the
Sigel Hotel, doing his best to look down at me as Best must have
glared at the miner.

47   Then my father said, "The guy suddenly pulls a knife, cuts Best across the gut, and slips behind the thick post." My father's knees buckle.

48   Best was not used to working in the camps, so he was out of his element and forgot to watch himself. He was too comfortable, my father would say, and should have reminded himself that Chickasaw was a rough mining camp and that the man he sought could be armed and was drunk, that he was not simply approaching a frightened hobo on top of a rushing train. At this point my father's voice became a little squeezed, imitating the pain of the knife wound, but he continued, "He cut Best clear across the stomach, and his guts bulged and began to spill. With his left arm Best reached down and pulled his own guts back in, and with the right drew his gun and shot the miner." My father was fully on his knees now, his arm and hand holding in intestines, his other arm raising a Colt revolver.

49   "He hit him in the mouth. Killed him deader than hell."

50   This is where the story of Charley Best generally ends, though sometimes my father tells how they took him by train to a hospital in Brookville, how he got mean after that. But with my father on his knees, clutching his stomach in agony, this is when Charley Best appeared, or should have. He could have been a little fellow, age having shrunken him, a glass of clay-colored liquor in front of him at the bar, his mustache trimmed to a salt-and-pepper line under his nose. He'd sit near the opposite end of the counter, listening to but not telling his own story.

51   Best wouldn't wear hunting clothes. He'd stand up and, pulling out his flannel shirttails, say, "That's just the way it happened." Then he'd raise his shirt quickly, and we'd see the brutish pucker circling his waist. When Best sat back down he would drain the liquor in front of him, no one noticing that his left arm rested across his lap and against his body, holding the organs in, still trying to get comfortable with the wound.

1996

Chapter

2

Description

Where the World Began

Margaret Laurence

A strange place it was, that place where the world began. A place 1
of incredible happenings, splendors, and revelations, despairs like
multitudinous pits of isolated hells. A place of shadow-spooki-
ness, inhabited by the unknowable dead. A place of jubilation and
of mourning, horrible and beautiful.

It was, in fact, a small prairie town. 2

Because that settlement and that land were my first and for 3
many years my only real knowledge of this planet, in some profound way they remain my world, my way of viewing. My eyes
were formed there. Towns like ours, set in a sea of land, have been
described thousands of times as dull, bleak, flat, uninteresting. I
have had it said to me that the railway trip across Canada is spectacular, except for the prairies, when it would be desirable to go to
sleep for several days, until the ordeal is over. I am always unable
to argue this point effectively. All I can say is—well, you really have
to live there to know that country. The town of my childhood could
be called bizarre, agonizingly repressive or cruel at times, and the
land in which it grew could be called harsh in the violence of its sea-
sonal changes. But never merely flat or uninteresting. Never dull.

In winter, we used to hitch rides on the back of the milk sleigh, 4
our moccasins squeaking and slithering on the hard rutted snow
of the roads, our hands in ice-bubbled mitts hanging onto the box
edge of the sleigh for dear life, while Bert grinned at us through

53

his great frosted mustache and shouted the horse into speed, daring us to stay put. Those mornings, rising, there would be the perpetual fascination of the frost feathers on windows, the ferns and flowers and eerie faces traced there during the night by unseen artists of the wind. Evenings, coming back from skating, the sky would be black but not dark, for you could see a cold glitter of stars from one side of the earth's rim to the other. And then the sometime astonishment when you saw the Northern Lights flaring across the sky, like the scrawled signature of God. After a blizzard, when the snowplow hadn't yet got through, school would be closed for the day, the assumption being that the town's young could not possibly flounder through five feet of snow in the pursuit of education. We would then gaily don snowshoes and flounder for miles out into the white dazzling deserts, in pursuit of a different kind of knowing. If you came back too close to night, through the woods at the foot of the town hill, the thin black branches of poplar and chokecherry now meringued with frost, sometimes you heard coyotes. Or maybe the banshee wolf-voices were really only inside your head.

5   Summers were scorching, and when no rain came and the wheat became bleached and dried before it headed, the faces of farmers and townsfolk would not smile much, and you took for granted, because it never seemed to have been any different, the frequent knocking at the back door and the young men standing there, mumbling or thrusting defiantly their requests for a drink of water and a sandwich if you could spare it. They were riding the freights, and you never knew where they had come from, or where they might end up, if anywhere. The Drought and Depression were like evil deities which had been there always. You understood and did not understand.

6   Yet the outside world had its continuing marvels. The poplar bluffs and the small river were filled and surrounded with a zillion different grasses, stones, and weed flowers. The meadowlark sang undaunted from the twanging telephone wires along the gravel highway. Once we found an old flat-bottomed scow, and launched her, poling along the shallow brown waters, mending her with wodges of hastily chewed Spearmint, grounding her among the tangles of yellow marsh marigolds that grew succu-

lently along the banks of the shrunken river, while the sun made
our skins smell dusty-warm.

My best friend lived in an apartment above some stores on 7
Main Street (its real name was Mountain Avenue, goodness knows
why), an elegant apartment with royal-blue velvet curtains. The
back roof, scarcely sloping at all, was corrugated tin, of a furnace-
like warmth on a July afternoon, and we would sit there drinking
lemonade and looking across the back lane at the Fire Hall. Sometimes our vigil would be rewarded. Oh joy! Somebody's house
burning down! We had an almost-perfect callousness in some
ways. Then the wooden tower's bronze bell would clonk and toll
like a thousand speeded funerals in a time of plague, and in a few
minutes the team of giant black horses would cannon forth, pulling
the fire wagon like some scarlet chariot of the Goths, while the fire-
men clung with one hand, adjusting their helmets as they went.

The oddities of the place were endless. An elderly lady used 8
to serve, as her afternoon tea offering to other ladies, soda biscuits
spread with peanut butter and topped with a whole marshmal-
low. Some considered this slightly eccentric, when compared with
chopped egg sandwiches, and admittedly talked about her behind
her back, but no one ever refused these delicacies or indicated to
her that they thought she had slipped a cog. Another lady dyed
her hair a bright and cherry orange, by strangers often mistaken at
twenty paces for a feather hat. My own beloved stepmother wore
a silver fox neckpiece, a whole pelt, *with the embalmed (?) head still
on.* My Ontario Irish grandfather said, "sparrow grass," a more interesting term than asparagus. The town dump was known as
"the nuisance grounds," a phrase fraught with weird connotations, as though the effluvia of our lives was beneath contempt but
at the same time was subtly threatening to the determined and
sometimes hysterical propriety of our ways.

Some oddities were, as idiom had it, "funny ha ha"; others 9
were "funny peculiar." Some were not so very funny at all. An old
man lived, deranged, in a shack in the valley. Perhaps he wasn't
even all that old, but to us he seemed a wild Methuselah figure,
shambling among the underbrush and the tall couchgrass, mutter-
ing indecipherable curses or blessings, a prophet who had forgotten his prophecies. Everyone in town knew him, but no one knew

him. He lived among us as though only occasionally and momentarily visible. The kids called him Andy Gump, and feared him. Some sought to prove their bravery by tormenting him. They were the medieval bear baiters, and he the lumbering bewildered bear, half blind, only rarely turning to snarl. Everything is to be found in a town like mine. Belsen, writ small but with the same ink.

10   All of us cast stones in one shape or another. In grade school, among the vulnerable and violet girls we were, the feared and despised were those few older girls from what was charmingly termed "the wrong side of the tracks." Tough in talk and tougher in muscle, they were said to be whores already. And may have been, that being about the only profession readily available to them.

11   The dead lived in that place, too. Not only the grandparents who had, in local parlance, "passed on" and who gloomed, bearded or bonneted, from the sepia photographs in old albums, but also the uncles, forever eighteen or nineteen, whose names were carved on the granite family stones in the cemetery, but whose bones lay in France. My own young mother lay in that graveyard, beside other dead of our kin, and when I was ten, my father, too, only forty, left the living town for the dead dwelling on the hill.

12   When I was eighteen, I couldn't wait to get out of that town, away from the prairies. I did not know then that I would carry the land and town all my life within my skull, that they would form the mainspring and source of the writing I was to do, wherever and however far away I might live.

13   This was my territory in the time of my youth, and in a sense my life since then has been an attempt to look at it, to come to terms with it. Stultifying to the mind it certainly could be, and sometimes was, but not to the imagination. It was many things, but it was never dull.

14   The same, I now see, could be said for Canada in general. Why on earth did generations of Canadians pretend to believe this country dull? We knew perfectly well it wasn't. Yet for so long we did not proclaim what we knew. If our upsurge of so-called nationalism seems odd or irrelevant to outsiders, and even to some of our own people (*what's all the fuss about?*), they might try to understand that for many years we valued ourselves insufficiently, living as we did under the huge shadows of those two dominating figures, Uncle Sam and Britannia. We have only just begun to

value ourselves, our land, our abilities. We have only just begun to
recognize our legends and to give shape to our myths.

There are, God knows, enough aspects to deplore about this 15
country. When I see the killing of our lakes and rivers with industrial wastes, I feel rage and despair. When I see our industries and
natural resources increasingly taken over by America, I feel an
overwhelming discouragement, especially as I cannot simply say
"damn Yankees." It should never be forgotten that it is we ourselves who have sold such a large amount of our birthright for a
mess of plastic Progress. When I saw the War Measures Act being
invoked in 1970, I lost forever the vestigial remains of the naïve
wish-belief that repression could not happen here, or would not.
And yet, of course, I had known all along in the deepest and often
hidden caves of the heart that anything can happen anywhere, for
the seeds of both man's freedom and his captivity are found everywhere, even in the microcosm of a prairie town. But in raging
against our injustices, our stupidities, I do so *as family*, as I did, and
still do in writing, about those aspects of my town which I hated
and which are always in some ways aspects of myself.

The land still draws me more than other lands. I have lived in 16
Africa and in England, but splendid as both can be, they do not
have the power to move me in the same way as, for example, that
part of southern Ontario where I spent four months last summer
in a cedar cabin beside a river. "Scratch a Canadian, and you find
a phony pioneer," I used to say to myself in warning. But all the
same it is true, I think, that we are not yet totally alienated from
physical earth, and let us only pray we do not become so. I once
thought that my lifelong fear and mistrust of cities made me a
kind of old-fashioned freak; now I see it differently.

The cabin has a long window across its front western wall, 17
and sitting at the oak table there in the mornings, I used to look
out at the river and at the tall trees beyond, green-gold in the early
light. The river was bronze; the sun caught it strangely, reflecting
upon its surface the near-shore sand ripples underneath. Suddenly, the crescenting of a fish, gone before the eye could clearly
give image to it. The old man next door said these leaping fish
were carp. Himself, he preferred muskie, for he was a real fisher-
man and the muskie gave him a fight. The wind most often blew
from the south, and the river flowed toward the south, so when

the water was windriffled, and the current was strong, the river seemed to be flowing both ways. I liked this, and interpreted it as an omen, a natural symbol.

18   A few years ago, when I was back in Winnipeg, I gave a talk at my old college. It was open to the public, and afterward a very old man came up to me and asked me if my maiden name had been Wemyss. I said yes, thinking he might have known my father or my grandfather. But no. "When I was a young lad," he said, "I once worked for your great-grandfather, Robert Wemyss, when he had the sheep ranch at Raeburn." I think that was a moment when I realized all over again something of great importance to me. My long-ago families came from Scotland and Ireland, but in a sense that no longer mattered so much. My true roots were here.

19   I am not very patriotic, in the usual meaning of that word. I cannot say "My country right or wrong" in any political, social, or literary context. But one thing is inalterable, for better or worse, for life.

20   This is where my world began. A world which includes the ancestors—both my own and other people's ancestors who become mine. A world which formed me, and continues to do so, even while I found it in some of its aspects, and continue to do so. A world which gave me my own lifework to do, because it was here that I learned the sight of my own particular eyes.

1976

The Metropolitan Cathedral in San Salvador

Joan Didion

1   During the week before I flew down to El Salvador a Salvadoran woman who works for my husband and me in Los Angeles gave me repeated instructions about what we must and must not do.

We must not go out at night. We must stay off the street whenever possible. We must never ride in buses or taxis, never leave the capital, never imagine that our passports would protect us. We must not even consider the hotel a safe place: people were killed in hotels. She spoke with considerable vehemence, because two of her brothers had been killed in Salvador in August of 1981, in their beds. The throats of both brothers had been slashed. Her father had been cut but stayed alive. Her mother had been beaten. Twelve of her other relatives, aunts and uncles and cousins, had been taken from their houses one night the same August, and their bodies had been found some time later, in a ditch. I assured her that we would remember, we would be careful, we would in fact be so careful that we would probably (trying for a light touch) spend all our time in church.

She became still more agitated, and I realized that I had spoken as a *norteamericana:* Churches had not been to this woman the neutral ground they had been to me. I must remember: Archbishop Romero killed saying mass in the chapel of the Divine Providence Hospital in San Salvador. I must remember: More than thirty people killed at Archbishop Romero's funeral in the Metropolitan Cathedral in San Salvador. I must remember: More than twenty people killed before that on the steps of the Metropolitan Cathedral. CBS had filmed it. It had been on television, the bodies jerking, those still alive crawling over the dead as they tried to get out of range. I must understand: The Church was dangerous. 2

I told her that I understood, that I knew all that, and I did, abstractly, but the specific meaning of the Church she knew eluded me until I was actually there, at the Metropolitan Cathedral in San Salvador, one afternoon when rain sluiced down its corrugated plastic windows and puddled around the supports of the Sony and Philips billboards near the steps. The effect of the Metropolitan Cathedral is immediate, and entirely literary. This is the cathedral that the late Archbishop Oscar Arnulfo Romero refused to finish, on the premise that the work of the Church took precedence over its display, and the high walls of raw concrete bristle with structural rods, rusting now, staining the concrete, sticking out at wrenched and violent angles. The wiring is exposed. Fluorescent tubes hang askew. The great high altar is backed by 3 warped plyboard. The cross on the altar is of bare incandescent bulbs, but the bulbs, that afternoon, were unlit: there was in fact no light at all on the main altar, no light on the cross, no light on the globe of the world that showed the northern American continent in gray and the southern in white; no light on the dove above the globe, *Salvador del Mundo.* In this vast brutalist space that was the cathedral, the unlit altar seemed to offer a single ineluctable message: At this time and in this place the light of the world could be construed as out, off, extinguished.

4   In many ways the Metropolitan Cathedral is an authentic piece of political art, a statement for El Salvador as *Guernica* was for Spain. It is quite devoid of sentimental relief. There are no decorative or architectural references to familiar parables, in fact no stories at all, not even the Stations of the Cross. On the afternoon I was there the flowers laid on the altar were dead. There were no traces of normal parish activity. The doors were open to the barricaded main steps, and down the steps there was a spill of red paint, lest anyone forget the blood shed there. Here and there on the cheap linoleum inside the cathedral there was what seemed to be actual blood, dried in spots, the kind of spots dropped by a slow hemorrhage, or by a woman who does not know or does not care that she is menstruating.

5   There were several women in the cathedral during the hour or so I spent there, a young woman with a baby, an older woman in house slippers, a few others, all in black. One of the women walked the aisles as if by compulsion, up and down, across and back, crooning loudly as she walked. Another knelt without moving at the tomb of Archbishop Romero in the right transept. "Loor a Monsenor Romero," the crude needlepoint tapestry by the tomb read, "Praise to Monsignor Romero from the Mothers of the Imprisoned, the Disappeared, and the Murdered," the *Comité de Madres y Familiares de Presos, Desaparecidos, y Asesinados Politicos de El Salvador.*

6   The tomb itself was covered with offerings and petitions, notes decorated with motifs cut from greeting cards and cartoons. I recall one with figures cut from a Bugs Bunny strip, and another with a pencil drawing of a baby in a crib. The baby in this drawing seemed to be receiving medication or fluid or blood intra-

venously, through the IV line shown on its wrist. I studied the notes for a while and then went back and looked again at the un-lit altar, and at the red paint on the main steps, from which it was possible to see the guardsmen on the balcony of the National Palace hunching back to avoid the rain. Many Salvadorans are offended by the Metropolitan Cathedral, which is as it should be, because the place remains perhaps the only unambiguous political statement in El Salvador, a metaphorical bomb in the ultimate power station.

1983

Fifth Avenue, Uptown

James Baldwin

There is a housing project standing now where the house in which 1 we grew up once stood, and one of those stunted city trees is snarling where our doorway used to be. This is on the rehabili-tated side of the avenue. The other side of the avenue—for progress takes time—has not been rehabilitated yet and it looks exactly as it looked in the days when we sat with our noses pressed against the windowpane, longing to be allowed to go "across the street." The grocery store which gave us credit is still there, and there can be no doubt that it is still giving credit. The people in the project certainly need it—far more, indeed, than they ever needed the project. The last time I passed by, the Jewish pro-prietor was still standing among his shelves, looking sadder and heavier but scarcely any older. Farther down the block stands the shoe-repair store in which our shoes were repaired until repara-tion became impossible and in which, then, we bought all our "new" ones. The Negro proprietor is still in the window, head down, working at the leather.

2   These two, I imagine, could tell a long tale if they would (perhaps they would be glad to if they could), having watched so
many, for so long, struggling in the fishhooks, the barbed wire, of
this avenue.

3   The avenue is elsewhere the renowned and elegant Fifth. The
area I am describing, which, in today's gang parlance, would be
called "the turf," is bounded by Lenox Avenue on the west, the
Harlem River on the east, 135th Street on the north, and 130th
Street on the south. We never lived beyond these boundaries; this
is where we grew up. Walking along 145th Street—for example—
familiar as it is, and similar, does not have the same impact because I do not know any of the people on the block. But when I
turn east on 131st Street and Lenox Avenue, there is first a soda-
pop joint, then a shoeshine "parlor," then a grocery store, then a
dry cleaners', then the houses. All along the street there are people
who watched me grow up, people who grew up with me, people
I watched grow up along with my brothers and sisters; and, sometimes in my arms, sometimes underfoot, sometimes at my shoulder—or on it—their children, a riot, a forest of children, who include my nieces and nephews.

4   When we reach the end of this long block, we find ourselves on
wide, filthy, hostile Fifth Avenue, facing that project which hangs
over the avenue like a monument to the folly, and the cowardice,
of good intentions. All along the block, for anyone who knows it,
are immense human gaps, like craters. These gaps are not created
merely by those who have moved away, inevitably into some other
ghetto; or by those who have risen, almost always into a greater capacity for self-loathing and self-delusion; or yet by those who, by
whatever means—World War II, the Korean war, a policeman's
gun or billy, a gang war, a brawl, madness, an overdose of heroin,
or, simply, unnatural exhaustion—are dead. I am talking about
those who are left, and I am talking principally about the young.
What are they doing? Well, some, a minority, are fanatical church-
goers, members of the more extreme of the Holy Roller sects. Many,
many more are "moslems," by affiliation or sympathy, that is to say
that they are united by nothing more—and nothing less—than a
hatred of the white world and all its works. They are present, for
example, at every Buy Black street-corner meeting—meetings in

which the speaker urges his hearers to cease trading with white
men and establish a separate economy. Neither the speaker nor his
hearers can possibly do this, of course, since Negroes do not own
General Motors or RCA or the A & P, nor, indeed, do they own
more than a wholly insufficient fraction of anything else in Harlem
(those who *do* own anything are more interested in their profits
than in their fellows). But these meetings nevertheless keep alive in
the participators a certain pride of bitterness without which, however futile this bitterness may be, they could scarcely remain alive
at all. Many have given up. They stay home and watch the TV
screen, living on the earnings of their parents, cousins, brothers, or
uncles, and only leave the house to go to the movies or to the nearest bar. "How're you making it?" one may ask, running into them
along the block, or in the bar. "Oh, I'm TV-ing it"; with the saddest,
sweetest, most shamefaced of smiles, and from a great distance.
This distance one is compelled to respect; anyone who has traveled
so far will not easily be dragged again into the world. There are further retreats, of course, than the TV screen or the bar. There are
those who are simply sitting on their stoops, "stoned," animated
for a moment only, and hideously, by the approach of someone
who may lend them the money for a "fix." Or by the approach of
someone from whom they can purchase it, one of the shrewd ones,
on the way to prison or just coming out.

And the others, who have avoided all of these deaths, get up   5
in the morning and go downtown to meet "the man." They work
in the white man's world all day and come home in the evening to
this fetid block. They struggle to instill in their children some private sense of honor or dignity which will help the child to survive.
This means, of course, that they must struggle, stolidly, inces-
santly, to keep this sense alive in themselves, in spite of the insults,
the indifference, and the cruelty they are certain to encounter in
their working day. They patiently browbeat the landlord into fixing the heat, the plaster, the plumbing; this demands prodigious
patience; nor is patience usually enough. In trying to make their
hovels habitable, they are perpetually throwing good money after
bad. Such frustration, so long endured, is driving many strong,
admirable men and women whose only crime is color to the very
gates of paranoia.

6   One remembers them from another time—playing handball
in the playground, going to church, wondering if they were going
to be promoted at school. One remembers them going off to war—
gladly, to escape this block. One remembers their return. Perhaps
one remembers their wedding day. And one sees where the girl is
now—vainly looking for salvation from some other embittered,
trussed, and struggling boy—and sees the all-but-abandoned children in the streets.

1948

The Death
of the Moth

Virginia Woolf

change color of trees
welcome spring.

1   Moths that fly by day are not properly to be called moths; they do
not excite that pleasant sense of dark autumn nights and ivy-blos-
som which the commonest yellow-underwing asleep in the
shadow of the curtain never fails to rouse in us. They are hybrid
creatures, neither gay like butterflies nor sombre like their own
species. Nevertheless the present specimen, with his narrow hay-
coloured wings, fringed with a tassel of the same colour, seemed
to be content with life. It was a pleasant morning, mid-September,
mild, benignant, yet with a keener breath than that of the summer
months. The plough was already scoring the field opposite the
window, and where the share had been, the earth was pressed flat
and gleamed with moisture. Such vigour came rolling in from the
fields and the down beyond that it was difficult to keep the eyes
strictly turned upon the book. The rooks too were keeping one of
their annual festivities; soaring round the tree tops until it looked
as if a vast net with thousands of black knots in it had been cast up
into the air; which, after a few moments sank slowly down upon
the trees until every twig seemed to have a knot at the end of it.

Then, suddenly, the net would be thrown into the air again in a wider circle this time, with the utmost clamour and vociferation, as though to be thrown into the air and settle slowly down upon the tree tops were a tremendously exciting experience.

The same energy which inspired the rooks, the ploughmen, the horses, and even, it seemed, the lean bare-backed downs, sent the moth fluttering from side to side of his square of the window-pane. One could not help watching him. One was, indeed, conscious of a queer feeling of pity for him. The possibilities of pleasure seemed that morning so enormous and so various that to have only a moth's part in life, and a day moth's at that, appeared a hard fate, and his zest in enjoying his meagre opportunities to the full, pathetic. He flew vigorously to one corner of his compartment, and, after waiting there a second, flew across to the other. What remained for him but to fly to a third corner and then to a fourth? That was all he could do, in spite of the size of the downs, the width of the sky, the far-off smoke of houses, and the romantic voice, now and then, of a steamer out at sea. What he could do he did. Watching him, it seemed as if a fibre, very thin but pure, of the enormous energy of the world had been thrust into his frail and diminutive body. As often as he crossed the pane, I could fancy that a thread of vital light became visible. He was little or nothing but life.

Yet, because he was so small, and so simple a form of the energy that was rolling in at the open window and driving its way through so many narrow and intricate corridors in my own brain and in those of other human beings, there was something marvellous as well as pathetic about him. It was as if someone had taken a tiny bead of pure life and decking it as lightly as possible with down and feathers, had set it dancing and zig-zagging to show us the true nature of life. Thus displayed one could not get over the strangeness of it. One is apt to forget all about life, seeing it humped and bossed and garnished and cumbered so that it has to move with the greatest circumspection and dignity. Again, the thought of all that life might have been had he been born in any other shape caused one to view his simple activities with a kind of pity.

After a time, tired by his dancing apparently, he settled on the window ledge in the sun, and, the queer spectacle being at an end,

I forgot about him. Then, looking up, my eye was caught by him. He was trying to resume his dancing, but seemed either so stiff or so awkward that he could only flutter to the bottom of the windowpane; and when he tried to fly across it he failed. Being intent on other matters I watched these futile attempts for a time without thinking, unconsciously waiting for him to resume his flight, as one waits for a machine, that has stopped momentarily, to start again without considering the reason of its failure. After perhaps a seventh attempt he slipped from the wooden ledge and fell, fluttering his wings, on to his back on the window sill. The helplessness of his attitude roused me. It flashed upon me that he was in difficulties; he could no longer raise himself; his legs struggled vainly. But, as I stretched out a pencil, meaning to help him to right himself, it came over me that the failure and awkwardness were the approach of death. I laid the pencil down again.

The legs agitated themselves once more. I looked as if for the enemy against which he struggled. I looked out of doors. What had happened there? Presumably it was midday, and work in the fields had stopped. Stillness and quiet had replaced the previous animation. The birds had taken themselves off to feed in the brooks. The horses stood still. Yet the power was there all the same, massed outside, indifferent, impersonal, not attending to anything in particular. Somehow it was opposed to the little hay-coloured moth. It was useless to try to do anything. One could only watch the extraordinary efforts made by those tiny legs against an oncoming doom which could, had it chosen, have submerged an entire city, not merely a city, but masses of human beings; nothing, I knew, had any chance against death. Nevertheless after a pause of exhaustion the legs fluttered again. It was superb this last protest, and so frantic that he succeeded at last in righting himself. One's sympathies, of course, were all on the side of life. Also, when there was nobody to care or to know, this gigantic effort on the part of an insignificant little moth, against a power of such magnitude, to retain what no one else valued or desired to keep, moved one strangely. Again, somehow, one saw life, a pure bead. I lifted the pencil again, useless though I knew it to be. But even as I did so, the unmistakable tokens of death showed themselves. The body relaxed, and instantly grew stiff. The struggle was over. The insignificant little creature now knew death. As I looked at the dead moth, this minute wayside triumph of so great a force over so mean an antagonist filled me with wonder. Just as life had been strange a few minutes before, so death was now as strange. The moth having righted himself now lay most decently and uncomplainingly composed. O yes, he seemed to say, death is stronger than I am.

1942

The Way to Rainy Mountain

N. Scott Momaday

A single knoll rises out of the plain in Oklahoma, north and west of   1
the Wichita Range. For my people, the Kiowas, it is an old landmark, and they gave it the name Rainy Mountain. The hardest
weather in the world is there. Winter brings blizzards, hot tornadic
winds arise in the spring, and in summer the prairie is an anvil's
edge. The grass turns brittle and brown, and it cracks beneath your
feet. There are green belts along the rivers and creeks, linear groves
of hickory and pecan, willow and witch hazel. At a distance in July
or August the steaming foliage seems almost to writhe in fire. Great
green-and-yellow grasshoppers are everywhere in the tall grass,
popping up like corn to sting the flesh, and tortoises crawl about
on the red earth, going nowhere in the plenty of time. Loneliness is
an aspect of the land. All things in the plain are isolate; there is no
confusion of objects in the eye, but *one* hill or *one* tree or *one* man.
To look upon that landscape in the early morning, with the sun at
your back, is to lose the sense of proportion. Your imagination
comes to life, and this, you think, is where Creation was begun.

I returned to Rainy Mountain in July. My grandmother had   2
died in the spring, and I wanted to be at her grave. She had lived

to be very old and at last infirm. Her only living daughter was with her when she died, and I was told that in death her face was that of a child.

3   I like to think of her as a child. When she was born, the Kiowas were living that last great moment of their history. For more than a hundred years they had controlled the open range from the Smoky Hill River to the Red, from the headwaters of the Canadian to the fork of the Arkansas and Cimarron. In alliance with the Comanches, they had ruled the whole of the southern Plains. War was their sacred business, and they were among the finest horsemen the world has ever known. But warfare for the Kiowas was preeminently a matter of disposition rather than of survival, and they never understood the grim, unrelenting advance of the U.S. Cavalry. When at last, divided and ill-provisioned, they were driven onto the Staked Plains in the cold rains of autumn, they fell into panic. In Palo Duro Canyon they abandoned their crucial stores to pillage and had nothing then but their lives. In order to save themselves, they surrendered to the soldiers at Fort Sill and were imprisoned in the old stone corral that now stands as a military museum. My grandmother was spared the humiliation of those high gray walls by eight or ten years, but she must have known from birth the affliction of defeat, the dark brooding of old warriors.

4   Her name was Aho, and she belonged to the last culture to evolve in North America. Her forebears came down from the high country in western Montana nearly three centuries ago. They were a mountain people, a mysterious tribe of hunters whose language has never been positively classified in any major group. In the late seventeenth century they began a long migration to the south and east. It was a long journey toward the dawn, and it led to a golden age. Along the way the Kiowas were befriended by the Crows, who gave them the culture and religion of the Plains. They acquired horses, and their ancient nomadic spirit was suddenly free of the ground. They acquired Tai-me, the sacred Sun Dance doll, from that moment the object and symbol of their worship, and so shared in the divinity of the sun. Not least, they acquired the sense of destiny, therefore courage and pride. When they entered upon the southern Plains, they had been transformed. No longer were

they slaves to the simple necessity of survival; they were a lordly
and dangerous society of fighters and thieves, hunters and priests
of the sun. According to their origin myth, they entered the world
through a hollow log. From one point of view, their migration was
the fruit of an old prophecy, for indeed they emerged from a sun-
less world.

Although my grandmother lived out her long life in the 5
shadow of Rainy Mountain, the immense landscape of the continental interior lay like memory in her blood. She could tell of the
Crows, whom she had never seen, and of the Black Hills, where
she had never been. I wanted to see in reality what she had seen
more perfectly in the mind's eye, and traveled fifteen hundred
miles to begin my pilgrimage.

Yellowstone, it seemed to me, was the top of the world, a re- 6
gion of deep lakes and dark timber, canyons and waterfalls. But,
beautiful as it is, one might have the sense of confinement there.
The skyline in all directions is close at hand, the high wall of the
woods and deep cleavages of shade. There is a perfect freedom in
the mountains, but it belongs to the eagle and the elk, the badger
and the bear. The Kiowas reckoned their stature by the distance
they could see, and they were bent and blind in the wilderness.

Descending eastward, the highland meadows are a stairway 7
to the plain. In July the inland slope of the Rockies is luxuriant
with flax and buckwheat, stonecrop and larkspur. The earth un-
folds and the limit of the land recedes. Clusters of trees and animals grazing far in the distance cause the vision to reach away and
wonder to build upon the mind. The sun follows a longer course
in the day, and the sky is immense beyond all comparison. The
great billowing clouds that sail upon it are shadows that move
upon the grain like water, dividing light. Farther down, in the land
of the Crows and Blackfeet, the plain is yellow. Sweet clover takes
hold of the hills and bends upon itself to cover and seal the soil.
There the Kiowas paused on their way; they had come to the place
where they must change their lives. The sun is at home on the
plains. Precisely there does it have the certain character of a god.
When the Kiowas came to the land of the Crows, they could see
the dark lees of the hills at dawn across the Bighorn River, the pro-
fusion of light on the grain shelves, the oldest deity ranging after

the solstices. Not yet would they veer southward to the caldron of the land that lay below; they must wean their blood from the northern winter and hold the mountains a while longer in their view. They bore Tai-me in procession to the east.

8   A dark mist lay over the Black Hills, and the land was like iron. At the top of a ridge I caught sight of Devil's Tower upthrust against the gray sky as if in the birth of time the core of the earth had broken through its crust and the motion of the world was begun. There are things in nature that engender an awful quiet in the heart of man; Devil's Tower is one of them. Two centuries ago, because they could not do otherwise, the Kiowas made a legend at the base of the rock. My grandmother said:

> Eight children were there at play, seven sisters and their brother. Suddenly the boy was struck dumb; he trembled and began to run upon his hands and feet. His fingers became claws, and his body was covered with fur. Directly there was a bear where the boy had been. The sisters were terrified; they ran, and the bear after them. They came to the stump of a great tree, and the tree spoke to them. It bade them climb upon it, and as they did so, it began to rise into the air. The bear came to kill them, but they were just beyond its reach. It reared against the tree and scored the bark all around with its claws. The seven sisters were borne into the sky, and they became the stars of the Big Dipper.

From that moment, and so long as the legend lives, the Kiowas have kinsmen in the night sky. Whatever they were in the mountains, they could be no more. However tenuous their well-being, however much they had suffered and would suffer again, they had found a way out of the wilderness.

9   My grandmother had a reverence for the sun, a holy regard that now is all but gone out of mankind. There was a wariness in her, and an ancient awe. She was a Christian in her later years, but she had come a long way about, and she never forgot her birthright. As a child she had been to the Sun Dances; she had taken part in those annual rites, and by them she had learned the restoration of her people in the presence of Tai-me. She was about seven when the last Kiowa Sun Dance was held in 1887 on the Washita River above Rainy Mountain Creek. The buffalo were gone. In order to consummate the ancient sacrifice—to impale the

head of a buffalo bull upon the medicine tree—a delegation of old men journeyed into Texas, there to beg and barter for an animal from the Goodnight herd. She was ten when the Kiowas came together for the last time as a living Sun Dance culture. They could find no buffalo; they had to hang an old hide from the sacred tree. Before the dance could begin, a company of soldiers rode out from Fort Sill under orders to disperse the tribe. Forbidden without cause the essential act of their faith, having seen the wild herds slaughtered and left to rot upon the ground, the Kiowas backed away forever from the medicine tree. That was July 20, 1890, at the great bend of the Washita. My grandmother was there. Without bitterness, and for as long as she lived, she bore a vision of deicide.

Now that I can have her only in memory, I see my grandmother in the several postures that were peculiar to her: standing at the wood stove on a winter morning and turning meat in a great iron skillet; sitting at the south window, bent above her beadwork, and afterwards, when her vision had failed, looking down for a long time into the fold of her hands; going out upon a cane, very slowly as she did when the weight of age came upon her; praying. I remember her most often at prayer. She made long, rambling prayers out of suffering and hope, having seen many things. I was never sure that I had the right to hear, so exclusive were they of all mere custom and company. The last time I saw her she prayed standing by the side of her bed at night, naked to the waist, the light of a kerosene lamp moving upon her dark skin. Her long, black hair, always drawn and braided in the day, lay upon her shoulders and against her breasts like a shawl. I do not speak Kiowa, and I never understood her prayers, but there was something inherently sad in the sound, some merest hesitation upon the syllables of sorrow. She began in a high and descending pitch, exhausting her breath to silence; then again and again—and always the same intensity of effort, of something that is, and is not, like urgency in the human voice. Transported so in the dancing light among the shadows of her room, she seemed beyond the reach of time. But that was illusion; I think I knew then that I should not see her again.

1969

Alias Benowitz
Shoe Repair

David Quammen

1   I first heard about George Ochenski from a friend of mine who happens to be president of the Montana River-Snorkelers Association. We were in a fancy restaurant, as I recall, and there was wine involved. Ochenski had come to my friend's attention in the course of his (the friend's) presidential duties, which are in strict point of fact nonexistent. I should explain that the MRSA presidency is a purely honorary title, self-bestowed actually, because the MRSA is a mythical organization. This is all quite different, please note, from labeling the organization itself nonexistent. Certainly the Montana River-Snorkelers Association does exist (mainly over wine and beer at various bars and restaurants, occasionally also around a campfire); it just isn't *real*. An actual mythical entity, then, the MRSA, of roughly the same ontological status as the NCAA national championship in football, or the domino theory of international relations. You should look into this fellow Ochenski, my friend told me. He can be reached care of Benowitz Shoe Repair, in a tiny town called Southern Cross, up in the Flint Mountains above Anaconda. Have some more cabernet, I said. But sure enough it turned out to be true. Benowitz Shoe Repair is another mythical entity, existent in its own way but not real. George Ochenski is both mythical and real. Are you with me so far?

2   George Ochenski must certainly be the preeminent river-snorkeler in the Rocky Mountains. He has talent, commitment, infectious enthusiasm, broad experience, state-of-the-art equipment, and a measure of lunatic daring. He has precious little competition. Most important, he has self-abnegating dedication to a larger purpose.

3   Sometimes you have to snorkel a river, Ochenski believes, in order to save it.

4   So dedicated is George Ochenski, and so scornful of risk, that—if necessary to make a point—he is willing even to snorkel the Clark Fork River downstream from the Anaconda smelter.

Now a river-snorkeler (in case this isn't self-evident) is someone who swims downstream in a river with his face under water, enjoying the ride, watching the scenery, breathing through his little tube. A lazy, hypnotic pastime best practiced on pellucid trout streams in midsummer. A few of us have been toying at it for years.

But George Ochenski does not toy. He jimmies himself into a full wet suit, adds fins and a hood and neoprene gloves and a fanny pack holding three cans of beer, pulls a pair of skateboarding knee pads into place, defogs his mask, and jumps into rivers. Gentle rivers and raging whitewater monsters. Last year, for instance, he did thirty-eight miles of the Salmon in Idaho without benefit of a boat. Also last year, he leapt into the Quake Lake trench—an earthquake-contorted stretch of the Madison River famous for biting kayaks in half—and nearly died. On that run his mask was ripped off six times while he tumbled head over teakettle through a garden of sharp boulders; the trench, George admits today, was a miscalculation. In Montana this kind of behavior does not pass unnoticed. By word, and more discreetly by the looks on their faces, people frequently tell him: *Son, you must be out of your everlovin' skull.* But they said that to Orville Wright, and they were wrong. Then again, they said it to Evel Knievel, and they were right. George Ochenski figures somewhere in between.

He has an enduring though ambivalent attraction to what he himself classifies "death sports." Huge squinting grin from George as he acknowledges this ambivalence. Mountaineering. Iceclimbing. Scuba. Never a major injury, never a bad accident—unless you count the time he fell 600 feet down a steep rock slope in the Alaska Range and did a self-arrest on his nose. Back in those years he traveled exotically for serious climbing, with generous sponsorship from the equipment people, and took part in the first successful ascent of the west face of Alaska's Mt. Hayes. Scaled some breathtaking frozen waterfalls. Around the same time, a consummate autodidact, he turned himself into an expert cobbler, because he wasn't satisfied with the professional repair work on his climbing boots; before long he was doing work for his friends too, and they had rechristened him, whimsically and metonymically, "Benowitz Shoe Repair." Today he mostly stays close to the little wood-heated cabin at Southern Cross, in the front room of which stands a bass fiddle. The fiddle is a logical switch from tuba, which he played for thirteen years. Benowitz is a man of many skills.

8 Several years ago, in response to pressure both internal and external, he gave up the glorious climbing, thanked the sponsors, and settled down to being useful politically. He had come to feel that he owed something back to the mountains and rivers; meanwhile there happened to be a certain crisis brewing near home. He now makes his living as an editorial assistant to an author of textbooks on environmental science. The cabin is filled ceiling-high with an eclectic library. On one wall is a quote from Congressman Ron Dellums: "Democracy is not about being a damn spectator against the backdrop of tapdancing politicians swinging in the winds of expediency." By disposition, George is certainly no spectator. Some people, particularly of the opposition, might still take him on first impression for a wild-haired, good-timing, reckless flake. They would be grievously mistaken. George Ochenski has an excellent brain, he has chutzpah, he has focus.

9 And in a small trailer up the hill behind his own cabin, where the ash from his cook stove can't fuddle its circuits, he has an Apple II computer, its floppy discs full of damning information concerning the Anaconda Minerals Company.

10 On September 29, 1980, the Anaconda Company announced that it was closing its copper-smelting operations at the town of Anaconda. This came as a severe shock to the 1,000 smelter workers suddenly unemployed, and marked the end of a century of awesome environmental pillage. For one hundred years the Company had cut down forests, poisoned streams, smelted copper, piled up vast mounds of slag, and filled the air of the country with a sulfurous smog, in exchange for the regular paychecks dispensed. Now the economics of copper had shifted. Goodbye, thanks for everything. "The Company thought they could just lock the doors and walk away," says George Ochenski.

He and a few other Anaconda folk, some of them former 11
smelter workers, think otherwise. They are after the Company like
a fierce dog after a bear. They have formed an enraged-citizens'
organization, pressured the governor, pressured the senators,
pressured the EPA. They want more than goodbyes. They want
reclamation. They want accountability. At very least they want
precise information about the nature and magnitude of the poiso-
nous mess left behind.

With sulfur dioxide no longer pouring from the smelter stack, 12
the chief concern now is over toxic metals: lead, cadmium, mercury,
zinc, copper itself, and especially arsenic. One hundred years of copper-smelting have left various concentrations of some or all of these
in the waters, in the plants, in the soil, in the animals of the county.
George Ochenski and his compatriots want to know: *How much?*
How much was dumped in the ponds, how much was buried, how
much is still blowing free off the smelter site? How much is already
in our lungs and our bones? How much is ingested with each brown
trout from the Clark Fork River, if a person should be so lucky as to
catch one of the surviving fish, and so foolhardy as to eat it?

How much lead? How much cadmium? How much arsenic? 13
The Anaconda Company, no doubt, devoutly wishes that these
questions would go away.

Sometimes you have to snorkel a river in order to save it. 14
Guided by this dictum, George Ochenski loaded his gear into the
back of my car. It was late in the season, Labor Day weekend, with
the air already growing cool. We paused briefly, where the gravel
lane down from Southern Cross joined the larger road, to check
the Benowitz Shoe Repair mailbox. Then George led me off on a
pair of brief but illuminating tours.

We went to the Big Hole River, across the Continental Divide 15
from Anaconda and clear of the war zone over heavy metals. The Big
Hole is still a pellucid trout stream. We jimmied ourselves into wet
suits, added fins and hoods and neoprene gloves; I pulled George's
one extra skateboarding pad into position over my favorite knee.
Masks were defogged, snorkels adjusted, and we jumped in.

The view was beautiful. Trout and whitefish looked me in the 16
eye, aghast, and skittered away. Sculpins darted discreetly for

cover. I observed the differences in underwater behavior among three different species of stonefly. I gazed at the funnel webs of *Arctopsyche* caddisfly larvae, down between rocks in the fast water, that I had read about often but never before seen. I found a mayfly nymph equipped with an elephantine pair of tusks. We passed through a few modest sets of rapids, where the current abruptly accelerated and the boulders came at me like blitzing linebackers who must be straight-armed away. After two hours of cruising we were nearly hypothermic, but the experience had been delightful.

17   Our second tour was to the Clark Fork River, downstream from the settling ponds into which the Anaconda Company has voided its years of industrial offal. "We're off to snorkel the Clark Fork," George told a friend as we pulled out of town. The friend looked puzzled. Huge squinting grin from George. "Then we'll come back and glow in the dark."

18   We snorkeled a long section of the Clark Fork. Here the water was turbid, visibility was poor. The rocks of the stream bed were largely cemented together with silt, leaving no habitat for stoneflies or *Arctopsyche*. I didn't see a single fish. I didn't see a single insect. Some people claim that the Clark Fork today is actually much improved over its sorry condition two decades ago, before the Company adopted certain technical measures to mitigate the toxicity of its releases. Maybe those people are right. But I remain skeptical. The river I was swimming through, with my eyes open and my nose very close to the bottom, was definitely no basis for passing out congratulations.

19   This dramatic lack of vitality proves nothing, of course, about what causal role the smelter wastes, and the erosion from denuded hillsides around Anaconda, may or may not still be playing. It simply correlates. Consider it, if you wish to, purest coincidence. It is not, however, mythical. It is real.

20   Later Benowitz and I were careful to shower ourselves down with clean water. "River-snorkeling," he told me, and he should know, "is not supposed to be a death sport."

1985

My Father

Doris Lessing

We use our parents like recurring dreams, to be entered into when   1
needed; they are always there for love or for hate; but it occurs to
me that I was not always there for my father. I've written about
him before, but novels, stories, don't have to be "true." Writing
this article is difficult because it has to be "true." I knew him when
his best years were over.

There are photographs of him. The largest is of an officer in the   2
1914–18 war. A new uniform—buttoned, badged, strapped,
tabbed—confines a handsome, dark young man who holds himself stiffly to confront what he certainly thought of as his duty. His
eyes are steady, serious, and responsible, and show no signs of
what he became later. A photograph at sixteen is of a dark, intro-
spective youth with the same intent eyes. But it is his mouth you
notice—a heavily-jutting upper lip contradicts the rest of a regular face. His moustache was to hide it: "Had to do something—a
damned fleshy mouth. Always made me uncomfortable, that
mouth of mine."

Earlier a baby (eyes already alert) appears in a lace waterfall   3
that cascades from the pillowy bosom of a fat, plain woman to her
feet. It is the face of a head cook. "Lord, but my mother was a practical female—almost as bad as you!" as he used to say, or throw at
my mother in moments of exasperation. Beside her stands, or
droops, arms dangling, his father, the source of the dark, arresting
eyes, but otherwise masked by a long beard.

The birth certificate says: Born 3rd August, 1886, Walton Villa,   4
Creffield Road, S. Mary at the Wall, R.S.D. Name, Alfred Cook.
Name and surname of Father: Alfred Cook Tayler. Name and
maiden name of Mother: Caroline May Batley. Rank or Profession:
Bank Clerk. Colchester, Essex.

They were very poor. Clothes and boots were a problem. They   5
"made their own amusements." Books were mostly the Bible and
The Pilgrim's Progress. Every Saturday night they bathed in a hip-
bath in front of the kitchen fire. No servants. Church three times

on Sundays. "Lord, when I think of those Sundays! I dreaded them all week, like a nightmare coming at you full tilt and no escape." But he rabbited with ferrets along the lanes and fields, bird-nested, stole fruit, picked nuts and mushrooms, paid visits to the blacksmith and the mill and rode a farmer's carthorse.

6   They ate economically, but when he got diabetes in his forties and subsisted on lean meat and lettuce leaves, he remembered suet puddings, treacle puddings, raisin and currant puddings, steak and kidney puddings, bread and butter puddings, "batter cooked in the gravy with the meat," potato cake, plum cake, butter cake, porridge with treacle, fruit tarts and pies, brawn, pig's trotters and pig's cheek and homesmoked ham and sausages. And "lashings of fresh butter and cream and eggs." He wondered if this diet had produced the diabetes, but said it was worth it.

7   There was an elder brother described by my father as: "Too damned clever by half. One of those quick, clever brains. Now I've always had a slow brain, but I get there in the end, damn it!"

8   The brothers went to a local school and the elder did well, but my father was beaten for being slow. They both became bank clerks in, I think, the Westminster Bank, and one must have found it congenial, for he became a manager, the "rich brother," who had cars and even a yacht. But my father did not like it, though he was conscientious. For instance, he changed his writing, letter by letter, because a senior criticised it. I never saw his unregenerate hand, but the one he created was elegant, spiky, careful. Did this mean he created a new personality for himself, hiding one he did not like, as he hid his "damned fleshy mouth"? I don't know.

9   Nor do I know when he left home to live in Luton, or why. He found family life too narrow? A safe guess—he found everything too narrow. His mother was too down-to-earth? He had to get away from his clever elder brother?

10   Being a young man in Luton was the best part of his life. It ended in 1914, so he had a decade of happiness. His reminiscences of it were all of pleasure, the delight of physical movement, of dancing in particular. All his girls were "a beautiful dancer, light as a feather." He played billiards and ping-pong (both for his country); he swam, boated, played cricket and football, went to picnics and horse races, sang at musical evenings. One family of a

mother and two daughters treated him "like a son only better. I didn't know whether I was in love with the mother or the daughters, but oh I did love going there; we had such good times." He was engaged to one daughter, then, for a time, to the other. An engagement was broken off because she was rude to a waiter. "I could not marry a woman who allowed herself to insult someone who was defenseless." He used to say to my wryly smiling mother: "Just as well I didn't marry either of *them*; they would never have stuck it out the way you have, old girl."

Just before he died he told me he had dreamed he was standing in a kitchen on a very high mountain holding X in his arms. "Ah, yes, that's what I've missed in my life. Now don't you let yourself be cheated out of life by the old dears. They take all the colour out of everything if you let them." [11]

But in that decade—"I'd walk 10, 15 miles to a dance two or three times a week and think nothing of it. Then I'd dance every dance and walk home again over the fields. Sometimes it was moonlight, but I liked the snow best all crisp and fresh. I loved walking back and getting into my digs just as the sun was rising. My little dog was so happy to see me, and I'd feed her, and make myself porridge and tea, then I'd wash and shave and go off to work." [12]

The boy who was beaten at school, who went too much to church, who carried the fear of poverty all his life, but who nevertheless was filled with the memories of country pleasures; the young bank clerk who worked such long hours for so little money, but who danced, sang, played, flirted—this naturally vigorous, sensuous being was killed in 1914, 1915, 1916. I think the best of my father died in that war, that his spirit was crippled by it. The people I've met, particularly the women, who knew him young, speak of his high spirits, his energy, his enjoyment of life. Also of his kindness, his compassion and—a word that keeps recurring—his wisdom. "Even when he was just a boy he understood things that you'd think even an old man would find it easy to condemn." I do not think these people would have easily recognised the ill, irritable, abstracted, hypochondriac man I knew. [13]

He "joined up" as an ordinary soldier out of a characteristically quirky scruple: it wasn't right to enjoy officers' privileges [14] when the Tommies had such a bad time. But he could not stick the communal latrines, the obligatory drinking, the collective visits to brothels, the jokes about girls. So next time he was offered a commission he took it.

15   His childhood and young man's memories, kept fluid, were added to, grew, as living memories do. But his war memories were congealed in stories that he told again and again, with the same words and gestures, in stereotyped phrases. They were anonymous, general, as if they had come out of a communal war memoir. He met a German in no-man's-land, but both slowly lowered their rifles and smiled and walked away. The Tommies were the salt of the earth, the British fighting men the best in the world. He had never known such comradeship. A certain brutal officer was shot in a sortie by his men, but the other officers, recognising rough justice, said nothing. He had known men intimately who saw the Angels at Mons. He wished he could force all the generals on both sides into the trenches for just one day, to see what the common soldiers endured—*that* would have ended the war at once.

16   There was an undercurrent of memories, dreams, and emotions much deeper, more personal. This dark region in him, fate-ruled, where nothing was true but horror, was expressed inarticulately, in brief, bitter exclamations or phrases of rage, incredulity, betrayal. The men who went to fight in that war believed it when they said it was to end war. My father believed it. And he was never able to reconcile his belief in his country with his anger at the cynicism of its leaders. And the anger, the sense of betrayal, strengthened as he grew old and ill.

17   But in 1914 he was naïve, the German atrocities in Belgium inflamed him, and he enlisted out of idealism, although he knew he would have a hard time. He knew because a fortuneteller told him. (He could be described as uncritically superstitious or as psychically gifted.) He would be in great danger twice, yet not die—he was being protected by a famous soldier who was his ancestor. "And sure enough, later I heard from the Little Aunties that the church records showed we were descended the backstairs way from the Duke of Wellington, or was it Marlborough? Damn it, I forget. But one of them would be beside me all through the war,

she said." (He was romantic, not only about this solicitous ghost, but also about being a descendant of the Huguenots, on the strength of the "e" in Tayler; and about "the wild blood" in his veins from a great uncle who, sent unjustly to prison for smuggling, came out of a ten-year sentence and earned it, very efficiently, along the coasts of Cornwall until he died.)

The luckiest thing that ever happened to my father, he said, 18 was getting his leg shattered by shrapnel ten days before Passchendaele. His whole company was killed. He knew he was going to be wounded because of the fortuneteller, who had said he would know. "I did not understand what she meant, but both times in the trenches, first when my appendix burst and I nearly died, and then just before Passchendaele, I felt for some days as if a thick, black velvet pall was settled over me. I can't tell you what it was like. Oh, it was awful, and the second time it was so bad I wrote to the old people and told them I was going to be killed."

His leg was cut off at mid-thigh, he was shell-shocked, he was 19 very ill for many months, with a prolonged depression afterwards. "You should always remember that sometimes people are all seething underneath. You don't know what terrible things people have to fight against. You should look at a person's eyes, that's how you tell. . . . When I was like that, after I lost my leg, I went to a nice doctor man and said I was going mad, but he said, don't worry, everyone locks up things like that. You don't know—horrible, horrible, awful things. I was afraid of myself, of what I used to dream. I wasn't myself at all."

In the Royal Free Hospital was my mother, Sister McVeagh. 20 He married his nurse which, as they both said often enough (though in different tones of voice), was just as well. That was 1919. He could not face being a bank clerk in England, he said, not after the trenches. Besides, England was too narrow and conventional. Besides, the civilians did not know what the soldiers had suffered, they didn't want to know, and now it wasn't done even to remember "The Great Unmentionable." He went off to the Imperial Bank of Persia, in which country I was born.

The house was beautiful, with great stone-floored high- 21 ceilinged rooms whose windows showed ranges of snow-streaked mountains. The gardens were full of roses, jasmine, pomegranates, walnuts. Kermanshah he spoke of with liking, but soon they went to Teheran, populous with "Embassy people," and my gregarious mother created a lively social life about which he was irritable even in recollection.

22   Irritableness—that note was first struck here, about Persia. He did not like, he said, "the graft and the corruption." But here it is time to try and describe something difficult—how a man's good qualities can also be his bad ones, or if not bad, a danger to him.

23   My father was honourable—he always knew exactly what that word meant. He had integrity. His "one does not do that sort of thing," his "no, it is *not* right," sounded throughout my child-hood and were final for all of us. I am sure it was true he wanted to leave Persia because of "the corruption." But it was also because he was already unconsciously longing for something freer, be-cause as a bank official he could not let go into the dream-logged personality that was waiting for him. And later in Rhodesia, too, what was best in him was also what prevented him from shaking away the shadows: it was always in the name of honesty or de-cency that he refused to take this step or that out of the slow de-cay of the family's fortunes.

24   In 1925 there was leave from Persia. That year in London there was an Empire Exhibition, and on the Southern Rhodesian stand some very fine maize cobs and a poster saying that fortunes could be made on maize at 25/ -a bag. So on an impulse, turning his back forever on England, washing his hands of the corruption of the East, my father collected all his capital, £800, I think, while my mother packed curtains from Liberty's, clothes from Harrods, visiting cards, a piano, Persian rugs, a governess and two small children.

25   Soon, there was my father in a cigar-shaped house of thatch and mud on the top of a kopje that overlooked in all directions a great system of mountains, rivers, valleys, while overhead the sky arched from horizon to empty horizon. This was a couple of hun-dred miles south from the Zambesi, a hundred or so west from Mozambique, in the district of Banket, so called because certain of its reefs were of the same formation as those called *banket* on the Rand. Lomagundi—gold country, tobacco country, maize coun-try—wild, almost empty. (The Africans had been turned off it into reserves.) Our neighbours were four, five, seven miles off. In front

of the house . . . no neighbours, nothing; no farms, just wild bush with two rivers but no fences to the mountains seven miles away. And beyond these mountains and bush again to the Portuguese border, over which "our boys" used to escape when wanted by the police for pass or other offences.

And then? There was bad luck. For instance, the price of maize 26 dropped from 25/- to 9/-a bag. The seasons were bad, prices bad, crops failed. This was the sort of thing that made it impossible for him ever to "get off the farm," which, he agreed with my mother, was what he most wanted to do.

It was an absurd country, he said. A man could "own" a farm 27 for years that was totally mortgaged to the Government and run from the Land Bank, meanwhile employing half-a-hundred Africans at 12/-a month and none of them knew how to do a day's work. Why, two farm labourers from Europe could do in a day what twenty of these ignorant black savages would take a week to do. (Yet he was proud that he had a name as a just employer, that he gave "a square deal.") Things got worse. A fortuneteller had told him that her heart ached when she saw the misery ahead for my father: this was the misery.

But it was my mother who suffered. After a period of neurotic 28 illness, which was a protest against her situation, she became brave and resourceful. But she never saw that her husband was not living in a real world, that he had made a captive of her common sense. We were always about to "get off the farm." A miracle would do it—a sweepstake, a goldmine, a legacy. And then? What a question! We would go to England where life would be normal with people coming in for musical evenings and nice supper parties at the Trocadero after a show. Poor woman, for the twenty years we were on the farm, she waited for when life would begin for her and for her children, for she never understood that what was a calamity for her was for them a blessing.

Meanwhile my father sank towards his death (at 61). Every- 29 thing changed in him. He had been a dandy and fastidious, now he hated to change out of shabby khaki. He had been sociable, now he was misanthropic. His body's disorders—soon diabetes and all kinds of stomach ailments—dominated him. He was brave about his wooden leg, and even went down mine shafts and climbed trees with it, but he walked clumsily and it irked him badly. He greyed fast, and slept more in the day, but would be awake half the night pondering about . . .

30   It could be gold divining. For ten years he experimented on private theories to do with the attractions and repulsions of metals. His whole soul went into it but his theories were wrong or he was *unlucky*—after all, if he had found a mine he would have had to leave the farm. It could be the relation between the minerals of the earth and of the moon; his decision to make infusions of all the plants on the farm and drink them himself in the interests of science; the criminal folly of the British Government in not realizing that the Germans and the Russians were conspiring as Anti-Christ to . . . the inevitability of war because no one would listen to Churchill, but it would be all right because God (by then he was a British Israelite) had destined Britain to rule the world; a prophecy said 10 million dead would surround Jerusalem—how would the corpses be cleared away?; people who wished to abolish flogging should be flogged; the natives understood nothing but a good beating; hanging must not be abolished because the Old Testament said "an eye for an eye and a tooth for a tooth. . . ."

31   Yet, as this side of him darkened, so that it seemed all his thoughts were of violence, illness, war, still no one dared to make an unkind comment in his presence or to gossip. Criticism of people, particularly of women, made him more and more uncomfortable till at last he burst out with: "It's all very well, but no one has the right to say that about another person."

32   In Africa, when the sun goes down, the stars spring up, all of them in their expected places, glittering and moving. In the rainy season, the sky flashed and thundered. In the dry season, the great dark hollow of night was lit by veld fires: the mountains burned through September and October in chains of red fire. Every night my father took out his chair to watch the sky and the mountains, smoking, silent, a thin shabby fly-away figure under the stars. "Makes you think—there are so many worlds up there, wouldn't really matter if we did blow ourselves up—plenty more where we came from."

33   The Second World War, so long foreseen by him, was a bad time. His son was in the Navy and in danger, and his daughter a

sorrow to him. He became very ill. More and more often it was necessary to drive him into Salisbury with him in a coma, or in danger of one, on the back seat. My mother moved him into a pretty little suburban house in town near the hospitals, where he took to his bed and a couple of years later died. For the most part he was unconscious under drugs. When awake he talked obsessively (a tongue licking a nagging sore place) about "the old war." Or he remembered his youth. "I've been dreaming—Lord, to see those horses come lickety-split down the course with their necks stretched out and the sun on their coats and everyone shouting. . . . I've been dreaming how I walked along the river in the mist as the sun was rising. . . . Lord, lord, lord, what a time that was, what good times we all had then, before the old war."

1956

Easter in Sicily*

Mary Taylor Simeti

Beyond the vague intention of ending up at Prizzi to see the dev- 1 ils dance on Easter afternoon, we have no set itinerary for the rest of the day and decide to drive east along the southern coast, turning or stopping at whim. And whim soon declares itself: only a short distance from Castelvetrano there are road signs indicating the turnoff for Selinunte, and it seems sinful not to make a stop when we have all the time in the world.

Selinunte is to me the least accessible of the Greek sites I have 2 seen in Sicily. The bare bones of a city sacked by man and toppled by earthquake lie in careless heaps on low cliffs overlooking the sea, building blocks abandoned by some infant Titan who has centuries since outgrown them. They are illegible in their very size, with the tourists clambering over the enormous fluted

*Editor's title.

drums of fallen columns like tiny, multicolored ants. Today it is very crowded; parking is difficult and the air rings with a many-tongued babble and with the nagging claxons of the tourist buses gathering their various broods. We mingle with the crowds, wander through the eastern temples, and stroll along the road that leads down into the river valley and up to the acropolis on the opposite cliff until the heat and the confusion persuade us to turn back.

3   Selinunte was a revelation the first time I came, exactly twenty years ago yesterday. Apart from Tonino and me there were no more than a dozen people here, and even these disappeared, swallowed up by the vast sweep of sea and plain and the immoderate proportions of the ruins. We sat for hours on some stones and stared out across sea and centuries, the sea of flowers in the foreground no less brilliant than the Mediterranean that sparkled in the distance. The *selinon,* the wild celery that gave the ancient city its name, was submerged by the red of the sulla, the yellow of mayflowers and mustard, the blue of bugloss and borage, bobbing and trembling under the insistent and noisy prodding of thousands of bees. It was my first immersion in the Sicilian spring, in its colors and its perfumes and its heat, a baptism that caught and held me convert. Today the flowers are still as beautiful, the sun perhaps even hotter, but the crowd and the confusion drown out the bees, and the ruins are silent, unable despite their size to cope with this Lilliputian invasion.

4   We continue eastward and then turn north on the road for Caltabellotta, which winds up over the ridge of low mountains that separates the southern coastal plain east of Selinunte from the rolling hills of the interior. These mountains are quite barren, with patches of vineyard or wheat exploiting the rare flat spaces, an occasional olive or almond tree clinging to the steep and rocky slopes, and, as closer inspection reveals, a sparse carpeting of the crouching, grasping plants of arid soil and high altitudes: Purple squill, delicate white clusters of star-of-Bethlehem, the single tiny yellow-and-brown orchids of the lutea family, and the many-flowered stalks of the *orchis italica,* bristling with minute pink tentacles.

5   The village of Caltabellotta lies at the summit of the highest mountain in this southern ridge, topped only by two great spurs

of rock that thrust up behind it like giant tusks. The streets are narrow and zigzag steeply up the hillside; a policeman directing all five cars' worth of traffic instructs us to park the car and continue on foot if we want to see the procession. Of course we do, so we quickly park and follow the main street up to a point where it splits, one fork leading farther up a very steep slope, the other curving down to the right into a tiny piazza. The "procession" is here—townspeople and bandsmen, their instruments tucked forgotten under their elbows, have gathered in a circle to cheer and applaud a dancing saint, a life-size plaster statue of the Archangel Michael, the town's patron. Michael, dressed in the armor of a Roman legionary, is leaning against a column that has been completely wrapped in purple phlox, with a young laurel tree tied next to it so that the purple flowers glow against the dark leaves. As in Tràpani and Castelvetrano, the flower-decked platform that bears the statue is mounted on two poles–in this case very long, thick wooden beams that of themselves must weigh an enormous amount—and requires some thirty hefty young men to carry it. But "carry" is not the right word: they rock and jostle and bounce the statue in the most extraordinary manner, accompanied and encouraged by a crescendo of cheering and clapping from the crowd that presses in around them. Sweat pouring off their faces, the young men push and pull still harder on their poles, and the Archangel rocks and sways and reels in a frenzied dance, until his porters can bear it no longer, the movement subsides into a faint bobbing, and the statue itself seems to pant as the men fight to catch their breath, still holding all the weight on their shoulders.

Bottles of water and beer are passed around, the band recovers 6 its role and starts to play again, and considerable maneuvering is necessary to effect the passage of the statue around the curve and into the main street, where it pauses at the foot of the rise, gathering strength. Meanwhile another statue arrives, a little winged cherub about two feet high, with platform, poles, and porters in proportion: a handful of boys about twelve years old bounce the baby statue about in great excitement, egged on by an amused crowd.

The music dies out, and, at a sign from one of the porters, the 7 drummer sounds a roll. On the final snap of the drumsticks the men charge up the street, running and stumbling with their heavy burden up a slope so steep that the statue seems almost horizontal. The cheers of the onlookers assist them over the top and around the corner, quickly followed by the angel, who bobs gaily and effortlessly up the rise in the wake of his big brother.

8   We too turn and climb. We have lost the statues, but echoes of their progress parallel to ours reach us at the street corners. A final hike up a street so sheer that the sidewalk is a flight of stairs brings us out onto the Piano della Matrice, the open square of the mother church, unexpectedly spectacular. In front of us a wide checkerboard of cobble and grass slopes gently up the steps of the Matrice, built by Count Roger after he took Caltabellotta from the Saracens in 1090. The weathered gray stone of the Norman church blends into the sharp-toothed rock that rises abruptly behind it. On the left-hand side of the square stands the chapel of San Michele, its Gothic portal garlanded in laurel branches, and next to it a gate and a stairway carved into the live rock lead off toward the second, bigger pinnacle, ringed by the trees of the town park where the ruins of the Norman castle lie.

9   Commotion rising from below tells us that Saint Michael is about to make his final assault on the mountain. The last steep rise is rendered more problematical by telephone wires and shop signs, and considerable measuring accompanied by animated discussion is necessary before a strategy can be agreed upon. At last somebody climbs out on a balcony and unties a laundry line, final directions are shouted out, and the group braces itself. Up they come, the initial momentum waning as they scramble up the cobbled street, their boots slipping and straining to find a grip on the polished stones. A final push and they burst into the square, where they bring up sharply, the statue swaying back and forth, evidently in some confusion as to where to go next.

10   One of the townsmen who has followed the progress of the statue explains to us that the municipal *pro loco* committee has decided that Caltabellotta should cash in on the "Easter in Sicily" tourist boom and has organized a new procession for the afternoon, a version of the Castelvetrano Aurora, but the details have not been thought out all that well, and no one knows whether Michael should spend his lunch hour in the Matrice or in the

chapel of San Michele, where the garlands declare a readiness to receive him sooner or later.

After a few false starts and some rather languishing discussion, Michael is carried up the steps and into the dark interior of the Matrice. We start to follow it, but a priest, heretofore absent from the scene, closes the door firmly in our faces. Lunchtime. The Matrice is closed, the chapel is closed, the gate to the castle is closed. The best we can do is climb up some stone steps that lead around behind the Matrice, to discover that the rock is sheltering a miniature Alpine meadow, shaded by pine trees whose sun-warmed resin fills the air and dotted with tiny daisies, the kind whose white petals have had their tips dipped in red. I remember the flowers from a French children's book I had when I was little, and it is surprising yet suitable to find their smiling faces here in the shadow of the Norman walls. The view from the meadow is spectacular: We can look north toward the mountains of Palermo across the whole of Sicily, the hills and valleys flattened from this height into a gentle pool of green, flecked with the white foam of the blossoming fruit trees.

The priest had something, however. Our stomachs call us to more prosaic questions. We discover that Caltabellotta offers a choice of two restaurants, one in the town itself and one just outside, around the back of the peak that rises above the castle ruins. Walking down toward the car we pass the first, which is occupied by a baptismal party and has no free tables. A winding road takes us out of town, past vegetable plots and tiny vineyards, to a huge baroque monastery, this too flanked by a cliff and by a charming restaurant with a trelised terrace. The proprietor is polite and extremely apologetic: A wedding reception is in progress, and there isn't a free chair in the place. Tonino, undaunted or perhaps desperate, asks if they couldn't fix us a little antipasto to go. After a brief wait the obliging host produces three foil-covered plates, a bottle of mineral water, and a round kilo loaf of fragrant, crusty bread. We drive back along the road a little way to a curve that offers space to park and some rocks to sit on. Our plates turn out to hold spicy olives, some slices of *prosciutto crudo* and of a peppery local salame, and two kinds of pecorino cheese, one fresh and mild, the other aged and sharper. With a bag of oranges from the car, the sun warm on our backs, the mountains rolling down at our feet to the southern coast and the sea beyond, where the heat haze clouds the horizon and hides Africa from view, we have as fine an Easter dinner as I have ever eaten.

13   The drive north to Prizzi, a rapid descent switchbacking down the north side of the mountain to the green valleys we had seen from above, takes us along luxuriant riverbeds, over hills of green wheat, past isolated pear and apple trees in bloom. The hedge rows are overflowing with flowers, unable to contain such a riot of color, such an exuberance of form and texture. It is difficult to believe that in the space of a few months the velvet softness of the wheat fields, shifting from emerald to chartreuse with the wind, will give way to bristling, colorless stubble; these are the hills that the Lampedusa family cross in the Visconti film of *The Leopard,* in blinding light and smothering dust, their carriages creaking to the shrill song of the locusts.

14   But the extravagant hand of spring is less and less successful in concealing the poverty of the agriculture the farther north we go. Our destination, the village of Prizzi, is quite high, slapped down on a hill of rock soil and stunted vegetation with none of the cozy shifting and filling with which most Sicilian towns have accommodated themselves to the bones of that island. The outskirts of the town are ringed with the usual half-finished houses, fruit of the emigrants' remittances, but once past them the streets are small and close and we are hard put to find a parking space and then to fight our way through the crowds that are thronging toward the center of town, the ranks of the Prizzitani being very much swollen by both foreign and Sicilian tourists. Tonino greets several of his students from the university, then most unexpectedly a hand claps down on my shoulder. It is Nicolò, a man who served on the school board with me. He is a native of Prizzi, a linesman for the telephone company, and after a period of technical schooling in Milan now lives in Palermo, where, fortified by his northern experience, he has become very active in the local section of the Communist party, in the neighborhood council, the trade union, and the school board. He proved a most unusual and valuable addition to the school board, able and willing to work on two levels in a way that is rare among Sicilians, ready to debate the ideological or educational implications of a policy decision and at

the same time to fix a light plug or repair a busted slide projector himself rather than trusting to the lengthy meanderings of the school bureaucracy. But today he is here in Prizzi to be with his family and to see the devils dance.

We are lucky to run into him. We have arrived too late for the distribution of the *cannateddi*, Prizzi's special Easter cakes, but Nicolò carries us off to the Circolo della Caccia, the Hunters' Club, which the Chamber of Commerce has been using as its headquarters for the occasion, and there he sets various cousins scurrying around to unearth some last undistributed *cannateddi* for us, oval cakes of biscuit dough braided about an egg. 15

Cannateddi in hand, we follow Nicolò out again and push our way along the main street, which dips sharply down, then rises again in the distance. Nicolò guides us to the lowest point in the street, where he tells us to stay put, this being a grandstand seat for watching the triumph of Good over Evil. The street is filled with people, strolling, talking, and shouting across from one crowded balcony to another. Here at the bottom we can look up in either direction at a sea of faces. A small and hornèd vortex is descending upon us from the eastern end: the devils are coming, accompanied by the clanking of their chains and the squealing and shouting of a swarm of little boys. There are three masked figures, two devils escorting Death. Death is dressed in yellow, a big, loose-fitting yellow jump suit and a yellow mask of soldered tin covering his whole head in the shape of a skull, in which have been cut eyeholes, a black dent for the nose, and a mouth grinning around a few long and crooked teeth. Under his arm is a crossbow with which he menaces the crowd. The devils have rust-colored jump suits, ample enough to accommodate a variety of figures over the years, and their masks are large, flat tin ovals, painted brown, with curved horns, long noses, and tongues sticking out from leering mouths. The backs of their heads and shoulders are covered by heavy, long-haired goat pelts, black for one, white for the other, a touch of the genuine that is somehow much more menacing than the masks themselves. The multicolored stripes of Adidas sneakers show underneath the baggy trouser legs. 16

Comfortable shoes are a must for the devils, whose loping, lolloping dance betrays considerable weariness. Well it may, says 17

Nicolò: they have been dancing ever since the hour of the Cruci-
fixion on Friday, chasing about the town making mischief and
teasing all they encounter. Nicolò was a devil one year and assures
us that the costumes are unbearably hot and heavy, especially on
a sunny day like today—the only thing that keeps you going is the
wine. Anyone whom Death manages to hit with his crossbow is
obliged to stand the devils a round at the nearest tavern, and if
Death is a good shot, they all have quite a bit under their jump
suits by the end of the day.

18   There is movement up at either end of the street, and for the
second time today we are shoved back against the buildings by
white-gloved policemen. The street is long and I can barely make
out the Madonna to the east, Christ to the west, and just hear the
loudest notes of the band. Down the hill come the forces of Good,
two angels in armor, with cardboard wings, red capes, ropes of
beads and gilt chains across their breasts, swords in hand, and
strange flat-topped helmets that Francesco is quick to notice have
been cut out from Alemagna panettone boxes. The devils at first
have the best of these bizarre apparitions; a brief skirmish leads to
a hasty retreat, and then a counterattack. Back and forth they run
and clash and feint as the statues continue their slow but steady
descent. The battlefield shrinks as the statues draw nearer, the
dance and the swordwork grow more and more frenzied as the
devils find themselves hemmed in between the advancing figures,
until a last and desperate leap marks the meeting between the
risen Christ and the rejoicing Madonna, and Death and the devils
fall to earth, vanquished and immobile.

19   This scene will be repeated four more times this evening, the
last time in the dark in the big piazza in front of the Matrice, at the
top of the hill. Nicolò urges us to stay, but it is a long way back to
Bosco and it is already half past five, so we say good-bye. Drunk
with all that we have seen, my cheeks burning from the sun and
wind, and my eyes watering, I can hardly take in the landscape we
drive through, nor do I notice where we are when Tonino turns his
attention from the road to give me a reproachful glance.

20   "When I was a boy, I spent all my time *avoiding* processions!"

1986

Chapter

Process

3

The Spider and the Wasp

Alexander Petrunkevitch

To hold its own in the struggle for existence, every species of animal must have a regular source of food, and if it happens to live on other animals, its survival may be very delicately balanced. The hunter cannot exist without the hunted; if the latter should perish from the earth, the former would, too. When the hunted also prey on some of the hunters, the matter may become complicated. 1

This is nowhere better illustrated than in the insect world. Think of the complexity of a situation such as the following: There is a certain wasp, *Pimpla inquisitor,* whose larvae feed on the larvae of the tussock moth. *Pimpla* larvae in turn serve as food for the larvae of a second wasp, and the latter in their turn nourish still a third wasp. What subtle balance between fertility and mortality must exist in the case of each of these four species to prevent the extinction of all of them! An excess of mortality over fertility in a single member of the group would ultimately wipe out all four. 2

This is not a unique case. The two great orders of insects, Hymenoptera and Diptera, are full of such examples of interrelationship. And the spiders (which are not insects but members of a separate order of anthropods) also are killers and victims of insects. 3

4   In the feeding and safeguarding of their progeny the insects and spiders exhibit some interesting analogies to reasoning and some crass examples of blind instinct. The case I propose to describe here is that of the tarantula spiders and their arch-enemy, the digger wasps of the genus Pepsis. It is a classic example of what looks like intelligence pitted against instinct—a strange situation in which the victim, though fully able to defend itself, submits unwittingly to its destruction.

5   A fertilized female tarantula lays from 200 to 400 eggs at a time; thus it is possible for a single tarantula to produce several thousand young. She takes no care of them beyond weaving a cocoon of silk to enclose the eggs. After they hatch, the young walk away, find convenient places in which to dig their burrows and spend the rest of their lives in solitude. Tarantulas feed mostly on insects and millipedes. Once their appetite is appeased, they digest the food for several days before eating again. Their sight is poor, being limited to sensing a change in the intensity of light and to the perception of moving objects. They apparently have little or no sense of hearing, for a hungry tarantula will pay no attention to a loudly chirping cricket placed in its cage unless the insect happens to touch one of its legs.

6   But all spiders, and especially hairy ones, have an extremely delicate sense of touch. Laboratory experiments prove that tarantulas can distinguish three types of touch: pressure against the body wall, stroking of the body hair, and riffling of certain very fine hairs on the legs called trichobothria. Pressure against the body, by a finger or the end of a pencil, causes the tarantula to move off slowly for a short distance. The touch excites no defensive response unless the approach is from above where the spider can see the motion, in which case it rises on its hind legs, lifts its front legs, opens its fangs and holds this threatening posture as long as the object continues to move. When the motion stops, the spider drops back to the ground, remains quiet for a few seconds and then moves slowly away.

7   The entire body of a tarantula, especially its legs, is thickly clothed with hair. Some of it is short and woolly, some long and stiff. Touching this body hair produces one of two distinct reactions. When the spider is hungry, it responds with an immediate

and swift attack. At the touch of a cricket's antennae the tarantula seizes the insect so swiftly that a motion picture taken at the rate of 64 frames per second shows only the result and not the process of capture. But when the spider is not hungry, the stimulation of its hairs merely causes it to shake the touched limb. An insect can walk under its hairy belly unharmed.

The trichobothria, very fine hairs growing from disklike mem- 8 branes on the legs, were once thought to be the spider's hearing organs, but we now know that they have nothing to do with sound. They are sensitive only to air movement. A light breeze makes them vibrate slowly without disturbing the common hair. When one blows gently on the trichobothria, the tarantula reacts with a quick jerk of its four front legs. If the front and hind legs are stimulated at the same time, the spider makes a sudden jump. This reaction is quite independent of the state of its appetite.

These three tactile responses—to pressure on the body wall, to 9 moving of the common hair and to flexing of the trichobothria— are so different from one another that there is no possibility of confusing them. They serve the tarantula adequately for most of its needs and enable it to avoid most annoyances and dangers. But they fail the spider completely when it meets its deadly enemy, the digger wasp Pepsis.

These solitary wasps are beautiful and formidable creatures. 10 Most species are either a deep shiny blue all over, or deep blue with rusty wings. The largest have a wing span of about four inches. They live on nectar. When excited, they give off a pungent odor—a warning that they are ready to attack. The sting is much worse than that of a bee or common wasp, and the pain and swelling last longer. In the adult stage the wasp lives only a few months. The female produces but a few eggs, one at a time at intervals of two or three days. For each egg the mother must provide one adult tarantula, alive but paralyzed. The tarantula must be of the correct species to nourish the larva. The mother wasp attaches the egg to the paralyzed spider's abdomen. Upon hatching from the egg, the larva is many hundreds of times smaller than its living but helpless victim. It eats no other food and drinks no water. By the time it has finished its single gargantuan meal and becomes ready for wasphood, nothing remains of the tarantula but its indigestible chitinous skeleton.

11   The mother wasp goes tarantula-hunting when the egg in her ovary is almost ready to be laid. Flying low over the ground late on a sunny afternoon, the wasp looks for its victim or for the mouth of a tarantula burrow, a round hole edged by a bit of silk. The sex of the spider makes no difference, but the mother is highly discriminating as to species. Each species of Pepsis requires a certain species of tarantula, and the wasp will not attack the wrong species. In a cage with a tarantula which is not its normal prey the wasp avoids the spider, and is usually killed by it in the night.

12   Yet when a wasp finds the correct species, it is the other way about. To identify the species the wasp apparently must explore the spider with her antennae. The tarantula shows an amazing tolerance to this exploration. The wasp crawls under it and walks over it without evoking any hostile response. The molestation is so great and so persistent that the tarantula often rises on all eight legs, as if it were on stilts. It may stand this way for several minutes. Meanwhile the wasp, having satisfied itself that the victim is of the right species, moves off a few inches to dig the spider's grave. Working vigorously with legs and jaws, it excavates a hole 8 to 10 inches deep with a diameter slightly larger than the spider's girth. Now and again the wasp pops out of the hole to make sure that the spider is still there.

13   When the grave is finished, the wasp returns to the tarantula to complete her ghastly enterprise. First she feels it all over once more with her antennae. Then her behavior becomes more aggressive. She bends her abdomen, protruding her sting, and searches for the soft membrane at the point where the spider's leg joins its body—the only spot where she can penetrate the horny skeleton. From time to time, as the exasperated spider slowly shifts ground, the wasp turns on her back and slides along with the aid of her wings, trying to get under the tarantula for a shot at the vital spot. During all this maneuvering, which can last for several minutes, the tarantula makes no move to save itself. Finally the wasp corners it against some obstruction and grasps one of its legs in her powerful jaws. Now at last the harassed spider tries a desperate but vain defense. The two contestants roll over and over on the ground. It is a terrifying sight and the outcome is always the same. The wasp finally manages to thrust her sting into the

soft spot and holds it there for a few seconds while she pumps in the poison. Almost immediately the tarantula falls paralyzed on its back. Its legs stop twitching; its heart stops beating, yet it is not dead, as is shown by the fact that if taken from the wasp it can be restored to some sensitivity by being kept in a moist chamber for several months.

After paralyzing the tarantula, the wasp cleans herself by 14 dragging her body along the ground and rubbing her feet, sucks the drop of blood oozing from the wound in the spider's abdomen, then grabs a leg of the flabby, helpless animal in her jaws and drags it down to the bottom of the grave. She stays there for many minutes, sometimes for several hours, and what she does all that time in the dark we do not know. Eventually she lays her egg and attaches it to the side of the spider's abdomen with a sticky secretion. Then she emerges, fills the grave with soil carried bit by bit in her jaws, and finally tramples the ground all around to hide any trace of the grave from prowlers. Then she flies away, leaving her descendant safely started in life.

In all this the behavior of the wasp evidently is qualitatively 15 different from that of the spider. The wasp acts like an intelligent animal. This is not to say that instinct plays no part or that she reasons as man does. But her actions are to the point; they are not automatic and can be modified to fit the situation. We do not know for certain how she identifies the tarantula—probably it is by some olfactory or chemo-tactile sense—but she does it purposefully and does not blindly tackle a wrong species.

On the other hand, the tarantula's behavior shows only con- 16 fusion. Evidently the wasp's pawing gives it no pleasure, for it tries to move away. That the wasp is not simulating sexual stimulation is certain, because male and female tarantulas react in the same way to its advances. That the spider is not anesthetized by some odorless secretion is easily shown by blowing lightly at the tarantula and making it jump suddenly. What, then, makes the tarantula behave as stupidly as it does?

No clear, simple answer is available. Possibly the stimulation 17 by the wasp's antennae is masked by a heavier pressure on the spider's body, so that it reacts as when prodded by a pencil. But the explanation may be much more complex. Initiative in attack is not in the nature of tarantulas; most species fight only when cornered so that escape is impossible. Their inherited patterns of behavior apparently prompt them to avoid problems rather than attack them. For example, spiders always weave their webs in three dimensions, and when a spider finds that there is insufficient space to attach certain threads in the third dimension, it leaves the place and seeks another, instead of finishing the web in a single plane. This urge to escape seems to arise under all circumstances, in all phases of life and to take the place of reasoning. For a spider to change the pattern of its web is as impossible as for an inexperienced man to build a bridge across a chasm obstructing his way.

18   In a way the instinctive urge to escape is not only easier but often more efficient than reasoning. The tarantula does exactly what is most efficient in all cases except in an encounter with a ruthless and determined attacker dependent for the existence of her own species on killing as many tarantulas as she can lay eggs. Perhaps in this case the spider follows its usual pattern of trying to escape, instead of seizing and killing the wasp, because it is not aware of its danger. In any case, the survival of the tarantula species as a whole is protected by the fact that the spider is much more fertile than the wasp.

1952

How to Cook a Carp

Euell Gibbons

1   When I was a lad of about eighteen, my brother and I were working on a cattle ranch in New Mexico that bordered on the Rio Grande. Most Americans think of the Rio Grande as a warm southern stream, but it rises among the high mountains of Colorado, and in the spring it is fed by melting snows. At this time of

the year, the water that rushed by the ranch was turbulent, icy-cold and so silt-laden as to be semisolid. "A little too thick to drink, and a little too thin to plow" was a common description of the waters of the Rio Grande.

A few species of fish inhabited this muddy water. Unfortu- 2 nately, the most common was great eight- to ten-pound carp, a fish that is considered very poor eating in this country, although the Germans and Asiatics have domesticated this fish, and have developed some varieties that are highly esteemed for the table.

On the ranch where we worked, there was a drainage ditch 3 that ran through the lower pasture and emptied its clear waters into the muddy Rio Grande. The carp swimming up the river would strike this clear warmer water and decide they preferred it to the cold mud they had been inhabiting. One spring day, a cowhand who had been riding that way reported that Clear Ditch was becoming crowded with huge carp.

On Sunday we decided to go fishing. Four of us armed our- 4 selves with pitchforks, saddled our horses and set out. Near the mouth of the ditch, the water was running about two feet deep and twelve to sixteen feet wide. There is a saying in that part of the country that you can't get a cowboy to do anything unless it can be done from the back of a horse, so we forced our mounts into the ditch and started wading them upstream, four abreast, herding the carp before us.

By the time we had ridden a mile upstream, the water was less 5 than a foot deep and so crystal clear that we could see our herd of several hundred carp still fleeing from the splashing, wading horses. As the water continued to shallow, our fish began to get panicky. A few of the boldest ones attempted to dart back past us and were impaled on pitchforks. We could see that the whole herd was getting restless and was about to stampede back downstream, so we piled off our horses into the shallow water to meet the charge. The water boiled about us as the huge fish swirled past us and we speared madly in every direction with our pitchforks, throwing each fish we managed to hit over the ditch bank. This was real fishing—cowhand style. The last of the fish herd was by us in a few minutes and it was all over, but we had caught a tremendous quantity of fish.

6   Back at the ranch house, after we had displayed our trophies, we began wondering what we were going to do with so many fish. This started a series of typical cowboy tall tales on "how to cook a carp." The best of these yarns was told by a grizzled old *vaquero*, who claimed he had made his great discovery when he ran out of food while camping on a tributary of the Rio Grande. He said that he had found the finest way to cook a carp was to plaster the whole fish with a thick coating of fresh cow manure and bury it in the hot ashes of a campfire. In an hour or two, he said, the casing of cow manure had become black and very hard. He then related how he had removed the fish from the fire, broken the hard shell with the butt of his Winchester and peeled it off. He said that as the manure came off the scales and skin adhered to it, leaving the baked fish, white and clean. He then ended by saying, "Of course, the carp still wasn't fit to eat, but the manure in which it was cooked tasted pretty good."

7   There were also some serious suggestions and experiments. The chief objection to the carp is that its flesh is full of many forked bones. One man said that he had enjoyed carp sliced very thin and fried so crisp that one could eat it, bones and all. He demonstrated, and you really could eat it without the bones bothering you, but it was still far from being an epicurean dish. One cowboy described the flavor as "a perfect blend of Rio Grande mud and rancid hog lard."

8   Another man said that he had eaten carp that had been cooked in a pressure cooker until the bones softened and became indistinguishable from the flesh. A pressure cooker is almost a necessity at that altitude, so we had one at the ranch house. We tried this method, and the result was barely edible. It tasted like the poorest possible grade of canned salmon flavored with a bit of mud. It was, however, highly appreciated by the dogs and cats on the ranch, and solved the problem of what to do with the bulk of the fish we had caught.

9   It was my brother who finally devised a method of cooking carp that not only made it fit for human consumption, but actually delicious. First, instead of merely scaling the fish, he skinned them. Then, taking a large pinch, where the meat was thickest, he worked his fingers and thumb into the flesh until he struck the

median bones, then he worked his thumb and fingers together and tore off a handful of meat. Using this tearing method, he could get two or three goodsized chunks of flesh from each side of the fish. He then heated a pot of bland vegetable shortening, rubbed the pieces of fish with salt and dropped them into the hot fat. He used no flour, meal, crumbs or seasoning other than salt. They cooked to a golden brown in a few minutes, and everyone pronounced them "mighty fine eating." The muddy flavor seemed to have been eliminated by removing the skin and the large bones. The forked bones were still there, but they had not been multiplied by cutting across them, and one only had to remove several bones still intact with the fork from each piece of fish.

For the remainder of that spring, every few days one or another of the cowboys would take a pitchfork and ride over to Clear Ditch and spear a mess of carp. On these evenings, my brother replaced the regular *cocinero* and we enjoyed some delicious fried carp. 10

The flavor of carp varies with the water from which it is caught. Many years after the above incidents I attended a fish fry at my brother's house. The main course was all of his own catching, and consisted of bass, catfish and carp, all from Elephant Butte Lake farther down the Rio Grande. All the fish were prepared exactly alike, except that the carp was pulled apart as described above, while the bass and catfish, being all twelve inches or less in length, were merely cleaned and fried whole. None of his guests knew one fish from another, yet all of them preferred the carp to the other kinds. These experiences have convinced me that the carp is really a fine food fish when properly prepared. 11

Carp can, of course, be caught in many ways besides spearing them with pitchforks from the back of a horse. In my adopted home state, Pennsylvania, they are classed as "trash fish" and one is allowed to take them almost any way. They will sometimes bite on worms, but they are vegetarians by preference and are more easily taken on dough balls. Some states allow the use of gill nets, and other states, because they would like to reduce the population of this unpopular fish, will issue special permits for the use of nets to catch carp. 12

13   A good forager will take advantage of the lax regulations on carp fishing while they last. When all fishermen realize that the carp is really a good food fish when prepared in the right way, maybe this outsized denizen of our rivers and lakes will no longer be considered a pest and will take his rightful place among our valued food and game fishes.

1962

Behind the Formaldehyde Curtain

Jessica Mitford

1 The drama begins to unfold with the arrival of the corpse at the mortuary.

2   Alas, poor Yorick! How surprised he would be to see how his counterpart of today is whisked off to a funeral parlor and is in short order sprayed, sliced, pierced, pickled, trussed, trimmed, creamed, waxed, painted, rouged and neatly dressed—transformed from a common corpse into a Beautiful Memory Picture. This process is known in the trade as embalming and restorative art, and is so universally employed in the United States and Canada that the funeral director does it routinely, without consulting corpse or kin. He regards as eccentric those few who are hardy enough to suggest that it might be dispensed with. Yet no law requires embalming, no religious doctrine commends it, nor is it dictated by considerations of health, sanitation, or even of personal daintiness. In no part of the world but in Northern America is it widely used. The purpose of embalming is to make the corpse presentable for viewing in a suitably costly container; and here too the funeral director routinely, without first consulting the family, prepares the body for public display.

Is all this legal? The processes to which a dead body may be ₃
subjected are after all to some extent circumscribed by law. In most
states, for instance, the signature of next of kin must be obtained
before an autopsy may be performed, before the deceased may be
cremated, before the body may be turned over to a medical school
for research purposes; or such provision must be made in the
decedent's will. In the case of embalming, no such permission is
required nor is it ever sought. A textbook, *The Principles and Practices of Embalming,* comments on this: "There is some question regarding the legality of much that is done within the preparation
room." The author points out that it would be most unusual for a
responsible member of a bereaved family to instruct the mortician,
in so many words, to *"embalm"* the body of a deceased relative.
The very term "embalming" is so seldom used that the mortician
must rely upon custom in the matter. The author concludes that
unless the family specifies otherwise, the act of entrusting the
body to the care of a funeral establishment carries with it an implied permission to go ahead and embalm.

Embalming is indeed a most extraordinary procedure, and ₄
one must wonder at the docility of Americans who each year pay
hundreds of millions of dollars for its perpetuation, blissfully ignorant of what it is all about, what is done, how it is done. Not one
in ten thousand has any idea of what actually takes place. Books
on the subject are extremely hard to come by. They are not to be
found in most libraries or bookshops.

In an era when huge television audiences watch surgical op- ₅
erations in the comfort of their living rooms, when, thanks to the
animated cartoon, the geography of the digestive system has become familiar territory even to the nursery school set, in a land
where the satisfaction of curiosity about almost all matters is a national pastime, the secrecy surrounding embalming can, surely,
hardly be attributed to the inherent gruesomeness of the subject.
Custom in this regard has within this century suffered a complete
reversal. In the early days of American embalming, when it was
performed in the home of the deceased, it was almost mandatory
for some relative to stay by the embalmer's side and witness the
procedure. Today, family members who might wish to be in attendance would certainly be dissuaded by the funeral director. All

others, except apprentices, are excluded by law from the preparation room.

6   A close look at what does actually take place may explain in
large measure the undertaker's intractable reticence concerning a
procedure that has become his major *raison d'être*. Is it possible he
fears that public information about embalming might lead patrons
to wonder if they really want this service? If the funeral men are
loath to discuss the subject outside the trade, the reader may, understandably, be equally loath to go on reading at this point. For
those who have the stomach for it, let us part the formaldehyde
curtain. . . .

7   The body is first laid out in the undertaker's morgue—or
rather, Mr. Jones is reposing in the preparation room—to be read-
ied to bid the world farewell.

8   The preparation room in any of the better funeral establish-
ments has the tiled and sterile look of a surgery, and indeed the
embalmer-restorative artist who does his chores there is beginning to adopt the term "dermasurgeon" (appropriately corrupted
by some mortician-writers as "demi-surgeon") to describe his calling. His equipment, consisting of scalpels, scissors, augers, for-
ceps, clamps, needles, pumps, tubes, bowls, and basins, is crudely
imitative of the surgeon's, as is his technique, acquired in a nine-
or twelve-month post-high school course in an embalming school.
He is supplied by an advanced chemical industry with a bewil-
dering array of fluids, sprays, pastes, oils, powders, creams, to fix
or soften tissue, shrink or distend it as needed, dry it here, restore
the moisture there. There are cosmetics, waxes and paints to fill
and cover features, even plaster of Paris to replace entire limbs.
There are ingenious aids to prop and stabilize the cadaver: A Vari-
Pose Head Rest, the Edwards Arm and Hand Positioner, the Repose Block (to support the shoulders during the embalming), and
the Throop Foot Positioner, which resembles an old-fashioned
stock.

9   Mr. John H. Eckels, president of the Eckels College of Mortuary Science, thus describes the first part of the embalming procedure: "In the hands of a skilled practitioner, this work may be
done in a comparatively short time and without mutilating the
body other than by slight incision—so slight that it scarcely would

cause serious inconvenience if made upon a living person. It is necessary to remove the blood, and doing this not only helps in the disinfecting, but removes the principal cause of disfigurements due to discoloration."

Another textbook discusses the all-important time element: "The earlier this is done, the better, for every hour that elapses between death and embalming will add to the problems and complications encountered. . . ." Just how soon should one get going on the embalming? The author tells us, "On the basis of such scanty information made available to this profession through its rudimentary and haphazard system of technical research, we must conclude that the best results are to be obtained if the subject is embalmed before life is completely extinct—that is, before cellular death has occurred. In the average case, this would mean within an hour after somatic death." For those who feel that there is something a little rudimentary, not to say haphazard, about this advice, a comforting thought is offered by another writer. Speaking of fears entertained in early days of premature burial, he points out, "One of the effects of embalming by chemical injection, however, has been to dispel fears of live burial." How true; once the blood is removed, chances of live burial are indeed remote.

To return to Mr. Jones, the blood is drained out through the veins and replaced by embalming fluid pumped in through the arteries. As noted in *The Principles and Practices of Embalming*, "every operator has a favorite injection and drainage point—a fact which becomes a handicap only if he fails or refuses to forsake his favorites when conditions demand it." Typical favorites are the carotid artery, femoral artery, jugular vein, subclavian vein. There are various choices of embalming fluid. If Flextone is used, it will produce a "mild, flexible rigidity. The skin retains a velvety softness, the tissues are rubbery and pliable. Ideal for women and children." It may be blended with B. and G. Products Company's Lyf-Lyk tint, which is guaranteed to reproduce "nature's own skin texture . . . the velvety appearance of living tissue." Suntone comes in three separate tints: Suntan; Special Cosmetic Tint, a pink shade "especially indicated for female subjects"; and Regular Cosmetic Tint, moderately pink.

12   About three to six gallons of a dyed and perfumed solution of formaldehyde, glycerin, borax, phenol, alcohol and water is soon circulating through Mr. Jones, whose mouth has been sewn together with a "needle directed upward between the upper lip and gum and brought out through the left nostril," with the corners raised slightly "for a more pleasant expression." If he should be bucktoothed, his teeth are cleaned with Bon Ami and coated with colorless nail polish. His eyes, meanwhile, are closed with flesh-tinted eye caps and eye cement.

13   The next step is to have at Mr. Jones with a thing called a trocar. This is a long, hollow needle attached to a tube. It is jabbed into the abdomen, poked around the entrails and chest cavity, the contents of which are pumped out and replaced with "cavity fluid." This done, and the hole in the abdomen sewn up, Mr. Jones's face is heavily creamed (to protect the skin from burns which may be caused by leakage of the chemicals), and he is covered with a sheet and left unmolested for a while. But not for long—there is more, much more, in store for him. He has been embalmed, but not yet restored, and the best time to start the restorative work is eight to ten hours after embalming, when the tissues have become firm and dry.

14   The object of all this attention to the corpse, it must be remembered, is to make it presentable for viewing in an attitude of healthy repose. "Our customs require the presentation of our dead in the semblance of normality . . . unmarred by the ravages of illness, disease or mutilation," says Mr. J. Sheridan Mayer in his *Restorative Art.* This is rather a large order since few people die in the full bloom of health, unravaged by illness and unmarked by some disfigurement. The funeral industry is equal to the challenge: "In some cases the gruesome appearance of a mutilated or disease-ridden subject may be quite discouraging. The task of restoration may seem impossible and shake the confidence of the embalmer. This is the time for intestinal fortitude and determination. Once the formative work is begun and affected tissues are cleaned or removed, all doubts of success vanish. It is surprising and gratifying to discover the results which may be obtained."

15   The embalmer, having allowed an appropriate interval to elapse, returns to the attack, but now he brings into play the skill

and equipment of sculptor and cosmetician. Is a hand missing? Casting one in plaster of Paris is a simple matter. "For replacement purposes, only a cast of the back of the hand is necessary; this is within the ability of the average operator and is quite adequate." If a lip or two, a nose or an ear should be missing, the embalmer has at hand a variety of restorative waxes with which to model replacements. Pores and skin texture are simulated by stippling with a little brush, and over this cosmetics are laid on. Head off? Decapitation cases are rather routinely handled. Ragged edges are trimmed, and head joined to torso with a series of splints, wires and sutures. It is a good idea to have a little something at the neck—a scarf or a high collar—when time for viewing comes. Swollen mouth? Cut out tissue as needed from inside the lips. If too much is removed, the surface contour can easily be restored by padding with cotton. Swollen necks and cheeks are reduced by removing tissue through vertical incisions made down each side of the neck. "When the deceased is casketed, the pillow will hide the suture incisions . . . as an extra precaution against leakage, the suture may be painted with liquid sealer."

The opposite condition is more likely to present itself—that of 16 emaciation. His hypodermic syringe now loaded with massage cream, the embalmer seeks out and fills the hollowed and sunken areas by injection. In this procedure the backs of the hands and fingers and the under-chin area should not be neglected.

Positioning the lips is a problem that recurrently challenges 17 the ingenuity of the embalmer. Closed too tightly, they tend to give a stern, even disapproving expression. Ideally, embalmers feel, the lips should give the impression of being ever so slightly parted, the upper lip protruding slightly for a more youthful appearance. This takes some engineering, however, as the lips tend to drift apart. Lip drift can sometimes be remedied by pushing one or two straight pins through the inner margin of the lower lip and then inserting them between the two front upper teeth. If Mr. Jones happens to have no teeth, the pins can just as easily be anchored in his Armstrong Face Former and Denture Replacer. Another method to maintain lip closure is to dislocate the lower jaw, which is then held in its new position by a wire run through holes which have been drilled through the upper and lower jaws at the midline. As the French are fond of saying, *il faut souffrir pour être belle.*

18   If Mr. Jones has died of jaundice, the embalming fluid will very likely turn him green. Does this deter the embalmer? Not if he has intestinal fortitude. Masking pastes and cosmetics are heavily laid on, burial garments and casket interiors are color-correlated with particular care, and Jones is displayed beneath rose-colored lights. Friends will say "How *well* he looks." Death by carbon monoxide, on the other hand, can be rather a good thing from the embalmer's viewpoint: "One advantage is the fact that this type of discoloration is an exaggerated form of a natural pink coloration." This is nice because the healthy glow is already present and needs but little attention.

19   The patching and filling completed, Mr. Jones is now shaved, washed and dressed. Cream-based cosmetic, available in pink, flesh, suntan, brunette and blond, is applied to his hands and face, his hair is shampooed and combed (and, in the case of Mrs. Jones, set), his hands manicured. For the horny-handed son of toil special care must be taken; cream should be applied to remove ingrained grime, and the nails cleaned. "If he were not in the habit of having them manicured in life, trimming and shaping is advised for better appearance—never questioned by kin."

20   Jones is now ready for casketing (this is the present participle of the verb "to casket"). In this operation his right shoulder should be depressed slightly "to turn the body a bit to the right and soften the appearance of lying flat on the back." Positioning the hands is a matter of importance, and special rubber positioning blocks may be used. The hands should be cupped slightly for a more life-like, relaxed appearance. Proper placement of the body requires a delicate sense of balance. It should lie as high as possible in the casket, yet not so high that the lid, when lowered, will hit the nose. On the other hand, we are cautioned, placing the body too low "creates the impression that the body is in a box."

21   Jones is next wheeled into the appointed slumber room where a few last touches may be added—his favorite pipe placed in his hand or, if he was a great reader, a book propped into position. (In the case of little Master Jones a Teddy bear may be clutched.) Here he will hold open house for a few days, visiting hours 10 AM to 9 PM.

All now being in readiness, the funeral director calls a staff 22 conference to make sure that each assistant knows his precise duties. Mr. Wilber Kriege writes: "This makes your staff feel that they are a part of the team, with a definite assignment that must be properly carried out if the whole plan is to succeed. You never heard of a football coach who failed to talk to his entire team before they go on the field. They have drilled on the plays they are to execute for hours and days, and yet the successful coach knows the importance of making even the bench-warming third-string substitute feel that he is important if the game is to be won." The winning of *this* game is predicated upon glass-smooth handling of the logistics. The funeral director has notified the pallbearers whose names were furnished by the family, has arranged for the presence of clergyman, organist, and soloist, has provided transportation for everybody, has organized and listed the flowers sent by friends. In *Psychology of Funeral Service* Mr. Edward A. Martin points out: "He may not always do as much as the family thinks he is doing, but it is his helpful guidance that they appreciate in knowing they are proceeding as they should. . . . The important thing is how well his services can be used to make the family believe they are giving unlimited expression to their own sentiment."

The religious service may be held in a church or in the chapel of 23 the funeral home; the funeral director vastly prefers the latter arrangement, for not only is it more convenient for him but it affords him the opportunity to show off his beautiful facilities to the gathered mourners. After the clergyman has had his say, the mourners queue up to file past the casket for a last look at the deceased. The family is *never* asked whether they want an open-casket ceremony; in the absence of their instruction to the contrary, this is taken for granted. Consequently well over 90 percent of all American funerals feature the open casket—a custom unknown in other parts of the world. Foreigners are astonished by it. An English woman living in San Francisco described her reaction in a letter to the writer:

> I myself have attended only one funeral here—that of an elderly fellow worker of mine. After the service I could not understand why everyone was walking towards the coffin (sorry, I mean casket), but thought I had better follow the crowd. It shook me rigid to get there and find the casket open and poor old Oscar lying

there in his brown tweed suit, wearing a suntan makeup and just the wrong shade of lipstick. If I had not been extremely fond of the old boy, I have a horrible feeling that I might have giggled. Then and there I decided that I could never face another American funeral—even dead.

24   The casket (which has been resting throughout the service on a Classic Beauty Ultra Metal Casket Bier) is now transferred by a hydraulically operated device called Porto-Lift to a balloon-tired, Glide Easy casket carriage which will wheel it to yet another conveyance, the Cadillac Funeral Coach. This may be lavender, cream, light green—anything but black. Interiors, of course, are color-correlated, "for the man who cannot stop short of perfection."

25   At graveside, the casket is lowered into the earth. This office, once the prerogative of friends of the deceased, is now performed by a patented mechanical lowering device. A "Lifetime Green" artificial grass mat is at the ready to conceal the sere earth, and overhead, to conceal the sky, is a portable Steril Chapel Tent ("resists the intense heat and humidity of summer and the terrific storms of winter . . . available in Silver Grey, Rose or Evergreen"). Now is the time for the ritual scattering of earth over the coffin, as the solemn words "earth to earth, ashes to ashes, dust to dust" are pronounced by the officiating cleric. This can today be accomplished "with a mere flick of the wrist with the Gordon Leak-Proof Earth Dispenser. No grasping of a handful of dirt, no soiled fingers. Simple, dignified, beautiful, reverent! The modern way!" The Gordon Earth Dispenser (at $5) is of nickel-plated brass construction. It is not only "attractive to the eye and long wearing"; it is also "one of the 'tools' for building better public relations" if presented as "an appropriate non-commercial gift" to the clergyman. It is shaped something like a saltshaker.

26   Untouched by human hand, the coffin and the earth are now united.

27   It is in the function of directing the participants through this maze of gadgetry that the funeral director has assigned to himself his relatively new role of "grief therapist." He has relieved the family of every detail, he has revamped the corpse to look like a living doll, he has arranged for it to nap for a few days in a slumber room, he has put on a well-oiled performance in which the

concept of *death* has played no part whatsoever—unless it was inconsiderately mentioned by the clergyman who conducted the religious service. He has done everything in his power to make the funeral a real pleasure for everybody concerned. He and his team have given their all to score an upset victory over death.

1963

Writing Drafts

Richard Marius

Finally the moment comes when you sit down to begin your first 1 draft. It is always a good idea at the start to list the points you want to cover. A list is not as elaborate as a formal outline. In writing your first list, don't bother to set items down in the order of importance. List your main points and trust your mind to organize them. You will probably make one list, study it, make another, study it, and perhaps make another. You can organize each list more completely than the last. This preliminary process may save you hours of starting and stopping.

Write with your list outline in front of you. Once you begin to 2 write, commit yourself to the task at hand. Do not get up until you have written for an hour. Write your thoughts quickly. Let one sentence give you an idea to develop in the next. Organization, grammar, spelling, and even clarity of sentences are not nearly as important as getting the first draft together. No matter how desperate you feel, keep going.

Always keep your mind open to new ideas that pop into your 3 head as you write. Let your list outline help you, but don't become a slave to it. Writers often start an essay with one topic in mind only to discover that another pushes the first one aside as they work. Ideas you had not even thought of before you began to write may pile onto your paper, and five or six pages into your first draft you may realize that you are going to write about something you did not imagine when you started.

4   If such a revelation comes, be grateful and accept it. But don't immediately tear up or erase your draft and start all over again. Make yourself keep on writing, developing these new ideas as they come. If you suddenly start all over again, you may break the train of thought that has given you the new topic. Let your thoughts follow your new thesis, sailing on that tack until the wind changes.

5   When you have said everything you can say in this draft, print it out if you are working on a computer. Get up from your desk and go sit in a chair somewhere else to read it without correcting anything. Then put it aside, preferably overnight. If possible, read your rough draft just before you go to sleep. Many psychological tests have shown that our minds organize and create while we sleep if we pack them full before bedtime. Study a draft just before sleep, and you may discover new ideas in the morning.

6   Be willing to make radical changes in your second draft. If your thesis changed while you were writing your first draft, you will base your second draft on this new subject. Even if your thesis has not changed, you may need to shift paragraphs around, eliminate paragraphs, or add new ones. Inexperienced writers often suppose that revising a paper means changing only a word or two or adding a sentence or two. This kind of editing is part of the writing process, but it is not the most important part. The most important part of rewriting is a willingness to turn the paper upside down, to shake out of it those ideas that interest you most, to set them in a form where they will interest the reader, too.

7   I mentioned earlier that some writers cut up their first drafts with a pair of scissors. They toss some paragraphs into the trash; others they paste up with rubber cement in the order that seems most logical and coherent. Afterward they type the whole thing through again, smoothing out the transitions, adding new material, getting new ideas as they work. The translation of the first draft into the second nearly always involves radical cutting and shifting around. Now and then you may firmly fix the order of your thoughts in your first draft, but I find that the order of my essays is seldom established until the second draft.

With the advent of computers the shifting around of parts of 8
the essays has become easy. We can cut and paste electronically
with a few strokes of the keyboard. We can also make back-up
copies of our earlier drafts so we can go back to them if we wish.
But as I said earlier, computers do not remove from us the necessity to think hard about revising.

Always be firm enough with yourself to cut out thoughts or 9
stories that have nothing to do with your thesis, even if they are
interesting. Cutting is the supreme test of a writer. You may create
a smashing paragraph or sentence only to discover later that it
does not help you make your point. You may develop six or seven
examples to illustrate a point and discover you need only one.

Now and then you may digress a little. If you digress too of- 10
ten or too far, readers will not follow you unless your facts, your
thoughts, and your style are so compelling that they are somehow driven to follow you. Not many writers can pull such digressions off, and most editors will cut out the digressions even
when they are interesting. In our hurried and harried time, most
readers get impatient with the rambling scenic route. They want
to take the most direct way to their destination. To appeal to
most of them, you must cut things that do not apply to your main
argument.

In your third draft, you can sharpen sentences, add informa- 11
tion here and there, cut some things, and attend to other details to
heighten the force of your writing. In the third draft, writing becomes a lot of fun (for most of us). By then you have usually decided what you want to say. You can now play a bit, finding just
the right word, choosing just the right sentence form, compressing
here, expanding there.

I find it helpful to put a printed draft down beside my key- 12
board and type the whole thing through again as a final draft, letting all the words run through my mind and fingers one more time
rather than merely deleting and inserting on the computer screen.
I wrote four drafts of the first edition of this book; I have preserved
the final draft of that edition on computer diskettes. But I am writing this draft by propping the first edition up here beside me and
typing it all over again. By comparing the first draft and the second draft, one can see how many changes I have made, most of
them unforeseen until I sat down here to work.

13   I have outlined here my own writing process. It works for me.
You must find the process that works for you. It may be different
from mine. A friend tells me that his writing process consists of
writing a sentence, agonizing over it, walking around the room,
thinking, sitting down, and writing the next sentence. He does
not revise very much. I think it unnecessarily painful to bleed out
prose that way, but he bleeds out enough to write what he needs
to write. Several of my friends tell me they cannot compose at a
typewriter; they must first write with a pencil on a yellow pad.
These are the people most likely to cut up their drafts with scissors and paste them together in a different form. They also tend
to be older. Most young writers are learning to compose at a keyboard, and they cannot imagine another way to write. Neither
can I—though on occasion yet I go back to my pencil for pages at
a time.

14   The main thing is to keep at it. B. F. Skinner has pointed out
that if you write only fifty words a night, you will produce a goodsized book every two or three years. That's not a bad record for any
writer. William Faulkner outlined the plot of his Nobel Prize–winning novel *A Fable* on a wall inside his house near Oxford, Mississippi. You can see it there to this day. Once he got the outline on the
wall, he sat down with his typewriter and wrote, following the outline to the end. If writing an outline on a kitchen wall does the trick
for you, do it. You can always repaint the wall if you must.

15   Think of writing as a process making its way toward a product—sometimes painfully. Don't imagine you must know everything you are going to say before you begin. Don't demean yourself and insult your readers by letting your first draft be your final
draft. Don't imagine that writing is easy or that you can do it without spending time on it. And don't let anything stand in your way
of doing it. Let your house get messy. Leave your magazines unread and your mail unanswered. Put off getting up for a drink of
water or a cup of tea. (Never mix alcohol with your writing; true,
lots of writers have become alcoholics, but it has not helped their
writing.) Don't make a telephone call. Don't straighten up your
desk. Sit down and write. And write, and write, and write.

1988

The Rules of the Game: Rodeo

Gretel Ehrlich

Instead of honeymooning in Paris, Patagonia, or the Sahara as we 1
had planned, my new husband and I drove through a series of blizzards to Oklahoma City. Each December the National Finals Rodeo
is held in a modern, multistoried colosseum next to buildings that
house banks and petroleum companies in a state whose flatness resembles a swimming pool filled not with water but with oil.

The National Finals is the "World Series of Professional 2
Rodeo," where not only the best cowboys but also the most ath-
letic horses and bucking stock compete. All year, rodeo cowboys
have been vying for the honor to ride here. They've been to Hous-
ton, Las Vegas, Pendleton, Tucson, Cheyenne, San Francisco, Cal-
gary; to as many as eighty rodeos in one season, sometimes making two or three on a day like the Fourth of July, and when the
results are tallied up (in money won, not points) the top fifteen riders in each event are invited to Oklahoma City.

We climbed to our peanut gallery seats just as Miss Rodeo 3
America, a lanky brunette swaddled in a lavender pantsuit,
gloves, and cowboy hat, loped across the arena. There was a hush
in the audience; all the hats swimming down in front of us, like
buoys, steadied and turned toward the chutes. "Out of chute number three, Pat Linger, a young cowboy from Miles City, Montana,
making his first appearance here on a little horse named
Dillinger." And as fast as these words sailed across the colosseum,
the first bareback horse bumped into the lights.

There's a traditional order to the four timed and three rough 4
stock events that make up a rodeo program. Bareback riders are
first, then steer wrestlers, team ropers, saddle bronc riders, barrel
racers, and finally, the bull riders.

After Pat Linger came Steve Dunham, J. C. Trujillo, Mickey 5
Young, and the defending champ, Bruce Ford on a horse named
Denver. Bareback riders do just that: they ride a horse with no sad-
dle, no halter, no rein, clutching only a handhold riveted into a

girth that goes around the horse's belly. A bareback rider's loose
style suggests a drunken, comic bout of lovemaking: he lies back
on the horse and, with each jump and jolt, flops delightfully, like
a libidinous Raggedy Andy, toes turned out, knees flexed, legs
spread and pumping, back arched, the back of his hat bumping
the horse's rump as if nodding, "Yes, let's do 'er again." My husband, who rode saddle broncs in amateur rodeos, explains it differently: "It's like riding a runaway bicycle down a steep hill and
lying on your back; you can't see where you're going or what's going to happen next."

6   Now the steer wrestlers shoot out of the box on their own
well-trained horses: There is a hazer on the right to keep the steer
running straight, the wrestler on the left, and the steer between
them. When the wrestler is neck and neck with the animal, he
slides sideways out of his saddle as if he's been stabbed in the ribs
and reaches for the horns. He's airborne for a second; then his
heels swing into the dirt, and with his arms around the horns, he
skids to a stop twisting the steer's head to one side so the animal
loses his balance and falls to the ground. It's a fast-paced game of
catch with a thousand-pound ball of horned flesh.

7   The team ropers are next. Most of them hail from the hilly, oak-
strewn valleys of California where dally roping originated.* Ropers
are the graceful technicians, performing their pas de deux (plus
steer) with a precision that begins to resemble a larger clarity—an
erudition. Header and heeler come out of the box at the same time,
steer between them, but the header acts first: He ropes the horns of
the steer, dallies up, turns off, and tries to position the steer for the
heeler who's been tagging behind this duo, loop clasped in his
armpit as if it were a hen. Then the heeler sets his generous,
unsweeping loop free and double-hocks the steer. It's a complicated
act which takes about six seconds. Concomitant with this speed and
skill is a feminine grace: they don't clutch their stiff loop or throw it
at the steer like a bag of dirty laundry the way I do, but hold it gently, delicately, as if it were a hoop of silk. One or two cranks and both
arm and loop vault forward, one becoming an appendage of the

*The word dally is a corruption of the Spanish *da la vuelta,* meaning to take a turn,
as with a rope around the saddle horn.

other, as if the tendons and pulse that travel through the wrist had lengthened and spun forward like fishing line until the loop sails down on the twin horns, then up under the hocks like a repeated embrace that tightens at the end before it releases.

The classic event at rodeo is saddle bronc riding. The young men look as serious as academicians: They perch spryly on their high-kicking mounts, their legs flicking forward and back, "charging the point" "going back to the cantle" in a rapid, staccato rhythm. When the horse is at the high point of his buck and the cowboy is stretched out, legs spurring above the horse's shoulder, rein-holding arm straight as a board in front, and free hand lifted behind, horse and man look like a propeller. Even their dismounts can look aeronautical: springing off the back of the horse, they land on their feet with a flourish—hat still on—as if they had been ejected mechanically from a burning plane long before the crash.

Barrel racing is the one women's event. Where the men are tender in their movements, as elegant as if Balanchine had been their coach, the women are prodigies of Wayne Gretzky, all speed, bully, and grit. When they charge into the arena, their hats fly off; they ride brazenly, elbows, knees, feet fluttering, and by the time they've careened around the second of three barrels, the whip they've had clenched between their teeth is passed to a hand, and on the home stretch they urge the horse to the finish line.

Calf ropers are the whiz kids of rodeo: They're expert on the horse and on the ground, and their horses are as quick-witted. The cowboy emerges from the box with a loop in his hand, a piggin' string in his mouth, coils and reins in the other, and a network of slack line strewn so thickly over horse and rider, they look as if they'd run through a tangle of kudzu before arriving in the arena. After roping the calf and jerking the slack in the rope, he jumps off the horse, sprints down the length of nylon, which the horse keeps taut, throws the calf down, and ties three legs together with the piggin' string. It's said of Roy Cooper, the defending calf-roping champion, that "even with pins and metal plates in his arm, he's known for the fastest groundwork in the business; when he springs down his rope to flank the calf, the resulting action is pure rodeo poetry." The six or seven separate movements he makes are so fluid they look like one continual unfolding.

11   Bull riding is last, and of all the events it's the only one truly dangerous. Bulls are difficult to ride: They're broadbacked, loose-skinned, and powerful. They don't jump balletically the way a horse does; they jerk and spin, and if you fall off, they'll try to gore you with a horn, kick, or trample you. Bull riders are built like the animals they ride: Low to the ground and hefty. They're the tough men on the rodeo circuit, and the flirts. Two of the current champs are city men: Charlie Samson is a small, shy black from Watts, and Bobby Del Vecchio, a brash Italian from the Bronx who always throws the audience a kiss after a ride with a Catskill-like show-manship not usually seen here. What a bull rider lacks in techni-cal virtuosity—you won't see the fast spurring action of a saddle bronc rider in this event—he makes up for in personal flamboy-ance, and because it's a deadlier game they're playing, you can see the belligerence rise up their necks and settle into their faces as the bull starts his first spin. Besides the bull and the cowboy, there are three other men in the ring—the rodeo clowns—who aren't there to make children laugh but to divert the bull from some of his deadlier tricks, and, when the rider bucks off, jump between the two—like secret service men—to save the cowboy's life.

12   Rodeo, like baseball, is an American sport and has been around almost as long. While Henry Chadwick was writing his first book of rules for the fledgling ball clubs in 1858, ranch hands were paying $25 a dare to a kid who would ride five outlaw horses from the rough string in a makeshift arena of wagons and carts. The first commercial rodeo in Wyoming was held in Lander in 1895, just nineteen years after the National League was formed. Baseball was just as popular as bucking and roping contests in the West, but no one in Cooperstown, New York, was riding broncs. And that's been part of the problem. After 124 years, rodeo is still misunderstood. Unlike baseball, it's a regional sport (although they do have rodeos in New Jersey, Florida, and other eastern states); it's derived from and stands for the western way of life and the western spirit. It doesn't have the universal appeal of a sport contrived solely for the competition and winning; there is no ball bandied about between opposing players.

13   Rodeo is the wild child of ranch work and embodies some of what ranching is all about. Horsemanship—not gunslinging—

was the pride of western men, and the chivalrous ethics they formulated, known as the western code, became the ground rules for every human game. Two great partnerships are celebrated in this Oklahoma arena: The indispensable one between man and animal that any rancher or cowboy takes on, enduring the joys and punishments of the alliance; and the one between man and man, cowboy and cowboy.

Though rodeo is an individualist's sport, it has everything to do 14 with teamwork. The cowboy who "covers" his bronc (stays on the full eight seconds) has become a team with that animal. The cowboys' competitive feelings amongst each other are so mixed with western tact as to appear ambivalent. When Bruce Ford, the bareback rider, won a go-round he said, "The hardest part of winning this year was taking it away from one of my best friends, Mickey Young, after he'd worked so hard all year." Stan Williamson, who'd just won the steer wrestling, said, "I just drew a better steer. I didn't want Butch to get a bad one. I just got lucky, I guess."

Ranchers, when working together, can be just as diplomatic. 15 They'll apologize if they cut in front of someone while cutting out a calf, and their thanks to each other at the end of the day has a formal sound. Like those westerners who still help each other out during branding and roundup, rodeo cowboys help each other in the chutes. A bull rider will steady the saddle bronc rider's horse, help measure out the rein or set the saddle, and a bareback rider might help the bull rider set his rigging and pull his rope. Ropers lend each other horses, as do barrel racers and steer wrestlers. This isn't a show they put on; they offer their help with the utmost goodwill and good-naturedness. Once, when a bucking horse fell over backward in the chute with my husband, his friend H.A., who rode bulls, jumped into the chute and pulled him out safely.

Another part of the "westernness" rodeo represents is the 16 drifting cowboys do. They're on the road much of their lives the way turn-of-the-century cowboys were on the trail, but these cowboys travel in style if they can—driving pink Lincolns and new pickups with a dozen fresh shirts hanging behind the driver, and the radio on.

Some ranchers look down on the sport of rodeo; they don't 17 want these "drugstore cowboys" getting all the attention and

glory. Besides, rodeo seems to have less and less to do with real
ranch work. Who ever heard of gathering cows on a bareback
horse with no bridle, or climbing on a herd bull? Ranchers are gen-
eralists—they have to know how to do many things—from jug-
gling the futures market to overhauling a tractor or curing viral
scours (diarrhea) in calves—while rodeo athletes are specialists.
Deep down, they probably feel envious of each other: The rancher
for the praise and big money; the rodeo cowboy for the stay-at-
home life among animals to which their sport only alludes.

18   People with no ranching background have even more difficulty with the sport. Every ride goes so fast, it's hard to see just
what happened, and perhaps because of the Hollywood mytholo-
gizing of the West which distorted rather than distilled western rituals, rodeo is often considered corny, anachronistic, and cruel to
animals. Quite the opposite is true. Rodeo cowboys are as sophis-
ticated athletically as Bjorn Borg or Fernando Valenzuela. That's
why they don't need to be from a ranch anymore, or to have grown
up riding horses. And to undo another myth, rodeo is not cruel to
animals. Compared to the arduous life of any "using horse" on a
cattle or dude ranch, a bucking horse leads the life of Riley. His actual work load for an entire year, i.e., the amount of time he spends
in the arena, totals approximately 4.6 minutes, and nothing done to
him in the arena or out could in any way be called cruel. These animals aren't bludgeoned into bucking; they love to buck. They're
bred to behave this way, they're athletes whose ability has been
nurtured and encouraged. Like the cowboys who compete at the
National Finals, the best bulls and horses from all the bucking
strings in the country are nominated to appear in Oklahoma, winning money along with their riders to pay their own way.

19   The National Finals run ten nights. Every contestant rides
every night, so it is easy to follow their progress and setbacks. One
evening we abandoned our rooftop seats and sat behind the
chutes to watch the saddle broncs ride. Behind the chutes two
cowboys are rubbing rosin—part of their staying power—behind
the saddle swells and on their Easter-egg-colored chaps which are
pink, blue, and light green with white fringe. Up above, standing
on the chute rungs, the stock contractors direct horse traffic: "Vel-

vet Drums" in chute #3, "Angel Sings" in #5, "Rusty" in #1. Rick Smith, Monty Henson, Bobby Berger, Brad Gjermudson, Mel Coleman, and friends climb the chutes. From where I'm sitting, it looks like a field hospital with five separate operating theaters, the cowboys, like surgeons, bent over their patients with sweaty brows and looks of concern. Horses are being haltered; cowboys are measuring out the long, braided reins, saddles are set: One cowboy pulls up on the swells again and again, repositioning his hornless saddle until it sits just right. When the chute boss nods to him and says, "Pull 'em up, boys," the ground crew tightens front and back cinches on the first horse to go, but very slowly so he won't panic in the chute as the cowboy eases himself down over the saddle, not sitting on it, just hovering there. "Okay, you're on." The chute boss nods to him again. Now he sits on the saddle, taking the rein in one hand, holding the top of the chute with the other. He flips the loose bottoms of his chaps over his shins, puts a foot in each stirrup, takes a breath, and nods. The chute gate swings open releasing a flood—not of water, but of flesh, groans, legs kicking. The horse lunges up and out in the first big jump like a wave breaking whose crest the cowboy rides, "marking out the horse," spurs well above the bronc's shoulders. In that first second under the lights, he finds what will be the rhythm of the ride. Once again he "charges the point," his legs pumping forward, then so far back his heels touch behind the cantle. For a moment he looks as though he were kneeling on air, then he's stretched out again, his whole body taut but released, free hand waving in back of his head like a palm frond, rein-holding hand thrust forward: *En garde!*" he seems to be saying, but he's airborne; he looks like a wing that has sprouted suddenly from the horse's broad back. Eight seconds. The whistle blows. He's covered the horse. Now two gentlemen dressed in white chaps and satin shirts gallop beside the bucking horse. The cowboy hands the rein to one and grabs the waist of the other—the flank strap on the bronc has been undone, so all three horses move at a run—and the pickup man from whom the cowboy is now dangling slows almost to a stop, letting him slide to his feet on the ground.

Rick Smith from Wyoming rides, looking pale and nervous in 20 his white shirt. He's bucked off and so are the brash Monty

"Hawkeye" Henson, and Butch Knowles, and Bud Pauley, but with such grace and aplomb, there is no shame. Bobby Berger, an Oklahoma cowboy, wins the go-round with a score of 83.

21   By the end of the evening we're tired, but in no way as exhausted as these young men who have ridden night after night. "I've never been so sore and had so much fun in my life," one first-time bull rider exclaims breathlessly. When the performance is over we walk across the street to the chic lobby of a hotel chock full of cowboys. Wives hurry through the crowd with freshly ironed shirts for tomorrow's ride, ropers carry their rope bags with them into the coffee shop, which is now filled with contestants, eating mild midnight suppers of scrambled eggs, their numbers hanging crookedly on their backs, their faces powdered with dust, and looking at this late hour prematurely old.

22   We drive back to the motel, where, the first night, they'd "never heard of us" even though we'd had reservations for a month. "Hey, it's our honeymoon," I told the night clerk and showed him the white ribbons my mother had tied around our duffel bag. He looked embarrassed, then surrendered another latecomer's room.

23   The rodeo finals in Oklahoma may be a better place to honeymoon than Paris. All week, we've observed some important rules of the game. A good rodeo, like a good marriage, or a musical instrument when played to the pitch of perfection, becomes more than what it started out to be. It is effort transformed into effortlessness; a balance becomes grace, the way love goes deep into friendship.

24   In the rough stock events such as the one we watched tonight, there is no victory over the horse or bull. The point of the match is not conquest but communion: The rhythm of two beings becoming one. Rodeo is not a sport of opposition; there is no scrimmage line here. No one bears malice—neither the animals, the stock contractors, nor the contestants; no one wants to get hurt. In this match of equal talents, it is only acceptance, surrender, respect, and spiritedness that make for the midair union of cowboy and horse. Not a bad thought when starting out fresh in a marriage.

1985

*Honey Harvest**

Sue Hubbell

I keep twenty hives of bees here in my home beeyard, but most of   1
my hives are scattered in outyards across the Ozarks, where I can
find the thickest stands of wild blackberries and other good things
for bees. I always have a waiting list of farmers who would like the
bees on their land, for the clover in their pastures is more abun-
dant when the bees are there to pollinate it.

One of the farmers, a third-generation Ozarker and a dairy-   2
man with a lively interest in bees, came over today for a look at
what my neighbors call my honey factory. My honey house contains a shiny array of stainless-steel tanks with clear plastic tubing
connecting them, a power uncapper for slicing open honey comb,
an extractor for spinning honey out of the comb, and a lot of machinery and equipment that whirs, thumps, hums, and looks very
special. The dairyman, shrewd in mountain ways, looked it all
over carefully and then observed, "Well . . . ll . . . ll, wouldn't say
for sure now, but it looks like a still to me."

There have been droughty years and cold wet ones when   3
flowers refused to bloom and I would have been better off with a
still back up here on my mountain top, but the weather this past
year was perfect from a bee's standpoint, and this August I ran
33,000 pounds of honey through my factory. This was nearly twice
the normal crop, and everything was overloaded, starting with
me. Neither I nor my equipment is set up to handle this sort of harvest, even with extra help.

I always need to hire someone, a strong young man who is not   4
afraid of being stung, to help me harvest the honey from the hives.

The honey I take is the surplus that the bees will not need for   5
the winter; they store it above their hives in wooden boxes called
supers. To take it from them, I stand behind each hive with a gaso-
line-powered machine called a bee-blower and blow the bees out
of the supers with a jet of air. Meanwhile, the strong young man

*Editor's title.

carries the supers, which weigh about sixty pounds each, and stacks them on pallets in the truck. There may be thirty to fifty supers in every outyard, and we have only about half an hour to get them off the hives, stacked and covered before the bees get really cross about what we are doing. The season to take the honey in this part of the country is summer's end, when the temperature is often above ninety-five degrees. The nature of the work and the temper of the bees require that we wear protective clothing while doing the job: a full set of coveralls, a zippered bee veil and leather gloves. Even a very strong young man works up a considerable sweat wrapped in a bee suit in hot weather hustling sixty-pound supers—being harassed by angry bees at the same time.

6   This year my helper has been Ky, my nephew, who wanted to learn something about bees and beekeeping. He is a sweet, gentle, cooperative giant of a young man who, because of a series of physical problems, lacks confidence in his own ability to get on in the world.

7   As soon as he arrived, I set about to desensitize him to bee stings. The first day, I put a piece of ice on his arm to numb it; then, holding the bee carefully by her head, I placed her abdomen on the numbed spot and let her sting him there. A bee's stinger is barbed and stays in the flesh, pulling loose from her body as she struggles to free herself. Lacking her stinger, the bee will live only a short time. The bulbous poison sac at the top of the stinger continues to pulsate after the bee has left, its muscles pumping the venom and forcing the barbed stinger deeper into the flesh.

8   I wanted Ky to have only a partial dose of venom that first day, so after a minute I scraped the stinger out with my fingernail and watched his reaction closely. A few people—about one percent of the population—are seriously sensitive to bee venom. Each sting they receive can cause a more severe reaction than the one before, reactions ranging from hives, difficulty in breathing and accelerated heartbeat, to choking, anaphylactic shock, and death. Ky had been stung a few times in his life and didn't think he was seriously allergic, but I wanted to make sure.

9   The spot where the stinger went in grew red and began to swell. This was a normal reaction, and so was the itchiness that Ky felt the next day. That time I let a bee sting him again, repeating the procedure, but leaving the stinger in his arm a full ten minutes,

until the venom sac was emptied. Again the spot was red, swollen and itchy, but had disappeared the next day. Thereafter Ky decided that he didn't need the ice cube any more, and began holding the bee himself to administer his own stings. I kept him at one sting a day until he had no redness or swelling from the full sting, and then had him increase to two stings daily. Again the greater amount of venom caused redness and swelling, but soon his body could tolerate them without an allergic reaction. I gradually had him build up to ten full stings a day with no reaction.

To encourage Ky, I had told him that what he was doing might   10
help protect him from the arthritis that runs in our family. Beekeepers generally believe that getting stung by bees is a healthy thing, and that bee venom alleviates the symptoms of arthritis. When I first began keeping bees, I supposed this to be just another one of the old wives' tales that make beekeeping such an entertaining occupation, but after my hands were stung the pain in my fingers disappeared and I too became a believer. Ky was polite, amused, and skeptical of what I told him, but he welcomed my taking a few companionable stings on my knuckles along with him.

In desensitizing Ky to bee venom, I had simply been inter-   11
ested in building up his tolerance to stings so that he could be an effective helper when we took the honey from the hives, for I knew that he would be stung frequently. But I discovered that there had been a secondary effect on Ky that was more important: He was enormously pleased with himself for having passed through what he evidently regarded as a rite of initiation. He was proud and delighted in telling other people about the whole process. He was now one tough guy.

I hoped he was prepared well enough for our first day of   12
work. I have had enough strong young men work for me to know what would happen the first day: He would be stung royally.

Some beekeepers insist that bees know their keeper—that   13
they won't sting that person, but *will* sting a stranger. This is nonsense, for summertime bees live only six weeks and I often open a particular hive less frequently than that, so I am usually a stranger to my bees; yet I am seldom stung. Others say that bees can sense fear or nervousness. I don't know if this is true or not, but I do know that bees' eyes are constructed in such a way that they can detect discontinuities and movement very well and stationary

objects less well. This means that a person near their hives who moves with rapid, jerky motions attracts their attention and will more often be blamed by the bees when their hives are being meddled with than will the person whose motions are calm and easy. It has been my experience that the strong young man I hire for the honey harvest is always stung unmercifully for the first few days while he is new to the process and a bit tense. Then he learns to become easier with the bees and settles down to his job. As he gains confidence and assurance, the bees calm down too, and by the end of the harvest he usually is only stung a few times a day.

14 I knew that Ky very much wanted to do a good job with me that initial day working in the outyards. I had explained the procedures we would follow in taking the honey from the hives, but of course they were new to him and he was anxious. The bees from the first hive I opened flung themselves on him. Most of the stingers could not penetrate his bee suit, but in the act of stinging a bee leaves a chemical trace that marks the person stung as an enemy, a chemical sign other bees can read easily. This sign was read by the bees in each new hive I opened, and soon Ky's bee suit began to look like a pincushion, bristling with stingers. In addition, the temperature was starting to climb and Ky was sweating. Honey oozing from combs broken between the supers was running down the front of his bee suit when he carried them to the truck. Honey and sweat made the suit cling to him, so that the stingers of angry bees could penetrate the suit and he could feel the prick of each one as it entered his skin. Hundreds of bees were assaulting him and finally drove him out of the beeyard, chasing him several hundred yards before they gave up the attack. There was little I could do to help him but try to complete the job quickly, so I took the supers off the next few hives myself, carried them to the truck and loaded them. Bravely, Ky returned to finish the last few hives. We tied down the load and drove away. His face was red with exertion when he unzipped his bee veil. He didn't have much to say as we drove to the next yard, but sat beside me gulping down ice water from the thermos bottle.

15 At the second yard the bees didn't bother Ky as we set up the equipment. I hoped that much of the chemical marker the bees had left on him had evaporated, but as soon as I began to open the

hives they were after him again. Soon a cloud of angry bees enveloped him, accompanying him to the truck and back. Because of the terrain, the truck had to be parked at an odd angle and Ky had to bend from the hips as he loaded it, stretching the fabric of the bee suit taut across the entire length of his back and rear, allowing the bees to sting through it easily. We couldn't talk over the noise of the beeblower's engine, but I was worried about how he was taking hundreds more stings. I was removing the bees from the supers as quickly as I could, but the yard was a good one and there were a lot of supers there.

In about an hour's time Ky carried and stacked what we later   16
weighed in as a load of 2,500 pounds. The temperature must have been nearly a hundred degrees. After he had stacked the last super, I drove the truck away from the hives and we tied down the load. Ky's long hair was plastered to his face and I couldn't see the expression on it, but I knew he had been pushed to his limits and I was concerned about him. He tried to brush some of the stingers out of the seat of his bee suit before he sat down next to me in the truck in an uncommonly gingerly way. Unzipping his bee veil, he tossed it aside, pushed the hair back from his sweaty face, reached for the thermos bottle, gave me a sunny and triumphant grin and said, "If I ever get arthritis of the ass, I'll know all that stuff you've been telling me is a lot of baloney."

1983

How to Paint
a Fresco

Adam Goodheart

Although it must be painted in a very short time, a fresco will last   1
a very long time—that is its great advantage. Many of the masterpieces of the golden age of fresco (from the 14th through the 18th

centuries) are as brilliant now as when they were first painted. If you want to fresco a cathedral or palazzo today, you may have a few problems—papal and ducal commissions are scarcer than they once were, and the great Renaissance masters are no longer accepting applications for apprenticeships. Fortunately, a few of their trade secrets have come down to us through the ages.

EQUIPMENT

2   *Lime*

Sand

Water

A trowel

Paper

A needle

A small bag of charcoal dust

The bristles of a white hog

The hair of bears, sables, and martens

The quills of vultures, geese, hens, and doves

Ocher, burnt grapevines, lapis lazuli

Egg yolks

Goat's milk

3   **1. Preparing the wall.** Cennino Cennini, a Tuscan master, advised pupils in 1437 to "begin by decking yourselves with this attire: Enthusiasm, Reverence, Obedience, and Constancy." You'd do better to deck yourself with some old clothes, though, since the first stage of the process is quite messy. Soak the wall thoroughly and coat it with coarse plaster, two parts sand to one part lime, leaving the surface uneven. (Andrea Pozzo, a 17th-century expert, recommended hiring a professional mason to do this, since "the lime makes a foul odor, which is injurious to the head.")

2. Tracing your design. You should already have extensive 4
drawings for your fresco—these will be much sought by scholars
and collectors in centuries to come. Make a full-size sketch, on
sturdy paper, of a section of the fresco that you can paint in a day.
Then go over the drawing with a needle, pricking holes along
every line. Lay a coat of fine plaster on a section of the wall corresponding to the location, size, and shape of the sketch, and press
the sketch against the plaster. Fill a loosely woven bag with charcoal dust and strike it lightly all over the surface of the paper. Now
peel the sketch off. Your design will be outlined in black dots on
the wet plaster, giving you a guide for the day's work.

3. Painting. Time is of the essence: You must paint the plas- 5
ter while it is wet, so that the pigments bind chemically with the
lime. That gives you about six hours, although some painters
had tricks to prolong drying. (Piero della Francesca packed the
plaster with wet rags; problem was, this left indentations that are
still visible after 500 years.) Use top-quality brushes. One 17th-
century Flemish master recommended those made of "fish hair"
(he probably meant seal fur), but most painters made brushes
from bear, marten, or sable hairs inserted in hollow quills. Cennini suggested the bristles of a white hog for the coarser work.
As for paints, every artist had his own favorite recipes, but all
agreed that mineral pigments such as ocher or ground stone
mixed with water were best. Avoid white lead. One 14th-century
Umbrian used it to paint a nursing infant; the lime turned the
white black and the milky babe into a "devilish changeling." A
few pigments, such as dark blue azurite (often used for the Virgin Mary's mantle), must be mixed with egg yolk or goat's milk
and added after the fresco is dry. Such colors will prove less
durable.

Money is a consideration in choosing materials. When 6
Michelangelo frescoed the Sistine ceiling, expenses came out of his
fee, so he used cheap blue smalt for the sky. Twenty years later,
when he did the *Last Judgment*, Michelangelo used semiprecious
lapis lazuli for blue, since the pope was paying for the paint. (He
made up for it by using burnt grapevines for black.)

7   **4. *Casualties of style*.** Realism, while a worthy goal, has its perils. Spinello Aretino, a 14th-century Tuscan, is said to have painted a fresco that depicted Lucifer with such hideous accuracy that the Evil One himself came to the artist in a dream and demanded an explanation. Spinello went half-mad with fear and died shortly thereafter. On the other hand, a Florentine woodcut from 1500 depicts a painter who has portrayed the Virgin so skillfully that when he falls off the scaffold, she reaches out of the fresco and saves him.

WARNING

8 Frescoing ceilings can be rough on your back. While working on the Sistine Chapel, Michelangelo wrote a poem complaining: "I've already grown a goiter at this drudgery . . . With my beard toward heaven . . . I am bent like a bow." Don't be discouraged, though. Bad posture is a small price to pay for immortality.

1995

Chapter

Definition

Women's Beauty: Put Down or Power Source?

Susan Sontag

For the Greeks, beauty was a virtue: A kind of excellence. Persons 1
then were assumed to be what we now have to call—lamely, envi-
ously—*whole* persons. If it did occur to the Greeks to distinguish between a person's "inside" and "outside," they still expected that inner beauty would be matched by beauty of the other kind. The
well-born young Athenians who gathered around Socrates found it
quite paradoxical that their hero was so intelligent, so brave, so honorable, so seductive—and so ugly. One of Socrates' main pedagogical acts was to be ugly—and teach those innocent, no doubt splendid—looking disciples of his how full of paradoxes life really was.

They may have resisted Socrates' lesson. We do not. Several 2
thousand years later, we are more wary of the enchantments of
beauty. We not only split off—with the greatest facility—the "inside" (character, intellect) from the "outside" (looks); but we are
actually surprised when someone who is beautiful is also intelligent, talented, good.

It was principally the influence of Christianity that deprived 3
beauty of the central place it had in classical ideals of human excellence. By limiting excellence (*virtus* in Latin) to *moral* virtue
only, Christianity set beauty adrift—as an alienated, arbitrary, superficial enchantment. And beauty has continued to lose prestige.

131

For close to two centuries it has become a convention to attribute
beauty to only one of the two sexes: The sex which, however Fair,
is always Second. Associating beauty with women has put beauty
even further on the defensive, morally.

4   A beautiful woman, we say in English. But a handsome man.
"Handsome" is the masculine equivalent of—and refusal of—a
compliment which has accumulated certain demeaning overtones,
by being reserved for women only. That one can call a man "beautiful" in French and in Italian suggests that Catholic countries—unlike those countries shaped by the Protestant version of Christianity—still retain some vestiges of the pagan admiration for beauty.
But the difference, if one exists, is of degree only. In every modern
country that is Christian or post-Christian, women *are* the beautiful
sex—to the detriment of the notion of beauty as well as of women.

5   To be called beautiful is thought to name something essential
to women's character and concerns. (In contrast to men—whose
essence is to be strong, or effective, or competent.) It does not take
someone in the throes of advanced feminist awareness to perceive
that the way women are taught to be involved with beauty encourages narcissism, reinforces dependence and immaturity.
Everybody (women and men) knows that. For it is "everybody," a
whole society, that has identified being feminine with caring
about how one *looks.* (In contrast to being masculine—which is
identified with caring about what one *is* and *does* and only secon-
darily, if at all, about how one looks.) Given these stereotypes, it is
no wonder that beauty enjoys, at best, a rather mixed reputation.

6   It is not, of course, the desire to be beautiful that is wrong but
the obligation to be—or to try. What is accepted by most women as
a flattering idealization of their sex is a way of making women feel
inferior to what they actually are—or normally grow to be. For the
ideal of beauty is administered as a form of self-oppression. Women
are taught to see their bodies in *parts,* and to evaluate each part sep-
arately. Breasts, feet, hips, waistline, neck, eyes, nose, complexion,
hair, and so on—each in turn is submitted to an anxious, fretful, often despairing scrutiny. Even if some pass muster, some will always
be found wanting. Nothing less than perfection will do.

7   In men, good looks is a whole, something taken in at a glance.
It does not need to be confirmed by giving measurements of dif-

ferent regions of the body, nobody encourages a man to dissect his appearance, feature by feature. As for perfection, that is considered trivial—almost unmanly. Indeed, in the ideally good-looking man a small imperfection or blemish is considered positively desirable. According to one movie critic (a woman) who is a declared Robert Redford fan, it is having that cluster of skin-colored moles on one cheek that saves Redford from being merely a "pretty face." Think of the depreciation of women—as well as of beauty—that is implied in that judgment.

"The privileges of beauty are immense," said Cocteau. To be sure, beauty is a form of power. And deservedly so. What is lamentable is that it is the only form of power that most women are encouraged to seek. This power is always conceived in relation to men; it is not the power to do but the power to attract. It is a power that negates itself. For this power is not one that can be chosen freely—at least, not by women—or renounced without social censure.

To preen, for a woman, can never be just a pleasure. It is also a duty. It is her work. If a woman does real work—and even if she has clambered up to a leading position in politics, law, medicine, business, or whatever—she is always under pressure to confess that she still works at being attractive. But in so far as she is keeping up as one of the Fair Sex, she brings under suspicion her very capacity to be objective, professional, authoritative, thoughtful. Damned if they do—women are. And damned if they don't.

One could hardly ask for more important evidence of the dangers of considering persons as split between what is "inside" and what is "outside" than that interminable half-comic half-tragic tale, the oppression of women. How easy it is to start off by defining women as caretakers of their surfaces, and then to disparage them (or find them adorable) for being "superficial." It is a crude trap, and it has worked for too long. But to get out of the trap requires that women get some critical distance from that excellence and privilege which is beauty, enough distance to see how much beauty itself has been abridged in order to prop up the mythology of the "feminine." There should be a way of saving beauty *from* women—and *for* them.

1975

What Is Poverty?

Jo Goodwin Parker

1 You ask me what is poverty? Listen to me. Here I am, dirty, smelly, and with no "proper" underwear on and with the stench of my rotting teeth near you. I will tell you. Listen to me. Listen without pity. I cannot use your pity. Listen with understanding. Put yourself in my dirty, worn out, ill-fitting shoes, and hear me.

2 Poverty is getting up every morning from a dirt- and illness-stained mattress. The sheets have long since been used for diapers. Poverty is living in a smell that never leaves. This is a smell of urine, sour milk, and spoiling food sometimes joined with the strong smell of long-cooked onions. Onions are cheap. If you have smelled this smell, you did not know how it came. It is the smell of the outdoor privy. It is the smell of young children who cannot walk the long dark way in the night. It is the smell of the mattresses where years of "accidents" have happened. It is the smell of the milk which has gone sour because the refrigerator long has not worked, and it costs money to get it fixed. It is the smell of rotting garbage. I could bury it, but where is the shovel? Shovels cost money.

3 Poverty is being tired. I have always been tired. They told me at the hospital when the last baby came that I had chronic anemia caused from poor diet, a bad case of worms, and that I needed a corrective operation. I listened politely—the poor are always polite. The poor always listen. They don't say that there is no money for iron pills, or better food, or worm medicine. The idea of an operation is frightening and costs so much that, if I had dared, I would have laughed. Who takes care of my children? Recovery from an operation takes a long time. I have three children. When I left them with "Granny" the last time I had a job, I came home to find the baby covered with fly specks, and a diaper that had not

been changed since I left. When the dried diaper came off, bits of my baby's flesh came with it. My other child was playing with a sharp bit of broken glass, and my oldest was playing alone at the edge of a lake. I made twenty-two dollars a week, and a good nursery school costs twenty dollars a week for three children. I quit my job.

Poverty is dirt. You can say in your clean clothes coming from   4
your clean house, "Anybody can be clean." Let me explain about housekeeping with no money. For breakfast I give my children grits with no oleo or cornbread without eggs and oleo. This does not use up many dishes. What dishes there are, I wash in cold water and with no soap. Even the cheapest soap has to be saved for the baby's diapers. Look at my hands, so cracked and red. Once I saved for two months to buy a jar of Vaseline for my hands and the baby's diaper rash. When I had saved enough, I went to buy it and the price had gone up two cents. The baby and I suffered on. I have to decide every day if I can bear to put my cracked sore hands into the cold water and strong soap. But you ask, why not hot water? Fuel costs money. If you have a wood fire it costs money. If you burn electricity, it costs money. Hot water is a luxury. I do not have luxuries. I know you will be surprised when I tell you how young I am. I look so much older. My back has been bent over the wash tubs every day for so long, I cannot remember when I ever did anything else. Every night I wash every stitch my school age child has on and just hope her clothes will be dry by morning.

Poverty is staying up all night on cold nights to watch the fire   5
knowing one spark on the newspaper covering the walls means your sleeping child dies in flames. In summer, poverty is watching gnats and flies devour your baby's tears when he cries. The screens are torn and you pay so little rent you know they will never be fixed. Poverty means insects in your food, in your nose, in your eyes, and crawling over you when you sleep. Poverty is hoping it never rains because diapers won't dry when it rains and soon you are using newspapers. Poverty is seeing your children forever with runny noses. Paper handkerchiefs cost money and all your rags you need for other things. Even more costly are antihistamines. Poverty is cooking without food and cleaning without soap.

6   <u>Poverty is asking for help.</u> Have you ever had to ask for help, knowing your children will suffer unless you get it? Think about asking for a loan from a relative, if this is the only way you can imagine asking for help. I will tell you how it feels. You find out where the office is that you are supposed to visit. You circle that block four or five times. Thinking of your children, you go in. Everyone is very busy. Finally, someone comes out and you tell her that you need help. That never is the person you need to see. You go see another person, and <u>after spilling the whole shame of your poverty all over the desk</u> between you, you find that this isn't the right office after all—you must repeat the whole process, and it never is any easier at the next place.

7   You have asked for help, and after all it has a cost. You are again told to wait. You are told why, but you don't really hear because of the <u>red cloud of shame and the rising cloud of</u> despair.

8   Poverty is remembering. It is remembering quitting school in junior high because "nice" children had been so cruel about my clothes and my smell. The attendance officer came. My mother told him I was pregnant. I wasn't, but she thought that I could get a job and help out. I had jobs off and on, but never long enough to learn anything. Mostly I remember being married. I was so young then. I am still young. For a time, we had all the things you have. There was a little house in another town, with hot water and everything. Then my husband lost his job. There was unemployment insurance for a while and what few jobs I could get. Soon, all our nice things were repossessed and we moved back here. I was pregnant then. This house didn't look so bad when we first moved in. Every week it gets worse. Nothing is ever fixed. We now had no money. There were a few odd jobs for my husband, but everything went for food then, as it does now. I don't know how we lived through three years and three babies, but we did. I'll tell you something, after the last baby I destroyed my marriage. It had been a good one, but could you keep on bringing children in this dirt? <u>Did you ever think how much it costs for any kind of birth</u> control? I knew my husband was leaving the day he left, but there were no goodbys between us. <u>I hope he has been able to climb out of this mess somewhere. He never could hope with us to drag him</u> down.

That's when I asked for help. When I got it, you know how 9
much it was? It was, and is, seventy-eight dollars a month for the
four of us; that is all I ever can get. Now you know why there is no
soap, no needles and thread, no hot water, no aspirin, no worm
medicine, no hand cream, no shampoo. None of these things forever and ever and ever. So that you can see clearly, I pay twenty dollars a month rent, and most of the rest goes for food. For grits and
cornmeal, and rice and milk and beans. I try my best to use only the
minimum electricity. If I use more, there is that much less for food.

Poverty is looking into a black future. Your children won't 10
play with my boys. They will turn to other boys who steal to get
what they want. I can already see them behind the bars of their
prison instead of behind the bars of my poverty. Or they will turn
to the freedom of alcohol or drugs, and find themselves enslaved.
And my daughter? At best, there is for her a life like mine.

But you say to me, there are schools. Yes, there are schools. My 11
children have no extra books, no magazines, no extra pencils, or
crayons, or paper and most important of all, they do not have
health. They have worms, they have infections, they have pink-
eye all summer. They do not sleep well on the floor, or with me in
my one bed. They do not suffer from hunger, my seventy-eight
dollars keeps us alive, but they do suffer from malnutrition. Oh
yes, I do remember what I was taught about health in school. It
doesn't do much good. In some places there is a surplus com-
modities program. Not here. The county said it cost too much.
There is a school lunch program. But I have two children who will
already be damaged by the time they get to school.

But, you say to me, there are health clinics. Yes, there are 12
health clinics and they are in the towns. I live out here eight miles
from town. I can walk that far (even if it is sixteen miles both
ways), but can my little children? My neighbor will take me when
he goes; but he expects to get paid, *one way or another*. I bet you
know my neighbor. He is that large man who spends his time at
the gas station, the barbershop, and the corner store complaining
about the government spending money on the immoral mothers
of illegitimate children.

Poverty is an acid that drips on pride until all pride is worn 13
away. Poverty is a chisel that chips on honor until honor is worn

away. Some of you say that you would do *something* in my situation, and maybe you would, for the first week or the first month, but for year after year after year?

14   Even the poor can dream. A dream of a time when there is money. Money for the right kinds of food, for worm medicine, for iron pills, for toothbrushes, for hand cream, for a hammer and nails and a bit of screening, for a shovel, for a bit of paint, for some sheeting, for needles and thread. Money to pay *in money* for a trip to town. And, oh, money for hot water and money for soap. A dream of when asking for help does not eat away the last bit of pride. When the office you visit is as nice as the offices of other governmental agencies, when there are enough workers to help you quickly, when workers do not quit in defeat and despair. When you have to tell your story to only one person, and that person can send you for other help and you don't have to prove your poverty over and over and over again.

15   I have come out of my despair to tell you this. Remember I did not come from another place or another time. Others like me are all around you. Look at us with an angry heart, anger that will help you help me. Anger that will let you tell of me. The poor are always silent. Can you be silent too?

1971

Faith of the Father

Sam Pickering

1 On weekdays Campbell's store was the center of life in the little Virginia town in which I spent summers and Christmas vacations. The post office was in a corner of the store, and the train station was across the road. In the morning men gathered on Campbell's porch and drank coffee while they waited for the train to Richmond. Late in the afternoon, families appeared. While waiting for

their husbands, women bought groceries, mailed letters, and visited with one another. Children ate cups of ice cream and played in the woods behind the store. Sometimes a work train was on the siding, and the engineer filled his cab with children and took them for short trips down the track. On weekends life shifted from the store to St. Paul's Church. Built in a grove of pine trees in the nineteenth century, St. Paul's was a small, white clapboard building. A Sunday School wing added to the church in the 1920s jutted out into the graveyard. Beyond the graveyard was a field in which picnics were held and on the Fourth of July, the yearly Donkey Softball Game was played.

St. Paul's was familial and comfortable. Only a hundred 2 people attended regularly, and everyone knew everyone else and his business. What was private became public after the service as people gathered outside and talked for half an hour before going home to lunch. Behind the altar inside the church was a stained glass window showing Christ's ascension to heaven. A red carpet ran down the middle aisle, and worn, gold cushions covered the pews. On the walls were plaques in memory of parishioners killed in foreign wars or who had made large donations to the building fund. In summer the minister put fans out on the pews. Donated by a local undertaker, the fans were shaped like spades. On them, besides the undertaker's name and telephone number, were pictures of Christ performing miracles: Walking on water, healing the lame, and raising Lazarus from the dead.

Holidays and funerals were special at St. Paul's. Funerals 3 were occasions for reminiscing and telling stories. When an irascible old lady died and her daughter had "Gone to Jesus" inscribed on her tombstone, her son-in-law was heard to say "poor Jesus"—or so the tale went at the funeral. Christmas Eve was always cold and snow usually fell. Inside the church at midnight, though, all was cheery and warm as the congregation sang the great Christmas hymns: "O Come, All Ye Faithful," "The First Noel," "O Little Town of Bethlehem," and "Hark! The Herald Angels Sing." The last hymn was "Silent Night." The service did not follow the prayer book; inspired by Christmas and eggnog, the congregation came to sing, not to pray. Bourbon was in the air, and when the altar boy lit the candles, it seemed a miracle that the first spark didn't send us all to heaven in a blue flame.

4   Easter was almost more joyous than Christmas. Men stuck greenery into their lapels and women blossomed in bright bonnets, some ordering hats not simply from Richmond but from Baltimore and Philadelphia. On a farm outside town lived Miss Emma and Miss Ida Catlin. Miss Emma was the practical sister, running the farm and bringing order wherever she went. Unlike Miss Emma, Miss Ida was shy. She read poetry and raised guinea fowl and at parties sat silently in a corner. Only on Easter was she outgoing; then like a day lily she bloomed triumphantly. No one else's Easter bonnet ever matched hers, and the congregation eagerly awaited her entrance which she always made just before the first hymn.

5   One year Miss Ida found a catalogue from a New York store which advertised hats and their accessories. For ten to twenty-five cents ladies could buy artificial flowers to stick into their bonnets. Miss Ida bought a counter full, and that Easter her head resembled a summer garden in bloom. Daffodils, zinnias, and black-eyed Susans hung yellow and red around the brim of her hat while in the middle stood a magnificent pink peony.

6   In all his glory Solomon could not have matched Miss Ida's bonnet. The congregation could not take its eyes off it; even the minister had trouble concentrating on his sermon. After the last hymn, everyone hurried out of the church, eager to get a better look at Miss Ida's hat. As she came out, the altar boy began ringing the bell. Alas, the noise frightened pigeons who had recently begun to nest and they shot out of the steeple. The congregation scattered, but the flowers on Miss Ida's hat hung over her eyes, and she did not see the pigeons until it was too late and the peony had been ruined.

7   Miss Ida acted like nothing had happened. She greeted everyone and asked about their healths and the healths of absent members of families. People tried not to look at her hat but were not very successful. For two Sundays Miss Ida's "accident" was the main subject of after-church conversation; then it was forgotten for almost a year. But, as Easter approached

again, people remembered the hat. They wondered what Miss Ida would wear to church. Some people speculated that since she was a shy, poetic person, she wouldn't come. Even the minister had doubts. To reassure Miss Ida, he and his sons borrowed ladders two weeks before Easter, and climbing to the top of the steeple, chased the pigeons away and sealed off their nesting place with chicken wire.

Easter Sunday seemed to confirm the fears of those who 8 doubted Miss Ida would appear. The choir assembled in the rear of the church without her. Half-heartedly the congregation sang the processional hymn, "Hail Thee, Festival Day." Miss Ida's absence had taken something bright from our lives, and as we sat down after singing, Easter seemed sadly ordinary.

We were people of little faith. Just as the minister reached the 9 altar and turned to face us, there was a stir at the back of the church. Silently the minister raised his right hand and pointed toward the door. Miss Ida had arrived. She was wearing the same hat she wore the year before; only the peony was missing. In its place was a wonderful sunflower; from one side hung a black and yellow garden spider building a web while fluttering above was a mourning cloak, black wings, dotted with blue and a yellow border running around the edges. Our hearts leaped up, and at the end of the service people in Richmond must have heard us singing "Christ the Lord Is Risen Today."

St. Paul's was the church of my childhood, that storied time 10 when I thought little about religion but knew that Jesus loved me, yes, because the Bible told me so. In the Morning Prayer of life I mixed faith and fairy tale, thinking God a kindly giant, holding in his hands, as the song put it, the corners of the earth and the strength of the hills. Thirty years have passed since I last saw St. Paul's, and I have come down from the cool upland pastures and the safe fold of childhood to the hot lowlands. Instead of being neatly tucked away in a huge hand, the world now seems to bound erratically, smooth and slippery, forever beyond the grasp of even the most magical deity. Would that it were not so, and my imagination could find a way through his gates, as the prayer says, with thanksgiving. Often I wonder what happened to the "faith of our fathers." Why if it endured dungeon, fire, and sword in others, did it weaken so within me?

11   For me religion is a matter of story and community, a congregation rising together to look at an Easter Bonnet, unconsciously seeing it as an emblem of hope and vitality, indeed of the Resurrection itself. For me religion ought to be more concerned with people than ideas, creating soft feeling rather than sharp thought. Often I associate religion with small, backwater towns in which tale binds folk one to another. Here in a university in which people are separated by idea rather than linked by story, religion doesn't have a natural place. In the absence of community, ceremony becomes important. Changeable and always controversial, subject to dispassionate analysis, ceremony doesn't tie people together like accounts of pigeons and peonies and thus doesn't promote good feeling and finally love for this world and hope for the next. Often when I am discouraged, I turn for sustenance, not to formal faith with articled ceremony but to memory, a chalice winey with story.

12   Not long ago I thought about Beagon Hackett, a Baptist minister in Carthage, Tennessee. Born in Bagdad in Jackson County, Beagon answered the call early in life. Before he was sixteen, he had preached in all the little towns in Jackson County: Antioch, Nameless, McCoinsville, Liberty, and Gum Springs. Although popular in country churches, Beagon's specialty was the all-day revival, picnic, and baptizing, usually held back in the woods near places like Seven Knobs, Booger Hill, Backbone Ridge, Chigger Hollow, and Twelve Corners. Beagon made such a name that the big Baptist church in Carthage selected him as minister. Once in Carthage, Beagon tempered his faith to suit the mood of the county seat. Only once a year did he hold a meeting out of doors. For his first four or five years in Carthage, he led a revival near Dripping Rock Bluff across Hell Bend on the Caney Fork River, the spot being selected for name not location.

13   The narrows of the river were swift and deep, and crossing Hell Bend was dangerous, a danger Beagon celebrated, first reminding the faithful that Jesus was a fisher of men and then buoying their spirits up on a raft of watery Christian song: "Shall We

Gather at the River," "The Rock That Is Higher Than I," and "Sweet By and By." Beagon's meetings across the Caney Fork were a success with people traveling from as far as Macon and Trousdale counties to be baptized. But then one spring Gummert Capron or Doodlebug Healy, depending on whose memory is accurate, became frightened in mid-river and tipping over a rowboat changed "Throw Out the Life-Line" from word to deed. If Homer Nye had not grabbed Clara Jakeways by the hair, the dark waters, as the hymn puts it, would have swept her to eternity's shore. As it turned out Clara's salvation turned into romance, and three months later she and Nye were married, much to the disappointment of Silas Jakeways who owned a sawmill and the Eagle Iron Works and who disapproved of Nye, until that time an itinerant bricklayer. Clara, Silas was reported to have said, would "have been better off if love hadn't lifted her from the deep to become the wife of a no-account." Whatever the case, however, Beagon never led another revival across Hell Bend; instead he stayed dry on the Carthage side of the Caney Fork, once a year holding a temperate affair, more Sunday outing than revival, on Myers Bottom.

After Beagon had been in Carthage for twenty years, he grew heavy and dignified. No longer would he preside at river baptizings. In his church he erected, as Silas Jakeways said "a marble birdbath," a baptismal font, copied from one he saw in an Episcopal Church at Monteagle. In Carthage, though, pretension was always liable to be tipped over, if not by simple-minded folk like Gummert Capron or Doodlebug Healy, then by daily life. Addicted to drink, Horace Armitage, the disreputable brother of Benbow Armitage, occasionally cut hair at King's Barber Shop. One morning after a long night of carousing at Enos Mayfield's in South Carthage, Horace was a bit shaky, and while shaving Beagon cut him slightly on the chin. "That's what comes of taking too much to drink," said Beagon, holding a towel to his chin. "Yes, sir, Reverend," Horace replied, "Alcohol does make the skin tender."

1985

Erotica and Pornography

Gloria Steinem

1   Human beings are the only animals that experience the same sex drive at times when we can—and cannot—conceive.

2   Just as we developed uniquely human capacities for language, planning, memory, and invention along our evolutionary path, we also developed sexuality as a form of expression, a way of communicating that is separable from our need for sex as a way of perpetuating ourselves. For humans alone, sexuality can be and often is primarily a way of bonding, of giving and receiving pleasure, bridging differentness, discovering sameness, and communicating emotion.

3   We developed this and other human gifts through our ability to change our environment, adapt physically, and in the long run, to affect our own evolution. But as an emotional result of this spiraling path away from other animals, we seem to alternate between periods of exploring our unique abilities to change new boundaries and feelings of loneliness in the unknown that we ourselves have created; a fear that sometimes sends us back to the comfort of the animal world by encouraging us to exaggerate our sameness.

4   The separation of "play" from "work," for instance, is a problem only in the human world. So is the difference between art and nature, or an intellectual accomplishment and a physical one. As a result, we celebrate play, art, and invention as leaps into the unknown; but any imbalance can send us back to nostalgia for our primate past and the conviction that the basics of work, nature, and physical labor are somehow more worthwhile or even moral.

5   In the same way, we have explored our sexuality as separable from conception: A pleasurable, empathetic bridge to strangers of the same species. We have even invented contraception—a skill that has probably existed in some form since our ancestors figured out the process of birth—in order to extend this uniquely human difference. Yet we also have times of atavistic suspicion that sex is

not complete—or even legal or intended-by-god—if it cannot end in conception.

No wonder the concepts of "erotica" and "pornography" can be 6 so crucially different, and yet so confused. Both assume that sexuality can be separated from conception, and therefore can be used to carry a personal message. That's a major reason why, even in our current culture, both may be called equally "shocking" or legally "obscene," a word whose Latin derivative means "dirty, containing filth." This gross condemnation of all sexuality that isn't harnessed to childbirth and marriage has been increased by the current backlash against women's progress. Out of fear that the whole patriarchal structure might be upset if women really had the autonomous power to decide our reproductive futures (that is, if we controlled the most basic means of production), right-wing groups are not only denouncing prochoice abortion literature as "pornographic," but are trying to stop the sending of all contraceptive information through the mails by invoking obscenity laws. In fact, Phyllis Schlafly recently denounced the entire Women's Movement as "obscene."

Not surprisingly, this religious, visceral backlash has a secu- 7 lar, intellectual counterpart that relies heavily on applying the "natural" behavior of the animal world to humans. That is questionable in itself, but these Lionel Tigerish studies make their political purpose even more clear in the particular animals they select and the habits they choose to emphasize. The message is that females should accept their "destiny" of being sexually dependent and devote themselves to bearing and rearing their young.

Defending against such reaction in turn leads to another 8 temptation: To merely reverse the terms, and declare that *all* nonprocreative sex is good. In fact, however, this human activity can be as constructive or destructive, moral or immoral, as any other. Sex as communication can send messages as different as life and death; even the origins of "erotica" and "pornography" reflect that fact. After all, "erotica" is rooted in *eros* or passionate love, and thus in the idea of positive choice, free will, the yearning for a particular person. (Interestingly, the definition of erotica leaves open the question of gender.) "Pornography" begins with a root meaning "prostitution" or "female captives," thus letting us know that the subject is not mutual love, or love at all, but domination and violence against women. (Though, of course, homosexual pornography may imitate this violence by putting a man in the "feminine" role of victim.) It ends with a root meaning "writing about" or "description of" which puts still more distance between subject and object, and replaces a spontaneous yearning for closeness with objectification and a voyeur.

9   The difference is clear in the words. It becomes even more so by example.

10   Look at any photo or film of people making love; really making love. The images may be diverse, but there is usually a sensuality and touch and warmth, an acceptance of bodies and nerve endings. There is always a spontaneous sense of people who are there because they *want* to be, out of shared pleasure.

11   Now look at any depiction of sex in which there is clear force, or an unequal power that spells coercion. It may be very blatant, with weapons or torture or bondage, wounds and bruises, some clear humiliation, or an adult's sexual power being used over a child. It may be much more subtle: A physical attitude of conqueror and victim, the use of race or class difference to imply the same thing, perhaps a very unequal nudity, with one person exposed and vulnerable while the other is clothed. In either case, there is no sense of equal choice or equal power.

12   The first is erotic: A mutually pleasurable, sexual expression between people who have enough power to be there by positive choice. It may or may not strike the sense-memory in the viewer, or be creative enough to make the unknown seem real; but it doesn't require us to identify with a conqueror or a victim. It is truly sensuous, and may give us a contagion of pleasure.

13   The second is pornographic: Its message is violence, dominance, and conquest. It is sex being used to reinforce some inequality, or to create one, or to tell us the lie that pain and humiliation (ours or someone else's) are really the same as pleasure. If we are to feel anything, we must identify with conqueror or victim. That means we can only experience pleasure through the adoption of some degree of sadism or masochism. It also means that we may feel diminished by the role of conqueror, or enraged, humiliated, and vengeful by sharing identity with the victim.

Perhaps one could simply say that erotica is about sexuality, 14
but pornography is about power and sex-as-weapon—in the same
way we have come to understand that rape is about violence, and
not really about sexuality at all.

Yes, it's true that there are women who have been forced by 15
violent families and dominating men to confuse love with pain; so
much so that they have become masochists. (A fact that in no way
excuses those who administer such pain.) But the truth is that, for
most women—and for men with enough humanity to imagine
themselves into the predicament of women—true pornography
could serve as aversion therapy for sex.

Of course, there will always be personal differences about what 16
is and is not erotic, and there may be cultural differences for a long
time to come. Many women feel that sex makes them vulnerable and
therefore may continue to need more sense of personal connection
and safety before allowing any erotic feelings. We now find competence and expertise erotic in men, but that may pass as we develop
those qualities in ourselves. Men, on the other hand, may continue
to feel less vulnerable, and therefore more open to such potential
danger as sex with strangers. As some men replace the need for submission from childlike women with the pleasure of cooperation
from equals, they may find a partner's competence to be erotic, too.

Such group changes plus individual differences will continue 17
to be reflected in sexual love between people of the same gender,
as well as between women and men. The point is not to dictate
sameness, but to discover ourselves and each other through sexuality that is an exploring, pleasurable, empathetic part of our lives;
a human sexuality that is unchained both from unwanted preg-
nancies and from violence.

But that is a hope, not a reality. At the moment, fear of change 18
is increasing both the indiscriminate repression of all nonprocreative sex in the religious and "conservative" male world, and the
pornographic vengeance against women's sexuality in the secular
world of "liberal" and "radical" men. It's almost futuristic to debate what is and is not truly erotic, when many women are again
being forced into compulsory motherhood, and the number of
pornographic murders, tortures, and woman-hating images are
on the increase in both popular culture and real life.

19   It's a familiar division: Wife or whore, "good" woman who is constantly vulnerable to pregnancy or "bad" woman who is unprotected from violence. *Both* roles would be upset if we were to control our own sexuality. And that's exactly what we must do.

20   In spite of all our atavistic suspicions and training for the "natural" role of motherhood, we took up the complicated battle for reproductive freedom. Our bodies had borne the health burden of endless births and poor abortions, and we had a greater motive for separating sexuality and conception.

21   Now we have to take up the equally complex burden of explaining that all nonprocreative sex is *not* alike. We have a motive: Our right to a uniquely human sexuality, and sometimes even to survival. As it is, our bodies have too rarely been enough our own to develop erotica in our own lives, much less in art and literature. And our bodies have too often been the objects of pornography and the womanhating, violent practice that it preaches. Consider also our spirits that break a little each time we see ourselves in chains or full labial display for the conquering male viewer, bruised or on our knees, screaming a real or pretended pain to delight the sadist, pretending to enjoy what we don't enjoy, to be blind to the images of our sisters that really haunt us—humiliated often enough ourselves by the truly obscene idea that sex and the domination of women must be combined.

22   Sexuality *is* human, free, separate—and so are we.

23   But until we untangle the lethal confusion of sex with violence, there will be more pornography and less erotica. There will be little murders in our beds—and very little love.

1978

Good Souls

Dorothy Parker

1 All about us, living in our very families, it may be, there exists a race of curious creatures. Outwardly, they possess no marked peculiarities; in fact, at a hasty glance, they may be readily mistaken

for regular human beings. They are built after the popular design;
they have the usual number of features, arranged in the conventional manner; they offer no variations on the general run of
things in their habits of dressing, eating, and carrying on their
business.

Yet, between them and the rest of the civilized world, there ₂
stretches an impassable barrier. Though they live in the very thick
of the human race, they are forever isolated from it. They are fated
to go through life, congenital pariahs. They live out their little
lives, mingling with the world, yet never a part of it.

They are, in short, Good Souls.   ₃

And the piteous thing about them is that they are wholly un- ₄
conscious of their condition. A Good Soul thinks he is just like anyone else. Nothing could convince him otherwise. It is heartrend-
ing to see him, going cheerfully about, even whistling or
humming as he goes, all unconscious of his terrible plight. The utmost he can receive from the world is an attitude of good-hu-
mored patience, a perfunctory word of approbation, a praising
with faint damns, so to speak—yet he firmly believes that everything is all right with him.

There is no accounting for Good Souls.   ₅

They spring up anywhere. They will suddenly appear in fam- ₆
ilies which, for generations, have had no slightest stigma attached
to them. Possibly they are throw-backs. There is scarcely a family
without at least one Good Soul somewhere in it at the present moment—maybe in the form of an elderly aunt, an unmarried sister,
an unsuccessful brother, an indigent cousin. No household is complete without one.

The Good Soul begins early; he will show signs of his condi- ₇
tion in extreme youth. Go now to the nearest window, and look
out on the little children playing so happily below. Any group of
youngsters that you may happen to see will do perfectly. Do you
observe the child whom all the other little dears make "it" in their
merry games? Do you follow the child from whom the other little
ones snatch the cherished candy, to consume it before his stream-
ing eyes? Can you get a good look at the child whose precious toys
are borrowed for indefinite periods by the other playful youngsters, and are returned to him in fragments? Do you see the child
upon whom all the other kiddies play their complete repertory of

childhood's winsome pranks—throwing bags of water on him, running away and hiding from him, shouting his name in quaint rhymes, chalking coarse legends on his unsuspecting back?

8   Mark that child well. He is going to be a Good Soul when he grows up.

9   Thus does the doomed child go through early youth and adolescence. So does he progress towards the fulfillment of his destiny. And then, some day, when he is under discussion, someone will say of him, "Well, he means well, anyway." That settles it. For him, that is the end. Those words have branded him with the indelible mark of his pariahdom. He has come into his majority; he is a full-fledged Good Soul.

10   The activities of the adult of the species are familiar to us all. When you are ill, who is it that hastens to your bedside bearing molds of blanc-mange, which, from infancy, you have hated with unspeakable loathing? As usual, you are way ahead of me, gentle reader—it is indeed the Good Soul. It is the Good Souls who efficiently smooth out your pillow when you have just worked it into the comfortable shape, who creak about the room on noisy tiptoe, who tenderly lay on your fevered brow damp cloths which drip ceaselessly down your neck. It is they who ask, every other minute, if there isn't something that they can do for you. It is they who, at great personal sacrifice, spend long hours sitting beside your bed, reading aloud the continued stories in the *Woman's Home Companion*, or chatting cozily on the increase in the city's death rate.

11   In health, as in illness, they are always right there, ready to befriend you. No sooner do you sit down, than they exclaim that they can see you aren't comfortable in that chair, and insist on your changing places with them. It is the Good Souls who just *know* that you don't like your tea that way, and who bear it masterfully away from you to alter it with cream and sugar until it is a complete stranger to you. At the table, it is they who always feel that their grapefruit is better than yours and who have to be restrained almost forcibly from exchanging with you. In a restaurant the waiter invariably makes a mistake and brings them something which they did not order—and which they refuse to have changed, choking it down with a wistful smile. It is they who

cause traffic blocks, by standing in subway entrances arguing altruistically as to who is to pay the fare.

At the theater, should they be members of a box-party, it is the Good Souls who insist on occupying the rear chairs; if the seats are in the orchestra, they worry audibly, all through the performance, about their being able to see better than you, until finally in desperation you grant their plea and change seats with them. If, by so doing, they can bring a little discomfort on themselves—sit in a draught, say, or behind a pillar—then their happiness is complete. To feel the genial glow of martyrdom—that is all they ask of life. . . .

The lives of Good Souls are crowded with Occasions, each with its own ritual which must be solemnly followed. On Mother's Day, Good Souls conscientiously wear carnations; on St. Patrick's Day, they faithfully don boutonnieres of shamrocks; on Columbus Day, they carefully pin on miniature Italian flags. Every feast must be celebrated by the sending out of cards—Valentine's Day, Arbor Day, Groundhog Day, and all the other important festivals, each is duly observed. They have a perfect genius for discovering appropriate cards of greeting for the event. It must take hours of research.

If it's too long a time between holidays, then the Good Soul will send little cards or little mementoes, just by way of surprises. He is strong on surprises, anyway. It delights him to drop in unexpectedly on his friends. Who has not known the joy of those evenings when some Good Soul just runs in, as a surprise? It is particularly effective when a chosen company of other guests happens to be present—enough for two tables of bridge, say. This means that the Good Soul must sit wistfully by, patiently watching the progress of the rubber, or else must cut in at intervals, volubly voicing his desolation at causing so much inconvenience, and apologizing constantly during the evening.

His conversation, admirable though it is, never receives its just due of attention and appreciation. He is one of those who believe and frequently quote the exemplary precept that there is good in everybody; hanging in his bedchamber is the whimsically phrased, yet vital, statement, done in burned leather—"There is so much good in the worst of us and so much bad in the best of us that it hardly behooves any of us to talk about the rest of us." This, too, he archly quotes on appropriate occasions. Two or three may be gathered together, intimately discussing some mutual acquaintance. It is just getting really absorbing, when comes the Good Soul, to utter his dutiful, "We mustn't judge harshly—after all, we must always remember that many times our own actions may be misconstrued." Somehow, after several of these little reminders, there seems to be a general waning of interest; the little gathering breaks up, inventing quaint excuses to get away and discuss the thing more fully, adding a few really good details, some place where the Good Soul will not follow. While the Good Soul pitifully ignorant of their evil purpose glows with the warmth of conscious virtue, and settles himself to read the Contributors' Club, in the *Atlantic Monthly,* with a sense of duty well done. . . .

16   Good Souls are no mean humorists. They have a time-honored formula of fun-making, which must be faithfully followed. Certain words or phrases must be whimsically distorted every time they are used. "Over the river," they dutifully say, whenever they take their leave. "Don't you cast any asparagus on me," they warn, archly; and they never fail to speak of "three times in concussion." According to their ritual, these screaming phrases must be repeated several times, for the most telling effect, and are invariably followed by hearty laughter from the speaker, to whom they seem eternally new.

17   Perhaps the most congenial role of the Good Soul is that of advice-giver. He loves to take people aside and have serious little personal talks, all for their own good. He thinks it only right to point out faults or bad habits which are, perhaps unconsciously, growing on them. He goes home and laboriously writes long, intricate letters, invariably beginning, "Although you may feel that this is no affair of mine, I think that you really ought to know," and so on, indefinitely. In his desire to help, he reminds one irresistibly of Marcelline, who used to try so pathetically and so fruitlessly to be of some assistance in arranging the circus arena, and who brought such misfortunes on his own innocent person thereby.

18   The Good Souls will, doubtless, gain their reward in Heaven; on this earth, certainly, theirs is what is technically known as a rough deal. The most hideous outrages are perpetrated on them.

"Oh, he won't mind," people say. "He's a Good Soul." And then they proceed to heap the rankest impositions upon him. When Good Souls give a party, people who have accepted weeks in advance call up at the last second and refuse, without the shadow of an excuse save that of a subsequent engagement. Other people are invited to all sorts of entertaining affairs; the Good Soul, unasked, waves them a cheery good-bye and hopes wistfully that they will have a good time. His is the uncomfortable seat in the motor car; he is the one to ride backwards in the train; he is the one who is always chosen to solicit subscriptions and make up deficits. People borrow his money, steal his servants, lose his golf balls, use him as a sort of errand boy, leave him flat whenever something more attractive offers—and carry it all off with their cheerful slogan, "Oh, he won't mind—he's a Good Soul."

And that's just it—Good Souls never do mind. After each 19 fresh atrocity they are more cheerful, forgiving and virtuous, if possible, than they were before. There is simply no keeping them down—back they come, with their little gifts, and their little words of advice, and their little endeavors to be of service, always anxious for more.

Yes, there can be no doubt about it—their reward will come to 20 them in the next world.

Would that they were even now enjoying it!   21

1919

Fire in the Sky

Claudia Glenn Dowling

Nights are long and bitter in the polar winters, but the compensa- 1 tions can be spectacular: The skies blaze in a display of energy called the aurora borealis in the Arctic, aurora australis in the Antarctic. Ancient tribes who saw the lights believed they were caused by the bonfires of spirits; today we know that awe-inspiring physical forces create the heavenly arrays. And we're about to know more: A hardy breed of scientists—who don't mind odd hours or sub-zero temperatures—are investigating the powerful magnetic storms hidden within the aurora's glory. A few years ago some of these researchers put up a sign outside their University of Alaska lab near the tiny village of Poker Flats. It said it all: "Center for the Study of Something which, on the face of it, might seem trivial, but on closer examination takes on Global Significance."

2   Auroras are born on the sun, where thermonuclear storms tear apart hydrogen atoms, blasting protons and electrons toward earth at up to 1,000 miles per second. As this solar wind approaches earth's magnetic field, particles are drawn to the poles like iron filings to the ends of a bar magnet. When the particles collide with gases in the earth's atmosphere, they create electrical discharges that glow purple, green, red and white. The effect is similar to the collision of electrons and gases inside a color television tube.

3   The beauty of an auroral storm hides its violence—the release of millions of amperes of electricity, 20 times that found in a bolt of lightning. Surges within auroras, called substorms, tap energy trapped by the earth's magnetic field on the side of the planet away from the sun. One physicist poetically calls this energy pool earth's "electromagnetic soul."

4   A series of such storms knocked out power in all of Quebec as well as several U.S. states in 1989. Earlier this year surges damaged two communications satellites. NASA researchers theorize that the substorms, which produce nitrogen oxides, may also damage the ozone layer above the poles. No one knows what effect the electrical charge may have on human beings, although Japanese travel agencies book tours to the Arctic specifically for couples who believe that their chances of conceiving a child are better under the aurora.

5   Lately, interest in mapping and predicting substorms has led to increased government spending. (That may be why, not long ago, the sign at Poker Flats was changed to read: "This facility is uniquely dedicated to studies of the aurora borealis and other atmospheric research studies for the paying customer such as the National Aeronautics and Space Administration, the United States

Air Force . . . .") Last month NASA launched a satellite—dubbed Wind—to monitor the solar wind as it howls toward earth. Another, called Polar, the size of a school bus, is planned to orbit closer to the planet, photographing auroras with sensitive cameras. Next year Russia will launch two similar probes. And in November a consortium of European nations will open a radar installation in Spitsbergen, Norway, with high-powered dishes that will collect information about the velocity, density and temperature of solar particles. A European satellite that is designed to circle the Arctic will collect similar data from above.

Still, a nonscientific observer need only be in the right place at   6 the right time to study this natural wonder. A jargon-filled recorded message from the National Oceanic and Atmospheric Administration in Boulder, Colo. (303-497-3235), tells aficionados when conditions are favorable for a good show. Although the aurora can be seen year-round—the atmosphere is always being bombarded by the solar wind—and is sometimes visible as far away as the equator, it occurs most often in the extreme north and south and is easiest to see on a clear, dark winter night. Photographer Norbert Rosing's favorite site is Churchill, Manitoba, where winter skies are cloudless 80 percent of the time. There, every February and March, he waits in the cold, warming his film with his car heater so it won't crack. "When you see the northern lights," he says, "you're in love."

1994

Stop Murdering the Language

John Leo

If you doubt that word games are becoming crucial to our social   1 and political struggles, listen to Derek Humphry. A leading figure in the euthanasia movement, Humphry says his side lost at the polls in Washington State last fall largely because it lost the battle over language. The pro-euthanasia campaigners talked broadly about "aid in dying." But the media and public, Humphry says, "used the real words with relish"—suicide and euthanasia—and Initiative 119 went down.

2   In passing, Humphry pointed out the vagueness of "aid in dying." It can mean, he says, "anything from a physician's lethal injection all the way to holding hands with a dying patient and saying, 'I love you.' " Anyone who stretches a phrase to cover both killing and moral support is a serious player in the language games.

3   This is, in fact, a big trend in the fast-growing field of language manipulation. Specific terms give way to ever broader and gassier ones. "Blind" or "legally blind" was replaced by "visually impaired," which includes everyone who wears glasses. "Child abuse" now seems to cover almost anything a parent or a parental figure can do wrong. "Substance abusers" (formerly addicts and winos) now include any person who overuses or misuses anything at all. William Lutz, editor of the *Quarterly Review of Doublespeak*, says, "The whole world is composed of substance. . . . This doesn't promote clarity of discussion."

4   More often word stretching occurs for frankly polemic reasons. "Family has been stretched to make nonfamilies eligible for various family benefits. Now the word is seriously used to refer to group renters, childless couples and even single people living alone. To circumvent zoning restrictions, two groups of recovering alcoholics in Cherry Hill, N.J., insisted they were families. A spokesman said, "Residents consider themselves a family, and no other family in the country has to announce itself or explain itself." As in "Alice in Wonderland," the word means what the speaker wants it to mean.

5   Another popular form of stretching is to associate some low-level complaint with a higher-level one involving violence, thus presumably startling everyone into paying attention. A *Washington Post* columnist complained recently about "intellectual genocide" in D.C. public schools, meaning that students aren't taught well and aren't learning basic skills. Betty Friedan regularly complains about the media's "symbolic annihilation of women" (she

means there still aren't enough news stories by and about women). A Manhattan man, dying of AIDS, said his death should be seen as "a form of political assassination" (he means Bush should have spent more on AIDS).

These stretching exercises are often more than publicity-grab- 6
bing hyperbole. Sometimes they are conscious attempts to ratchet up a minor offense into a major one. Ogling a woman, once considered harmless, or merely rude, is considered sexual harassment now and is often mentioned in the same breath as rape. Notice how the University of Minnesota's definition of sexual harassment blurs all lines between a glance, lack of sensitivity, serious harassment and rape: "Sexual harassment can be as blatant as rape or as subtle as a look. Harassment . . . often consists of callous insensitivity to the experience of women."

The verbal work of folding the entire category of harassment 7
into the category of rape goes on all the time. "Sexual harassment is a subtle rape," a psychologist named John Gottman told the *New York Times*. "Sexual harassment is a subset of rape with overtones of blackmail and extortion," columnist Carole Agus told her readers in *New York Newsday*.

Looser definitions keep blurring categories. The term "domes- 8
tic violence," for instance, once referred to physical assault in the home. Now it includes psychological abuse. Lenore Walker, a specialist in the field, defines wife battering to include bullying and manipulation ("making women do things they otherwise wouldn't . . . by eroding their self-esteem"). This mimics what happened when some definitions of date rape were expanded to include "psychological coercion," presumably including wheedling and pleading for sex.

A similar blurring occurs in the hate crime field. Often it's not 9
very clear whether we are talking about violence or nonviolence, crimes or noncriminal bias incidents, serious social offenses or minor and ambiguous run-ins. The National Institute Against Prejudice and Violence in Baltimore keeps feeding the media statistics on campus "ethnoviolence," but it defines violence to include slurs, graffiti and perceptions of slights (e.g., "I went to talk to someone who was black, and his friend stared at me the whole time as though she didn't want me there"). The effect of this tactic

is to increase alarm about what's happening on campus and to raise doubts about the aims and methods of the statistics keepers.

10   The constant use of violent language for nonviolent incidents reflects the current tensions among races and between sexes. But it probably also helps magnify those tensions by linking minor incidents to major assaults and putting everyone on full-time alert for offense. It's one price we're paying for these polemic word games.

1993

Chapter

Classification and Division

5

Cinematypes

Susan Allen Toth

Aaron takes me only to art films. That's what I call them, anyway: 1
strange movies with vague poetic images I don't always understand, long dreamy movies about a distant Technicolor past, even
longer black-and-white movies about the general meaningless-
ness of life. We do not go unless at least one reputable critic has
found the cinematography superb. We went to *The Devil's Eye,* and
Aaron turned to me in the middle and said, "My God, this is
funny." I do not think he was pleased.

When Aaron and I go to the movies, we drive our cars sepa- 2
rately and meet by the box office. Inside the theater he sits tentatively in his seat, ready to move if he can't see well, poised to leave
if the film is disappointing. He leans away from me, careful not to
touch the bare flesh of his arm against the bare flesh of mine.
Sometimes he leans so far I am afraid he may be touching the
woman on his other side. If the movie is very good, he leans forward, too, peering between the heads of the couple in front of us.
The light from the screen bounces off his glasses; he gleams with
intensity, sitting there on the edge of his seat, watching the screen.
Once I tapped him on the arm so I could whisper a comment in his
ear. He jumped.

After *Belle de Jour* Aaron said he wanted to ask me if he could 3
stay overnight. "But I can't," he shook his head mournfully before
I had a chance to answer, "because I know I never sleep well in
strange beds." Then he apologized for asking. "It's just that after
a film like that," he said, "I feel the need to assert myself."

4   Pete takes me only to movies that he thinks have redeeming social value. He doesn't call them "films." They tend to be about poverty, war, injustice, political corruption, struggling unions in the 1930s, and the military-industrial complex. Pete doesn't like propaganda movies, though, and he doesn't like to be too depressed, either. We stayed away from *The Sorrow and the Pity;* it would be, he said, just too much. Besides, he assured me, things are never that hopeless. So most of the movies we see are made in Hollywood. Because they are always topical, these movies offer what Pete calls "food for thought." When we saw *Coming Home,* Pete's jaw set so firmly with the first half-hour that I knew we would end up at Poppin' Fresh Pies afterward.

5   When Pete and I go to the movies, we take turns driving so no one owes anyone else anything. We leave the car far from the theater so we don't have to pay for a parking space. If it's raining or snowing, Pete offers to let me off at the door, but I can tell he'll feel better if I go with him while he finds a spot, so we share the walk too. Inside the theater Pete will hold my hand when I get scared if I ask him. He puts my hand firmly on his knee and covers it completely with his own hand. His knee never twitches. After a while, when the scary part is past, he loosens his hand slightly and I know that is a signal to take mine away. He sits companionably close, letting his jacket just touch my sweater, but he does not infringe. He thinks I ought to know he is there if I need him.

6   One night, after *The China Syndrome,* I asked Pete if he wouldn't like to stay for a second drink, even though it was past midnight. He thought a while about that, considering my offer from all possible angles, but finally he said no. Relationships today, he said, have a tendency to move too quickly.

7   Sam likes movies that are entertaining. By that he means movies that Will Jones in the *Minneapolis Tribune* loved and either *Time* or *Newsweek* rather liked; also movies that do not have sappy love stories, are not musicals, do not have subtitles, and will not force him to think. He does not go to movies to think. He liked *California Suite* and *The Seduction of Joe Tynan,* though the plots, he said, could have been zippier. He saw it all coming too far in advance, and that took the fun out. He doesn't like to know what is

going to happen. "I just want my brain to be tickled," he says. It is very hard for me to pick out movies for Sam.

When Sam takes me to the movies, he pays for everything. He 8 thinks that's what a man ought to do. But I buy my own popcorn, because he doesn't approve of it; the grease might smear his flannel slacks. Inside the theater, Sam makes himself comfortable. He takes off his jacket, puts one arm around me, and all during the movie he plays with my hand, stroking my palm, beating a small tattoo on my wrist. Although he watches the movie intently, his body operates on instinct. Once I inclined my head and kissed him lightly just behind his ear. He beat a faster tattoo on my wrist, quick and musical, but he didn't look away from the screen.

When Sam takes me home from the movies, he stands outside 9 my door and kisses me long and hard. He would like to come in, he says regretfully, but his steady girlfriend in Duluth wouldn't like it. When the *Tribune* gives a movie four stars, he has to save it to see with her. Otherwise her feelings might be hurt.

I go to some movies by myself. On rainy Sunday afternoons I 10 often sneak into a revival house or a college auditorium for old Technicolor musicals, *Kiss Me Kate, Seven Brides for Seven Brothers, Calamity Jane,* even, once, *The Sound of Music*. Wearing saggy jeans so I can prop my feet on the seat in front, I sit toward the rear where no one can see me. I eat large handfuls of popcorn with double butter. Once the movie starts, I feel completely at home. Howard Keel and I are old friends; I grin back at him on the screen. I know the sound tracks by heart. Sometimes when I get really carried away I hum along with Kathryn Grayson, remembering how I once thought I would fill out a formal like that. I am rather glad now I never did. Skirts whirl, feet tap, acrobatic young men perform impossible feats, and then the camera dissolves into a dream sequence I know I can comfortably follow. It is not, thank God, Bergman.

If I can't find an old musical, I settle for Hepburn and Tracy, 11 vintage Grant or Gable, on adventurous days Claudette Colbert or James Stewart. Before I buy my ticket I make sure it will all end happily. If necessary, I ask the girl at the box office. I have never seen *Stella Dallas* or *Intermezzo*. Over the years I have developed other peccadilloes: I will, for example, see anything that is redeemed by Thelma Ritter. At the end of *Daddy Long Legs* I wait happily for the scene when Fred Clark, no longer angry, at last pours Thelma a convivial drink. They smile at each other. I smile at them, I feel they are smiling at me. In the movies I go to by myself, the men and women always like each other.

1980

The Climythology of America

David M. Ludlum

1 History is full of myths, and so is climatology. Every generation of historians gives rise to a revisionist school that reinterprets the past in light of new material and facts. Sometimes the revisions join the body of history; other times they are revised by the next generation. Overall, the process leads to a richer and more truthful history.

2   The settlement of America produced a series of myths about the climate of different regions of our country. Even before the first British settlements in North America, Europeans held certain concepts concerning the supposed climate of the New World, and those concepts greatly influenced their efforts to establish colonies from Newfoundland to the Carolinas.

3   Once the seaboard was occupied, new myths arose about the lands west of the Allegheny Mountains. Other unfounded beliefs appeared to influence the occupation of the Mississippi Valley and Great Plains until, in the last decade of the nineteenth century, the land office in Washington officially declared the frontier closed, though much territory remained unsettled. Most of this, however, was thought to be wasteland unsuitable for cultivation. This belief would be dispelled in the next century by the introduction of scientific methods of agriculture and the construction of huge irrigation projects.

THE EQUAL-LATITUDE MYTH

The intellectual content of climatology had made little progress 4
from the time of Ptolemy, the Greek astronomer and geographer
of the second century A.D., to the year 1601, which marked the beginning of the century of colonization of North America by the
English and the French. The concept of *clima,* or parallel bands
around the world which shared comparable temperatures and
hence weather conditions, was the generally accepted view of
global arrangements. So much so, in fact, that the word clima was
used by English writers interchangeably with "latitude." This
gave rise to what I shall call the equal-latitude myth.

The planners and backers of the new colonies held to the 5
classical view of the distribution of global temperatures and
thus were greatly surprised and chagrined when their environmental expectations were not met by the realities of the New
World. The French were perplexed by the harsh winter conditions they met in Nova Scotia and the St. Lawrence Valley because both lay at the same latitudes as northern and central
France. The British ultimately gave up constant efforts to settle
Newfoundland in the early years of the seventeenth century because of the severe winters, despite the fact that it lay at the
same latitude as southernmost England, where winters were
usually moderate in temperature.

The history of all the British colonies from Maine to the Car- 6
olinas ran much the same. The commercial backers of each colony
expressed surprise and dismay that these settlements, though at
the latitudes of France and Spain, could not produce the exotic
agricultural products of those countries.

Believing Virginia to have a Mediterranean climate, the pro- 7
prietors tried silk culture until the realities of the winter killed all
hopes of producing such a tropical product.

Almost a century passed before the backers of the colonies re- 8
alized that the American climate differed from the European at the
same latitudes. By the beginning of the eighteenth century, a more
realistic viewpoint prevailed about the climate of the New World.
Facts replaced the equal-latitude myth.

THE CLIMATE CHANGE MYTH

9 During the first two centuries of settlement of the American seaboard, a popular misconception arose about the observed climate. Where were the record snows of yesteryear? Why did we not have the harsh winters so often mentioned by grandfather and great-grandfather? Many homespun philosophers pondered these questions and suggested answers. Though no actual facts were brought forth, most colonists believed that conditions had grown milder and that the seasons had changed, with spring coming later and autumn lasting longer.

10 These ideas were expressed in an article by Dr. Hugh Williamson of North Carolina in the first issue of the *Transactions of the American Philosophical Society* in 1771: "An attempt to account for the change observed in the Middle Colonies in North America."

11 Williamson's thesis was that the cutting down of the forests for farms and settlements had produced a warming of the soil for two reasons. First, the felling of the trees allowed easterly winds to penetrate more deeply into the country, bringing temperate marine influences inland. Second, the bare soil received and stored more solar heat than did forested lands, and snow melted more quickly when exposed to direct sunlight.

12 In addition, some colonials suggested that the rise of urban communities with heated buildings and smokepots was leading to a milder climate, as they claimed had occurred in Europe. These ideas were the first of many about climate change that were to arise and claim a body of believers among Americans.

THE OHIO COUNTRY MYTH

13 After almost 200 years of English settlement along the Atlantic seaboard, the vast interior of the North American continent remained a *terra incognita* as far as an exact knowledge of its geography and climate was concerned. The French had sent voyageurs, couriers de bois and missionaries deep into the interior, but their first-hand knowledge of the conditions encountered did not reach the seaboard-bound British. Though the barrier of

the Appalachian Mountains was breached during the war years that marked the closing decades of the eighteenth century, few scientific men went westward to observe and report on the physical and atmospheric geography of the interior.

A vigorous controversy as to the nature of the climate of the 14 Ohio Country beyond the Allegheny Mountains arose as the century drew to a close and continued to spark lively arguments well into the next century. The controversy became known as the Ohio Country myth.

Between October 1795 and June 1796, Constantin Francois de 15 Chaseboeuf, Comte de Volney, traveled from Washington, D.C., to Vincennes on the Wabash River in Indiana. He was familiar with Jefferson's view, expressed in his *Notes on the State of Virginia*, that the annual temperature west of the mountains was several degrees warmer than at the same latitude east of the mountains along the Atlantic seaboard. Jefferson based his opinion on the different types of plants thriving on opposite sides of the mountains. Volney's seeming confirmation of Jefferson's opinion received wide dissemination in the *View of the Climate and Soil of the United States*, published in London and Paris in 1804.

The first refutation of the ideas promulgated by Volney came 16 from Dr. Daniel Drake in *Notices Concerning Cincinnati*, published in 1810, which produced actual comparative temperature readings. Others soon took up their scientific cudgels. In an address before the Albany Institute in 1823, Dr. Lewis Beck took each of Volney's statements and demolished them with facts from more recent material.

William Darby, in his *View of the United States: Historical, Geo-* 17 *graphical and Statistical* (1828), referred to Volney's "by no means innoxious vulgar error." As late as 1842, Dr. Samuel Forry, in the first climatological survey to employ meteorological observations, felt constrained to criticize Volney's opinions as being "barren of precise data."

In 1857, Lorin Blodget put the Ohio Country myth to final rest 18 in his comprehensive *Climatology of the United States:* "The early distinction between the Atlantic States and the Mississippi has been quite dropped, as the progress of observation has shown them to be essentially the same, or to differ only in unimportant particulars."

THE GREAT AMERICAN DESERT MYTH

19 "When I was a schoolboy my map of the United States showed between the Missouri River and the Rocky Mountains a long, broad white blotch, upon which was printed in small capitals 'THE GREAT AMERICAN DESERT—UNEXPLORED.'" So wrote Colonel Richard Irving Dodge in 1877 when commencing his revealing survey, *The Great Plains of the Great West*. He concluded: "What was then 'unexplored' is now almost thoroughly known. What was regarded as a desert supports, in some portions, thriving populations. The blotch of thirty years ago is now known as 'The Plains.'"

20 Sergeant John Ordway, who had accompanied Lewis and Clark in 1804, had stated ". . . this country may with propriety be called the Deserts of North America." Captain Zebulon Pike in exploring the headwaters of the Arkansas River had declared that ". . . these vast plains of the western hemisphere may become in time as celebrated as the sandy deserts of Africa." And Major Stephen H. Long had written, ". . . the Great Desert at the Base of the Rocky Mountains . . . is almost wholly unfit for cultivation, and of course uninhabitable. . . ."

21 When Lorin Blodget published his comprehensive *Climatology of the United States* in 1857, he marked a zone running east of the 100° W meridian on his precipitation chart "the eastern limit of the dry plains," and labeled the area of western Kansas and Nebraska "the Desert Plains."

22 Following the Civil War, a counterattack was launched on the pessimistic opinion about the future of the plains. The pressure for new lands to settle caused a change of view regarding the farming possibilities of the plains west of the Missouri River. Optimistic projections were penned by enthusiastic travelers, booster-type editors and eager business promoters. Their hopes were bolstered by several years of above-normal rainfall in the late 1860s and early 1870s. The concept that "Rain Follows the Plough" was broadcast in chamber-of-commerce style by agricultural improvement societies and business enterprises. This was the "Garden Myth"—that planting trees and crops on the dry plains would result in increased rainfall in a self-perpetuating manner. The climate pendulum, however, underwent several swings from adequate to inadequate rainfall until a nadir was reached in the late

1880s and early 1890s, resulting in disaster for the many cattle ranchers and the abandonment of farming in much of western Kansas and western Nebraska.

The occupation of the central plains by farmers, the western 23 plains by cattlemen, the mountains by miners, and the Pacific Northwest by lumbermen brought more adequate knowledge of the actual climates of these regions. The filling in of the nation's climatological charts was completed about 1890, when the availability of free land ended and the frontier was considered closed.

THE SOUTHERN CALIFORNIA HEALTH MYTH

During the first 30 years of American settlement Southern Cali- 24 fornia remained a frontier country with ranching and agriculture dominating the economy. The last two decades of the century, however, brought a change. Promoters and developers exploited the region's prime natural attraction, a beneficent climate, to make it the health frontier of the United States. Its favorable features were widely promoted in a tidal wave of publicity, and hordes of Easterners responded by migrating to the promised land in search of restored health. Thanks to man's ingenuity, the barren outlands had suddenly become habitable and even attractive.

During the decades from 1850 to 1880, native Angelenos 25 might have been forgiven for doubting their climate would turn out to be the most promising feature of the region. Damaging floods occurred in 1862 and 1868, devastating droughts came in 1862–64 and 1876–77, and a long spell of recurrent cold weather in the late 1870s and early 1880s set many still-standing date records for coldness. In addition, a destructive earthquake struck in 1857 and every year there were "tremblos."

Despite the lack of knowledge of the effect of California's cli- 26 mate on disease, publicity for the region's salubrity soon poured forth. A pamphlet entitled *Southern California: The Italy of America* claimed for the area the "only perfect climate in the world and the grandest scenery under the sun." *The Los Angeles Star* in 1872 carried an article, "Land of Glorious Sunsets," which was considered by historian Oscar O. Winther (in 1946) as "the opening trumpet blast of a climate promotion campaign that has not ended."

27   Concerted efforts to attract visitors and settlers became an increasingly active industry in the 1880s. The local Chamber of Commerce was careful to point out that not all parts of California enjoyed the salubrious climate claimed for the southern region. The results soon became apparent. A great boom in real estate and business developed in the mid-1880s, similar to those previously experienced in other sections of the western frontier country.

28   In the 1890s, climate continued to be the principal pitch of promotion agencies. In 1892, the Southern California Information Bureau asserted: "... we sell the climate at so much an acre and throw in the land." To a complaint that the region had nothing to sell except climate, one enthusiast declared: "That's right, and we sell it, too—$10 for an acre of land, $490 an acre for the climate."

29   The health angle and longevity prospects were emphasized in the promotional publications of the 1890s. Dr. Peter C. Remondino stated the extreme claim for the region in his book, *The Mediterranean Shores of America: Southern California:* "from my personal observations, I can say that at least an extra ten years' lease on life is gained by a removal to this coast from the Eastern States; not ten years to be added with its extra weight of age and infirmity, but ten years more with additional benefit of feeling ten years younger during the time."

30   They came at first by the thousands, and finally by the millions; today more than 15 million people live in Southern California where a century ago there were only 32,000.

31   Ironically, the concentration of population with attendant urban sprawl and congested freeways affected the climate in a way none of its promoters of the late 1800s foresaw. The effusions of millions of combustion engines, trapped in the area's natural basins by the almost daily inversions in the lower atmosphere, have created smog conditions detrimental to health.

ALASKAN CLIMYTHOLOGY

32 The bill for $7,200,000 to pay for Alaska "loosed a storm in the House of Representatives. I shall not attempt to say whether it was a hurricane or tornado, but it was accompanied by a lot of wind,

by a great flood—a flood of oratory and some verbal thunder," declared Senator Ernest Gruening at a meeting of the American Meteorological Society at the University of Alaska on June 27, 1962. The former Russian colony was portrayed as "a frozen waste with a savage climate, where little or nothing could grow, and where few could or would live."

Typical of the statements of these pioneer climythologists was that of Benjamin F. Loan of St. Louis, who declared: 33

". . . the acquisition of this inhospitable and barren waste will never add a dollar to the wealth of our country or furnish any homes to our people. It is utterly worthless. . . . To suppose that anyone would leave the United States . . . to seek a home . . . in the regions of perpetual snow is simply to suppose such a person insane." 34

Another climatic pessimist, Representative Orange Ferris of Glens Falls, New York, asserted that Alaska "is a barren and unproductive region covered with ice and snow" and "will never be populated by an enterprising people." 35

A representative from New York, Dennis McCarthy of Syracuse, cited "reports that every foot of the soil of Alaska is frozen from five to six feet in depth" and ventured that his colleagues would soon hear that Greenland was on the market. 36

And the minority report of the House Committee on Foreign Relations, in a scathing denunciation, declared Alaska "had no capacity as an agricultural country . . . no value as a mineral country . . . its timber generally of poor quality and growing upon inaccessible mountains . . . its fur trade . . . of insignificant value, and, will speedily come to an end . . . the fisheries of doubtful value . . . in a climate unfit for the habitation of civilized men." 37

Today, Alaska supports a population of more than one half million people and an annual economy worth more than $9 billion. 38

1987

Predictable Crises
of Adulthood

Gail Sheehy

1   We are not unlike a particularly hardy crustacean. The lobster
grows by developing and shedding a series of hard, protective
shells. Each time it expands from within, the confining shell must
be sloughed off. It is left exposed and vulnerable until, in time, a
new covering grows to replace the old.

2   With each passage from one stage of human growth to the
next we, too, must shed a protective structure. We are left exposed
and vulnerable—but also yeasty and embryonic again, capable of
stretching in ways we hadn't known before. These sheddings may
take several years or more. Coming out of each passage, though,
we enter a longer and more stable period in which we can expect
relative tranquility and a sense of equilibrium regained. . . .

3   As we shall see, each person engages the steps of development in his or her own characteristic *step-style*. Some people never
complete the whole sequence. And none of us "solves" with one
step—by jumping out of the parental home into a job or marriage,
for example—the problems in separating from the caregivers of
childhood. Nor do we "achieve" autonomy once and for all by
converting our dreams into concrete goals, even when we attain
those goals. The central issues or tasks of one period are never
fully completed, tied up, and cast aside. But when they lose their
primacy and the current life structure has served its purpose, we
are ready to move on to the next period.

4   Can one catch up? What might look to others like listless-
ness, contrariness, a maddening refusal to face up to an obvious
task may be a person's own unique detour that will bring him
out later on the other side. Developmental gains won can later
be lost—and rewon. It's plausible, though it can't be proven,
that the mastery of one set of tasks fortifies us for the next period and the next set of challenges. But it's important not to
think too mechanistically. Machines work by units. The bureaucracy (supposedly) works step by step. Human beings, thank

God, have an individual inner dynamic that can never be precisely coded.

Although I have indicated the ages when Americans are likely 5 to go through each stage, and the differences between men and women where they are striking, do not take the ages too seriously. The stages are the thing, and most particularly the sequence.

Here is the briefest outline of the developmental ladder. 6

PULLING UP ROOTS

Before 18, the motto is loud and clear: "I have to get away from my 7 parents." But the words are seldom connected to action. Generally still safely part of our families, even if away at school, we feel our autonomy to be subject to erosion from moment to moment.

After 18, we begin Pulling Up Roots in earnest. College, mili- 8 tary service, and short-term travels are all customary vehicles our society provides for the first round trips between family and a base of one's own. In the attempt to separate our view of the world from our family's view, despite vigorous protestations to the contrary—"I know exactly what I want!"—we cast about for any beliefs we can call our own. And in the process of testing those beliefs we are often drawn to fads, preferably those most mysterious and inaccessible to our parents.

Whatever tentative memberships we try out in the world, the 9 fear haunts us that we are really kids who cannot take care of ourselves. We cover that fear with acts of defiance and mimicked confidence. For allies to replace our parents, we turn to our contemporaries. They become conspirators. So long as their perspective meshes with our own, they are able to substitute for the sanctuary of the family. But that doesn't last very long. And the instant they diverge from the shaky ideals of "our group," they are seen as betrayers. Rebounds to the family are common between the ages of 18 and 22.

The tasks of this passage are to locate ourselves in a peer 10 group role, a sex role, an anticipated occupation, an ideology or world view. As a result, we gather the impetus to leave home physically and the identity to *begin* leaving home emotionally.

11   Even as one part of us seeks to be an individual, another part longs to restore the safety and comfort of merging with another. Thus one of the most popular myths of this passage is: We can piggyback our development by attaching to a Stronger One. But people who marry during this time often prolong financial and emotional ties to the family and relatives that impede them from becoming self-sufficient.

12   A stormy passage through the Pulling Up Roots years will probably facilitate the normal progression of the adult life cycle. If one doesn't have an identity crisis at this point, it will erupt during a later transition, when the penalties may be harder to bear.

THE TRYING TWENTIES

13   The Trying Twenties confront us with the question of how to take hold in the adult world. Our focus shifts from the interior turmoils of late adolescence—"Who am I?" "What is truth?"—and we become almost totally preoccupied with working out the externals. "How do I put my aspirations into effect?" "What is the best way to start?" "Where do I go?" "Who can help me?" "How did *you* do it?"

14   In this period, which is longer and more stable compared with the passage that leads to it, the tasks are as enormous as they are exhilarating: To shape a Dream, that vision of ourselves which will generate energy, aliveness, and hope. To prepare for a lifework. To find a mentor if possible. And to form the capacity for intimacy without losing in the process whatever consistency of self we have thus far mustered. The first test structure must be erected around the life we choose to try.

15   Doing what we "should" is the most pervasive theme of the twenties. The "shoulds" are largely defined by family models, the press of the culture, or the prejudices of our peers. If the prevailing cultural instructions are that one should get married and settle down behind one's own door, a nuclear family is born. If instead the peers insist that one should do one's own thing, the 25-year-old is likely to harness himself onto a Harley-Davidson and burn up Route 66 in the commitment to have no commitments.

One of the terrifying aspects of the twenties is the inner con- 16
viction that the choices we make are irrevocable. It is largely a false
fear. Change is quite possible, and some alteration of our original
choices is probably inevitable.

Two impulses, as always, are at work. One is to build a firm, 17
safe structure for the future by making strong commitments, to
"be set." Yet people who slip into a ready-made form without
much self-examination are likely to find themselves *locked* in.

The other urge is to explore and experiment, keeping any 18
structure tentative and therefore easily reversible. Taken to the extreme, these are people who skip from one trial job and one limited personal encounter to another, spending their twenties in the
transient state.

Although the choices of our twenties are not irrevocable, they 19
do set in motion a Life Pattern. Some of us follow the lock-in pattern, others the transient pattern, the wunderkind pattern, the
caregiver pattern, and there are a number of others. Such patterns
strongly influence the particular questions raised for each person
during each passage. . . .

Buoyed by powerful illusions and belief in the power of the 20
will, we commonly insist in our twenties that what we have chosen to do is the one true course in life. Our backs go up at the merest hint that we are like our parents, that two decades of parental
training might be reflected in our current actions and attitudes.

"Not me," is the motto, "I'm different."
21

CATCH-30

Impatient with devoting ourselves to the "shoulds," a new vital- 22
ity springs from within as we approach 30. Men and women alike
speak of feeling too narrow and restricted. They blame all sorts of
things, but what the restrictions boil down to are the outgrowth of
career and personal choices of the twenties. They may have been
choices perfectly suited to that stage. But now the fit feels different. Some inner aspect that was left out is striving to be taken into
account. Important new choices must be made, and commitments
altered or deepened. The work involves great change, turmoil,

and often crisis—a simultaneous feeling of rock bottom and the urge to bust out.

23   One common response is the tearing up of the life we spent most of our twenties putting together. It may mean striking out on a secondary road toward a new vision or converting a dream of "running for president" into a more realistic goal. The single person feels a push to find a partner. The woman who was previously content at home with children chafes to venture into the world. The childless couple reconsiders children. And almost everyone who is married, especially those married for seven years, feels a discontent.

24   If the discontent doesn't lead to a divorce, it will, or should, call for a serious review of the marriage and of each partner's aspirations in their Catch-30 condition. The gist of that condition was expressed by a 29-year-old associate with a Wall Street law firm:

25   "I'm considering leaving the firm. I've been there four years now; I'm getting good feedback, but I have no clients of my own. I feel weak. If I wait much longer, it will be too late, too close to that fateful time of decision on whether or not to become a partner. I'm success-oriented. But the concept of being 55 years old and stuck in a monotonous job drives me wild. It drives me crazy now, just a little bit. I'd say that 85 percent of the time I thoroughly enjoy my work. But when I get a screwball case, I come away from court saying, 'What am I doing here?' It's a *visceral* reaction that I'm wasting my time. I'm trying to find some way to make a social contribution or a slot in city government. I keep saying, 'There's something more.' "

26   Besides the push to broaden himself professionally, there is a wish to expand his personal life. He wants two or three more children. "The concept of a home has become very meaningful to me, a place to get away from troubles and relax. I love my son in a way I could not have anticipated. I never could live alone."

27   Consumed with the work of making his own critical lifesteering decisions, he demonstrates the essential shift at this age: An absolute requirement to be more self-concerned. The self has new value now that his competency has been proved.

28   His wife is struggling with her own age-30 priorities. She wants to go to law school, but he wants more children. If she is going to stay home, she wants him to make more time for the family instead

of taking on even wider professional commitments. His view of the bind, of what he would most like from his wife, is this:

"I'd like not to be bothered. It sounds cruel, but I'd like not to 29 have to worry about what she's going to do next week. Which is why I've told her several times that I think she should do something. Go back to school and get a degree in social work or geography or whatever. Hopefully that would fulfill her, and then I wouldn't have to worry about her line of problems. I want her to be decisive about herself."

The trouble with his advice to his wife is that it comes out of 30 concern with *his* convenience, rather than with *her* development. She quickly picks up on this lack of goodwill: He is trying to dispose of her. At the same time, he refuses her the same latitude to be "selfish" in making an independent decision to broaden her horizons. Both perceive a lack of mutuality. And that is what Catch-30 is all about for the couple.

ROOTING AND EXTENDING

Life becomes less provisional, more rational and orderly in the 31 early thirties. We begin to settle down in the full sense. Most of us begin putting down roots and sending out new shoots. People buy houses and become very earnest about climbing career ladders. Men in particular concern themselves with "making it." Satisfaction with marriage generally goes downhill in the thirties (for those who have remained together) compared with the highly valued, vision-supporting marriage of the twenties. This coincides with the couple's reduced social life outside the family and the in-turned focus on raising their children.

THE DEADLINE DECADE

In the middle of the thirties we come upon a crossroads. We have 32 reached the halfway mark. Yet even as we are reaching our prime, we begin to see there is a place where it finishes. Time starts to squeeze.

33   The loss of youth, the faltering of physical powers we have always taken for granted, the fading purpose of stereotyped roles by
which we have thus far identified ourselves, the spiritual dilemma
of having no absolute answers—any or all of these shocks can give
this passage the character of crisis. Such thoughts usher in a
decade between 35 and 45 that can be called the Deadline Decade.
It is a time of both danger and opportunity. All of us have the
chance to rework the narrow identity by which we defined ourselves in the first half of life. And those of us who make the most
of the opportunity will have a full-out authenticity crisis.

34   To come through this authenticity crisis, we must reexamine
our purposes and reevaluate how to spend our resources from now
on. "Why am I doing all this? What do I really believe in?" No matter what we have been doing, there will be parts of ourselves that
have been suppressed and now need to find expression. "Bad"
feelings will demand acknowledgment along with the good.

35   It is frightening to step off onto the treacherous footbridge
leading to the second half of life. We can't take everything with us
on this journey through uncertainty. Along the way, we discover
that we are alone. We no longer have to ask permission because we
are the providers of our own safety. We must learn to give ourselves permission. We stumble upon feminine or masculine aspects of our natures that up to this time have usually been masked.
There is grieving to be done because an old self is dying. By taking in our suppressed and even our unwanted parts, we prepare
at the gut level for the reintegration of an identity that is ours and
ours alone—not some artificial form put together to please the culture or our mates. It is a dark passage at the beginning. But by dis-
assembling ourselves, we can glimpse the light and gather our
parts into a renewal.

36   Women sense this inner crossroads earlier than men do. The
time pinch often prompts a woman to stop and take an all-
points survey at age 35. Whatever options she has already
played out, she feels a "my last chance" urgency to review those
options she has set aside and those that aging and biology will
close off in the now *foreseeable* future. For all her qualms and
confusion about where to start looking for a new future, she
usually enjoys an exhilaration of release. Assertiveness begins
rising. There are so many firsts ahead.

Men, too, feel the time push in the mid-thirties. Most men re-   37
spond by pressing down harder on the career accelerator. It's "my
last chance" to pull away from the pack. It is no longer enough to
be the loyal junior executive, the promising young novelist, the
lawyer who does a little *pro bono* work on the side. He wants now
to become part of top management, to be recognized as an established writer, or an active politician with his own legislative program. With some chagrin, he discovers that he has been too anxious to please and too vulnerable to criticism. He wants to put
together his own ship.

During this period of intense concentration on external ad-   38
vancement, it is common for men to be unaware of the more difficult, gut issues that are propelling them forward. The survey that
was neglected at 35 becomes a crucible at 40. Whatever rung of
achievement he has reached, the man of 40 usually feels stale, restless, burdened, and unappreciated. He worries about his health.
He wonders, "Is this all there is?" He may make a series of depar-
tures from well-established lifelong base lines, including marriage.
More and more men are seeking second careers in midlife. Some
become self-destructive. And many men in their forties experience
a major shift of emphasis away from pouring all their energies into
their own advancement. A more tender, feeling side comes into
play. They become interested in developing an ethical self.

RENEWAL OR RESIGNATION

Somewhere in the mid-forties, equilibrium is regained. A new sta-   39
bility is achieved, which may be more or less satisfying.

If one has refused to budge through the midlife transition,   40
the sense of staleness will calcify into resignation. One by one,
the safety and supports will be withdrawn from the person who
is standing still. Parents will become children; children will become strangers; a mate will grow away or go away; the career
will become just a job—and each of these events will be felt as
an abandonment. The crisis will probably emerge again around
50. And although its wallop will be greater, the jolt may be just
what is needed to prod the resigned middle-ager toward seeking revitalization.

41   On the other hand . . .

42   If we have confronted ourselves in the middle passage and found a renewal of purpose around which we are eager to build a more authentic life structure, these may well be the best years. Personal happiness takes a sharp turn upward for partners who can now accept the fact: "I cannot expect *anyone* to fully understand me." Parents can be forgiven for the burdens of our childhood. Children can be let go without leaving us in collapsed silence. At 50, there is a new warmth and mellowing. Friends become more important than ever, but so does privacy. Since it is so often proclaimed by people past midlife, the motto of this stage might be "No more bullshit."

1976

Why Nothing Is "Wrong" Anymore

Meg Greenfield

1   There has been an awful lot of talk about sin, crime, and plain old antisocial behavior this summer—drugs and pornography at home, terror and brutality abroad. Maybe it's just the heat; or maybe these categories of conduct (sin, crime, etc.) are really on the rise. What strikes me is our curiously deficient, not to say defective, way of talking about them. We don't seem to have a word anymore for "wrong" in the moral sense, as in, for example, "theft is wrong."

2   Let me quickly qualify. There is surely no shortage of people condemning other people on such grounds, especially their political opponents or characters they just don't care for. Name-calling is still very much in vogue. But where the concept of wrong is really important—as a guide to one's own behavior or that of one's own side in some dispute—it is missing; and this is as true of those on the religious right who are going around pronouncing great

masses of us sinners as it is of their principal antagonists, those on the secular left who can forgive or "understand" just about anything so long as it has not been perpetrated by a right-winger.

There is a fairly awesome literature that attempts to explain ₃ how we have changed as a people with the advent of psychiatry, the weakening of religious institutions and so forth, but you don't need to address these matters to take note of a simple fact. As a guide and a standard to live by, you don't hear so much about "right and wrong" these days. The very notion is considered politically, not to say personally, embarrassing, since it has such a repressive, Neanderthal ring to it. So we have developed a broad range of alternatives to "right and wrong." I'll name a few.

Right and stupid: This is the one you use when your candidate gets ₄ *caught stealing, or, for that matter, when anyone on your side does something reprehensible. "It was really so dumb of him"—head must shake here—"I just can't understand it." Bad is dumb, breathtakingly dumb and therefore unfathomable; so, conveniently enough, the effort to fathom it might just as well be called off. This one had a big play during Watergate and has had mini-revivals ever since whenever congressmen and senators investigating administration crimes turn out to be guilty of something similar themselves.*

Right and not necessarily unconstitutional: I don't know at ₅ *quite what point along the way we came to this one, the avoidance of admitting that something is wrong by pointing out that it is not specifically or even inferentially prohibited by the Constitution or, for that matter, mentioned by name in the criminal code or the Ten Commandments. The various parties that prevail in civil-liberty and civil-rights disputes before the Supreme Court have gotten quite good at making this spurious connection: It is legally permissible, therefore it is morally acceptable, possibly even good. But both as individuals and as a society we do things every day that we know to be wrong even though they may not fall within the class of legally punishable acts or tickets to eternal damnation.*

Right and sick: Crime or lesser wrongdoing defined as physical ₆ *and/or psychological disorder—this one has been around for ages now and as long ago as 1957 was made the butt of a great joke in the "Gee Officer Krupke!" song in "West Side Story." Still, I think no one could have foreseen the degree to which an originally reasonable and humane assumption (that some of what once was regarded as wrongdoing is committed by people acting out of ailment rather than moral choice) would be seized upon and exploited to exonerate every kind of misfeasance. This route is a particular favorite of caught-out officeholders who, when there is at last no other recourse, hold a press conference, announce that they are "sick" in some wise and throw themselves and their generally stunned families on our mercy. At which point it becomes gross to pick on them; instead we are exhorted to admire them for their "courage."*

7   ***Right and only to be expected:*** *You could call this the tit-for-tat school; it is related to the argument that holds moral wrongdoing to be evidence of sickness, but it is much more pervasive and insidious these days. In fact it is probably the most popular dodge, being used to justify, or at least avoid owning up to, every kind of lapse: The other guy, or sometimes just plain circumstance, "asked for it." For instance, I think most of us could agree that setting fire to live people, no matter what their political offense, is—dare I say it?—wrong. Yet if it is done by those for whom we have sympathy in a conflict, there is a tendency to extenuate or disbelieve it, receiving it less as evidence of wrongdoing on our side than as evidence of the severity of the provocation or as enemy-supplied disinformation. Thus the hesitation of many in the antiapartheid movement to confront the brutality of so-called "necklacing," and thus the immediate leap of Sen. Jesse Helms to the defense of the Chilean government after the horrifying incineration of protesters there.*

8   ***Right and complex:*** *This one hardly takes a moment to describe; you know it well. "Complex" is the new "controversial," a word used as "controversial" was for so long to flag trouble of some unspecified, dismaying sort that the speaker doesn't want to have to step up to. "Well, you know, it's very complex. . . ." I still can't get this one out of my own vocabulary.*

9   In addition to these various sophistries, we also have created a rash of "ethics committees" in our government, of course, whose function seems to be to dither around writing rules that allow people who have clearly done wrong—and should have known it and probably did—to get away because the rules don't cover their offense (see Right and not necessarily unconstitutional). But we don't need any more committees or artful dodges for that matter.

As I listen to the moral arguments swirling about us this summer I become ever more persuaded that our real problem is this: the "still, small voice" of conscience has become far too small—and utterly still.

1986

Four Kinds of Reading

Donald Hall

Everywhere one meets the idea that reading is an activity desirable in itself. It is understandable that publishers and librarians—and even writers—should promote this assumption, but it is strange that the idea should have general currency. People surround the idea of reading with piety, and do not take into account the purpose of reading or the value of what is being read. Teachers and parents praise the child who reads, and praise themselves, whether the text be *The Reader's Digest* or *Moby Dick*. The advent of TV has increased the false values ascribed to reading, since TV provides a vulgar alternative. But this piety is silly; and most reading is no more cultural nor intellectual nor imaginative than shooting pool or watching *What's My Line*.   1

It is worth asking how the act of reading became something to value in itself, as opposed for instance to the act of conversation or the act of taking a walk. Mass literacy is a recent phenomenon, and I suggest that the aura which decorates reading is a relic of the importance of reading to our great-great-grandparents. Literacy used to be a mark of social distinction, separating a small portion of humanity from the rest. The farm laborer who was ambitious for his children did not daydream that they would become schoolteachers or doctors; he daydreamed that they would learn to read, and that a world would therefore open up to them in which they did not have to labor in the fields fourteen hours a day for six days a week   2 in order to buy salt and cotton. On the next rank of society, ample time for reading meant that the reader was free from the necessity to spend most of his waking hours making a living. This sort of attitude shades into the contemporary man's boast of his wife's cultural activities. When he says that his wife is interested in books and music and pictures, he is not only enclosing the arts in a female world, he is saying that he is rich enough to provide her with the leisure to do nothing. Reading is an inactivity, and therefore a badge of social class. Of course, these reasons for the piety attached to reading are never acknowledged. They show themselves in the shape of our attitudes toward books; reading gives off an air of gentility.

3   It seems to me possible to name four kinds of reading, each with a characteristic manner and purpose. The first is reading for information—reading to learn about a trade, or politics, or how to accomplish something. We read a newspaper this way, or most textbooks, or directions on how to assemble a bicycle. With most of this material, the reader can learn to scan the page quickly, coming up with what he needs and ignoring what is irrelevant to him, like the rhythm of the sentence, or the play of metaphor. Courses in speed reading can help us read for this purpose, training the eye to jump quickly across the page. If we read the *New York Times* with the attention we should give a novel or a poem, we will have time for nothing else, and our mind will be cluttered with clichés and dead metaphor. Quick eye-reading is a necessity to anyone who wants to keep up with what's happening, or learn much of what has happened in the past. The amount of reflection, which interrupts and slows down the reading, depends on the material.

4   But it is not the same activity as reading literature. There ought to be another word. If we read a work of literature properly, we read slowly, and we *hear* all the words. If our lips do not actually move, it's only laziness. The muscles in our throat move, and come together when we see the word "squeeze." We hear the sounds so accurately that if a syllable is missing in a line of poetry we hear the lack, though we may not know what we are lacking. In prose we accept the rhythms, and hear the adjacent sounds. We also register a track of feeling through the metaphors and associations of words. Careless writing prevents this sort of attention, and becomes offensive. But the great writers reward it. Only by the full exercise of

our powers to receive language can we absorb their intelligence and their imagination. This kind of reading goes through the ear—though the eye takes in the print, and decodes it into sound—to the throat and the understanding, and it can never be quick. It is slow and sensual, a deep pleasure that begins with touch and ends with the sort of comprehension that we associate with dream.

Too many intellectuals read in order to reduce images to ab- 5 stractions. One reads philosophy slowly, as if it were literature, but much time must be spent with the eyes turned away from the page, reflecting on the text. To read literature this way is to turn it into something it is not—to concepts clothed in character, or philosophy sugar-coated. I think that most literary intellectuals read this way, including brighter professors of English, with the result that they miss literature completely, and concern themselves with a minor discipline called the history of ideas. I remember a course in Chaucer at my university in which the final exam required the identification of a hundred or more fragments of Chaucer, none as long as a line. If you like poetry, and read Chaucer through a couple of times slowly, you found yourself knowing them all. If you were a literary intellectual, well-informed about the great chain of being, chances are you had a difficult time. To read literature is to be intimately involved with the words on the page, and never to think of them as the embodiments of ideas which can be expressed in other terms. On the other hand, intellectual writing—closer to mathematics on a continuum that has at its opposite pole lyric poetry—requires intellectual reading, which is slow because it is reflective and because the reader must pause to evaluate concepts.

But most of the reading which is praised for itself is neither 6 literary nor intellectual. It is narcotic. Novels, stories, and biographies—historical sagas, monthly regurgitations of book clubs, four- and five-thousand word daydreams of the magazines—these are the opium of the suburbs. The drug is not harmful except to the addict himself, and is no more injurious to him than Johnny Carson or a bridge club, but it is nothing to be proud of. This reading is the automated daydream, the mild trip of the housewife and the tired businessman, interested not in experience and feeling but in turning off the possibilities of experience and feeling. Great literature, if we read it well, opens us up to the world, and makes us more sensitive to it, as if we acquired eyes that could see through walls and ears that could hear the smallest sounds. But by narcotic reading, one can reduce great literature to the level of *The Valley of the Dolls*. One can read *Anna Karenina* passively and inattentively, and float down the river of lethargy as if one were reading a confession magazine: "I Spurned My Husband for a Count."

7   I think that everyone reads for narcosis occasionally, and perhaps most consistently in late adolescence, when great readers are born. I remember reading to shut the world out, away at a school where I did not want to be; I invented a word for my disease: "Bibliolepsy," on the analogy of narcolepsy. But after a while the books became a window on the world, and not a screen against it. This change doesn't always happen. I think that late adolescent narcotic reading accounts for some of the badness of English departments. As a college student, the boy loves reading and majors in English because he would be reading anyway. Deciding on a career, he takes up English teaching for the same reason. Then in graduate school he is trained to be a scholar, which is painful and irrelevant, and finds he must write papers and publish them to be a Professor—and at about this time he no longer requires reading for narcosis, and he is left with nothing but a Ph.D. and the prospect of fifty years of teaching literature; and he does not even like literature.

8   Narcotic reading survives the impact of television, because this type of reading has even less reality than melodrama; that is, the reader is in control: Once the characters reach into the reader's feelings, he is able to stop reading, or glance away, or superimpose his own daydream. The trouble with television is that it embodies its own daydream. Literature is often valued precisely because of its distance from the tangible. Some readers prefer looking into the text of a play to seeing it performed. Reading a play, it is possible to stage it oneself by an imaginative act; but it is also possible to remove it from real people. Here is Virginia Woolf, who was lavish in her praise of the act of reading, talking about reading a play rather than seeing it: "Certainly there is a good deal to be said for reading *Twelfth Night* in the book if the book can be read in a garden, with no sound but the thud of an apple falling to the earth, or of the wind ruffling the branches of the trees." She sets her own

stage; the play is called *Virginia Woolf Reads Twelfth Night in a Garden.* Piety moves into narcissism, and the high metaphors of Shakespeare's lines dwindle into the flowers of an English garden; actors in ruffles wither, while the wind ruffles branches.

1968

Growing Up Asian in America

Kesaya E. Noda

Sometimes when I was growing up, my identity seemed to hurtle   1
toward me and paste itself right to my face. I felt that way, en-
countering the stereotypes of my race perpetuated by non-Japan-
ese people (primarily white) who may or may not have had contact with other Japanese in America. "You don't like cheese, do
you?" someone would ask. "I know your people don't like
cheese." Sometimes questions came making allusions to history.
That was another aspect of the identity. Events that had happened
quite apart from the me who stood silent in that moment connected my face with an incomprehensible past. "Your parents
were in California? Were they in those camps during the war?"
And sometimes there were phrases or nicknames: "Lotus Blos-
som." I was sometimes addressed or referred to as racially Japanese, sometimes as Japanese-American, and sometimes as an Asian
woman. Confusions and distortions abounded.

How is one to know and define oneself? From the inside—   2
within a context that is self-defined, from a grounding in community and a connection with culture and history that are comfortably accepted? Or from the outside—within terms of messages
received from the media and people who are often ignorant? Even
as an adult I can still see two sides of my face and past. I can see
from the inside out, in freedom. And I can see from the outside in,
driven by the old voices of childhood and lost in anger and fear.

I AM RACIALLY JAPANESE

3   A voice from my childhood says: "You are other. You are less than. You are unalterably alien." This voice has its own history. We have indeed been seen as other and alien since the early years of our arrival in the United States. The very first immigrants were welcomed and sought as laborers to replace the dwindling numbers of Chinese, whose influx had been cut off by the Chinese Exclusion Act of 1882. The Japanese fell natural heir to the same anti-Asian prejudice that had arisen against the Chinese. As soon as they began striking for better wages, they were no longer welcomed.

4   I can see myself today as a person historically defined by law and custom as being forever alien. Being neither "free white," nor "African," our people in California were deemed "aliens, ineligible for citizenship," no matter how long they intended to stay here. Aliens ineligible for citizenship were prohibited from owning, buying, or leasing land. They did not and could not belong here. The voice in me remembers that I am always a *Japanese*-American in the eyes of many. A third-generation German-American is an American. A third-generation Japanese-American is a Japanese-American. Being Japanese means being a danger to the country during the war and knowing how to use chopsticks. I wear this history on my face.

5   I move to the other side. I see a different light and claim a different context. My race is a line that stretches across ocean and time to link me to the shrine where my grandmother was raised. Two high, white banners lift in the wind at the top of the stone steps leading to the shrine. It is time for the summer festival. Black characters are written against the sky as boldly as the clouds, as lightly as kites, as sharply as the big black crows I used to see above the fields in New Hampshire. At festival time there is liquor and food, ritual, discipline, and abandonment. There is music and drunkenness and invocation. There is hope. Another season has come. Another season has gone.

6   I am racially Japanese. I have a certain claim to this crazy place where the prayers intoned by a neighboring Shinto priest (standing in for my grandmother's nephew who is sick) are drowned out by the rehearsals for the pop singing contest in which most of the villagers will compete later that night. The village elders, the priest, and I stand respectfully upon the immaculate, shining

wooden floor of the outer shrine, bowing our heads before the hidden powers. During the patchy intervals when I can hear him, I notice the priest has a stutter. His voice flutters up to my ears only occasionally because two men and a woman are singing gustily into a microphone in the compound, testing the sound system. A pre-recorded tape of guitars, samisens, and drums accompanies them. Rock music and Shinto prayers. That night, to loud applause and cheers, a young man is given the award for the most *netsuretsu*—passionate, burning—rendition of a song. We roar our approval of the reward. Never mind that his voice had wandered and slid, now slightly above, now slightly below the given line of the melody. Netsuretsu. Netsuretsu.

In the morning, my grandmother's sister kneels at the foot of the stone stairs to offer her morning prayers. She is too crippled to climb the stairs, so each morning she kneels here upon the path. She shuts her eyes for a few seconds, her motions as matter of fact as when she washes rice. I linger longer than she does, so reluctant to leave, savoring the connection I feel with my grandmother in America, the past, and the power that lives and shines in the morning sun.

Our family has served this shrine for generations. The family's need to protect this claim to identity and place outweighs any individual claim to any individual hope. I am Japanese.

I AM A JAPANESE-AMERICAN

"Weak." I hear the voice from my childhood years. "Passive," I hear. Our parents and grandparents were the ones who were put into those camps. They went without resistance; they offered cooperation as proof of loyalty to America. "Victim," I hear. And, "Silent."

Our parents are painted as hard workers who were socially uncomfortable and had difficulty expressing even the smallest opinion. Clean, quiet, motivated, and determined to match the American way; that is us, and that is the story of our time here.

"Why did you go into those camps?" I raged at my parents, frightened by my own inner silence and timidity. "Why didn't you do anything to resist? Why didn't you name it the injustice it was?" Couldn't our parents even think? Couldn't they? Why were we so passive?

12   I shift my vision and my stance. I am in California. My uncle is in the midst of the sweet potato harvest. He is pressed, trying to get the harvesting crews onto the field as quickly as possible, worried about the flow of equipment and people. His big pickup is pulled off to the side, motor running, door ajar. I see two tractors in the yard in front of an old shed; the flatbed harvesting platform on which the workers will stand has already been brought over from the other field. It's early morning. The workers stand loosely grouped and at ease, but my uncle looks as harried and tense as a police officer trying to unsnarl a New York City traffic jam. Driving toward the shed, I pull my car off the road to make way for an approaching tractor. The front wheels of the car sink luxuriously into the soft, white sand by the roadside and the car slides to a dreamy halt, tail still on the road. I try to move forward. I try to move back. The front bites contentedly into the sand, the back lifts itself at a jaunty angle. My uncle sees me and storms down the road, running. He is shouting before he is even near me.

13   "What's the matter with you?" he screams. "What the hell are you doing?" In his frenzy, he grabs his hat off his head and slashes it through the air across his knee. He is beside himself. "Don't you know how to drive in sand? What's the matter with you? You've blocked the whole roadway. How am I supposed to get my tractors out of here? Can't you use your head? You've cut off the whole roadway, and we've got to get out of here."

14   I stand on the road before him helplessly thinking. "No, I don't know how to drive in sand. I've never driven in sand."

15   "I'm sorry, uncle," I say, burying a smile beneath a look of sincere apology. I notice my deep amusement and my affection for him with great curiosity. I am usually devastated by anger. Not this time.

16   During the several years that follow I learn about the people and the place, and much more about what has happened in this California village where my parents grew up. The issei, our grandparents, made this settlement in the desert. Their first crops were eaten by rabbits and ravaged by insects. The land was so barren that men walking from house to house sometimes got lost. Women came here too. They bore children in 114-degree heat, then carried the babies with them into the fields to nurse when they reached the end of each row of grapes or other truck-farm crops.

I had had no idea what it meant to buy this kind of land and 17
make it grow green. Or how, when the war came, there was no
space at all for the subtlety of being who we were—Japanese-
Americans. Either/or was the way. I hadn't understood that people were literally afraid for their lives then, that their money had
been frozen in banks; that there was a five-mile travel limit; that
when the early evening curfew came and they were inside their
houses, some of them watched helplessly as people they knew
went into their barns to steal their belongings. The police were pa-
trolling the road, interested only in violators of curfew. There was
no help for them in the face of thievery. I had not been able to
imagine before what it must have felt like to be an American—to
know absolutely that one is an American—and yet to have almost
everyone else deny it. Not only deny it, but challenge that identity
with machine guns and troops of white American soldiers. In
those circumstances it was difficult to say, "I'm a Japanese-American," "American" had to do.

But now I can say that I am a Japanese-American. It means I 18
have a place here in this country, too. I have a place here on the
East Coast, where our neighbor is so much a part of our family that
my mother never passes her house at night without glancing at the
lights to see if she is home and safe; where my parents have hauled
hundreds of pounds of rocks from fields and arduously planted
Christmas trees and blueberries, lilacs, asparagus, and crab apples; where my father still dreams of angling a stream to a new bed
so that he can dig a pond in the field and fill it with water and fish.
"The neighbors already came for their Christmas tree?" he asks in
December. "Did they like it? Did they like it?"

I have a place on the West Coast where my relatives still farm, 19
where I heard the stories of feuds and backbiting, and where I saw
that people survived and flourished because fundamentally they
trusted and relied upon one another. A death in the family is not
just a death in a family; it is a death in the community. I saw people help each other with money, materials, labor, attention, and
time. I saw men gather once a year, without fail, to clean the
grounds of a ninety-year-old woman who had helped the community before, during, and after the war. I saw her remembering
them with birthday cards sent to each of their children.

20   I come from a people with a long memory and a distinctive grace. We live our thanks. And we are Americans. Japanese-Americans.

I AM A JAPANESE-AMERICAN WOMAN

21   Woman. The last piece of my identity. It has been easier by far for me to know myself in Japan and to see my place in America than it has been to accept my line of connection with my own mother. She was my dark self, a figure in whom I thought I saw all that I feared most in myself. Growing into womanhood and looking for some model of strength, I turned away from her. Of course, I could not find what I sought. I was looking for a black feminist or a white feminist. My mother is neither white nor black.

22   My mother is a woman who speaks with her life as much as with her tongue. I think of her with her own mother. Grandmother had Parkinson's disease and it had frozen her gait and set her fingers, tongue, and feet jerking and trembling in a terrible dance. My aunts and uncles wanted her to be able to live in her own home. They fed her, bathed her, dressed her, awoke at midnight to take her for one last trip to the bathroom. My aunts (her daughters-in-law) did most of the care, but my mother went from New Hampshire to California each summer to spend a month living with Grandmother, because she wanted to and because she wanted to give my aunts at least a small rest. During those hot summer days, mother lay on the couch watching the television or reading, cooking foods that Grandmother liked, and speaking little. Grandmother thrived under her care.

23   The time finally came when it was too dangerous for Grandmother to live alone. My relatives kept finding her on the floor beside her bed when they went to wake her in the mornings. My mother flew to California to help clean the house and make arrangements for Grandmother to enter a local nursing home. On her last day at home, while Grandmother was sitting in her big, overstuffed armchair, hair combed and wearing a green summer dress, my mother went to her and knelt at her feet. "Here, Mamma," she said. "I've polished your shoes." She lifted Grand-

mother's legs and helped her into the shiny black shoes. My Grandmother looked down and smiled slightly. She left her house walking, supported by her children, carrying her pocket book, and wearing her polished black shoes. "Look, Mamma," my mom had said, kneeling. "I've polished your shoes."

Just the other day, my mother came to Boston to visit. She had 24 recently lost a lot of weight and was pleased with her new shape and her feeling of good health. "Look at me, Kes," she exclaimed, turning toward me, front and back, as naked as the day she was born. I saw her small breasts and the wide, brown scar, belly button to pubic hair, that marked her because my brother and I were both born by Caesarean section. Her hips were small. I was not a large baby, but there was so little room for me in her that when she was carrying me she could not even begin to bend over toward the floor. She hated it, she said.

"Don't I look good? Don't you think I look good?"   25

I looked at my mother, smiling and as happy as she, thinking 26 of all the times I have seen her naked. I have seen both my parents naked throughout my life, as they have seen me. From childhood through adulthood we've had our naked moments, sharing baths, idle conversations picked up as we moved between showers and closets, hurried moments at the beginning of days, quiet moments at the end of days.

I know this to be Japanese, this ease with the physical, and it 27 makes me think of an old Japanese folk song. A young nursemaid, a fifteen-year-old girl, is singing a lullaby to a baby who is strapped to her back. The nursemaid has been sent as a servant to a place far from her own home. "We're the beggars," she says, "and they are the nice people. Nice people wear fine sashes. Nice clothes."

> If I should drop dead,
> bury me by the roadside!
> I'll give a flower
> to everyone who passes.

> What kind of flower?
> The cam-cam-camellia [tsun-tsun-tsubaki]
> watered by Heaven:
> alms water.

28   The nursemaid is the intersection of heaven and earth, the intersection of the human, the natural world, the body, and the soul. In this song, with clear eyes, she looks steadily at life, which is sometimes so very terrible and sad. I think of her while looking at my mother, who is standing on the red and purple carpet before me, laughing, without any clothes.

29   I am my mother's daughter. And I am myself.

30   I am a Japanese-American woman.

EPILOGUE

31   I recently heard a man from West Africa share some memories of his childhood. He was raised Muslim, but when he was a young man, he found himself deeply drawn to Christianity. He struggled against his inner impulse for years, trying to avoid the church yet feeling pushed to return to it again and again. "I would have done anything to avoid the change," he said. At last, he became Christian. Afterwards he was afraid to go home, fearing that he would not be accepted. The fear was groundless, he discovered, when at last he returned—he had separated himself, but his family and friends (all Muslim) had not separated themselves from him.

32   The man, who is now a professor of religion, said that in the Africa he knew as a child and a young man, pluralism was embraced rather than feared. There was "a kind of tolerance that did not deny your particularity," he said. He alluded to zestful, spontaneous debates that would sometimes loudly erupt between Muslims and Christians in the village's public spaces. His memories of an atheist who harangued the villagers when he came to visit them once a week moved me deeply. Perhaps the man was an agricultural advisor or inspector. He harassed the women. He would say: "Don't go to the fields! Don't even bother to go to the fields. Let God take care of you. He'll send you the food. If you believe in God, why do you need to work? You don't need to work! Let God put the seeds in the ground. Stay home."

33   The professor said, "The women laughed, you know? They just laughed. Their attitude was, 'Here is a child of God. When will he come home?' "

The storyteller, the professor of religion, smiled a most fantas- 34
tic tender smile as he told this story. "In my country, there is a deep
affirmation of the oneness of God," he said. "The atheist and the
women were having quite different experiences in their encounter,
though the atheist did not know this. He saw himself as quite separate from the women. But the women did not see themselves as
being separate from him. 'Here is a child of God,' they said. 'When
will he come home?' "

1989

The Truth about Lying

Judith Viorst

I've been wanting to write on a subject that intrigues and chal- 1
lenges me: The subject of lying. I've found it very difficult to do.
Everyone I've talked to has a quite intense and personal but often
rather intolerant point of view about what we can—and can never
never—tell lies about. I've finally reached the conclusion that I
can't present any ultimate conclusions, for too many people
would promptly disagree. Instead, I'd like to present a series of
moral puzzles, all concerned with lying. I'll tell you what I think
about them. Do you agree?

SOCIAL LIES

Most of the people I've talked with say that they find social lying 2
acceptable and necessary. They think it's the civilized way for folks
to behave. Without these little white lies, they say, our relationships
would be short and brutish and nasty. It's arrogant, they say, to insist on being so incorruptible and so brave that you cause other

people unnecessary embarrassment or pain by compulsively as-
sailing them with your honesty. I basically agree. What about you?

3   Will you say to people, when it simply isn't true, "I like your
new hairdo," "You're looking much better," "It's so nice to see
you," "I had a wonderful time"?

4   Will you praise hideous presents and homely kids?

5   Will you decline invitations with "We're busy that night—so
sorry we can't come," when the truth is you'd rather stay home
than dine with the So-and-sos?

6   And even though, as I do, you may prefer the polite evasion
of "You really cooked up a storm" instead of "The soup"—which
tastes like warmed-over coffee—"is wonderful," will you, if you
must, proclaim it wonderful?

7   There's one man I know who absolutely refuses to tell social lies.
"I can't play that game," he says; "I'm simply not made that way."
And his answer to the argument that saying nice things to someone
doesn't cost anything is, "Yes, it does—it destroys your credibility."
Now, he won't, unsolicited, offer his views on the painting you just
bought, but you don't ask his frank opinion unless you want *frank*,
and his silence at those moments when the rest of us liars are mut-
tering, "Isn't it lovely?" is, for the most part, eloquent enough. My
friend does not indulge in what he calls "flattery, false praise and
mellifluous comments." When others tell fibs he will not go along.
He says that social lying is lying, that little white lies are still lies. And
he feels that telling lies is morally wrong. What about you?

PEACE-KEEPING LIES

8   Many people tell peace-keeping lies; lies designed to avoid irritation or argument; lies designed to shelter the liar from possible
blame or pain; lies (or so it is rationalized) designed to keep trouble at bay without hurting anyone.

9   I tell these lies at times, and yet I always feel they're wrong. I
understand why we tell them, but still they feel wrong. And
whenever I lie so that someone won't disapprove of me or think
less of me or holler at me, I feel I'm a bit of a coward, I feel I'm
dodging responsibility, I feel . . . guilty. What about you?

Do you, when you're late for a date because you overslept, say 10 that you're late because you got caught in a traffic jam?

Do you, when you forget to call a friend, say that you called 11 several times but the line was busy?

Do you, when you didn't remember that it was your father's 12 birthday, say that his present must be delayed in the mail?

And when you're planning a weekend in New York City and 13 you're not in the mood to visit your mother, who lives there, do you conceal—with a lie, if you must—the fact that you'll be in New York? Or do you have the courage—or is it the cruelty?—to say, "I'll be in New York, but sorry—I don't plan on seeing you"?

(Dave and his wife Elaine have two quite different points of 14 view on this very subject. He calls her a coward. She says she's being wise. He says she must assert her right to visit New York sometimes and not see her mother. To which she always patiently replies: "Why should we have useless fights? My mother's too old to change. We get along much better when I lie to her.")

Finally, do you keep the peace by telling your husband lies on 15 the subject of money? Do you reduce what you really paid for your shoes? And in general do you find yourself ready, willing and able to lie to him when you make absurd mistakes or lose or break things?

"I used to have a romantic idea that part of intimacy was con- 16 fessing every dumb thing that you did to your husband. But after a couple of years of that," says Laura, "have I changed my mind!"

And having changed her mind, she finds herself telling peace- 17 keeping lies. And yes, I tell them too. What about you?

PROTECTIVE LIES

Protective lies are lies folks tell—often quite serious lies—because 18 they're convinced that the truth would be too damaging. They lie because they feel there are certain human values that supersede the wrong of having lied. They lie, not for personal gain, but because they believe it's for the good of the person they're lying to. They lie to those they love, to those who trust them most of all, on the grounds that breaking this trust is justified.

19   They may lie to their children on money or marital matters.

20   They may lie to the dying about the state of their health.

21   They may lie about adultery, and not—or so they insist—to save their own hide, but to save the heart and the pride of the men they are married to.

22   They may lie to their closest friend because the truth about her talents or son or psyche would be—or so they insist—utterly devastating.

23   I sometimes tell such lies, but I'm aware that it's quite presumptuous to claim I know what's best for others to know. That's called playing God. That's called manipulation and control. And we never can be sure, once we start to juggle lies, just where they'll land, exactly where they'll roll.

24   And furthermore, we may find ourselves lying in order to back up the lies that are backing up the lie we initially told.

25   And furthermore—let's be honest—if conditions were reversed, we certainly wouldn't want anyone lying to us.

26   Yet, having said all that, I still believe that there are times when protective lies must nonetheless be told. What about you?

27   If your Dad had a very bad heart and you had to tell him some bad family news, which would you choose: To tell him the truth or to lie?

28   If your former husband failed to send his monthly childsupport check and in other ways behaved like a total rat, would you allow your children—who believed he was simply wonderful—to continue to believe that he was wonderful?

29   If your dearly beloved brother selected a wife whom you deeply disliked, would you reveal your feelings or would you fake it?

30   And if you were asked, after making love, "And how was that for you?" would you reply, if it wasn't too good, "Not too good"?

31   Now, some would call a sex lie unimportant, little more than social lying, a simple act of courtesy that makes all human intercourse run smoothly. And some would say all sex lies are bad news and unacceptably protective. Because, says Ruth, "a man with an ego that fragile doesn't need your lies—he needs a psychiatrist." Still others feel that sex lies are indeed protective lies, more serious than simple social lying, and yet at times they tell them on the grounds that when it comes to matters sexual, everybody's ego is somewhat fragile.

"If most of the time things go well in sex," says Sue, "I think ₃₂ you're allowed to dissemble when they don't. I can't believe it's good to say, 'Last night was four stars, darling, but tonight's performance rates only a half.' "

I'm inclined to agree with Sue. What about you?   ₃₃

TRUST-KEEPING LIES

Another group of lies are trust-keeping lies, lies that involve trian- ₃₄ gulation, with *A* (that's you) telling lies to *B* on behalf of *C* (whose trust you'd promised to keep). Most people concede that once you've agreed not to betray a friend's confidence, you can't betray it, even if you must lie. But I've talked with people who don't want you telling them anything that they might be called on to lie about.

"I don't tell lies for myself," says Fran, "and I don't want to ₃₅ have to tell them for other people." Which means, she agrees, that if her best friend is having an affair, she absolutely doesn't want to know about it.

"Are you saying," her best friend asks, "that if I went off with ₃₆ a lover and I asked you to tell my husband I'd been with you, that you wouldn't lie for me, that you'd betray me?"

Fran is very pained but very adamant. "I wouldn't want to be- ₃₇ tray you, so . . . don't ask me."

Fran's best friend is shocked. What about you?   ₃₈

Do you believe you can have close friends if you're not pre- ₃₉ pared to receive their deepest secrets?

Do you believe you must always lie for your friends?   ₄₀

Do you believe, if your friend tells a secret that turns out to be ₄₁ quite immoral or illegal, that once you've promised to keep it, you must keep it?

And what if your friend were your boss—if you were perhaps ₄₂ one of the President's men—would you betray or lie for him over, say, Watergate?

As you can see, these issues get terribly sticky.   ₄₃

It's my belief that once we've promised to keep a trust, we ₄₄ must tell lies to keep it. I also believe that we can't tell Watergate lies. And if these two statements strike you as quite contradictory, you're right—they're quite contradictory. But for now they're the best I can do. What about you?

45   Some say that truth will out and thus you might as well tell the truth. Some say you can't regain the trust that lies lose. Some say that even though the truth may never be revealed, our lies pervert and damage our relationships. Some say . . . well, here's what some of them have to say.

46   "I'm a coward," says Grace, "about telling close people important, difficult truths. I find that I'm unable to carry it off. And so if something is bothering me, it keeps building up inside till I end up just not seeing them any more."

47   "I lie to my husband on sexual things, but I'm furious," says Joyce, "that he's too insensitive to know I'm lying."

48   "I suffer most from the misconception that children can't take the truth," says Emily. "But I'm starting to see that what's harder and more damaging for them is being told lies, is *not* being told the truth."

49   "I'm afraid," says Joan, "that we often wind up feeling a bit of contempt for the people we lie to."

50   And then there are those who have no talent for lying.

51   "Over the years, I tried to lie," a friend of mine explained, "but I always got found out and I always got punished. I guess I gave myself away because I feel guilty about any kind of lying. It looks as if I'm stuck with telling the truth."

52   For those of us, however, who are good at telling lies, for those of us who lie and don't get caught, the question of whether or not to lie can be a hard and serious moral problem. I liked the remark of a friend of mine who said, "I'm willing to lie. But just as a last resort—the truth's always better."

53   "Because," he explained, "though others may completely accept the lie I'm telling, I don't."

54   I tend to feel that way too.

55   What about you?

1981

Comparison and Contrast

6

Grant and Lee: A Study in Contrasts

Bruce Catton

When Ulysses S. Grant and Robert E. Lee met in the parlor of a 1 modest house at Appomattox Court House, Virginia, on April 9, 1865, to work out the terms for the surrender of Lee's Army of Northern Virginia, a great chapter in American life came to a close, and a great new chapter began.

These men were bringing the Civil War to its virtual finish. To 2 be sure, other armies had yet to surrender, and for a few days the fugitive Confederate government would struggle desperately and vainly, trying to find some way to go on living now that its chief support was gone. But in effect it was all over when Grant and Lee signed the papers. And the little room where they wrote out the terms was the scene of one of the poignant, dramatic contrasts in American history.

They were two strong men, these oddly different generals, 3 and they represented the strengths of two conflicting currents that, through them, had come into final collision.

Back of Robert E. Lee was the notion that the old aristocratic 4 concept might somehow survive and be dominant in American life.

Lee was tidewater Virginia, and in his background were family, 5 culture, and tradition . . . the age of chivalry transplanted to a New World which was making its own legends and its own myths. He embodied a way of life that had come down through the age of knighthood and the English country squire. America was a land

199

that was beginning all over again, dedicated to nothing much more complicated than the rather hazy belief that all men had equal rights, and should have an equal chance in the world. In such a land Lee stood for the feeling that it was somehow of advantage to human society to have a pronounced inequality in the social structure. There should be a leisure class, backed by ownership of land; in turn, society itself should be keyed to the land as the chief source of wealth and influence. It would bring forth (according to this ideal) a class of men with a strong sense of obligation to the community; men who lived not to gain advantage for themselves, but to meet the solemn obligations which had been laid on them by the very fact that they were privileged. From them the country would get its leadership; to them it could look for the higher values—of thought, of conduct, of personal deportment—to give it strength and virtue.

6   Lee embodied the noblest elements of this aristocratic ideal. Through him, the landed nobility justified itself. For four years, the Southern states had fought a desperate war to uphold the ideals for which Lee stood. In the end, it almost seemed as if the Confederacy fought for Lee; as if he himself was the Confederacy . . . the best thing that the way of life for which the Confederacy stood could ever have to offer. He had passed into legend before Appomattox. Thousands of tired, underfed, poorly clothed Confederate soldiers, long-since past the simple enthusiasm of the early days of the struggle, somehow considered Lee the symbol of everything for which they had been willing to die. But they could not quite put this feeling into words. If the Lost Cause, sanctified by so much heroism and so many deaths, had a living justification, its justification was General Lee.

7   Grant, the son of a tanner on the Western frontier, was everything Lee was not. He had come up the hard way, and embodied nothing in particular except the eternal toughness and sinewy fiber of the men who grew up beyond the mountains. He was one of a body of men who owed reverence and obeisance to no one, who were self-reliant to a fault, who cared hardly anything for the past but who had a sharp eye for the future.

8   These frontier men were the precise opposites of the tidewater aristocrats. Back of them, in the great surge that had taken people over the Alleghenies and into the opening Western coun-

try, there was a deep, implicit dissatisfaction with a past that had settled into grooves. They stood for democracy, not from any reasoned conclusion about the proper ordering of human society, but simply because they had grown up in the middle of democracy and knew how it worked. Their society might have privileges, but they would be privileges each man had won for himself. Forms and patterns meant nothing. No man was born to anything, except perhaps to a chance to show how far he could rise. Life was competition.

Yet along with this feeling had come a deep sense of belonging to a national community. The Westerner who developed a farm, opened a shop or set up in business as a trader, could hope to prosper only as his own community prospered—and his community ran from the Atlantic to the Pacific and from Canada down to Mexico. If the land was settled, with towns and highways and accessible markets, he could better himself. He saw his fate in terms of the nation's own destiny. As its horizons expanded, so did his. He had, in other words, an acute dollars-and-cents stake in the continued growth and development of his country. 9

And that, perhaps, is where the contrast between Grant and Lee becomes most striking. The Virginia aristocrat, inevitably, saw himself in relation to his own region. He lived in a static society which could endure almost anything except change. Instinctively, his first loyalty would go to the locality in which that society existed. He would fight to the limit of endurance to defend it, because in defending it he was defending everything that gave his own life its deepest meaning. 10

The Westerner, on the other hand, would fight with an equal tenacity for the broader concept of society. He fought so because everything he lived by was tied to growth, expansion, and a constantly widening horizon. What he lived by would survive or fall with the nation itself. He could not possibly stand by unmoved in the face of an attempt to destroy the Union. He would combat it with everything he had, because he could only see it as an effort to cut the ground out from under his feet. 11

So Grant and Lee were in complete contrast, representing two diametrically opposed elements in American life. Grant was the 12 modern man emerging; beyond him, ready to come on the stage, was the great age of steel and machinery, of crowded cities and a restless, burgeoning vitality. Lee might have ridden down from the old age of chivalry, lance in hand, silken banner fluttering over his head. Each man was the perfect champion of his cause, drawing both his strengths and his weaknesses from the people he led.

13   Yet it was not all contrast, after all. Different as they were—in background, in personality, in underlying aspiration—these two great soldiers had much in common. Under everything else, they were marvelous fighters. Furthermore, their fighting qualities were really very much alike.

14   Each man had, to begin with, the great virtue of utter tenacity and fidelity. Grant fought his way down the Mississippi Valley in spite of acute personal discouragement and profound military handicaps. Lee hung on in the trenches at Petersburg after hope itself had died. In each man there was an indomitable quality . . . the born fighter's refusal to give up as long as he can still remain on his feet and lift his two fists.

15   Daring and resourcefulness they had, too; the ability to think faster and move faster than the enemy. These were the qualities which gave Lee the dazzling campaigns of Second Manassas and Chancellorsville and won Vicksburg for Grant.

16   Lastly, and perhaps greatest of all, there was the ability, at the end, to turn quickly from war to peace once the fighting was over. Out of the way these two men behaved at Appomattox came the possibility of a peace of reconciliation. It was a possibility not wholly realized, in the years to come, but which did, in the end, help the two sections to become one nation again . . . after a war whose bitterness might have seemed to make such a reunion wholly impossible. No part of either man's life became him more than the part he played in their brief meeting in the McLean house at Appomattox. Their behavior there put all succeeding generations of Americans in their debt. Two great Americans, Grant and Lee—very different, yet under everything very much alike. Their encounter at Appomattox was one of the great moments of American history.

1958

Talk in the Intimate Relationship: His and Hers

Deborah Tannen

Male-female conversation is cross-cultural communication. Culture is simply a network of habits and patterns gleaned from past experience, and women and men have different past experiences. From the time they're born, they're treated differently, talked to differently, and talk differently as a result. Boys and girls grow up in different worlds, even if they grow up in the same house. And as adults they travel in different worlds, reinforcing patterns established in childhood. These cultural differences include different expectations about the role of talk in relationships and how it fulfills that role. 1

Everyone knows that as a relationship becomes long-term, its terms change. But women and men often differ in how they expect them to change. Many women feel, "After all this time, you should know what I want without my telling you." Many men feel, "After all this time, we should be able to tell each other what we want." 2

These incongruent expectations capture one of the key differences between men and women. Communication is always a matter of balancing conflicting needs for involvement and independence. Though everyone has both these needs, women often have a relatively greater need for involvement, and men a relatively greater need for independence. Being understood without saying what you mean gives a payoff in involvement, and that is why women value it so highly. 3

If you want to be understood without saying what you mean explicitly in words, you must convey meaning somewhere else—in how words are spoken, or by metamessages. Thus it stands to reason that women are often more attuned than men to the metamessages of talk. When women surmise meaning in this way, it seems mysterious to men, who call it "women's intuition" (if 4 they think it's right) or "reading things in" (if they think it's wrong). Indeed, it could be wrong, since metamessages are not on record. And even if it is right, there is still the question of scale: How significant are the metamessages that are there?

5   Metamessages are a form of indirectness. Women are more likely to be indirect, and to try to reach agreement by negotiation. Another way to understand this preference is that negotiation allows a display of solidarity, which women prefer to the display of power (even though the aim may be the same—getting what you want). Unfortunately, power and solidarity are bought with the same currency: Ways of talking intended to create solidarity have the simultaneous effect of framing power differences. When they think they're being nice, women often end up appearing deferential and unsure of themselves or of what they want.

6   When styles differ, misunderstandings are always rife. As their differing styles create misunderstandings, women and men try to clear them up by talking things out. These pitfalls are compounded in talks between men and women because they have different ways of going about talking things out, and different assumptions about the significance of going about it.

7   Sylvia and Harry celebrated their fiftieth wedding anniversary at a mountain resort. Some of the guests were at the resort for the whole weekend, others just for the evening of the celebration: A cocktail party followed by a sit-down dinner. The manager of the dining room approached Sylvia during dinner. "Since there's so much food tonight," he said, "and the hotel prepared a fancy dessert and everyone already ate at the cocktail party anyway, how about cutting and serving the anniversary cake at lunch tomorrow?" Sylvia asked the advice of the others at her table. All the men agreed: "Sure, that makes sense. Save the cake for tomorrow." All the women disagreed: "No, the party is tonight. Serve the cake tonight." The men were focusing on the message: The cake as food. The women were thinking of the metamessage: Serving a special cake frames an occasion as a celebration.

8   Why are women more attuned to metamessages? Because they are more focused on involvement, that is, on relationships among people, and it is through metamessages that relationships among people are established and maintained. If you want to take

the temperature and check the vital signs of a relationship, the barometers to check are its metamessages: What is said and how.

Everyone can see these signals, but whether or not we pay at- 9 tention to them is another matter—a matter of being sensitized. Once you are sensitized, you can't roll your antennae back in; they're stuck in the extended position.

When interpreting meaning, it is possible to pick up signals 10 that weren't intentionally sent out, like an innocent flock of birds on a radar screen. The birds are there—and the signals women pick up are there—but they may not mean what the interpreter thinks they mean. For example, Maryellen looks at Larry and asks, "What's wrong?" because his brow is furrowed. Since he was only thinking about lunch, her expression of concern makes him feel under scrutiny.

The difference in focus on messages and metamessages can 11 give men and women different points of view on almost any com- ment. Harriet complains to Morton, "Why don't you ask me how my day was?" He replies, "If you have something to tell me, tell me. Why do you have to be invited?" The reason is that she wants the metamessage of interest: Evidence that he cares how her day was, regardless of whether or not she has something to tell.

A lot of trouble is caused between women and men by, of all 12 things, pronouns. Women often feel hurt when their partners use "I" or "me" in a situation in which they would use "we" or "us." When Morton announces, "I think I'll go for a walk," Harriet feels specifically uninvited, though Morton later claims she would have been welcome to join him. She felt locked out by his use of "I" and his omission of an invitation: "Would you like to come?" Metamessages can be seen in what is not said as well as what is said.

It's difficult to straighten out such misunderstandings be- 13 cause each one feels convinced of the logic of his or her position and the illogic—or irresponsibility—of the other's. Harriet knows that she always asks Morton how his day was, and that she'd never announce, "I'm going for a walk," without inviting him to join her. If he talks differently to her, it must be that he feels dif- ferently. But Morton wouldn't feel unloved if Harriet didn't ask about his day, and he would feel free to ask, "Can I come along?"

if she announced she was taking a walk. So he can't believe she is justified in feeling responses he knows he wouldn't have.

14   These processes are dramatized with chilling yet absurdly amusing authenticity in Jules Feiffer's play *Grown Ups*. To get a closer look at what happens when men and women focus on different levels of talk in talking things out, let's look at what happens in this play.

15   Jake criticizes Louise for not responding when their daughter, Edie, called her. His comment leads to a fight even though they're both aware that this one incident is not in itself important.

> JAKE: Look, I don't care if it's important or not, when a kid calls its mother the mother should answer.
> LOUISE: Now I'm a bad mother.
> JAKE: I didn't say that.
> LOUISE: It's in your stare.
> JAKE: Is that another thing you know? My stare?

Louise ignores Jake's message—the question of whether or not she responded when Edie called—and goes for the metamessage: His implication that she's a bad mother, which Jake insistently disclaims. When Louise explains the signals she's reacting to, Jake not only discounts them but is angered at being held accountable not for what he said but for how he looked—his stare.

16   As the play goes on, Jake and Louise replay and intensify these patterns:

> LOUISE: If I'm such a terrible mother, do you want a divorce?
> JAKE: I do not think you're a terrible mother and no, thank you, I do not want a divorce. Why is it that whenever I bring up any difference between us you ask me if I want a divorce?

The more he denies any meaning beyond the message, the more she blows it up, the more adamantly he denies it, and so on:

> JAKE: I have brought up one thing that you do with Edie that I don't think you notice that I have noticed for some time but which I have deliberately not brought up before because I had hoped you would notice it for your-

self and stop doing it and also—frankly, baby, I have
to say this—I knew if I brought it up we'd get into exactly the kind of circular argument we're in right now.
And I wanted to avoid it. But I haven't and we're in it,
so now, with your permission, I'd like to talk about it.

LOUISE: You don't see how that puts me down?

JAKE: What?

LOUISE: If you think I'm so stupid why do you go on living
with me?

JAKE: *Dammit! Why can't anything ever be simple around here?!*

It can't be simple because Louise and Jake are responding to different levels of communication. As in Bateson's example of the
dual-control electric blanket with crossed wires, each one intensi-
fies the energy going to a different aspect of the problem. Jake tries
to clarify his point by over-elaborating it, which gives Louise further evidence that he's condescending to her, making it even less
likely that she will address his point rather than his condescension.

What pushes Jake and Louise beyond anger to rage is their 17
different perspectives on metamessages. His refusal to admit that
his statements have implications and overtones denies her authority over her own feelings. Her attempts to interpret what he
didn't say and put the metamessage into the message makes him
feel she's putting words into his mouth—denying his authority
over his own meaning.

The same thing happens when Louise tells Jake that he is be- 18
ing manipulated by Edie:

LOUISE: Why don't you ever make her come to see you? Why
do you always go to her?

JAKE: You want me to play power games with a nine year
old? I want her to know I'm interested in her. Someone around here has to show interest in her.

LOUISE: You love her more than I do.

JAKE: I didn't say that.

LOUISE: Yes, you did.

JAKE: You don't know how to listen. You have never
learned how to listen. It's as if listening to you is a
foreign language.

Again, Louise responds to his implication—this time, that he loves
Edie more because he runs when she calls. And yet again, Jake
cries literal meaning, denying he meant any more than he said.

19   Throughout their argument, the point to Louise is her feelings—that Jake makes her feel put down—but to him the point is
her actions—that she doesn't always respond when Edie calls:

LOUISE: You talk about what I do to Edie, what do you think
        you do to me?

JAKE: This is not the time to go into what we do to each
        other.

20   Since she will talk only about the metamessage, and he will
talk only about the message, neither can get satisfaction from their
talk, and they end up where they started—only angrier:

JAKE: That's not the point!

LOUISE: It's my point.

JAKE: It's hopeless!

LOUISE: Then get a divorce.

American conventional wisdom (and many of our parents and
English teachers) tell us that meaning is conveyed by words, so
men who tend to be literal about words are supported by conventional wisdom. They may not simply deny but actually miss the
cues that are sent by how words are spoken. If they sense something about it, they may nonetheless discount what they sense. After all, it wasn't said. Sometimes that's a dodge—a plausible defense rather than a gut feeling. But sometimes it is a sincere
conviction. Women are also likely to doubt the reality of what they
sense. If they don't doubt it in their guts, they nonetheless may
lack the arguments to support their position and thus are reduced
to repeating, "You said it. You did so." Knowing that metamessages are a real and fundamental part of communication makes it
easier to understand and justify what they feel.

21   An article in a popular newspaper reports that one of the five
most common complaints of wives about their husbands is "He
doesn't listen to me anymore." Another is "He doesn't talk to me
anymore." Political scientist Andrew Hacker noted that lack of
communication, while high on women's lists of reasons for di-

vorce, is much less often mentioned by men. Since couples are parties to the same conversations, why are women more dissatisfied with them than men? Because what they expect is different, as well as what they see as the significance of talk itself.

First, let's consider the complaint "He doesn't talk to me."   22

One of the most common stereotypes of American men is the   23 strong silent type. Jack Kroll, writing about Henry Fonda on the occasion of his death, used the phrases "quiet power," "abashed silences," "combustible catatonia," and "sense of power held in check." He explained that Fonda's goal was not to let anyone see "the wheels go around," not to let the "machinery" show. According to Kroll, the resulting silence was effective on stage but devastating to Fonda's family.

The image of a silent father is common and is often the model   24 for the lover or husband. But what attracts us can become flypaper to which we are unhappily stuck. Many women find the strong silent type to be a lure as a lover but a lug as a husband. Nancy Schoenberger begins a poem with the lines "It was your silence that hooked me,/so like my father's." Adrienne Rich refers in a poem to the "husband who is frustratingly mute." Despite the initial attraction of such quintessentially male silence, it may begin to feel, to a woman in a long-term relationship, like a brick wall against which she is banging her head.

In addition to these images of male and female behavior—   25 both the result and the cause of them—are differences in how women and men view the role of talk in relationships as well as how talk accomplishes its purpose. These differences have their roots in the settings in which men and women learn to have conversations among their peers, growing up.

Children whose parents have foreign accents don't speak with   26 accents. They learn to talk like their peers. Little girls and little boys learn how to have conversations as they learn how to pronounce words from their playmates. Between the ages of five and fifteen, when children are learning to have conversations, they play mostly with friends of their own sex. So it's not surprising that they learn different ways of having and using conversations.

Anthropologists Daniel Maltz and Ruth Borker point out that   27 boys and girls socialize differently. Little girls tend to play in small groups or, even more common, in pairs. Their social life usually centers around a best friend, and friendships are made, maintained, and broken by talk—especially "secrets." If a little girl tells her friend's secret to another little girl, she may find herself with a new best friend. The secrets themselves may or may not be important, but the fact of telling them is all-important. It's hard for newcomers to get into these tight groups, but anyone who is admitted is treated as an equal. Girls like to play cooperatively; if they can't cooperate, the group breaks up.

28   Little boys tend to play in larger groups, often outdoors, and they spend more time doing things than talking. It's easy for boys to get into the group, but not everyone is accepted as an equal. Once in the group, boys must jockey for their status in it. One of the most important ways they do this is through talk: Verbal display such as telling stories and jokes, challenging and sidetracking the verbal displays of other boys, and withstanding other boys' challenges in order to maintain their own story—and status. Their talk is often competitive talk about who is best at what.

29   Feiffer's play is ironically named *Grown Ups* because adult men and women struggling to communicate often sound like children: "You said so!" "I did not!" The reason is that when they grow up, women and men keep the divergent attitudes and habits they learned as children—which they don't recognize as attitudes and habits but simply take for granted as ways of talking.

30   Women want their partners to be a new and improved version of a best friend. This gives them a soft spot for men who tell them secrets. As Jack Nicholson once advised a guy in a movie: "Tell her about your troubled childhood—that always gets 'em." Men expect to do things together and don't feel anything is missing if they don't have heart-to-heart talks all the time.

31   If they do have heart-to-heart talks, the meaning of those talks may be opposite for men and women. To many women, the relationship is working as long as they can talk things out. To many men, the relationship isn't working out if they have to keep working it over. If she keeps trying to get talks going to save the relationship, and he keeps trying to avoid them because he sees them as weakening it, then each one's efforts to preserve the relationship appear to the other as reckless endangerment.

If talks (of any kind) do get going, men's and women's ideas 32 about how to conduct them may be very different. For example, Dora is feeling comfortable and close to Tom. She settles into a chair after dinner and begins to tell him about a problem at work. She expects him to ask questions to show he's interested; reassure her that he understands and that what she feels is normal; and return the intimacy by telling her a problem of his. Instead, Tom sidetracks her story, cracks jokes about it, questions her interpretation of the problem, and gives her advice about how to solve it and avoid such problems in the future.

All of these responses, natural to men, are unexpected to 33 women, who interpret them in terms of their own habits—negatively. When Tom comments on side issues or cracks jokes, Dora thinks he doesn't care about what she's saying and isn't really listening. If he challenges her reading of what went on, she feels he is criticizing her and telling her she's crazy, when what she wants is to be reassured that she's not. If he tells her how to solve the problem, it makes her feel as if she's the patient to his doctor—a metamessage of condescension, echoing male one-upmanship compared to the female etiquette of equality. Because he doesn't volunteer information about his problems, she feels he's implying he doesn't have any.

His way of responding to her bid for intimacy makes her feel 34 distant from him. She tries harder to regain intimacy the only way she knows how—by revealing more and more about herself. He tries harder by giving more insistent advice. The more problems she exposes, the more incompetent she feels, until they both see her as emotionally draining and problem-ridden. When his efforts to help aren't appreciated, he wonders why she asks for his advice if she doesn't want to take it . . . .

When women talk about what seems obviously interesting to 35 them, their conversations often include reports of conversations. Tone of voice, timing, intonation, and wording are all re-created in the telling in order to explain—dramatize, really—the experience that is being reported. If men tell about an incident and give a brief summary instead of recreating what was said and how, the women often feel that the essence of the experience is being omitted. If the woman asks, "What exactly did he say?," and "How did he say it?," the man probably can't remember. If she continues to press him, he may feel as if he's being grilled.

36   All these different habits have repercussions when the man and the woman are talking about their relationship. He feels out of his element, even one down. She claims to recall exactly what he said, and what she said, and in what sequence, and she wants him to account for what he said. He can hardly account for it since he has forgotten exactly what was said—if not the whole conversation. She secretly suspects he's only pretending not to remember, and he secretly suspects that she's making up the details.

37   One woman reported such a problem as being a matter of her boyfriend's poor memory. It is unlikely, however, that his problem was poor memory in general. The question is what types of material each person remembers or forgets.

38   Frances was sitting at her kitchen table talking to Edward, when the toaster did something funny. Edward began to explain why it did it. Frances tried to pay attention, but very early in his explanation, she realized she was completely lost. She felt very stupid. And indications were that he thought so too.

39   Later that day they were taking a walk. He was telling her about a difficult situation in his office that involved a complex network of interrelationships among a large number of people. Suddenly he stopped and said, "I'm sure you can't keep track of all these people." "Of course I can," she said, and she retraced his story with all the characters in place, all the details right. He was genuinely impressed. She felt very smart.

40   How could Frances be both smart and stupid? Did she have a good memory or a bad one? Frances's and Edward's abilities to follow, remember, and recount depended on the subject—and paralleled her parents' abilities to follow and remember. Whenever Frances told her parents about people in her life, her mother could follow with no problem, but her father got lost as soon as she introduced a second character. "Now who was that?" he'd ask. "Your boss?" "No, my boss is Susan. This was my friend." Often he'd still be in the previous story. But whenever she told them about her work, it was her mother who would get lost as soon as she mentioned a second step: "That was your tech report?" "No, I handed my tech report in last month. This was a special project."

Frances's mother and father, like many men and women, had 41
honed their listening and remembering skills in different arenas.
Their experience talking to other men and other women gave
them practice in following different kinds of talk.

Knowing whether and how we are likely to report events later 42
influences whether and how we pay attention when they happen.
As women listen to and take part in conversations, knowing they
may talk about them later makes them more likely to pay attention
to exactly what is said and how. Since most men aren't in the habit
of making such reports, they are less likely to pay much attention
at the time. On the other hand, many women aren't in the habit of
paying attention to scientific explanations and facts because they
don't expect to have to perform in public by reciting them—just as
those who aren't in the habit of entertaining others by telling jokes
"can't" remember jokes they've heard, even though they listened
carefully enough to enjoy them.

So women's conversations with their women friends keep 43
them in training for talking about their relationships with men,
but many men come to such conversations with no training at
all—and an uncomfortable sense that this really isn't their event.

Most of us place enormous emphasis on the importance of a 44
primary relationship. We regard the ability to maintain such relationships as a sign of mental health—our contemporary metaphor
for being a good person.

Yet our expectations of such relationships are nearly—maybe 45
in fact—impossible. When primary relationships are between
women and men, male-female differences contribute to the impossibility. We expect partners to be both romantic interests and
best friends. Though women and men may have fairly similar expectations for romantic interests, obscuring their differences when
relationships begin, they have very different ideas about how to be
friends, and these are the differences that mount over time.

In conversations between friends who are not lovers, small 46
misunderstandings can be passed over or diffused by breaks in
contact. But in the context of a primary relationship, differences
can't be ignored, and the pressure cooker of continued contact
keeps both people stewing in the juice of accumulated minor
misunderstandings. And stylistic differences are sure to cause

misunderstandings—not, ironically, in matters such as sharing values and interests or understanding each other's philosophies of life. These large and significant yet palpable issues can be talked about and agreed on. It is far harder to achieve congruence—and much more surprising and troubling that it is hard—in the simple day-to-day matters of the automatic rhythms and nuances of talk. Nothing in our backgrounds or in the media (the present-day counterpart to religion or grandparents' teachings) prepares us for this failure. If two people share so much in terms of point of view and basic values, how can they continually get into fights about insignificant matters?

47   If you find yourself in such a situation and you don't know about differences in conversational style, you assume something's wrong with your partner, or you for having chosen your partner. At best, if you are forward thinking and generous minded, you may absolve individuals and blame the relationship. But if you know about differences in conversational style, you can accept that there are differences in habits and assumptions about how to have conversation, show interest, be considerate, and so on. You may not always correctly interpret your partner's intentions, but you will know that if you get a negative impression, it may not be what was intended—and neither are your responses unfounded. If he says he really is interested even though he doesn't seem to be, maybe you should believe what he says and not what you sense.

48   Sometimes explaining assumptions can help. If a man starts to tell a woman what to do to solve her problem, she may say, "Thanks for the advice but I really don't want to be told what to do. I just want you to listen and say you understand." A man might want to explain, "If I challenge you, it's not to prove you wrong; it's just my way of paying attention to what you're telling me." Both may try either or both to modify their ways of talking and to try to accept what the other does. The important thing is to know that what seem like bad intentions may really be good intentions expressed in a different conversational style. We have to give up our conviction that, as Robin Lakoff put it, "Love means never having to say 'What do you mean?' "

1986

Two Views of the Mississippi

Mark Twain

Now when I had mastered the language of this water, and had 1
come to know every trifling feature that bordered the great river
as familiarly as I knew the letters of the alphabet, I had made a
valuable acquisition. But I had lost something, too. I had lost
something which could never be restored to me while I lived. All
the grace, the beauty, the poetry, had gone out of the majestic river!
I still keep in mind a certain wonderful sunset which I witnessed
when steamboating was new to me. A broad expanse of the river
was turned to blood; in the middle distance the red hue bright-
ened into gold, through which a solitary log came floating black
and conspicuous; in one place a long, slanting mark lay sparkling
upon the water; in another the surface was broken by boiling,
tumbling rings, that were as many-tinted as an opal; where the
ruddy flush was faintest, was a smooth spot that was covered with
graceful circles and radiating lines, ever so delicately traced; the
shore on our left was densely wooded, and the somber shadow
that fell from this forest was broken in one place by a long, ruffled
trail that shone like silver; and high above the forest wall a clean-
stemmed dead tree waved a single leafy bough that glowed like a
flame in the unobstructed splendor that was flowing from the sun.
There were graceful curves, reflected images, woody heights, soft
distances; and over the whole scene, far and near, the dissolving
lights drifted steadily, enriching it every passing moment with
new marvels of coloring.

I stood like one bewitched. I drank it in, in a speechless rap- 2
ture. The world was new to me, and I had never seen anything
like this at home. But as I have said, a day came when I began to
cease from noting the glories and the charms which the moon and
the sun and the twilight wrought upon the river's face; another
day came when I ceased altogether to note them. Then, if that
sunset scene had been repeated, I should have looked upon it
without rapture, and should have commented upon it, inwardly,

after this fashion: "This sun means that we are going to have wind tomorrow; that floating log means that the river is rising, small thanks to it; that slanting mark on the water refers to a bluff reef which is going to kill somebody's steamboat one of these nights, if it keeps on stretching out like that; those tumbling 'boils' show a dissolving bar and a changing channel there; the lines and circles in the slick water over yonder are a warning that that troublesome place is shoaling up dangerously; that silver streak in the shadow of the forest is the 'break' from a new snag, and he has located himself in the very best place he could have found to fish for steamboats; that tall dead tree, with a single living branch, is not going to last long, and then how is a body ever going to get through this blind place at night without the friendly old landmark?"

3   No, the romance and beauty were all gone from the river. All the value any feature of it had for me now was the amount of usefulness it could furnish toward compassing the safe piloting of a steamboat. Since those days, I have pitied doctors from my heart. What does the lovely flush in a beauty's cheek mean to a doctor but a "break" that ripples above some deadly disease? Are not all her visible charms sown thick with what are to him the signs and symbols of hidden decay? Does he ever see her beauty at all, or doesn't he simply view her professionally, and comment upon her unwholesome condition all to himself? And doesn't he sometimes wonder whether he has gained most or lost most by learning his trade?

1883

The Rewards of Living a Solitary Life

May Sarton

The other day an acquaintance of mine, a gregarious and charm- 1
ing man, told me he had found himself unexpectedly alone in
New York for an hour or two between appointments. He went to
the Whitney and spent the "empty" time looking at things in solitary bliss. For him it proved to be a shock nearly as great as falling
in love to discover that he could enjoy himself so much alone.

What had he been afraid of, I asked myself? That, suddenly 2
alone, he would discover that he bored himself, or that there was,
quite simply, no self there to meet? But having taken the plunge,
he is now on the brink of adventure; he is about to be launched
into his own inner space, space as immense, unexplored and
sometimes frightening as outer space to the astronaut. His every
perception will come to him with a new freshness and, for a time,
seem startlingly original. For anyone who can see things for himself with a naked eye becomes, for a moment or two, something of
a genius. With another human being present vision becomes double vision, inevitably. We are busy wondering, what does my companion see or think of this, and what do I think of it? The original
impact gets lost, or diffused.

"Music I heard with you was more than music." Exactly. 3
And therefore music *itself* can only be heard alone. Solitude is
the salt of personhood. It brings out the authentic flavor of every
experience.

"Alone one is never lonely: The spirit adventures, walking / 4
In a quiet garden, in a cool house, abiding single there."

Loneliness is most acutely felt with other people, for with oth- 5
ers, even with a lover sometimes, we suffer from our differences of
taste, temperament, mood. Human intercourse often demands that
we soften the edge of perception, or withdraw at the very instant
of personal truth for fear of hurting, or of being inappropriately

present, which is to say naked, in a social situation. Alone we can afford to be wholly whatever we are, and to feel whatever we feel absolutely. That is a great luxury!

6   For me the most interesting thing about a solitary life, and mine has been that for the last twenty years, is that it becomes increasingly rewarding. When I can wake up and watch the sun rise over the ocean, as I do most days, and know that I have an entire day ahead, uninterrupted, in which to write a few pages, take a walk with my dog, lie down in the afternoon for a long think (why does one think better in a horizontal position?), read and listen to music, I am flooded with happiness.

7   I am lonely only when I am overtired, when I have worked too long without a break, when for the time being I feel empty and need filling up. And I am lonely sometimes when I come back home after a lecture trip, when I have seen a lot of people and talked a lot, and am full to the brim with experience that needs to be sorted out.

8   Then for a little while the house feels huge and empty, and I wonder where my self is hiding. It has to be recaptured slowly by watering the plants, perhaps, and looking again at each one as though it were a person, by feeding the two cats, by cooking a meal.

9   It takes a while, as I watch the surf blowing up in fountains at the end of the field, but the moment comes when the world falls away, and the self emerges again from the deep unconscious, bringing back all I have recently experienced to be explored and slowly understood, when I can converse again with my hidden powers, and so grow, and so be renewed, till death do us part.

1946

Neat People vs.
Sloppy People

Suzanne Britt

I've finally figured out the difference between neat people and   1
sloppy people. The distinction is, as always, moral. Neat people
are lazier and meaner than sloppy people.

   Sloppy people, you see, are not really sloppy. Their sloppiness   2
is merely the unfortunate consequence of their extreme moral rec-
titude. Sloppy people carry in their mind's eye a heavenly vision,
a precise plan, that is so stupendous, so perfect, it can't be
achieved in this world or the next.

   Sloppy people live in Never-Never Land. Someday is their   3
métier. Someday they are planning to alphabetize all their books
and set up home catalogs. Someday they will go through their
wardrobes and mark certain items for tentative mending and certain items for passing on to relatives of similar shape and size.
Someday sloppy people will make family scrapbooks into which
they will put newspaper clippings, postcards, locks of hair, and
the dried corsage from their senior prom. Someday they will file
everything on the surface of their desks, including the cash receipts from coffee purchases at the snack shop. Someday they will
sit down and read all the back issues of the *New Yorker*.

   For all these noble reasons and more, sloppy people never get   4
neat. They aim too high and wide. They save everything, planning
someday to file, order, and straighten out the world. But while
these ambitious plans take clearer and clearer shape in their heads,
the books spill from the shelves onto the floor, the clothes pile up
in the hamper and closet, the family mementos accumulate in
every drawer, the surface of the desk is buried under mounds of
paper and the unread magazines threaten to reach the ceiling.

   Sloppy people can't bear to part with anything. They give lov-   5
ing attention to every detail. When sloppy people say they're going to tackle the surface of the desk, they really mean it. Not a paper will go unturned; not a rubber band will go unboxed. Four
hours or two weeks into the excavation, the desk looks exactly the

same, primarily because the sloppy person is meticulously creating new piles of papers with new headings and scrupulously stopping to read all the old book catalogs before he throws them away. A neat person would just bulldoze the desk.

6   Neat people are bums and clods at heart. They have cavalier attitudes toward possessions, including family heirlooms. Everything is just another dustcatcher to them. If anything collects dust, it's got to go and that's that. Neat people will toy with the idea of throwing the children out of the house just to cut down on the clutter.

7   Neat people don't care about process. They like results. What they want to do is get the whole thing over with so they can sit down and watch the rasslin' on TV. Neat people operate on two unvarying principles: Never handle any item twice, and throw everything away.

8   The only thing messy in a neat person's house is the trash can. The minute something comes to a neat person's hand, he will look at it, try to decide if it has immediate use and, finding none, throw it in the trash.

9   Neat people are especially vicious with mail. They never go through their mail unless they are standing directly over a trash can. If the trash can is beside the mailbox, even better. All ads, catalogs, pleas for charitable contributions, church bulletins and money-saving coupons go straight into the trash can without being opened. All letters from home, postcards from Europe, bills and paychecks are opened, immediately responded to, then dropped in the trash can. Neat people keep their receipts only for tax purposes. That's it. No sentimental salvaging of birthday cards or the last letter a dying relative ever wrote. Into the trash it goes.

10   Neat people place neatness above everything, even economics. They are incredibly wasteful. Neat people throw away several toys every time they walk through the den. I knew a neat person once who threw away a perfectly good dish drainer because it had mold on it. The drainer was too much trouble to wash. And neat people sell their furniture when they move. They will sell a La-Z-Boy recliner while you are reclining in it.

11   Neat people are no good to borrow from. Neat people buy everything in expensive little single portions. They get their flour and sugar in two-pound bags. They wouldn't consider clipping a

coupon, saving a leftover, reusing plastic nondairy whipped cream containers or rinsing off tin foil and draping it over the unmoldy dish drainer. You can never borrow a neat person's newspaper to see what's playing at the movies. Neat people have the paper all wadded up and in the trash by 7:05 A.M.

Neat people cut a clean swath through the organic as well as the inorganic world. People, animals, and things are all one to them. They are so insensitive. After they've finished with the pantry, the medicine cabinet, and the attic, they will throw out the red geranium (too many leaves), sell the dog (too many fleas), and send the children off to boarding school (too many scuffmarks on the hardwood floors).

a kind of flowers   *rough mode*

allegation

1983

At the Mercy of the Cure

Mark Mathabane

精神錯乱

Upon returning to Dowling in the new year, 1982, I found a letter from home waiting for me with the miraculous news: My mother had finally been cured of her insanity. I was overwhelmed with joy. The contents of the letter related how Aunt Queen, the *isangoma,* had spent over a year treating my mother. She was said to have used *muti* (tribal medicine), consisting of special herbs, bark, and roots—and divination, a seeing into the past and future using bones.   *prediction*

Apparently my mother's kindness had done her in. While in South Africa she had, against my protestations and those of the family, taken in as boarders from the Giyani homeland in the Northern Transvaal a tall, raw-boned *nyanga* (medicine man) with bloodshot eyes, named Mathebula, and his family of five. They had nowhere else to go. The shack became home for about fifteen

small wooden house

people; some slept under the tables, others curled up in corners and near the stove; there was no privacy. My mother had made it clear that their moving in with us was only a temporary measure, to provide them a roof over their heads while they hunted for their own shack. When months passed without the Mathebulas making any attempts at finding alternative housing, my mother had politely requested them to leave. This angered the wizard, a proud and chauvinistic man. Nonetheless he speedily constructed a shack in one of the rat-infested alleyways. But he never forgave my mother.

3   From strands of my mother's hair and pieces of her clothing, which he had gathered while he lived in our house, he allegedly concocted his voodoo and drove my mother mad. It took Aunt Queen almost a year to piece together what she deemed a "dastardly plot." Daily, out in the yard, under the hot African sun, with my mother seated cross-legged across from her, my aunt shook bones and tossed them onto the ground. From interpreting their final positions she believed that she was able to name the sorcerer and the method he used to bewitch my mother. To a Western mind this of course sounds incredible and primitive. But witchcraft is a time-honored tradition among many African tribes, where convenient scapegoats are always blamed for events which, through limited knowledge and technology, seem inexplicable. Belief in witchcraft can be compared to a Westerner's belief in astrology holding answers to man's future and fate.

4   "Now you know the truth," Aunt Queen said to my mother at the end of her confinement, when she was finally cured. The two spoke in Tsonga. "What do you want me to do?"

5   "Protect my family from further mischief."

6   "Is that all?"

7   "That's all."

8   "Don't you want revenge? Are you simply going to let him go scot-free?"

9   "I'm not a witch. I'm a child of God. I harbor no malice toward him or his family. I seek no revenge." My mother, despite her belief in witchcraft, still considered the Christian God to be all-powerful. This position of course had its contradictions, and since this episode occurred I have pointed them out to her from time to time.

She has modified her beliefs and is now more under the sway of Christianity.

"But your ancestors must be satisfied," Aunt Queen said. 10 "And what about the pain he caused you? Do you know that he intended to kill you?"

"But Christ prevented that. He led me to you and gave you the 11 power to cure me."

"You know, Mudjaji [my mother's maiden name], you're so 12 loving that it's impossible for me to understand why anyone would want to harm you. The only thing left for me to do to complete your cure and prevent a relapse is to send the mischief back to its perpetrator." It was believed that no cure of witchcraft was complete until the black magic had reverted to the sorcerer.

"Please don't do anything that would harm him or his fam- 13 ily," my mother pleaded.

"The gods will decide," Aunt Queen said. 14

Two weeks after my mother returned to Alexandra, the sor- 15 cerer's favorite son was stabbed to death during an argument in a *shebeen*. Hardly had he been buried when another of his sons was stabbed to death by *tsotsis* (gangsters) during a robbery and dumped in a ditch. My mother felt remorse over the deaths and grieved for the sorcerer's family. Aunt Queen told her that there was nothing she could have done to prevent their fate.

Here I was in America, in the heart of Western civilization it- 16 self, having to grapple with the reality or unreality of witchcraft. I remember how my mother's incredible story tested my "civilized mentality," my Western education, my dependency on reason, my faith in science and philosophy. But in the end I realized that her insanity, of course, had rational causes, just as did Uncle Piet's gambling, matrimonial problems, my father's alcoholism, and the family's poverty—all of which they tended to blame on witchcraft. Either my mother's undiagnosed and untreated diabetes or the oppressive conditions under which she lived, or a combination of the two, had deranged her. Aunt Queen was the tribal equivalent of a shrink. Her "magical" treatments of diseases owed much to the power of suggestion and her keen knowledge of the medicinal effects of certain herbs, bark, leaves, and roots, from which, it has been discovered, a good deal of Western medicine has gained real remedies. As for the deaths of the Wizard's sons, this was, of course, pure coincidence, since Alexandra, especially the neighborhood in which my family lived, was an extremely violent place: On one weekend over a dozen murders were committed.

17   I realized all this from the knowledge I had gained since coming to America and discovering that there was a branch of medicine of which I had been completely ignorant while I lived in South Africa: Psychoanalysis and psychiatry. The inhuman suffering experienced by blacks under apartheid had devastating effects on their mental and physical well-being. Given the primitive state of health care in the ghettos, endemic illiteracy, and the sway of tribal beliefs, my mother and most blacks were ignorant of causal relationships. They therefore blamed witchcraft for mental illnesses like schizophrenia and paranoia; diseases like malnutrition and tuberculosis; problems like unemployment, alcoholism, and gambling; and unlucky coincidences, such as being arrested during a pass raid while neighbors escaped, or being fired from a job. Their lack of access to qualified medical doctors, psychotherapists, and social workers forced them to rely on the dubious and often dangerous "cures" of *isangomas,* especially since such "cures" at least offered the victim much-needed psychological relief.

18   Superstition is present in Western societies as well, astrology being one example. Some people also blame their misfortunes on the Devil. And many govern their lives through card-reading and palmistry, and rely on charlatans to cure them of cancer, AIDS, blindness, varicose veins, and other diseases. Until education dispelled my ignorance and fortified my reason I was to a degree superstitious and believed in witchcraft.

19   The psychological problems experienced by blacks in South African ghettos are somewhat similar to those experienced by inmates of concentration camps during the Second World War. *From Death-Camp to Existentialism,* by Viktor E. Frankl, explains how psychotic behavior can become a "normal" way of life, a means of survival, for helpless people whose sense of identity and self-worth are under constant attack by an all-powerful oppressor. Jews in concentration camps were at the mercy of their Nazi guards, just as blacks in the ghettos of South Africa are at the mercy of apartheid's Gestapo-like police. Some victims of oppres-

sion even come to identify with their oppressors and persecute with relish their own kind. There are cases of Jews, known as Capos, who, in return for special privileges like food and cigarettes doled out by SS guards, treated other Jews sadistically and even herded them into crematoriums and gas chambers. In South Africa black policemen, in return for special privileges such as better housing, residential permits, and passbooks for relatives, shoot and kill unarmed black protesters, torture them in jail, uproot black communities under the homeland policy, and launch brutal raids into the ghettos to enforce Kafkaesque apartheid laws. Such are the evil consequences of unbearable pressures.

1989

Discordant Fruit

Lydia Minatoya

Once, in a cross-cultural training manual, I came across a riddle.   1
In Japan, a young man and woman meet and fall in love. They decide they would like to marry. The young man goes to his mother and describes the situation. "I will visit the girl's family," says the mother. "I will seek their approval." After some time, a meeting between mothers is arranged. The boy's mother goes to the girl's ancestral house. The girl's mother has prepared tea. The women talk about the fine spring weather: Will this be a good year for cherry blossoms? The girl's mother serves a plate of fruit. Bananas are sliced and displayed in an exquisite design. Marriage never is mentioned. After the tea, the boy's mother goes home. "I am so sorry," she tells her son. "The other family has declined the match."

In the training manual, the following question was posed.   2
How did the boy's mother know the marriage was unacceptable? That is easy, I thought when I read it. To a Japanese, the answer is obvious. Bananas do not go well with tea.

3   All of my life, I have been fluent in communicating through discordant fruit.

4   "You're not serious about applying to be a foreign exchange student!" exclaims a high school teacher. "The point is to sponsor an *American* kid." On my application, I deliberately misspell the teacher's name. I cross it out with an unsightly splotch. "Take that you mean narrow man," I gloat in triumph.

5   "Your mother is so deferential, so *quiet*," says a boyfriend. "Women like that drive me crazy." *His* mother is an attorney. That morning, I scorch his scrambled eggs. I hide the sports section of the Sunday news. "No insight, loudmouth fool," I mutter. Vengeance, I think, is mine.

6   The Japanese raise their daughters differently than their sons. "*Gambatte!*" they exhort their sons. "Have courage, be like the carp, swim upstream!" "*Kiotsukete*," they caution their daughters. "Be careful, be modest, keep safe."

7   In the old stories, men are warriors: Fierce and bold. But a lady never lunges to slash the throat of an assailant. Instead, she writes a poem about harsh winter; how it can snap a slender stalk. Then she kills *herself* in protest. How the old stories galled me!

8   My mother was raised in a world such as this, in a house of tradition and myth. And although she has traveled across continents, oceans, and time, although she considers herself a modern woman—a believer in the sunlight of science—it is a world that surrounds her still. Feudal Japan floats around my mother. Like an unwanted pool of ectoplasm, it quivers with supernatural might. It followed her into our American home and governed my girlhood life.

9   And so, I was shaped. In that feudal code, all females were silent and yielding. Even their possessions were accorded more rights. For, if mistreated, belongings were granted an annual holiday when they could spring into life and complain.

10   And so, I was haunted. If I left my clothes on the floor, or my bicycle in the rain; if I yanked on my comb with roughness; if it splintered and lost its teeth (and I did these things often and deliberately, trying to challenge their spell); then my misdeeds pursued me in dreams.

11   Emitting a hair-raising keening, my mittens would mourn for their mates. The floors I had scuffed, the doors I had slammed,

herded me into the street. Broken dishes and dulled scissors joined them to form a large, shrill, and reproachful parade of dutiful ill-treated items. How I envied white children and the simple absolution of a spanking.

While other children were learning that in America you get 12 what you ask for, I was being henpecked by inanimate objects. While other children were learning to speak their minds, I was locked in a losing struggle for dominance with my clothing, my toys, and my tools.

The objects meant me no harm; they meant to humble and ed- 13 ucate me. "Ownership," they told me "means obligation, caretaking, reciprocity." And although I was a resistant student, in time I was trained. Well-maintained, my possessions live long, useful, and mercifully quiet lives of service.

The consequence, however, is that I cannot view my belong- 14 ings as mere conveniences. They cannot serve as simple time-savers. For me, acquisitiveness holds little allure. The indebtedness is much too great.

I am a woman who apologizes to her furniture. "Excuse me," 15 I say when I bump into a chair. My voice resonates with solicitude. In America, such behavior is viewed as slightly loony.

I am a woman caught between standards of East and West. "I 16 disagree," I say to elders, to the men in my life. My voice rises and cracks with shame. "Razor-tongue," relatives say with the pleasure of knowing. "No wonder she still is unmarried."

All these incongruities came flooding back while visiting my 17 Japanese family. The pull to be deferent. The push to be bold. The tension and richness between.

In the evening, after we left the patriarch's house, Sachikosan 18 prepared a feast. She kneeled before us, cooking a huge skillet of sukiyaki. She plucked plump morsels of tender beef from the pot and popped them onto my plate. Her teenaged daughters slipped shyly in and out of the room, bearing flasks of sake and platters of sushi.

Tadao-san, Yoshi, Mark, and I were seated at the table. 19 Sachiko-san and the girls ate in the kitchen. "Where are the other women?" Mark asked Yoshi. "Yuri-chan is the guest," he replied. "She is being paid the house's high honor."

20 Loosened by the sake, chaffing from days of communicating only with me or through me, Mark bombarded Yoshi with questions. Did Yoshi like American rock and roll? Who were his favorite performers?

21 Uncomfortable with being the focus of attention, Yoshi attempted to generalize every query. "How familiar are Japanese youth with popular American music?" he translated for Tadao-san.

22 But Tadao-san was not fooled. Excluded in his own house, shunned in favor of his translator, Tadao-san grew increasingly irritable.

23 "How long has this one been riding autobikes?" he suddenly interjected. "Has he ever had an accident? Would he know how to make repairs should the autobike become disabled?"

24 At first, the American in me grinned. Clearly Tadao-san had grown weary of his subordinate role. He was asserting his authority. "How are you providing for Yuri-chan's safety?" his questions implied. "Do not forget you are welcome only in so far as you provide service to members of my house."

25 But quickly, the Japanese in me surfaced. The evening was not going smoothly and I was responsible.

26 "You're putting Yoshi on the spot!" I hissed into Mark's ear. "After all, he is not your host. Address your comments to the household head and try to act with more deference!"

27 "No kidding!" exclaimed Mark. He thought everything had been going along just fine.

28 I smiled apologetically at Yoshi and Tadao-san. My annoyance and bossy instructiveness had not gone unnoticed. I flushed mightily. I knew my behavior was most unseemly for a lady.

29 "So Tadao-san," said Mark heartily, "what do you think about all these protests of American military presence in Japan?"

30 Yoshi reeled in horror. How could he translate, with delicacy, such an openly confrontational question?

31 "Don't you think it's a little, uhmmm, *ungrateful?*" continued Mark. "After all, by picking up the bill for your country's defense, America has allowed Japan to become an economic competitor."

"How can you be so rude!" I croaked in anger. I staggered un- ₃₂
der the responsibility of having brought a boor into the ancestral
house.

"Relax. You're overreacting," snapped Mark. "Besides, this ₃₃
is my conversation." Mark was growing tired of my conduct
coaching. I could hardly blame him. Only a few days earlier, as
we sat in a coffee shop and I instructed him on the proper
method of ordering, I had overheard a comment. *"Rimokon,"* a
woman had murmured to her companion. She had nodded in
Mark's direction. *Rimokon* is a shortened form of *rimoto-kon-
tororu*. It is the Japanese pronunciation of remote control: Slang
for a henpecked man.

Tadao-san looked questioningly at Yoshi. What was the mean- ₃₄
ing of all this clamor? Yoshi rushed to translate.

"This is a most difficult question," said Tadao-san after hear- ₃₅
ing an edited translation.

I cringed. When a Japanese says a question is difficult he is re- ₃₆
questing release from an uncomfortable situation.

"I work on a military base," said Mark, "and the sentiment is ₃₇
that Japan is complaining about a free ride."

I wished we never had left the subject of rock and roll. I ₃₈
wished I were not the honored guest. I wished I was with Sachiko-
san, in the refuge of the kitchen.

Tadao-san and Yoshi caucused for a while. "Some Japanese ₃₉
believe that America's motives are not fully benevolent," said
Yoshi. His voice hesitated with the task of defusing the situation.
"They say Americans do not fully view Asians as people. Japan
and her people are expendable. Perhaps the point is not to defend
Japan but rather to move the site of possible conflict. Asia may be
a buffer zone. If war is based from Japan, South Korea, or the
Philippines, the soil and civilians of these countries, not America,
would be the first at risk."

"I don't know about that," muttered Mark.   ₄₀

"In each country, there are prejudices," said Tadao-san. "We ₄₁
Japanese are prejudiced against the Koreans. I have read your history. Has there not been discrimination against Japanese in America? Is there not discrimination today?"

42   "No," said Mark flatly.

43   "Of course there is!" I cried. We argued hotly for a minute.
Then, remembering that I was trying to act like a credit to my
mother's upbringing, I demurred.

44   "Mark and I share slight disagreement about this point," I
murmured with sudden modesty.

45   Perhaps Mark was right. Perhaps I was overreacting. Perhaps
among men, even in Japan, verbal confrontations and positioning
for power are acceptable social forms. Perhaps when two samurai
meet, they must engage in hostile sword play and find themselves
well matched, before they can be friends.

46   The exchange of political opinions left me shaken, but Mark,
Tadao-san, and Yoshi seemed unscathed. They raised their cups
and had a seemingly splendid time.

47   But then again, perhaps I was right. Before the evening ended,
Tadao-san slipped me an envelope. "In case you wish to leave the
autobike, to continue, alone, by train," he said. Inside, was a stag-
gering sum of money.

48   After midnight, Sachiko-san led me to her daughters' room. It
was the room of teenagers, a sweet jumble of stuffed animals and
pinups of popular singers. Several pencil sketches were carefully
mounted on one wall. Through a window, I saw the crescent moon.

     "Come Yuri-chan." Sachiko-san led me to the sketches. "Come
49   and see your past."

     The drawings were light, romantic renderings, of princesses
50   all gowned and gloved.

     "Your mother lived here briefly, when she was a girl,"
51   Sachiko-san explained. "These are her drawings. My daughters
found them in storage and thought them pretty." She paused in reflection. "Your young mother's dreams have been rescued and
honored, mounted here on my little ones' wall."

     Through the open window came the sound of a bamboo flute.
52   Sachiko-san looked at me with the warmth of a sister. She touched
my hair gently and smiled. "The hearts of young girls," she whispered to me, "their visions, forever, the same."

                                                              1992

Chapter

7

Illustration

Why Don't We Complain?

William F. Buckley, Jr.

It was the very last coach and the only empty seat on the entire 1
train, so there was no turning back. The problem was to breathe.
Outside, the temperature was below freezing. Inside the railroad
car the temperature must have been about 85 degrees. I took off
my overcoat, and a few minutes later my jacket, and noticed that
the car was flecked with the white shirts of the passengers. I soon
found my hand moving to loosen my tie. From one end of the car
to the other, as we rattled through Westchester County, we
sweated; but we did not moan.

I watched the train conductor appear at the head of the car. 2
"Tickets, all tickets, please!" In a more virile age, I thought, the
passengers would seize the conductor and strap him down on a
seat over the radiator to share the fate of his patrons. He shuf-
fled down the aisle, picking up tickets, punching commutation
cards. *No one addressed a word to him.* He approached my seat,
and I drew a deep breath of resolution. "Conductor," I began
with a considerable edge to my voice. . . . Instantly the doleful
eyes of my seatmate turned tiredly from his newspaper to fix me
with a resentful stare: What question could be so important as
to justify my sibilant intrusion into his stupor? I was shaken by
those eyes. I am incapable of making a discreet fuss, so I mum-
bled a question about what time we were due in Stamford (I did-
n't even ask whether it would be before or after dehydration

could be expected to set in), got my reply, and went back to my newspaper and to wiping my brow.

3   The conductor had nonchalantly walked down the gauntlet of eighty sweating American freemen, and not one of them had asked him to explain why the passengers in that car had been consigned to suffer. There is nothing to be done when the temperature *outdoors* is 85 degrees, and indoors the air conditioner has broken down; obviously when that happens there is nothing to do, except perhaps curse the day that one was born. But when the temperature outdoors is below freezing, it takes a positive act of will on somebody's part to set the temperature *indoors* at 85. Somewhere a valve was turned too far, a furnace overstocked, a thermostat maladjusted: Something that could easily be remedied by turning off the heat and allowing the great outdoors to come indoors. All this is so obvious. What is not obvious is what has happened to the American people.

4   It isn't just the commuters, whom we have come to visualize as a supine breed who have got on to the trick of suspending their sensory faculties twice a day while they submit to the creeping dissolution of the railroad industry. It isn't just they who have given up trying to rectify irrational vexations. It is the American people everywhere.

5   A few weeks ago at a large movie theatre I turned to my wife and said, "The picture is out of focus." "Be quiet," she answered. I obeyed. But a few minutes later I raised the point again, with mounting impatience. "It will be all right in a minute," she said apprehensively. (She would rather lose her eyesight than be around when I make one of my infrequent scenes.) I waited. It was *just* out of focus—not glaringly out, but out. My vision is 20-20, and I assume that is the vision, adjusted, of most people in the movie house. So, after hectoring my wife throughout the first reel, I finally prevailed upon her to admit that it was off, and very annoying. We then settled down, coming to rest on the presumption that: a) someone connected with the management of the theatre must soon notice the blur and make the correction; or b) that someone seated near the rear of the house would make the complaint in behalf of those of us up front; or c) that—any minute now—the entire house would ex-

plode into catcalls and foot stamping, calling dramatic attention to the irksome distortion.

What happened was nothing. The movie ended, as it had be- 6 gun *just* out of focus, and as we trooped out, we stretched our faces in a variety of contortions to accustom the eye to the shock of normal focus.

I think it is safe to say that everybody suffered on that occa- 7 sion. And I think it is safe to assume that everyone was expecting someone else to take the initiative in going back to speak to the manager. And it is probably true even that if we had supposed the movie would run right through the blurred image, someone surely would have summoned up the purposive indignation to get up out of his seat and file his complaint.

But notice that no one did. And the reason no one did is be- 8 cause we are all increasingly anxious in America to be unobtrusive, we are reluctant to make our voices heard, hesitant about claiming our rights; we are afraid that our cause is unjust, or that if it is not unjust, that it is ambiguous; or if not even that, that it is too trivial to justify the horrors of a confrontation with Authority; we will sit in an oven or endure a racking headache before undertaking a head-on, I'm-here-to-tell-you complaint. That tendency to passive compliance, to a heedless endurance, is something to keep one's eyes on—in sharp focus.

I myself can occasionally summon the courage to complain, 9 but I cannot, as I have intimated, complain softly. My own instinct is so strong to let the thing ride, to forget about it—to expect that someone will take the matter up, when the grievance is collective, in my behalf—that it is only when the provocation is at a very special key, whose vibrations touch simultaneously a complexus of nerves, allergies, and passions, that I catch fire and find the reserves of courage and assertiveness to speak up. When that happens, I get quite carried away. My blood gets hot, my brow wet, I become unbearably and unconscionably sarcastic and bellicose; I am girded for a total showdown.

Why should that be? Why could not I (or anyone else) on that 10 railroad coach have said simply to the conductor, "Sir"—I take that back: That sounds sarcastic—"Conductor, would you be good enough to turn down the heat? I am extremely hot. In fact, I tend to get hot every time the temperature reaches 85 degr—" Strike that last sentence. Just end it with the simple statement that you are extremely hot, and let the conductor infer the cause.

11   Every New Year's Eve I resolve to do something about the Milquetoast in me and vow to speak up, calmly, for my rights, and for the betterment of our society, on every appropriate occasion. Entering last New Year's Eve I was fortified in my resolve because that morning at breakfast I had had to ask the waitress three times for a glass of milk. She finally brought it—after I had finished my eggs, which is when I don't want it any more. I did not have the manliness to order her to take the milk back, but settled instead for a cowardly sulk, and ostentatiously refused to drink the milk—though I later paid for it—rather than state plainly to the hostess, as I should have, why I had not drunk it, and would not pay for it.

12   So by the time the New Year ushered out the Old, riding in on my morning's indignation and stimulated by the gastric juices of resolution that flow so faithfully on New Year's Eve, I rendered my vow. Henceforward I would conquer my shyness, my despicable disposition to supineness. I would speak out like a man against the unnecessary annoyances of our time.

13   Forty-eight hours later, I was standing in line at the ski repair store in Pico Peak, Vermont. All I needed, to get on with my skiing, was the loan, for one minute, of a small screwdriver, to tighten a loose binding. Behind the counter in the workshop were two men. One was industriously engaged in servicing the complicated requirements of a young lady at the head of the line, and obviously he would be tied up for quite a while. The other—"Jiggs," his workmate called him—was a middle-aged man, who sat in a chair puffing a pipe, exchanging small talk with his working partner. My pulse began its telltale acceleration. The minutes ticked on. I stared at the idle shopkeeper, hoping to shame him into action, but he was impervious to my telepathic reproof and continued his small talk with his friend, brazenly insensitive to the nervous demands of six good men who were raring to ski.

14   Suddenly my New Year's Eve resolution struck me. It was now or never. I broke from my place in line and marched to the counter. I was going to control myself. I dug my nails into my palms. My effort was only partially successful.

"If you are not too busy," I said icily, "would you mind hand- 15
ing me a screwdriver?"

Work stopped and everyone turned his eyes on me, and I ex- 16
perienced that mortification I always feel when I am the center of
centripetal shafts of curiosity, resentment, perplexity.

But the worst was yet to come. "I am sorry, sir," said Jiggs def- 17
erentially, moving the pipe from his mouth. "I am not supposed to
move. I have just had a heart attack." That was the signal for a
great whirring noise that descended from heaven. We looked,
stricken, out the window, and it appeared as though a cyclone had
suddenly focused on the snowy courtyard between the shop and
the ski lift. Suddenly a gigantic army helicopter materialized, and
hovered down to a landing. Two men jumped out of the plane carrying a stretcher, tore into the ski shop, and lifted the shopkeeper
onto the stretcher. Jiggs bade his companion goodby, was whisked
out the door, into the plane, up to the heavens, down—we
learned—to a nearby army hospital. I looked up manfully—into a
score of maneating eyes. I put the experience down as a reversal.

As I write this, on an airplane, I have run out of paper and 18
need to reach into my briefcase under my legs for more. I cannot
do this until my empty lunch tray is removed from my lap. I arrested the stewardess as she passed empty-handed down the aisle
on the way to the kitchen to fetch the lunch trays for the passengers up forward who haven't been served yet. "Would you please
take my tray?" "Just a *moment, sir!*" she said, and marched on
sternly. Shall I tell her that since she is headed for the kitchen *anyway,* it could not delay the feeding of the other passengers by more
than two seconds necessary to stash away my empty tray? Or remind her that not fifteen minutes ago she spoke unctuously into
the loudspeaker the words undoubtedly devised by the airline's
highly paid public relations counselor: "If there is anything I or
Miss French can do for you to make your trip more enjoyable,
please let us—" I have run out of paper.

I think the observable reluctance of the majority of Americans 19
to assert themselves in minor matters is related to our increased
sense of helplessness in an age of technology and centralized political and economic power. For generations, Americans who were
too hot, or too cold, got up and did something about it. Now we

call the plumber, or the electrician, or the furnace man. The habit
of looking after our own needs obviously had something to do
with the assertiveness that characterized the American family familiar to readers of American literature. With the technification of
life goes our direct responsibility for our material environment,
and we are conditioned to adopt a position of helplessness not
only as regards the broken air conditioner, but as regards the over-
heated train. It takes an expert to fix the former, but not the latter;
yet these distinctions, as we withdraw into helplessness, tend to
fade away.

20   Our notorious political apathy is a related phenomenon.
Every year, whether the Republican or the Democratic Party is in
office, more and more power drains away from the individual to
feed vast reservoirs in far-off places; and we have less and less say
about the shape of events which shape our future. From this alien-
ation of personal power comes the sense of resignation with which
we accept the political dispensations of a powerful government
whose hold upon us continues to increase.

21   An editor of a national weekly news magazine told me a few
years ago that as few as a dozen letters of protest against an editorial stance of his magazine was enough to convene a plenipo-
tentiary meeting of the board of editors to review policy. "So few
people complain, or make their voices heard," he explained to me,
"that we assume a dozen letters represent the inarticulated views
of thousands of readers." In the past ten years, he said, the volume
of mail has noticeably decreased, even though the circulation of
his magazine has risen.

22   When our voices are finally mute, when we have finally suppressed the natural instinct to complain, whether the vexation is trivial or grave, we shall have become automatons, incapable of feeling.
When Premier Khrushchev first came to this country late in 1959 he
was primed, we are informed, to experience the bitter resentment of
the American people against his tyranny, against his persecutions,
against the movement which is responsible for the great number of
American deaths in Korea, for billions in taxes every year, and for life
everlasting on the brink of disaster; but Khrushchev was pleasantly
surprised, and reported back to the Russian people that he had been
met with overwhelming cordiality (read: apathy), except, to be sure,

for "a few fascists who followed me around with their wretched
posters, and should be horsewhipped."

I may be crazy, but I say there would have been lots more 23
posters in a society where train temperatures in the dead of winter are not allowed to climb to 85 degrees without complaint.

1961

A Few Kind Words
for Superstition

Robertson Davies

In grave discussions of "the renaissance of the irrational" in our 1
time, superstition does not figure largely as a serious challenge to
reason or science. Parapsychology, UFO's, miracle cures, tran-
scendental meditation and all the paths to instant enlightenment
are condemned, but superstition is merely deplored. Is it because
it has an unacknowledged hold on so many of us?

Few people will admit to being superstitious; it implies 2
naïveté or ignorance. But I live in the middle of a large university,
and I see superstition in its four manifestations, alive and flour-
ishing among people who are indisputably rational and learned.

You did not know that superstition takes four forms? Theolo- 3
gians assure us that it does. First is what they call Vain Observances,
such as not walking under a ladder, and that kind of thing. Yet I saw
a deeply learned professor of anthropology, who had spilled some
salt, throwing a pinch of it over his left shoulder; when I asked him
why, he replied, with a wink, that it was "to hit the Devil in the eye."
I did not question him further about his belief in the Devil: but I noticed that he did not smile until I asked him what he was doing.

The second form is Divination, or consulting oracles. Another 4
learned professor I know, who would scorn to settle a problem by
tossing a coin (which is a humble appeal to Fate to declare itself),

told me quite seriously that he had resolved a matter related to university affairs by consulting the I Ching. And why not? There are thousands of people on this continent who appeal to the I Ching, and their general level of education seems to absolve them of superstition. Almost, but not quite. The I Ching, to the embarrassment of rationalists, often gives excellent advice.

5   The third form is Idolatry, and universities can show plenty of that. If you have ever supervised a large examination room, you know how many jujus, lucky coins and other bringers of luck are placed on the desks of the candidates. Modest idolatry, but what else can you call it?

6   The fourth form is Improper Worship of the True God. A while ago, I learned that every day, for several days, a $2 bill (in Canada we have $2 bills, regarded by some people as unlucky) had been tucked under a candlestick on the altar of a college chapel. Investigation revealed that an engineering student, worried about a girl, thought that bribery of the Deity might help. When I talked with him, he did not think he was pricing God cheap, because he could afford no more. A reasonable argument, but perhaps God was proud that week, for the scientific oracle went against him.

7   Superstition seems to run, a submerged river of crude religion, below the surface of human consciousness. It has done so for as long as we have any chronicle of human behavior, and although I cannot prove it, I doubt if it is more prevalent today than it has always been. Superstition, the theologians tell us, comes from the Latin *supersisto*, meaning to stand in terror of the Deity. Most people keep their terror within bounds, but they cannot root it out, nor do they seem to want to do so.

8   The more the teaching of formal religion declines, or takes a sociological form, the less God appears to great numbers of people as a God of Love, resuming his older form of a watchful, minatory power, to be placated and cajoled. Superstition makes its appearance, apparently unbidden, very early in life, when children fear that stepping on cracks in the sidewalk will bring ill fortune. It may persist even among the greatly learned and devout, as in the case of Dr. Samuel Johnson, who felt it necessary to touch posts that he passed in the street. The psychoanalysts have their explanation, but calling a superstition a compulsion neurosis does not banish it.

Many superstitions are so widespread and so old that they ₉ must have risen from a depth of the human mind that is indifferent to race or creed. Orthodox Jews place a charm on their door-posts; so do (or did) the Chinese. Some peoples of Middle Europe believe that when a man sneezes, his soul, for that moment, is absent from his body, and they hasten to bless him, lest the soul be seized by the Devil. How did the Melanesians come by the same idea? Superstition seems to have a link with some body of belief that far antedates the religions we know—religions which have no place for such comforting little ceremonies and charities.

People who like disagreeable historical comparisons recall ₁₀ that when Rome was in decline, superstition proliferated wildly, and that something of the same sort is happening in our Western world today. They point to the popularity of astrology, and it is true that sober newspapers that would scorn to deal in love philters carry astrology columns and the fashion magazines count them among their most popular features. But when has astrology not been popular? No use saying science discredits it. When has the heart of man given a damn for science?

Superstition in general is linked to man's yearning to know ₁₁ his fate, and to have some hand in deciding it. When my mother was a child, she innocently joined her Roman Catholic friends in killing spiders on July 11, until she learned that this was done to ensure heavy rain the day following, the anniversary of the Battle of Boyne, when the Orangemen would hold their parade. I knew an Italian, a good scientist, who watched every morning before leaving his house, so that the first person he met would not be a priest or a nun, as this would certainly bring bad luck.

I am not one to stand aloof from the rest of humanity in this ₁₂ matter, for when I was a university student, a gypsy woman with a child in her arms used to appear every year at examination time, and ask a shilling of anyone who touched the Lucky Baby; that swarthy infant cost me four shillings altogether, and I never failed an examination. Of course, I did it merely for the joke—or so I thought then. Now, I am humbler.

1978

Handwritten annotation in top margin:
Great Lakes
1-800-236-4300
ask reduction
programs
3.5

Fecundity

Annie Dillard

1 I have to look at the landscape of the blue-green world again. Just think: In all the clean beautiful reaches of the solar system, our planet alone is a blot; our planet alone has death. I have to acknowledge that the sea is a cup of death and the land is a stained altar stone. We the living are survivors huddled on flotsam, living on jetsam. We are escapees. We wake in terror, eat in hunger, sleep with a mouthful of blood.

2 Death: W. C. Fields called death "the Fellow in the Bright Nightgown." He shuffles around the house in all the corners I've forgotten, all the halls I dare not call to mind or visit for fear I'll glimpse the hem of his shabby, dazzling gown disappearing around a turn. This is the monster evolution loves. How could it be?

3 The faster death goes, the faster evolution goes. If an aphid lays a million eggs, several might survive. Now, my right hand, in all its human cunning, could not make one aphid in a thousand years. But these aphid eggs—which run less than a dime a dozen, which run absolutely free—can make aphids as effortlessly as the sea makes waves. Wonderful things, wasted. It's a wretched system. Arthur Stanley Eddington, the British physicist and astronomer who died in 1944, suggested that all of "Nature" could conceivably run on the same deranged scheme. "If indeed she has no greater aim than to provide a home for her greatest experiment, Man, it would be just like her methods to scatter a million stars whereof one might haply achieve her purpose." I doubt very much that this is the aim, but it seems clear on all fronts that this is the method.

4 Say you are the manager of the Southern Railroad. You figure that you need three engines for a stretch of track between Lynchburg and Danville. It's a mighty steep grade. So at fantastic effort and expense you have your shops make nine thousand engines. Each engine must be fashioned just so, every rivet and bolt secure, every wire twisted and wrapped, every needle on every indicator sensitive and accurate.

You send all nine thousand of them out on the runs. Although there are engineers at the throttles, no one is manning the switches. The engines crash, collide, derail, jump, jam, burn . . . At the end of the massacre you have three engines, which is what the run could support in the first place. There are few enough of them that they can stay out of each others' paths.

You go to your board of directors and show them what you've done. And what are they going to say? You know what they're going to say. They're going to say: It's a hell of a way to run a railroad.

Is it a better way to run a universe?

Evolution loves death more than it loves you or me. This is easy to write, easy to read, and hard to believe. The words are simple, the concept clear—but you don't believe it, do you? Nor do I. How could I, when we're both so lovable? Are my values then so diametrically opposed to those that nature preserves? This is the key point.

Must I then part ways with the only world I know? I had thought to live by the side of the creek in order to shape my life to its free flow. But I seem to have reached a point where I must draw the line. It looks as though the creek is not buoying me up but dragging me down. Look: Cock Robin may die the most gruesome of slow deaths, and nature is no less pleased; the sun comes up, the creek rolls on, the survivors still sing. I cannot feel that way about your death, nor you about mine, nor either of us about the robin's—nor even the barnacles'. We value the individual supremely, and nature values him not a whit. It looks for the moment as though I might have to reject this creek life unless I want to be utterly brutalized. Is human culture with its values my only real home after all? Can it possibly be that I should move my anchor-hold to the side of a library? This direction of thought brings me abruptly to a fork in the road where I stand paralyzed, unwilling to go on, for both ways lead to madness.

Either this world, my mother, is a monster, or I myself am a freak.

Consider the former: The world is a monster. Any three-year-old can see how unsatisfactory and clumsy is this whole business of reproducing and dying by the billions. We have not yet encountered any god who is as merciful as a man who flicks a beetle over on its feet. There is not a people in the world who behaves as badly as praying mantises. But wait, you say, there is no right and wrong in nature; right and wrong is a human concept. Precisely: We are moral creatures, then, in an amoral world. The universe that suckled us is a monster that does not care if we live or die— does not care if it itself grinds to a halt. It is fixed and blind, a robot programmed to kill. We are free and seeing; we can only try to outwit it at every turn to save our skins.

12   This view requires that a monstrous world running on chance and death, careening blindly from nowhere to nowhere, somehow produced wonderful us. I came from the world, I crawled out of a sea of amino acids, and now I must whirl around and shake my fist at that sea and cry Shame! If I value anything at all, then I must blindfold my eyes when I near the Swiss Alps. We must as a culture dissemble our telescopes and settle down to back-slapping. We little blobs of soft tissue crawling around on this one planet's skin are right, and the whole universe is wrong.

13   Or consider the alternative.

14   Julian of Norwich, the great English anchorite and theologian, cited, in the manner of the prophets, these words from God: "See, I am God: See, I am in all things: See, I never lift my hands off my works, nor ever shall, without end . . . How should anything be amiss?" But now not even the simplest and best of us sees things the way Julian did. It seems to us that plenty is amiss. So much is amiss that I must consider the second fork in the road, that creation itself is blamelessly, benevolently askew by its very free nature, and that it is only human feeling that is freakishly amiss. The frog that the giant water bug sucked had, presumably, a rush of pure feeling for about a second, before its brain turned to broth. I, however, have been sapped by various strong feelings about the incident almost daily for several years.

15   Do the barnacle larvae care? Does the lacewing who eats her eggs care? If they do not care, then why am I making all this fuss? If I am a freak, then why don't I hush?

16   Our excessive emotions are so patently painful and harmful to us as a species that I can hardly believe that they evolved. Other creatures manage to have effective matings and even stable societies without great emotions, and they have a bonus in that they need not

ever mourn. (But some higher animals have emotions that we think are similar to ours: Dogs, elephants, otters, and the sea mammals mourn their dead. Why do that to an otter? What creator could be so cruel, not to kill otters, but to let them care?) It would seem that emotions are the curse, not death—emotions that appear to have devolved upon a few freaks as a special curse from Malevolence.

All right then. It is our emotions that are amiss. We are freaks, 17 the world is fine, and let us all go have lobotomies to restore us to a natural state. We can leave the library then, go back to the creek lobotomized, and live on its banks as untroubled as any muskrat or reed. You first.

Of the two ridiculous alternatives, I rather favor the second. 18 Although it is true that we are moral creatures in an amoral world, the world's amorality does not make it a monster. Rather, I am the freak. Perhaps I don't need a lobotomy, but I could use some calming down, and the creek is just the place for it. I must go down to the creek again. It is where I belong, although as I become closer to it, my fellows appear more and more freakish, and my home in the library more and more limited. Imperceptibly at first, and now consciously, I shy away from the arts, from the human emotional stew. I read what the men with telescopes and microscopes have to say about the landscape. I read about the polar ice, and I drive myself deeper and deeper into exile from my own kind. But, since I cannot avoid the library altogether—the human culture that taught me to speak in its tongue—I bring human values to the creek, and so save myself from being brutalized.

What I have been after all along is not an explanation but a 19 picture. This is the way the world is, altar and cup, lit by the fire from a star that has only begun to die. My rage and shock at the pain and death of individuals of my kind is the old, old mystery, as old as man, but forever fresh, and completely unanswerable. My reservations about the fecundity and waste of life among other creatures is, however, mere squeamishness. After all, I'm the one having the nightmares. It is true that many of the creatures live and die abominably, but I am not called upon to pass judgment. Nor am I called upon to live in that same way, and those creatures who are are mercifully unconscious.

20   I don't want to cut this too short. Let me pull the camera back and look at that fork in the road from a distance, in the larger context of the speckled and twining world. It could be that the fork will disappear, or that I will see it to be but one of many interstices in a network, so that it is impossible to say which line is the main part and which is the fork.

21   The picture of fecundity and its excesses and of the pressures of growth and its accidents is of course no different from the picture I painted before of the world as an intricate texture of a bizarre variety of forms. Only now the shadows are deeper. Extravagance takes on a sinister, wastrel air, and exuberance blithers. When I added the dimension of time to the landscape of the world, I saw how freedom grew the beauties and horrors from the same live branch. This landscape is the same as that one, with a few more details added, and a different emphasis. I see squashes expanding with pressure and a hunk of wood rapt on the desert floor. The rye plant and the Bronx ailanthus are literally killing themselves to make seeds, and the animals to lay eggs. Instead of one goldfish swimming in its intricate bowl, I see tons and tons of goldfish laying and eating billions and billions of eggs. The point of all the eggs is of course to make goldfish one by one—nature loves the *idea* of the individual, if not the individual himself—and the point of a goldfish is pizzazz. This is familiar ground. I merely failed to mention that it is death that is spinning the globe.

22   It is harder to take, but surely it's been thought about. I cannot really get very exercised over the hideous appearance and habits of some deep-sea jellies and fishes, and I exercise easy. But about the topic of my own death I am decidedly touchy. Nevertheless, the two phenomena are two branches of the same creek, the creek that waters the world. Its source is freedom, and its network of branches is infinite. The graceful mockingbird that falls drinks there and sips in the same drop a beauty that waters its eyes and a death that fledges and flies. The petals of tulips are flaps of the same doomed water that swells and hatches in the ichneumon's gut.

23   That something is everywhere and always amiss is part of the very stuff of creation. It is as though each clay form had baked into it, fired into it, a blue streak of nonbeing, a shaded emptiness like a bubble that not only shapes its very structure but that also causes

it to list and ultimately explode. We could have planned things more mercifully, perhaps, but our plan would never get off the drawing board until we agreed to the very compromising terms that are the only ones that being offers.

The world has signed a pact with the devil; it had to. It is a 24 covenant to which every thing, even every hydrogen atom, is bound. The terms are clear: If you want to live, you have to die; you cannot have mountains and creeks without space, and space is a beauty married to a blind man. The blind man is Freedom, or Time, and he does not go anywhere without his great dog Death. The world came into being with the signing of the contract. A scientist calls it the Second Law of Thermodynamics. A poet says, "The force that through the green fuse drives the flower/Drives my green age." This is what we know. The rest is gravy.

Patterns of Eating

Peter Farb and George Armelagos

Among the important societal rules that represent one component 1 of cuisine are table manners. As a socially instilled form of conduct, they reveal the attitudes typical of a society. Changes in table manners through time, as they have been documented for western Europe, likewise reflect fundamental changes in human relationships. Medieval courtiers saw their table manners as distinguishing them from crude peasants; but by modern standards, the manners were not exactly refined. Feudal lords used their unwashed hands to scoop food from a common bowl and they passed around a single goblet from which all drank. A finger or two would be extended while eating, so as to be kept free of grease and thus available for the next course, or for dipping into spices and condiments—possibly accounting for today's "polite" custom of extending the finger while holding a spoon or small fork. Soups and sauces were commonly drunk by lifting the bowl to the mouth; several diners frequently ate from the same bread trencher. Even lords and nobles would toss gnawed bones back into the common dish, wolf down their food, spit onto the table (preferred conduct called for spitting under it), and blew their noses into the tablecloth.

2   By about the beginning of the sixteenth century, table manners began to move in the direction of today's standards. The importance attached to them is indicated by the phenomenal success of a treatise, *On Civility in Children*, by the philosopher Erasmus, which appeared in 1530; reprinted more than thirty times in the next six years, it also appeared in numerous translations. Erasmus' idea of good table manners was far from modern, but it did represent an advance. He believed, for example, that an upper class diner was distinguished by putting only three fingers of one hand into the bowl, instead of the entire hand in the manner of the lower class. Wait a few moments after being seated before you dip into it, he advises. Do not poke around in your dish, but take the first piece you touch. Do not put chewed food from the mouth back on your plate; instead, throw it under the table or behind your chair.

3   By the time of Erasmus, the changing table manners reveal a fundamental shift in society. People no longer ate from the same dish or drank from the same goblet, but were divided from one another by a new wall of constraint. Once the spontaneous, direct, and informal manners of the Middle Ages had been repressed, people began to feel shame. Defecation and urination were now regarded as private activities; handkerchiefs came into use for blowing the nose; nightclothes were now worn, and bedrooms were set apart as private areas. Before the sixteenth century, even nobles ate in their vast kitchens; only then did a special room designated for eating come into use away from the bloody sides of meat, the animals about to be slaughtered, and the bustling servants. These new inhibitions became the essence of "civilized" behavior, distinguishing adults from children, the upper classes from the lower, and Europeans from the "savages" then being discovered around the world. Restraint in eating habits became more marked in the centuries that followed. By about 1800, napkins were in common use, and before long they were placed on the

thighs rather than wrapped around the neck; coffee and tea were no longer slurped out of the saucer; bread was genteelly broken into small pieces with the fingers rather than cut into large chunks with a knife.

Numerous paintings that depict meals—with subjects such as the Last Supper, the wedding at Cana, or Herod's feast—show what dining tables looked like before the seventeenth century. Forks were not depicted until about 1600 (when Jacopo Bassano painted one in a Last Supper), and very few spoons were shown. At least one knife is always depicted—an especially large one when it is the only one available for all the guests—but small individual knives were often at each place. Tin disks or oval pieces of wood had already replaced the bread trenchers. This change in eating utensils typified the new table manners in Europe. (In many other parts of the world, no utensils at all were used. In the Near East, for example, it was traditional to bring food to the mouth with the fingers of the right hand, the left being unacceptable because it was reserved for wiping the buttocks.) Utensils were employed in part because of a change in the attitude toward meat. During the Middle Ages, whole sides of meat, or even an entire dead animal, had been brought to the table and then carved in view of the diners. Beginning in the seventeenth century, at first in France but later elsewhere, the practice began to go out of fashion. One reason was that the family was ceasing to be a production unit that did its own slaughtering; as that function was transferred to specialists outside the home, the family became essentially a consumption unit. In addition, the size of the family was decreasing, and consequently whole animals, or even large parts of them, were uneconomical. The cuisines of Europe reflected these social and economic changes. The animal origin of meat dishes was concealed by the arts of preparation. Meat itself became distasteful to look upon, and carving was moved out of sight to the kitchen. Comparable changes had already taken place in Chinese cuisine, with meat being cut up beforehand, unobserved by the diners. England was an exception to the change in Europe, and in its former colonies—the United States, Canada, Australia, and South Africa—the custom has persisted of bringing a joint of meat to the table to be carved.

5   Once carving was no longer considered a necessary skill
among the well-bred, changes inevitably took place in the use of
the knife, unquestionably the earliest utensil used for manipu-
lating food. (In fact, the earliest English cookbooks were not so
much guides to recipes as guides to carving meat.) The attitude
of diners toward the knife, going back to the Middle Ages and
the Renaissance, had always been ambivalent. The knife served
as a utensil, but it offered a potential threat because it was also a
weapon. Thus taboos were increasingly placed upon its use: It
was to be held by the point with the blunt handle presented; it
was not to be placed anywhere near the face; and most important, the uses to which it was put were sharply restricted. It was
not to be used for cutting soft foods such as boiled eggs or fish,
or round ones such as potatoes, or to be lifted from the table for
courses that did not need it. In short, good table manners in Europe gradually removed the threatening aspect of the knife from
social occasions. A similar change had taken place much earlier
in China when the warrior was supplanted by the scholar as a
cultural model. The knife was banished completely from the
table in favor of chopsticks, which is why the Chinese came to
regard Europeans as barbarians at their table who "eat with
swords."

6   The fork in particular enabled Europeans to separate themselves from the eating process, even avoiding manual contact
with their food. When the fork first appeared in Europe, toward
the end of the Middle Ages, it was used solely as an instrument
for lifting chunks from the common bowl. Beginning in the sixteenth century, the fork was increasingly used by members of the
upper classes—first in Italy, then in France, and finally in Germany and England. By then, social relations in western Europe
had so changed that a utensil was needed to spare diners from the
"uncivilized" and distasteful necessity of picking up food and
putting it into the mouth with the fingers. The addition of the fork
to the table was once said to be for reasons of hygiene, but this
cannot be true. By the sixteenth century people were no longer
eating from a common bowl but from their own plates, and since
they also washed their hands before meals, their fingers were
now every bit as hygienic as a fork would have been. Nor can the

reason for the adoption of the fork be connected with the wish not to soil the long ruff that was worn on the sleeve at the time, since the fork was also adopted in various countries where ruffs were not then in fashion.

Along with the appearance of the fork, all table utensils be- 7 gan to change and proliferate from the sixteenth century onward. Soup was no longer eaten directly from the dish, but each diner used an individual spoon for that purpose. When a diner wanted a second helping from the serving dish, a ladle or a fresh spoon was used. More and more special utensils were developed for each kind of food: Soup spoons, oyster forks, salad forks, two-tined fondue forks, blunt butter knives, special utensils for various desserts and kinds of fruit, each one differently shaped, of a different size, with differently numbered prongs and with blunt or serrated edges. The present European pattern eventually emerged, in which each person is provided with a table setting of as many as a dozen utensils at a full-course meal. With that, the separation of the human body from the taking of food became virtually complete. Good table manners dictated that even the cobs of maize were to be held by prongs inserted in each end, and the bones of lamb chops covered by ruffled paper pantalettes. Only under special conditions—as when Western people consciously imitate an earlier stage in culture at a picnic, fish fry, cookout, or campfire—do they still tear food apart with their fingers and their teeth, in a nostalgic reenactment of eating behaviors long vanished.

Today's neighborhood barbecue recreates a world of sharing 8 and hospitality that becomes rarer each year. We regard as a curiosity the behavior of hunters in exotic regions. But every year millions of North Americans take to the woods and lakes to kill a wide variety of animals—with a difference, of course: What hunters do for survival we do for sport (and also for proof of masculinity, for male bonding, and for various psychological rewards). Like hunters, too, we stuff ourselves almost whenever food is available. Nibbling on a roasted ear of maize gives us, in addition to nutrients, the satisfaction of participating in culturally simpler ways. A festive meal, however, is still thought of in Victorian terms, with the dominant male officiating over the roast, the dominant female apportioning vegetables, the extended family gathered around the table, with everything in its proper place—a revered picture, as indeed it was so painted by Norman Rockwell, yet one that becomes less accurate with each year that passes.

1980

The Anthropology of Manners

Edward T. Hall

> The Goops they lick their fingers
> and the Goops they lick their knives;
> They spill their broth on the table cloth—
> Oh, they lead disgusting lives.
> The Goops they talk while eating,
> and loud and fast they chew;
> And that is why I'm glad that I
> am not a Goop—are you?

1 In Gelett Burgess' classic on the Goops we have an example of what anthropologists call "an enculturating device"—a means of conditioning the young to life in our society. Having been taught the lesson of the goops from childhood (with or without the aid of Mr. Burgess) Americans are shocked when they go abroad and discover whole groups of people behaving like goops—eating with their fingers, making noises and talking while eating. When this happens, we may (1) remark on the barbarousness or quaintness of the "natives" (a term cordially disliked all over the world) or (2) try to discover the nature and meaning of the differences in behavior. One rather quickly discovers that what is good manners

in one context may be bad in the next. It is to this point that I would like to address myself.

The subject of manners is complex; if it were not, there would 2 not be so many injured feelings and so much misunderstanding in international circles everywhere. In any society the code of manners tends to sum up the culture—to be a frame of reference for all behavior. Emily Post goes so far as to say: "There is not a single thing that we do, or say, or choose, or use, or even think, that does not follow or break one of the exactions of taste, or tact, or ethics of good manners, or etiquette—call it what you will." Unfortunately many of the most important standards of acceptable behavior in different cultures are elusive: They are intangible, undefined and unwritten.

An Arab diplomat who recently arrived in the U.S. from the 3 Middle East attended a banquet which lasted several hours. When it was over, he met a fellow countryman outside and suggested they go get something to eat, as he was starving. His friend, who had been in this country for some time, laughed and said: "But, Habib, didn't you know that if you say, 'No, thank you,' they think you really don't want any?" In an Arab country etiquette dictates that the person being served must refuse the proffered dish several times, while his host urges him repeatedly to partake. The other side of the coin is that Americans in the Middle East, until they learn better, stagger away from banquets having eaten more than they want or is good for them.

When a public-health movie of a baby being bathed in a 4 bathinette was shown in India recently, the Indian women who saw it were visibly offended. They wondered how people could be so inhuman as to bathe a child in stagnant (not running) water. Americans in Iran soon learn not to indulge themselves in their penchant for chucking infants under the chin and remarking on the color of their eyes, for the mother has to pay to have the "evil eye" removed. We also learn that in the Middle East you don't hand people things with your left hand, because it is unclean. In India we learn not to touch another person, and in Southeast Asia we learn that the head is sacred.

In the interest of intercultural understanding various U.S. Gov- 5 ernment agencies have hired anthropologists from time to time as

[handwritten note: unquestioning can lead to offensive behavior?]

technical experts. The Sta̶   ̶oneered
in the attempt to bring sci̶   ̶omplex
problem. It began by offer̶   ̶e an intensive four-week course f̶   ̶ facilities were expanded to incl̶   ̶el.

6   The anthropologist's jo̶   ̶ion to
obvious taboos or to coach̶   ̶ss behavior that have very little̶   ̶d not
need an anthropologist to p̶   ̶instance, that it is insulting to ask a foreigner: "How much is this in real money?" Where
technical advice is most needed is in the interpretation of the unconscious aspects of a culture—the things people do automatically without being aware of the full implications of what they
have done. For example, an ambassador who has been kept waiting for more than half an hour by a foreign visitor needs to understand that if his visitor "just mutters an apology" this is not
necessarily an insult. The time system in the foreign country may
be composed of different basic units, so that the visitor is not as
late as he may appear to us. You must know the time system of the
country to know at what point apologies are really due.

7   Twenty years of experience in working with Americans in
foreign lands convinces me that the real problem in preparing
them to work overseas is not with taboos, which they catch on to
rather quickly, but rather with whole congeries of habits and attitudes which anthropologists have only recently begun to describe systematically.

8   Can you remember tying your shoes this morning? Could you
give the rules for when it is proper to call another person by his
first name? Could you describe the gestures you make in conversation? These examples illustrate how much of our behavior is
"out of awareness," and how easy it is to get into trouble in another culture.

9   Nobody is continually aware of the quality of his own voice,
the subtleties of stress and intonation that color the meaning of his
words or the posture and distance he assumes in talking to another person. Yet all these are taken as cues to the real nature of an
utterance, regardless of what the words say. A simple illustration
is the meaning in the tone of voice. In the U.S. we raise our voices
not only when we are angry but also when we want to emphasize

a point, when we are more than a certain distance from another person, when we are concluding a meeting and so on. But to the Chinese, for instance, overloudness of the voice is most characteristically associated with anger and loss of self-control. Whenever we become really interested in something, they are apt to have the feeling we are angry, in spite of many years' experience with us. Very likely most of their interviews with us, however cordial, seem to end on a sour note when we exclaim heartily: "WELL, I'M CERTAINLY GLAD YOU DROPPED IN, MR. WONG."

The Latin Americans, who as a rule take business seriously, do 10 not understand our mixing business with informality and recreation. We like to put our feet up on the desk. If a stranger enters the office, we take our feet down. If it turns out that the stranger and we have a lot in common, up go the feet again—a cue to the other fellow that we feel at ease. If the office boy enters, the feet stay up; if the boss enters and our relationship with him is a little strained at the moment, they go down. To a Latin American this whole behavior is shocking. All he sees in it is insult or just plain rudeness.

Differences in attitudes toward space—what would be terri- 11 toriality in lower forms of life—raise a number of other interesting points. U.S. women who go to live in Latin America all complain about the "waste" of space in the houses. On the other hand, U.S. visitors to the Middle East complain about crowding, in the houses and on the streetcars and buses. Everywhere we go space seems to be distorted. When we see a gardener in the mountains of Italy planting a single row on each of six separate terraces, we wonder why he spreads out his crop so that he has to spend half his time climbing up and down. We overlook the complex chain of communication that would be broken if he didn't cultivate alongside his brothers and his cousin and if he didn't pass his neighbors and talk to them as he moves from one terrace to the next.

A colleague of mine was caught in a snowstorm while travel- 12 ing with companions in the mountains of Lebanon. They stopped at the next house and asked to be put up for the night. The house had only one room. Instead of distributing the guests around the room, their host placed them next to the pallet where he slept with his wife—so close that they almost touched the couple. To have done otherwise in that country would have been unnatural and unfriendly. In the U.S. we distribute ourselves more evenly than many other people. We have strong feelings about touching and being crowded; in a streetcar, bus or elevator we draw ourselves in. Toward a person who relaxes and lets himself come into full contact with others in a crowded place we usually feel reactions that could not be printed on this page. It takes years for us to train our children not to crowd and lean on us. We tell them to stand up, that it is rude to slouch, not to sit so close or not to "breathe down our necks." After a while they get the point. By the time we Americans are in our teens we can tell what relationship exists between a man and woman by how they walk or sit together.

13   In Latin America, where touching is more common and the basic units of space seem to be smaller, the wide automobiles made in the U.S. pose problems. People don't know where to sit. North Americans are disturbed by how close the Latin Americans stand when they converse. "Why do they have to get so close when they talk to you?" "They're so pushy." "I don't know what it is, but it's something in the way they stand next to you." And so on. The Latin Americans, for their part, complain that people in the U.S. are distant and cold—*retraídos* (withdrawing and uncommunicative).

14   An analysis of the handling of space during conversations shows the following: A U.S. male brought up in the Northeast stands 18 to 20 inches away when talking face to face to a man he does not know very well; talking to a woman under similar circumstances, he increases the distance about four inches. A distance of only eight to 13 inches between males is considered either very aggressive or indicative of a closeness of a type we do not ordinarily want to think about. Yet in many parts of Latin America and the Middle East distances which are almost sexual in connotation are the only ones at which people can talk comfortably. In Cuba, for instance, there is nothing suggestive in a man's talking to an educated woman at a distance of 13 inches. If you are a Latin American, talking to a North American at the distance he insists on maintaining is like trying to talk across a room.

15   To get a more vivid idea of this problem of the comfortable distance, try starting a conversation with a person eight or 10 feet away or one separated from you by a wide obstruction in a store or other public place. Any normally encultured person can't help trying to close up the space, even to the extent of climbing over benches or walking around tables to arrive within comfort-

able distance. U.S. businessmen working in Latin America try to prevent people from getting uncomfortably close by barricading themselves behind desks, typewriters or the like, but their Latin American office visitors will often climb up on desks or over chairs and put up with loss of dignity in order to establish a spatial context in which interaction can take place for them.

The interesting thing is that neither party is specifically aware of what is wrong when the distance is not right. They merely have vague feelings of discomfort or anxiety. As the Latin American approaches and the North American backs away, both parties take offense without knowing why. When a North American, having had the problem pointed out to him, permits the Latin American to get close enough, he will immediately notice that the latter seems much more at ease. **16**

My own studies of space and time have engendered considerable cooperation and interest on the part of friends and colleagues. One case recently reported to me had to do with a group of seven-year-olds in a crowded Sunday-school classroom. The children kept fighting. Without knowing quite what was involved, the teacher had them moved to a larger room. The fighting stopped. It is interesting to speculate as to what would have happened had the children been moved to a smaller room. **17**

The embarrassment about intimacy in space applies also to the matter of addressing people by name. Finding the proper distance in the use of names is even more difficult than in space, because the rules for first-naming are unbelievably complex. As a rule we tend to stay on the "mister" level too long with Latins and some others, but very often we swing into first naming too quickly, which amounts to talking down to them. Whereas in the U.S. we use Mr. with the surname, in Latin America the first and last names are used together and señor (Sr.) is a title. Thus when one says, "My name is Sr. So-and-So," it is interpreted to mean, "I am the Honorable, his Excellency So-and-So." It is no wonder that when we stand away, barricade ourselves behind our desks (usually a reflection of status) and call ourselves mister, our friends to the south wonder about our so-called "good neighbor" policy and think of us as either high-hat or unbelievably rude. Fortunately most North Americans learn some of these things after living in Latin America for a while, but the aversion to being touched and **18** to touching sometimes persists after 15 or more years of residence and even under such conditions as intermarriage.

19   The difference in sense of time is another thing of which we are not aware. An Iranian, for instance, is not taught that it is rude to be late in the same way that we in the U.S. are. In a general way we are conscious of this, but we fail to realize that their time system is structured differently from ours. The different cultures simply place different values on the time units.

20   Thus let us take as a typical case of the North European time system (which has regional variations) the situation in the urban eastern U.S.. A middle-class businessman meeting another of equivalent rank will ordinarily be aware of being two minutes early or late. If he is three minutes late, it will be noted as significant but usually neither will say anything. If four minutes late, he will mutter something by way of apology; at five minutes he will utter a full sentence of apology. In other words, the major unit is a five-minute block. Fifteen minutes is the smallest significant period for all sorts of arrangements and it is used very commonly. A half hour of course is very significant, and if you spend three quarters of an hour or an hour, either the business you transact or the relationship must be important. Normally it is an insult to keep a public figure or a person of significantly higher status than yourself waiting even two or three minutes, though the person of higher position can keep you waiting or even break an appointment.

21   Now among urban Arabs in the Eastern Mediterranean, to take an illustrative case of another time system, the unit that corresponds to our five-minute period is 15 minutes. Thus when an Arab arrives nearly 30 minutes after the set time, by his reckoning he isn't even "10 minutes" late yet (in our time units). Stated differently, the Arab's tardiness will not amount to one significant period (15 minutes in our system). An American normally will wait no longer than 30 minutes (two significant periods) for another person to turn up in the middle of the day. Thereby he often unwittingly insults people in the Middle East who want to be his friends.

22   How long is one expected to stay when making a duty call at a friend's house in the U.S.? While there are regional variations, I have observed that the minimum is very close to 45 minutes, even in the face of pressing commitments elsewhere, such as a roast in

the oven. We may think we can get away in 30 minutes by saying something about only stopping for "a minute," but usually we discover that we don't feel comfortable about leaving until 45 minutes have elapsed. I am referring to afternoon social calls; evening calls last much longer and operate according to a different system. In Arab countries an American paying a duty call at the house of a desert sheik causes consternation if he gets up to leave after half a day. There a duty call lasts three days—the first day to prepare the feast, the second for the feast itself and the third to taper off and say farewell. In the first half day the sheik has barely had time to slaughter the sheep for the feast. The guest's departure would leave the host frustrated.

There is a well-known story of a tribesman who came to 23 Kabul, the capital of Afghanistan, to meet his brother. Failing to find him, he asked the merchants in the market place to tell his brother where he could be found if the brother showed up. A year later the tribesman returned and looked again. It developed that he and his brother had agreed to meet in Kabul but had failed to specify what year! If the Afghan time system were structured similarly to our own, which it apparently is not, the brother would not offer a full sentence of apology until he was five years late.

Informal units of time such as "just a minute," "a while," 24 "later," "a long time," "a spell," "a long, long time," "years" and so on provide us with the culturological equivalent of Evil-Eye Fleegle's "double-whammy" (in *Li'l Abner*). Yet these expressions are not as imprecise as they seem. Any American who has worked in an office with someone else for six months can usually tell within five minutes when that person will be back if he says, "I'll be gone for a while." It is simply a matter of learning from experience the individual's system of time indicators. A reader who is interested in communications theory can fruitfully speculate for a while on the very wonderful way in which culture provides the means whereby the receiver puts back all the redundant material that was stripped from such a message. Spelled out, the message might go somewhat as follows: "I am going downtown to see So-and-So about the Such-and-Such contract, but I don't know what the traffic conditions will be like or how long it will take me to get a place to park nor do I know what shape So-and-So will be in today, but taking all this into account I think I will be out of the office about an hour but don't like to commit myself, so if anyone calls you can say I'm not sure how long I will be; in any event I expect to be back before 4 o'clock."

25   Few of us realize how much we rely on built-in patterns to interpret messages of this sort. An Iranian friend of mine who came to live in the U.S. was hurt and puzzled for the first few years. The new friends he met and liked would say on parting: "Well, I'll see you later." He mournfully complained: "I kept expecting to see them, but the 'later' never came." Strangely enough we ourselves are exasperated when a Mexican can't tell us precisely what he means when he uses the expression *mañana*.

26   The role of the anthropologist in preparing people for service overseas is to open their eyes and sensitize them to the subtle qualities of behavior—tone of voice, gestures, space and time relationships—that so often build up feelings of frustration and hostility in other people with a different culture. Whether we are going to live in a particular foreign country or travel in many, we need a frame of reference that will enable us to observe and learn the significance of differences in manners. Progress is being made in this anthropological study, but it is also showing us how little is known about human behavior.

1955

Distancing the Homeless

Jonathan Kozol

1   It is commonly believed by many journalists and politicians that the homeless of America are, in large part, former patients of large mental hospitals who were deinstitutionalized in the 1970s—the consequence, it is sometimes said, of misguided liberal opinion,

which favored the treatment of such persons in community-based centers. It is argued that this policy, and the subsequent failure of society to build such centers or to provide them in sufficient number, is the primary cause of homelessness in the United States.

Those who work among the homeless do not find that explanation satisfactory. While conceding that a certain number of the homeless are, or have been, mentally unwell, they believe that, in the case of most unsheltered people, the primary reason is economic rather than clinical. The cause of homelessness, they say with disarming logic, is the lack of homes and of income with which to rent or acquire them.

They point to the loss of traditional jobs in industry (2,000,000 every year since 1980) and to the fact that half of those who are laid off end up in work that pays a poverty-level wage. They point to the parallel growth of poverty in families with children, noting that children, who represent one quarter of our population, make up 40 percent of the poor; since 1968, the number of children in poverty has grown by 3,000,000, while welfare benefits to families with children have declined by 35 percent.

And they note, too, that these developments have coincided with a time in which the shortage of low-income housing has intensified as the gentrification of our major cities has accelerated. Half a million units of low-income housing have been lost each year to condominium conversion as well as to arson, demolition, or abandonment. Between 1978 and 1980, median rents climbed 30 percent for people in the lowest income sector, driving many of these families into the streets. After 1980, rents rose at even faster rates. In Boston, between 1982 and 1984, over 80 percent of the housing units renting below $300 disappeared, while the number of units renting above $600 nearly tripled.

Hard numbers, in this instance, would appear to be of greater help than psychiatric labels in telling us why so many people become homeless. Eight million American families now pay half or more of their income for rent or a mortgage. Six million more, unable to pay rent at all, live doubled up with others. At the same time, federal support for low-income housing dropped from $30 billion (1980) to $9 billion (1986). Under Presidents Ford and Carter, 500,000 subsidized private housing units were constructed. By President Reagan's second term, the number had dropped to 25,000. "We're getting out of the housing business, period," said a deputy assistant secretary of the Department of Housing and Urban Development in 1985.

6   One year later, the *Washington Post* reported that the number of homeless families in Washington, D.C., had grown by 500 percent over the previous 12 months. In New York City, the waiting list for public housing now contains 200,000 names. The waiting is 18 years.

7   Why, in the face of these statistics, are we impelled to find a psychiatric explanation for the growth of homelessness in the United States?

8   A misconception, once it is implanted in the popular imagination, is not easy to uproot, particularly when it serves a useful social role. The notion that the homeless are largely psychotics who belong in institutions, rather than victims of displacement at the hands of enterprising realtors, spares us from the need to offer realistic solutions to the fact of deep and widening extremes of wealth and poverty in the United States. It also enables us to tell ourselves that the despair of homeless people bears no intimate connection to the privileged existence we enjoy—when, for example, we rent or purchase one of those restored townhouses that once provided shelter for people now huddled in the street.

9   But there may be another reason to assign labels to the destitute. Terming economic victims "psychotic" or "disordered" helps to place them at a distance. It says that they aren't quite like us— and, more important, that we could not be like them. The plight of homeless families is a nightmare. It may not seem natural to try to banish human beings from our midst, but it is natural to try to banish nightmares from our minds.

10   So the rituals of clinical contamination proceed uninterrupted by the economic facts described above. Research that addresses homelessness as an *injustice* rather than as a medical *misfortune* does not win the funding of foundations. And the research which is funded, defining the narrowed borders of permissible debate, diverts our attention from the antecedent to the secondary cause of homelessness. Thus it is that perfectly ordinary women whom I know in New York City—people whose depression or anxiety is

a realistic consequence of months and even years in crowded shelters or the streets—are interrogated by invasive research scholars in an effort to decode their poverty, to find clinical categories for their despair and terror, to identify the secret failing that lies hidden in their psyche.

Many pregnant women without homes are denied prenatal 11 care because they constantly travel from one shelter to another. Many are anemic. Many are denied essential dietary supplements by recent federal cuts. As a consequence, some of their children do not live to see their second year of life. Do these mothers sometimes show signs of stress? Do they appear disorganized, depressed, disordered? Frequently. They are immobilized by pain, traumatized by fear. So it is no surprise that when researchers enter the scene to ask them how they "feel," the resulting reports tell us that the homeless are emotionally unwell. The reports do not tell us we have *made* these people ill. They do not tell us that illness is a natural response to intolerable conditions. Nor do they tell us of the strength and the resilience that so many of these people still retain despite the miseries they must endure. They set these men and women apart in capsules labeled "personality disorder" or "psychotic," where they no longer threaten our complacence.

I visited Haiti not many years ago, when the Duvalier family 12 was still in power. If an American scholar were to have made a psychological study of the homeless families living in the streets of Port-au-Prince—sleeping amidst rotten garbage, bathing in open sewers—and if he were to return to the United States to tell us that the reasons for their destitution were "behavioral problems" or "a lack of mental health," we would be properly suspicious. Knowledgeable Haitians would not merely be suspicious. They would be enraged. Even to initiate such research when economic and political explanations present themselves so starkly would appear grotesque. It is no less so in the United States.

One of the more influential studies of this nature was carried 13 out in 1985 by Ellen Bassuk, a psychiatrist at Harvard University. Drawing upon interviews with eight homeless parents, Dr. Bassuk contends, according to the *Boston Globe*, that "90 percent [of these people] have problems other than housing and poverty that are so acute they would be unable to live successfully on their own." She also precludes the possibility that illness, where it does exist, may be provoked by destitution. "Our data," she writes, "suggest that mental illness tends to precede homelessness." She concedes that living in the streets can make a homeless person's mental illness worse; but she insists upon the fact of prior illness.

14   The executive director of the Massachusetts Commission on Children and Youth believes that Dr. Bassuk's estimate is far too high. The staff of Massachusetts Human Services Secretary Phillip Johnston believes the appropriate number is closer to 10 percent.

15   In defending her research, Bassuk challenges such critics by claiming that they do not have data to refute her. This may be true. Advocates for the homeless do not receive funds to defend the sanity of the people they represent. In placing the burden of proof upon them, Dr. Bassuk has created an extraordinary dialectic: How does one prove that people aren't unwell? What homeless mother would consent to enter a procedure that might "prove" her mental health? What overburdened shelter operator would divert scarce funds to such an exercise? It is an unnatural, offensive, and dehumanizing challenge.

16   Dr. Bassuk's work, however, isn't the issue I want to raise here; the issue is the use or misuse of that work by critics of the poor. For example, in a widely syndicated essay published in 1986, the newspaper columnist Charles Krauthammer argued that the homeless are essentially a deranged segment of the population and that we must find the "political will" to isolate them from society. We must do this, he said, "whether they like it or not." Arguing even against the marginal benefits of homeless shelters, Krauthammer wrote: "There is a better alternative, however, though no one dares speak its name." Krauthammer dares: That better alternative, he said, is "asylum."

17   One of Mr. Krauthammer's colleagues at the *Washington Post*, the columnist George Will, perceives the homeless as a threat to public cleanliness and argues that they ought to be consigned to places where we need not see them. "It is," he says, "simply a matter of public hygiene" to put them out of sight. Another journalist, Charles Murray, writing from the vantage point of a social Darwinist, recommends the restoration of the almshouses of the 1800s. "Granted Dickensian horror stories about almshouses," he begins, there were nonetheless "good almshouses"; he proposes

"a good correctional 'halfway house'" as a proper shelter for a mother and child with no means of self-support.

In the face of such declarations, the voices of those who work 18 with and know the poor are harder to hear.

Manhattan Borough President David Dinkins made the fol- 19 lowing observation on the basis of a study commissioned in 1986: "No facts support the belief that addiction or behavioral problems occur with more frequency in the homeless family population than in a similar socioeconomic population. Homeless families are not demographically different from other public assistance families when they enter the shelter system . . . Family homelessness is typically a housing and income problem: The unavailability of affordable housing and the inadequacy of public assistance income."

In a "hypothetical world," write James Wright and Julie Lam 20 of the University of Massachusetts, "where there were no alcoholics, no drug addicts, no mentally ill, no deinstitutionalization, . . . indeed, no personal social pathologies at all, there would still be a formidable homelessness problem, simply because at this stage in American history, there is not enough low-income housing" to accommodate the poor.

New York State's respected commissioner of social services, 21 Cesar Perales, makes the point in fewer words: "Homelessness is less and less a result of personal failure, and more and more is caused by larger forces. There is no longer affordable housing in New York City for people of poor and modest means."

Even the words of medical practitioners who care for homeless 22 people have been curiously ignored. A study published by the Massachusetts Medical Society, for instance, has noted that the most frequent illnesses among a sample of the homeless population, after alcohol and drug use, are trauma (31 percent), upper respiratory disorders (28 percent), limb disorders (19 percent), mental illness (16 percent), skin diseases (15 percent), hypertension (14 percent), and neurological illnesses (12 percent). (Excluded from this tabulation are lead poisoning, malnutrition, acute diarrhea, and other illnesses especially common among homeless infants and small children.) Why, we may ask, of all these calamities, does mental illness command so much political and press attention? The answer may be that the label of mental illness places the destitute outside the sphere of ordinary life. It personalizes an anguish that is public in its genesis; it individualizes a misery that is both general in cause and general in application.

23   The rate of tuberculosis among the homeless is believed to be 10 times that of the general population. Asthma, I have learned in countless interviews, is one of the most common causes of discomfort in the shelters. Compulsive smoking, exacerbated by the crowding and the tension, is more common in the shelters than in any place that I have visited except prison. Infected and untreated sores, scabies, diarrhea, poorly set limbs, protruding elbows, awkwardly distorted wrists, bleeding gums, impacted teeth, and other untreated dental problems are so common among children in the shelters that one rapidly forgets their presence. Hunger and emaciation are everywhere. Children as well as adults can bring to mind the photographs of people found in camps for refugees of war in 1945. But these miseries bear no stigma, and mental illness does. It conveys a stigma in the Soviet Union. It conveys a stigma in the United States. In both nations the label is used, whether as a matter of deliberate policy or not, to isolate and treat as special cases those who, by deed or word or sheer presence, represent a threat to national complacence. The two situations are obviously not identical, but they are enough alike to give Americans reason for concern.

24   Last summer, some 28,000 homeless people were afforded shelter by the city of New York. Of this number, 12,000 were children and 6,000 were parents living together in families. The average child was six years old, the average parent 27. A typical homeless family included a mother with two or three children, but in about one-fifth of these families two parents were present. Roughly 10,000 single persons, then, made up the remainder of the population of the city's shelters.

25   These proportions vary somewhat from one area of the nation to another. In all areas, however, families are the fastest-growing sector of the homeless population, and in the Northeast they are by far the largest sector already. In Massachusetts, three-fourths of the homeless now are families with children; in certain parts of Massachusetts—Attleboro and Northampton, for example—the proportion reaches 90 percent. Two-thirds of the homeless children studied recently in Boston were less than five years old.

Of an estimated two to three million homeless people nation- 26
wide, about 500,000 are dependent children, according to Robert
Hayes, counsel to the National Coalition for the Homeless. Including their parents, at least 750,000 homeless people in America
are family members.

What is to be made, then, of the supposition that the homeless 27
are primarily the former residents of mental hospitals, persons
who were carelessly released during the 1970s? Many of them are,
to be sure. Among the older men and women in the streets and
shelters, as many as one-third (some believe as many as one-half)
may be chronically disturbed, and a number of these people were
deinstitutionalized during the 1970s. But in a city like New York,
where nearly half the homeless are small children with an average
age of six, to operate on the basis of such a supposition makes no
sense. Their parents, with an average age of 27, are not likely to
have been hospitalized in the 1970s, either.

Nor is it easy to assume, as was once the case, that single 28
men—those who come closer to fitting the stereotype of the homeless vagrant, the drifting alcoholic of an earlier age—are the former residents of mental hospitals. The age of homeless men has
dropped in recent years; many of them are only 21 to 28 years old.
Fifty percent of homeless men in New York City shelters in 1984
were there for the first time. Most had previously had homes and
jobs. Many had never before needed public aid.

A frequently cited set of figures tells us that in 1955, the aver- 29
age daily census of nonfederal psychiatric institutions was
677,000, and that by 1984, the number had dropped to 151,000.
Subtract the second number from the first, conventional logic tells
us, and we have an explanation for the homelessness of half a million people. A closer look at the same number offers us a different
lesson.

The sharpest decline in the average daily census of these insti- 30
tutions occurred prior to 1978, and the largest part of that decline,
in fact, appeared at least a decade earlier. From 677,000 in 1955, the
census dropped to 378,000 in 1972. The 1974 census was 307,000. In
1976 it was 230,000; in 1977 it was 211,000; and in 1978 it was
190,000. In no year since 1978 has the average daily census dropped
by more than 9,000 persons, and in the six-year period from 1978

to 1984, the total decline was 39,000 persons. Compared with a decline of 300,000 from 1955 to 1972, and of nearly 200,000 more from 1972 to 1978, the number is small. But the years since 1980 are the period in which the present homeless crisis surfaced. Only since 1983 have homeless individuals overflowed the shelters.

31   If the large numbers of the homeless lived in hospitals before they reappeared in subway stations and in public shelters, we need to ask where they were and what they had been doing from 1972 to 1980. Were they living under bridges? Were they waiting out the decade in the basements of deserted buildings?

32   No. The bulk of those who had been psychiatric patients and were released from hospitals during the 1960s and early 1970s had been living in the meantime in low-income housing, many in skid-row hotels or boarding houses. Such housing—commonly known as SRO (single-room occupancy) units—was drastically diminished by the gentrification of our cities that began in 1970. Almost 50 percent of SRO housing was replaced by luxury apartments or by office buildings between 1970 and 1980, and the remaining units have been disappearing at even faster rates. As recently as 1986, after New York City had issued a prohibition against conversion of such housing, a well-known developer hired a demolition team to destroy a building in Times Square that had previously been home to indigent people. The demolition took place in the middle of the night. In order to avoid imprisonment, the developer was allowed to make a philanthropic gift to homeless people as a token of atonement. This incident, bizarre as it appears, reminds us that the profit motive for displacement of the poor is very great in every major city. It also indicates a more realistic explanation for the growth of homelessness during the 1980s.

33   Even for those persons who are ill and were deinstitutionalized during the decades before 1980, the precipitating cause of homelessness in 1987 is not illness but loss of housing. SRO housing, unattractive as it may have been, offered low-cost sanctuaries for the homeless, providing a degree of safety and mutual support for those who lived within them. They were a demeaning version of the community health centers that society had promised; they were the de facto "halfway houses" of the 1970s. For these people

too, then—at most half of the homeless single persons in America—the cause of homelessness is lack of housing.

A writer in the *New York Times* describes a homeless woman 34 standing on a traffic island in Manhattan. "She was evicted from her small room in the hotel just across the street," and she is determined to get revenge. Until she does, "nothing will move her from that spot. . . . Her argumentativeness and her angry fixation on revenge, along with the apparent absence of hallucinations, mark her as a paranoid." Most physicians, I imagine, would be more reserved in passing judgment with so little evidence, but this author makes his diagnosis without hesitation. "The paranoids of the street," he says, "are among the most difficult to help."

Perhaps so. But does it depend on who is offering the help? Is 35 anyone offering to help this woman get back her home? Is it crazy to seek vengeance for being thrown into the street? The absence of anger, some psychiatrists believe, might indicate much greater illness.

The same observer sees additional symptoms of pathology 36 ("negative symptoms," he calls them) in the fact that many homeless persons demonstrate a "gross deterioration in their personal hygiene" and grooming, leading to "indifference" and "apathy." Having just identified one woman as unhealthy because she is so far from being "indifferent" as to seek revenge, he now sees apathy as evidence of illness; so consistency is not what we are looking for in this account. But how much less indifferent might the homeless be if those who decide their fate were less indifferent themselves? How might their grooming and hygiene be improved if they were permitted access to a public toilet?

In New York City, as in many cities, homeless people are de- 37 nied the right to wash in public bathrooms, to store their few belongings in a public locker, or, in certain cases, to make use of public toilets altogether. Shaving, cleaning of clothes, and other forms of hygiene are prohibited in the men's room of Grand Central Station. The terminal's three hundred lockers, used in former times by homeless people to secure their goods, were removed in 1986 as "a threat to public safety," according to a study made by the New York City Council.

38   At 1:30 every morning, homeless people are ejected from the station. Many once attempted to take refuge on the ramp that leads to Forty-Second Street because it was protected from the street by wooden doors and thus provided some degree of warmth. But the station management responded to this challenge in two ways. The ramp was mopped with a strong mixture of ammonia to produce a noxious smell, and when the people sleeping there brought cardboard boxes and newspapers to protect them from the fumes, the entrance doors were chained wide open. Temperatures dropped some nights to 10 degrees. Having driven these people to the streets, city officials subsequently determined that their willingness to risk exposure to cold weather could be taken as further evidence of mental illness.

39   At Pennsylvania Station in New York, homeless women are denied the use of toilets. Amtrak police come by and herd them off each hour on the hour. In June 1985, Amtrak officials issued this directive to police: "It is the policy of Amtrak to not allow the homeless and undesirables to remain. . . . Officers are encouraged to eject all undesirables. . . . Now is the time to train and educate them that their presence will not be tolerated as cold weather sets in." In an internal memo, according to CBS, an Amtrak official asked flatly: "Can't we get rid of this trash?"

40   I have spent many nights in conversation with the women who are huddled in the corridors and near the doorway of the public toilets in Penn Station. Many are young. Most are cogent. Few are dressed in the familiar rags suggested by the term *bag ladies*. Unable to bathe or use the toilets in the station, almost all are in conditions of intolerable physical distress. The sight of clusters of police officers, mostly male, guarding a toilet from use by homeless women speaks volumes about the public conscience of New York.

41   Where do these women defecate? How do they bathe? What will we do when, in her physical distress, a woman finally disrobes in public and begins to urinate right on the floor? "Gross deterioration," someone will call it, evidence of mental illness. In the course of an impromptu survey in the streets last September, Mayor Koch observed a homeless woman who had soiled her own clothes. Not only was the woman crazy, said the mayor, but those

who differed with him on his diagnosis must be crazy, too. "I am the number one social worker in this town—with sanity," said he.

It may be that this woman was psychotic, but the mayor's 42 comment says a great deal more about his sense of revulsion and the moral climate of a decade in which words like these may be applauded than about her mental state.

A young man who had lost his job, then his family, then his 43 home, all in the summer of 1986, spoke with me for several hours in Grand Central Station on the weekend following Thanksgiving. "A year ago," he said, "I never thought that somebody like me would end up in a shelter. Nothing you've ever undergone prepares you. You walk into the place [a shelter on the Bowery]—the smell of sweat and urine hits you like a wall. Unwashed bodies and the look of absolute despair on many, many faces there would make you think you were in Dante's Hell. . . . What you fear is that you will be here forever. You do not know if it is ever going to end. You think to yourself: It is a dream and I will awake. Sometimes I think: It's an experiment. They are watching you to find out how much you can take. . . . I was a pretty stable man. Now I tremble when I meet somebody in the ordinary world. I'm trembling right now. . . . For me, the loss of work and loss of wife had left me rocking. Then the welfare regulations hit me. I began to feel that I would be reduced to trash. . . . Half the people that I know are suffering from chest infections and sleep deprivation. The lack of sleep leaves you debilitated, shaky. You exaggerate your fears. If a psychiatrist came along he'd say that I was crazy. But I was an ordinary man. There was nothing wrong with me. I lost my kids. I lost my home. Now would you say that I was crazy if I told you I was feeling sad?"

"If the plight of homeless adults is the shame of America," 44 writes Fred Hechinger in the *New York Times*, "the lives of homeless children are the nation's crime."

In November 1984, a fact already known to advocates for the 45 homeless was given brief attention by the press. Homeless families, the *New York Times* reported, "mostly mothers and young children, have been sleeping on chairs, counters, and floors of the city's emergency welfare offices." Reacting to such reports, the mayor declared: "The woman is sitting on a chair or on a floor. It is not because we didn't offer her a bed. We provide a shelter for every single person who knocks on our door." On the same day, however, the city reported that in the previous 11 weeks it had been unable to give shelter to 153 families, and in the subsequent year, 1985, the city later reported that about 2,000 children slept in welfare offices because of lack of shelter space.

46   Some 800 homeless infants in New York City, reported the National Coalition for the Homeless, "routinely go without sufficient food, cribs, health care, and diapers." The lives of these children "are put at risk," while "high-risk pregnant women" are repeatedly forced to sleep in unsafe "barracks shelters" or welfare offices called Emergency Assistance Units (EAUs). "Coalition monitors, making sporadic random checks, found eight women in their *ninth* month of pregnancy sleeping in EAUs. . . . Two women denied shelter began having labor contractions at the EAU." In one instance, the Legal Aid Society was forced to go to court after a woman lost her child by miscarriage while lying on the floor of a communal bathroom in a shelter which the courts had already declared unfit to house pregnant women.

47   The coalition also reported numerous cases in which homeless mothers were obliged to choose between purchasing food or diapers for their infants. Federal guidelines issued in 1986 deepened the nutrition crisis faced by mothers in the welfare shelters by counting the high rent paid to the owners of the buildings as a part of family income, rendering their residents ineligible for food stamps. Families I interviewed who had received as much as $150 in food stamps monthly in June 1986 were cut back to $33 before Christmas.

48   "Now you're hearing all kinds of horror stories," said President Reagan, "about the people that are going to be thrown out in the snow to hunger and [to] die of cold and so forth. . . . We haven't cut a single budget." But in the four years leading up to 1985, according to the *New Republic*, Aid to Families with Dependent Children had been cut by $4.8 billion, child nutrition programs by $5.2 billion, food stamps by $6.8 billion. The federal government's authority to help low-income families with housing assistance was cut from $30 billion to $11 billion in Reagan's first term. In his fiscal 1986 budget, the president proposed to cut that by an additional 95 percent.

"If even one American child is forced to go to bed hungry at 49 night," the president said on another occasion, "that is a national tragedy. We are too generous a people to allow this." But in the years since the president spoke these words, thousands of poor children in New York alone have gone to bed too sick to sleep and far too weak to rise the next morning to attend a public school. Thousands more have been unable to attend school at all because their homeless status compels them to move repeatedly from one temporary shelter to another. Even in the affluent suburbs outside New York City, hundreds of homeless children are obliged to ride as far as 60 miles twice a day in order to obtain an education in the public schools to which they were originally assigned before their families were displaced. Many of these children get to school too late to eat their breakfast; others are denied lunch at school because of federal cuts in feeding programs.

Many homeless children die—and others suffer brain dam- 50 age—as a direct consequence of federal cutbacks in prenatal programs, maternal nutrition, and other feeding programs. The parents of one such child shared with me the story of the year in which their child was delivered, lived, and died. The child, weighing just over four pounds at birth, grew deaf and blind soon after, and for these reasons had to stay in the hospital for several months. When he was released on Christmas Eve of 1984, his mother and father had no home. He lived with his parents in the shelters, subways, streets, and welfare offices of New York City for four winter months, and was readmitted to the hospital in time to die in May 1985.

When we met and spoke the following year, the father told me 51 that his wife had contemplated and even attempted suicide after the child's death, while he had entertained the thought of blowing up the welfare offices of New York City. I would tell him that to do so would be illegal and unwise. I would never tell him it was crazy.

"No one will be turned away," says the mayor of New York 52 City, as hundreds of young mothers with their infants are turned from the doors of shelters season after season. That may sound to some like denial of reality. "Now you're hearing all these stories," says the president of the United States as he denies that anyone is cold or hungry or unhoused. On another occasion he says that the

unsheltered "are homeless, you might say, by choice." That
sounds every bit as self-deceiving.

53   The woman standing on the traffic island screaming for revenge until her room has been restored to her sounds relatively
healthy by comparison. If 3,000,000 homeless people did the same,
and all at the same time, we might finally be forced to listen.

1988

On a Greek Holiday

Alice Bloom

1   The only interesting question on a trip for me is—what sustains
life elsewhere? How deep does it go? Can one see it? This hope,
this anticipation, is forcibly blocked. Henry Miller, in 193—, stood
in Epidarus, alone, in a "weird solitude," and felt the "great heart
of the world beat." We stand at Epidaurus with several thousand
others, some of whom are being called "my chickens" by their tour
guide who calls herself "your mother hen," whose counterpart,
this time at Delphi, explains several times that what is being
looked at is the "belly button of the world, okay? The Greeks
thought, this is the belly button of the world, okay?" "These stones
all look alike to me," someone grumbles. There is no help for it;
we're there with guidebooks ourselves; but this fact—tourism is
big business—and others, throw us back, unwilling, into contemplation of our own dull home-soul, our dull bodily comforts, our
own dull dwindling purse, our own dull resentments; because the
other—in this case, Greece—is either rapidly disappearing or else,
self-protective, is retreating so far it has disappeared. You can get
there, but you can't get at it.

2   For instance, a study of travel posters and brochures, which in
the process of setting dates and buying tickets always precedes a
trip, shows us, by projection into these pictured, toothy, tourist
bodies, having some gorgeous piece of ingestion: The yellow

beach, the mossy blue ruin, a dinner table laden with food and red wine of the region, dancing, skiing, golfing, shopping, waving to roadside natives as our rented car sails by, as though we only go to play, as though all we do here at home is work, as though, for two or four weeks abroad, we seek regression.

Also in the posters, but as part of the landscape, there are the 3 natives—whether Spanish, Greek, Irish, etc.—costumed as attractions, performing in bouzouki or bag-pipe bands, or doing some picturesque and nonindustrial piece of work such as fishing, weaving, selling colorful cheap goods in open-air markets, herding sheep or goats. The journey promised by the posters and brochures is a trip into everyone's imaginary past: One's own, drained of the normal childhood content of fear, death, space, hurt, abandonment, perplexity, and so forth, now presented as the salesmen think we think it should have been: One in which we only ate, slept, and played in the eternal sun under the doting care of benevolent elders.

And we are shown the benevolent elders, the imaginary na- 4 tives who also, for a handsome fee, exist now, in the present of the trip we are about to take. ("Take" is probably a more telling verb here than we think.) They exist in a past where they are pictured having grown cheerfully old and wise doing only harmless, enjoyable, preindustrial, clean, self-employed, open-air work, in pink crinkled cheeks, merry eyes, and wonderful quaint clothes, with baskets, nets, toyshaped boats, flower boxes, cottages, sheep crooks, country roads, whitewashed walls, tea shop signs, and other paraphernalia of the pastoral wish. I have never seen a travel poster showing natives of the country enjoying their own food or beaches or ski-jumps or hotel balconies; nor have I ever seen a travel poster showing the natives working the nightshift in the Citroën factory, either.

The natives in the posters (are they Swiss, Mexican, Chilean, 5 Turkish models?) are happy parent figures, or character dolls, and their faces, like the faces of the good parents we are supposed to have dreamed, show them pleased with their own lot, busy but not too busy with a job that they obviously like, content with each other, and warmly indulgent of our need to play, to be fed good, clean food on time, and to be tucked into a nice bed at the end of our little day. They are the childhood people that also existed in early grammar school readers, and nowhere else: Adults in your neighborhood, in the identifiable costumes of their humble tasks, transitional-object people, smiling milkman, friendly aproned store owner in his small friendly store, happy mailman happy to bring your happy mail, happy mommy, icons who make up a six-year-old's school-enforced dream town, who enjoy doing their nonindustrial, unmysterious tasks: Mail, milk, red apple, cooky, just for you, so you can learn to decipher: See, Jip, see.

6   A travel remark I have always savored came from someone surprised in love for a place, just returned from a month in the Far East (no longer tagged "the mysterious," I've noticed), and who was explaining this trip at a party. She said, "I just loved Japan. It was so authentic and Oriental." Few people would go quite so naked as that, but the charm of her feelings seemed just right. Perhaps she had expected Tokyo to be more or less a larger version of the Japanese Shop in the Tokyo Airport. It is somewhat surprising that she found it to be anything much more.

7   One of the hushed-tone moral superiority stories, the aren't-we-advanced stories told by those lucky enough to travel in Soviet Russia, has to do with that government's iron management of the trip. There are people who can't be met, buildings that can't be entered, upper story windows that can't be photographed, streets that can't be strolled, districts that can't be crossed, cities in which it is impossible to spend the night, and so on. However, our notions of who we are and what comforts we demand and what conditions we'll endure, plus any country's understandably garbled versions of who we are, what we want, and what we'll pay for, are far more rigid than the strictures of any politburo because such strictures don't say "This is you, this is what you must want," but "This is what you can't, under any circumstances, do." That, though it inhibits movement, and no doubt in some cases prevents a gathering of or understanding of some crucial or desired bit of information, has at least the large virtue of defining the tourist as potentially dangerous. What we meet most of the time, here and abroad, is a definition of ourselves as harmless, spoiled babies, of low endurance and little information, minimal curiosity, frozen in infancy, frozen in longing, terrified for our next square meal and

clean bed, and whose only potential danger is that we might refuse to be separated from our money.

Suppose, for a moment, that tourism—the largest "industry" 8 in Greece (it employs, even more than shipping, the most people)—were also the largest industry in America. Not just in Manhattan or Washington, D.C., or Disneyland or Disney World or at the Grand Canyon or Niagara Falls, but in every motel, hotel, restaurant, in every McDonald's and Colonel Sanders and Howard Johnson's and Mom & Pop's, in every bar and neighborhood hangout, truck stop, gas station, pharmacy, department store, museum, church, historical site, battleground, in every taxi, bus, subway, train, plane, in every public building, in post offices and banks and public bathrooms, on every street in every city, town, village and hamlet from West Jonesport, Maine, to Centralia, Illinois, to Parachute, Colorado, and every stop in between and beyond, just as it is in Greece: Tourists.

Suppose that every other business establishment across the 9 country therefore found it in their best interest to become a souvenir shop, selling cheap, mass-produced "gifts" for the tourists to take back home that, back home, would announce that they had visited America. What images would we mass produce for them? Millions of little bronzed Liberty Bells? Tepees? St. Louis Arches? Streetcars named "Desire"? Statues of Babe Ruth? of Liberty? of Daniel Boone? In Greece we saw miniature bottles of ouzo encased in tiny plastic replicas of the temple of Athena Nike. Could we do something so clever, and immediately recognizable, with miniatures of bourbon? Encase them in tiny plastic Washington Monuments? Lincoln Memorials? Would we feel misrepresented?

Third, suppose that a sizable portion of these tourists wanting 10 gifts, toilets, rooms, baths, meals, dollars, film, drinks, stamps, directions, are Greek; or else, let us suppose that we assumed, that whether actually Greek or not, wherever they come from they speak Greek as a second language. Assume, therefore, that our map and traffic and road signs, postings of instruction and information, advertisements, timetables, directions—"stop," "go," "hot," "cold," "men," "women," "open," "closed," "yes," "no,"— to name a few rudiments of life, plus all the menus in all those sandwich counters, truck stops, fast-food outlets, lunch rooms, and so forth, had to be in Greek as well as in English. We have never been, so far, an occupied country, whether by forces enemy or not. Undoubtedly, if we were, as an ongoing fact of our "in-season" summer months, we Americans, having to offer our multitudinous wares in Greek, would come up with items as hilarious as those we collected from the English side of Greek menus: Baygon and egs. Xamberger steake. Veat. Orange juise. Rost beef. Shrimp carry. Potoes, Spaggeti. Morcoroni. And our favorite, Fried Smooth Hound. (This turned out to be a harmless local fish, much to the disappointment of our children, born surrealists.)

11   Suppose that we had to post Bar Harbor, Plum Island, Chincoteague, Key West, Bay St. Louis, Galveston, Big Sur and Seattle beaches with "No Nakedness Allowed" signs, but that the Greeks and other tourists, freed from the cocoons of air-conditioned tour buses, armed with sun-oil in every degree of protection, rushed beachwards past the signs and stripped to their altogether, anyway? Would our police sit quietly in the shade and drink with other men and turn, literally, their khaki-clad rumps to the beach, as did the Greek police?

12   And food. Suppose we had to contrive to feed them, these hungry hordes? They will come here, as we go there, entrenched in their habits and encumbered with fears of being cheated, fears of indigestion, of recurrent allergies, of breaking their diets, of catching American trots, of being poisoned by our water, fattened by our grease and starch, put off by our feeding schedules, sickened by something weird or local. Suppose we decided, out of some semiconscious, unorganized, but national canniness, that what these tourists really want is our cobbled version of their national foods. Whom will we please: The English who want their teas at four, or the Italians who want supper at nine at night? Or both? And what will we cook and serve, and how will we spell it?

13   Or suppose they want to eat "American" food. What tastes like us? What flavors contain our typicality, our history, our heroes, our dirt, our speeches, our poets, our battles, our national shames? The hot dog? Corn on the cob? I have eaten, barring picnics and occasional abstention, probably about 130 meals in Greece. And Greek food, I feel somewhat qualified to say, contains their history, and tastes of sorrow and triumph, of olive oil and

blood, in about equal amounts. It is the most astounding and the most boring food that I, an eater, have ever eaten.

Greek food is tragic. Why? Because each bite is a chomp into 14 history, our history. Why? Because this lunch—small fish, cheese, olives, wine, bread—exactly this lunch, and tomorrow's lunch— fish, cheese, olives, wine, bread—has been eaten since the time of the glory that will someday be called Greece, the glory that existed for a moment, the glory that Greece was, and the glory that mankind—for Greece is that, not Greek, but mankind—might yet be. Each bite is archaeological, into fine layers of millennia: Fish, oil, cheese, wine, bread—in the partaking we join, on the back of the tongue, Amazon forces and single crazy saints, mythical men who married their mythical mothers, and men, and mothers, who today and tomorrow only dream of it.

One uses a big word like "timeless" with caution, if at all. But 15 there is nothing timely about two things in Greece; therefore it is not rhetorical to claim that, in Greece, the quality of the heat of the sun on the skin and the quality of the food in the mouth are perhaps as close as we can come to the taste of "timelessness." Along with the oldest human question—how can we make God happy?—this sun and this food are among the most ancient sensations recorded.

Under this summer sun every meal, beginning with breakfast, 16 is eaten in 100 degrees of heat and hotter—115, 120—by afternoon. The meal, any one of them, is composed of food that grows best in this climate and yet is entirely unsuited to it as daily refreshment. No one could possibly, certainly not a tourist, need this oil-soaked food for fuel in mid-July. It tastes and feels, though, like fuel: Heavy, shiny, slow-moving food, purple, brown, red—tomatoes, eggplants, fish, lamb, olives, black wine, blinding white cheese, much bread. We eat this three times a day; three times a day the tourists eat it and the Greeks eat it. Everyone seems to look forward to the next meal, and all around our table, where we eat again with relish, are others eating with relish, sometimes even with a look of reprieve and relief. And there is no escape from it. Who would risk whatever "shrimp carry" might be? There is no ordering some- thing else—a salad of lettuce for a change, or a thin chicken sand- wich. There is nothing but this food with its taste and texture of an- cient days, of old crimes, forbidden loves, of something tinny and resigned, something of both gluttony and renunciation.

17   In addition to being a tragic cuisine, a sacramental cuisine, it
is also practical, cheap, crude, and uninventive. The raw materials
are without equal: Eggplants hang with the burnish of Dutch interiors; the fish still flap as they are headed oilwards; the lamb
chop's mother befouls the yard next to your table; fruit so perfect,
so total, that the scent of a single peach in a paper bag perfumes
the whole room overnight and brings tears of love of God to the
eyes. On a walk into the hills, meadows of thyme and mint and
basil are idly crushed under heel. What happens to all this in the
pot is a miracle of transformation, of negligence or brutality; or
possibly, stubborn evidence of some otherwise lost political
knowledge of what draws out the best, most noble, and most
beautiful in the masses.

18   For the food is destroyed, each meal, in the process from vine
or net or garden to violent table. Its facts are these: It has always
been eaten thus, with the exception of the late-coming tomato. It
is—lamb, eggplant, olive, fish, white cheese—even now, perfectly
indigenous. It is plain cooking. It is cooked for hours, all day; oil
is poured on without restraint, discretion, or mercy. Every morsel
is the same temperature and consistency by the time it reaches the
palate. In a profound way, it is stupid food, overfeeding the flesh
while tasting as though one should renounce the flesh forever.

19   We did not, to be fair, eat in a single Greek home. However, we
were careful to eat where the Greeks ate, and the Greeks eat out—
in family groups, starched, ironed, slicked-down heads, whited
summer shoes, strictly disciplined children; or in tense, dark
groups of greedy, hasty men; which is how, as families or as men,
the Greeks travel through the day. From the second-story, open-
air, Greek-family-filled restaurant where we ate most of our meals
while on the island, we could, if we had a table near the edge,
throw our bread scraps, if we had any left over, straight down into
the blue-green sea for the melon and dove-colored fish to mouth;
and we could watch the evening sky turn from the day's bleached-
out white to a pale English blue, then to lime-green streaked with
apricot, and finally, with the fall of night, to a grape-purple that
rose, in that instant, up from the sea.

1983

Cause and Effect

8

How Do You Know It's Good?

Marya Mannes

Suppose there were no critics to tell us how to react to a picture, a play, or a new composition of music. Suppose we wandered innocent as the dawn into an art·exhibition of unsigned paintings. By what standards, by what values would we decide whether they were good or bad, talented or untalented, successes or failures? How can we ever know that what we think is right?

For the last fifteen or twenty years the fashion in criticism or appreciation of the arts has been to deny the existence of any valid criteria and to make the words "good" or "bad" irrelevant, immaterial, and inapplicable. There is no such thing, we are told, as a set of standards, first acquired through experience and knowledge and later imposed on the subject under discussion. This has been a popular approach, for it relieves the critic of the responsibility of judgment and the public of the necessity of knowledge. It pleases those resentful of disciplines, it flatters the empty-minded by calling them open-minded, it comforts the confused. Under the banner of democracy and the kind of equality which our forefathers did *not* mean, it says, in effect, "Who are you to tell us what *is* good or bad?" This is the same cry used so long and so effectively by the producers of mass media who insist that it is the public, not they, who decides what it wants to hear and see, and that for a critic to say that *this* program is bad and *this* program is good is purely a reflection of personal taste. Nobody recently has expressed this philosophy

279

more succinctly than Dr. Frank Stanton, the highly intelligent president of CBS television. At a hearing before the Federal Communications Commission, this phrase escaped him under questioning: "One man's mediocrity is another man's good program."

3   There is no better way of saying "No values are absolute." There is another important aspect to this philosophy of *laissez faire:* It is the fear, in all observers of all forms of art, of guessing wrong. This fear is well come by, for who has not heard of the contemporary outcries against artists who later were called great? Every age has its arbiters who do not grow with their times, who cannot tell evolution from revolution or the difference between frivolous faddism, amateurish experimentation, and profound and necessary change. Who wants to be caught *flagrante delicto* with an error of judgment as serious as this? It is far safer, and certainly easier, to look at a picture or a play or a poem and to say "This is hard to understand, but it may be good," or simply to welcome it as a new form. The word "new"—in our country especially—has magical connotations. What is new must be good; what is old is probably bad. And if a critic can describe the new in language that nobody can understand, he's safer still. If he has mastered the art of saying nothing with exquisite complexity, nobody can quote him later as saying anything.

4   But all these, I maintain, are forms of abdication from the responsibility of judgment. In creating, the artist commits himself; in appreciating, you have a commitment of your own. For after all, it is the audience which makes the arts. A climate of appreciation is essential to its flowering, and the higher the expectations of the public, the better the performance of the artist. Conversely, only a public ill-served by its critics could have accepted as art and as literature so much in these last years that has been neither. If anything goes, everything goes; and at the bottom of the junkpile lie the discarded standards too.

5   But what are these standards? How do you get them? How do you know they're the right ones? How can you make a clear pattern out of so many intangibles, including that greatest one, the very private I?

6   Well for one thing, it's fairly obvious that the more you read and see and hear, the more equipped you'll be to practice that art

of association which is at the basis of all understanding and judgment. The more you live and the more you look, the more aware you are of a consistent pattern—as universal as the stars, as the tides, as breathing, as night and day—underlying everything. I would call this pattern and this rhythm an order. Not order—*an* order. Within it exists an incredible diversity of forms. Without it lies chaos—the wild cells of destruction—sickness. It is in the end up to you to distinguish between the diversity that is health and the chaos that is sickness, and you can't do this without a process of association that can link a bar of Mozart with the corner of a Vermeer painting, or a Stravinsky score with a Picasso abstraction; or that can relate an aggressive act with a Franz Kline painting and a fit of coughing with a John Cage composition.

There is no accident in the fact that certain expressions of art 7 live for all time and that others die with the moment, and although you may not always define the reasons, you can ask the questions. What does an artist say that is timeless; how does he say it? How much is fashion, how much is merely reflection? Why is Sir Walter Scott so hard to read now, and Jane Austen not? Why is baroque right for one age and too effulgent for another?

Can a standard of craftsmanship apply to art of all ages, or 8 does each have its own, and different, definitions? You may have been aware, inadvertently, that craftsmanship has become a dirty word these years because, again, it implies standards—something done well or done badly. The result of this convenient avoidance is a plenitude of actors who can't project their voices, singers who can't phrase their songs, poets who can't communicate emotion, and writers who have no vocabulary—not to speak of painters who can't draw. The dogma now is that craftsmanship gets in the way of expression. You can do better if you don't know how you do it, let alone *what* you're doing.

I think it is time you helped reverse this trend by trying to re- 9 discover craft: The command of the chosen instrument, whether it is a brush, a word, or a voice. When you begin to detect the difference between freedom and sloppiness, between serious experimentation and egotherapy, between skill and slickness, between strength and violence, you are on your way to separating the sheep from the goats, a form of segregation denied us for quite a while. All you need to restore it is a small bundle of standards and a Geiger counter that detects fraud, and we might begin our tour of the arts in an area where both are urgently needed: Contemporary painting.

10   I don't know what's worse: To have to look at acres of bad art to find the little good, or to read what the critics say about it all. In no other field of expression has so much double-talk flourished, so much confusion prevailed, and so much nonsense been circulated: Further evidence of the close interdependence between the arts and the critical climate they inhabit. It will be my pleasure to share with you some of this double-talk so typical of our times.

11   Item one: Preface for a catalogue of an abstract painter:

12   "Time-bound meditation experiencing a life; sincere with plastic piety at the threshold of hallowed arcana; a striving for pure ideation giving shape to inner drive; formalized patterns where neural balances reach a fiction." End of quote. Know what this artist paints like now?

13   Item two: A review in the *Art News:*

14   ". . . a weird and disparate assortment of material, but the monstrosity which bloomed into his most recent cancer of aggregations is present in some form everywhere. . . ." Then, later, "A gluttony of things and processes terminated by a glorious constipation."

15   Item three, same magazine, review of an artist who welds automobile fragments into abstract shapes:

16   "Each fragment . . . is made an extreme of human exasperation, torn at and fought all the way, and has its rightness of form as if by accident. *Any technique that requires order or discipline would just be the human ego.* No, these must be egoless, uncontrolled, undesigned and different enough to give you a bang—fifty miles an hour around a telephone pole. . . ."

17   "Any technique that requires order or discipline would just be the human ego." What does he mean—"just be"? What are they really talking about? Is this journalism? Is it criticism? Or is it that other convenient abdication from standards of performance and judgment practiced by so many artists and critics that they, like certain writers who deal only in sickness and depravity, "reflect the chaos about them"? Again, whose chaos? Whose depravity?

I had always thought that the prime function of art was to cre- 18
ate order *out* of chaos—again, not the order of neatness or rigidity
or convention or artifice, but the order of clarity by which one will
and one vision could draw the essential truth out of apparent confusion. I still do. It is not enough to use parts of a car to convey the
brutality of the machine. This is as slavishly representative, and just
as easy, as arranging dried flowers under glass to convey nature.

Speaking of which, i.e., the use of real materials (burlap, old 19
gloves, bottletops) in lieu of pigment, this is what one critic had to
say about an exhibition of Assemblage at the Museum of Modern
Art last year:

> Spotted throughout the show are indisputable works of art, ac-
> counting for a quarter or even a half of the total display. But the
> remainder are works of non-art, anti-art, and art substitutes that
> are the aesthetic counterparts of the social deficiencies that land
> people in the clink on charges of vagrancy. These aesthetic bank-
> rupts ... have no legitimate ideological roof over their heads and
> not the price of a square intellectual meal, much less a spiritual
> sandwich, in their pockets.

I quote these words of John Canaday of the *New York Times* as 20
an example of the kind of criticism which puts responsibility to an
intelligent public above popularity with an intellectual coterie.
Canaday has the courage to say what he thinks and the capacity
to say it clearly: Two qualities notably absent from his profession.

Next to art, I would say that appreciation and evaluation in 21
the field of music is the most difficult. For it is rarely possible to
judge a new composition at one hearing only. What seems confusing or fragmented at first might well become clear and organic
a third time. Or it might not. The only salvation here for the listener is, again, an instinct born of experience and association
which allows him to separate intent from accident, design from
experimentation, and pretense from conviction. Much of contemporary music is, like its sister art, merely a reflection of the com-
poser's own fragmentation: An absorption in self and symbols at
the expense of communication with others. The artist, in short,
says to the public: If you don't understand this, it's because you're
dumb. I maintain that you are not. You may have to go part way

or even halfway to meet the artist, but if you must go the whole way, it's his fault, not yours. Hold fast to that. And remember it too when you read new poetry, that estranged sister of music.

> A multitude of causes, unknown to former times, are now acting with a combined force to blunt the discriminating powers of the mind, and, unfitting it for all voluntary exertion, to reduce it to a state of almost savage torpor. The most effective of these causes are the great national events which are daily taking place and the increasing accumulation of men in cities, where the uniformity of their occupations produces a craving for extraordinary incident, which the rapid communication of intelligence hourly gratifies. To this tendency of life and manners, the literature and theatrical exhibitions of the country have conformed themselves.

22   This startlingly applicable comment was written in the year 1800 by William Wordsworth in the preface to his "Lyrical Ballads"; and it has been cited by Edwin Muir in his recently published book "The Estate of Poetry." Muir states that poetry's effective range and influence have diminished alarmingly in the modern world. He believes in the inherent and indestructible qualities of the human mind and the great and permanent objects that act upon it, and suggests that the audience will increase when "poetry loses what obscurity is left in it by attempting greater themes, for great themes have to be stated clearly." If you keep that firmly in mind and resist, in Muir's words, "the vast dissemination of secondary objects that isolate us from the natural world," you have gone a long way toward equipping yourself for the examination of any work of art.

23   When you come to theatre, in this extremely hasty tour of the arts, you can approach it on two different levels. You can bring to it anticipation and innocence, giving yourself up, as it were, to the life on the stage and reacting to it emotionally, if the play is good, or listlessly, if the play is boring; a part of the audience organism that expresses its favor by silence or laughter and its disfavor by coughing and rustling. Or you can bring to it certain critical faculties that may heighten, rather than diminish, your enjoyment.

24   You can ask yourselves whether the actors are truly in their parts or merely projecting themselves; whether the scenery helps or hurts the mood; whether the playwright is honest with himself,

his characters, and you. Somewhere along the line you can learn to distinguish between the true creative act and the false arbitrary gesture; between fresh observation and stale cliché; between the avant-garde play that is pretentious drivel and the avant-garde play that finds new ways to say old truths.

Purpose and craftsmanship—end and means—these are the keys to your judgment in all the arts. What is this painter trying to say when he slashes a broad band of black across a white canvas and lets the edges dribble down? Is it a statement of violence? Is it a self-portrait? If it is *one* of these, has he made you believe it? Or is this a gesture of the ego or a form of therapy? If it shocks you, what does it shock you into?

And what of this tight little painting of bright flowers in a vase? Is the painter saying anything new about flowers? Is it different from a million other canvases of flowers? Has it any life, any meaning, beyond its statement? Is there any pleasure in its forms or texture? The question is not whether a thing is abstract or representational, whether it is "modern" or conventional. The question, inexorably, is whether it is good. And this is a decision which only you, on the basis of instinct, experience, and association, can make for yourself. It takes independence and courage. It involves, moreover, the risk of wrong decision and the humility, after the passage of time, of recognizing it as such. As we grow and change and learn, our attitudes can change too, and what we once thought obscure or "difficult" can later emerge as coherent and illuminating. Entrenched prejudices, obdurate opinions are as sterile as no opinions at all.

Yet standards there are, timeless as the universe itself. And when you have committed yourself to them, you have acquired a passport to that elusive but immutable realm of truth. Keep it with you in the forests of bewilderment. And never be afraid to speak up.

1962

Pain is Not the Ultimate Enemy

Norman Cousins

1   Americans are probably the most pain-conscious people on the face of the earth. For years we have had it drummed into us—in print, on radio, over television, in everyday conversation—that any hint of pain is to be banished as though it were the ultimate evil. As a result, we are becoming a nation of pill-grabbers and hypochondriacs, escalating the slightest ache into a searing ordeal.

2   We know very little about pain and what we don't know makes it hurt all the more. Indeed, no form of illiteracy in the United States is so widespread or costly as ignorance about pain— what it is, what causes it, how to deal with it without panic. Almost everyone can rattle off the names of at least a dozen drugs that can deaden pain from every conceivable cause—all the way from headaches to hemorrhoids. There is far less knowledge about the fact that about 90 percent of pain is self-limiting, that it is not always an indication of poor health, and that, most frequently, it is the result of tension, stress, worry, idleness, boredom, frustration, suppressed rage, insufficient sleep, overeating, poorly balanced diet, smoking, excessive drinking, inadequate exercise, stale air, or any of the other abuses encountered by the human body in modern society.

3   The most ignored fact of all about pain is that the best way to eliminate it is to eliminate the abuse. Instead, many people reach almost instinctively for the painkillers—aspirins, barbiturates, codeines, tranquilizers, sleeping pills, and dozens of other analgesics or desensitizing drugs.

4   Most doctors are profoundly troubled over the extent to which the medical profession today is taking on the trappings of a pain-killing industry. Their offices are overloaded with people who are morbidly but mistakenly convinced that something dreadful is about to happen to them. It is all too evident that the campaign to get people to run to a doctor at the first sign of pain has boomeranged. Physicians find it difficult to give adequate at-

tention to patients genuinely in need of expert diagnosis and treatment because their time is soaked up by people who have nothing wrong with them except a temporary indisposition or a psychogenic ache.

Patients tend to feel indignant and insulted if the physician tells ₅ them he can find no organic cause of pain. They tend to interpret the term "psychogenic" to mean that they are complaining of nonexistent symptoms. They need to be educated about the fact that many forms of pain have no underlying physical cause but are the result, as mentioned earlier, of tension, stress, or hostile factors in the general environment. Sometimes a pain may be a manifestation of "conversion hysteria" . . . the name given by Jean Charcot to physical symptoms that have their origins in emotional disturbances.

Obviously, it is folly for an individual to ignore symptoms that ₆ could be a warning of a potentially serious illness. Some people are so terrified of getting bad news from a doctor that they allow their malaise to worsen, sometimes past the point of no return. Total neglect is not the answer to hypochondria. The only answer has to be increased education about the way the human body works, so that more people will be able to steer an intelligent course between promiscuous pill-popping and irresponsible disregard of genuine symptoms.

Of all forms of pain, none is more important for the individ- ₇ ual to understand than the "threshold" variety. Almost everyone has a telltale ache that is triggered whenever tension or fatigue reaches a certain point. It can take the form of a migraine-type headache or a squeezing pain deep in the abdomen or cramps or a pain in the lower back or even pain in the joints. The individual who has learned how to make the correlation between such threshold pains and their cause doesn't panic when they occur; he or she does something about relieving the stress and tension. Then, if the pain persists despite the absence of apparent cause, the individual will telephone the doctor.

If ignorance about the nature of pain is widespread, ignorance ₈ about the way pain-killing drugs work is even more so. What is not generally understood is that many of the vaunted pain-killing drugs conceal the pain without correcting the underlying condition. They deaden the mechanism in the body that alerts the brain to the fact that something may be wrong. The body can pay a high price for suppression of pain without regard to its basic cause.

9   Professional athletes are sometimes severely disadvantaged by trainers whose job it is to keep them in action. The more famous the athlete, the greater the risk that he or she may be subjected to extreme medical measures when injury strikes. The star baseball pitcher whose arm is sore because of a torn muscle or tissue damage may need sustained rest more than anything else. But his team is battling for a place in the World Series; so the trainer or team doctor, called upon to work his magic, reaches for a strong dose of Butazolidine or other powerful pain suppressants. Presto, the pain disappears! The pitcher takes his place on the mound and does superbly. That could be the last game, however, in which he is able to throw a ball with full strength. The drugs didn't repair the torn muscle or cause the damaged tissue to heal. What they did was to mask the pain, enabling the pitcher to throw hard, further damaging the torn muscle. Little wonder that so many star athletes are cut down in their prime, more the victims of overzealous treatment of their injuries than of the injuries themselves.

10   The king of all painkillers, of course, is aspirin. The U.S. Food and Drug Administration permits aspirin to be sold without prescription, but the drug, contrary to popular belief, can be dangerous and, in sustained doses, potentially lethal. Aspirin is self-administered by more people than any other drug in the world. Some people are aspirin-poppers, taking ten or more a day. What they don't know is that the smallest dose can cause internal bleeding. Even more serious perhaps is the fact that aspirin is antagonistic to collagen, which has a key role in the formation of connective tissue. Since many forms of arthritis involve disintegration of the connective tissues, the steady use of aspirin can actually intensify the underlying arthritic condition.

11   Aspirin is not the only pain-killing drug, of course, that is known to have dangerous side effects. Dr. Daphne A. Roe, of Cornell University, at a medical meeting in New York City in 1974, presented startling evidence of a wide range of hazards associated with sedatives and other pain suppressants. Some of these drugs seriously interfere with the ability of the body to metabolize food properly, producing malnutrition. In some instances, there is also

the danger of bone-marrow depression, interfering with the ability of the body to replenish its blood supply.

Pain-killing drugs are among the greatest advances in the history of medicine. Properly used, they can be a boon in alleviating suffering and in treating disease. But their indiscriminate and promiscuous use is making psychological cripples and chronic ailers out of millions of people. The unremitting barrage of advertising for pain-killing drugs, especially over television, has set the stage for a mass anxiety neurosis. Almost from the moment children are old enough to sit upright in front of a television screen, they are being indoctrinated into the hypochondriac's clamorous and morbid world. Little wonder so many people fear pain more than death itself. 12

It might be a good idea if concerned physicians and educators could get together to make knowledge about pain an important part of the regular school curriculum. As for the populace at large, perhaps some of the same techniques used by public-service agencies to make people cancer-conscious can be used to counteract the growing terror of pain and illness in general. People ought to know that nothing is more remarkable about the human body than its recuperative drive, given a modicum of respect. If our broadcasting stations cannot provide equal time for responses to the pain-killing advertisements, they might at least set aside a few minutes each day for common-sense remarks on the subject of pain. As for the Food and Drug Administration, it might be interesting to know why an agency that has energetically warned the American people against taking vitamins without prescriptions is doing so little to control over-the-counter sales each year of billions of pain-killing pills, some of which can do more harm than the pain they are supposed to suppress. 13

1979

Watching the Grasshopper Get the Goodies

Ellen Goodman

1 I don't usually play the great American game called Categories. There are already too many ways to divide us into opposing teams, according to age, race, sex and favorite flavors. Every time we turn around, someone is telling us that the whole country is made up of those who drive pick-up trucks and those who do not, and then analyzing what this means in terms of the Middle East.

2 Still, it occurs to me that if we want to figure out why people are angry right now, it's not a bad idea to see ourselves as a nation of planners and nonplanners. It's the planners these days who are feeling penalized, right down to their box score at the bank.

3 The part of us which is most visibly and vocally infuriated by inflation, for example, isn't our liberal or conservative side but, rather, our planning side. Inflation devastates our attempts to control our futures—to budget and predict and expect. It particularly makes fools out of the people who saved then to buy now. To a certain extent, it rewards instant gratification and makes a joke out of our traditional notions of preparation.

4 It is no news bulletin that the people who dove over their heads into the real-estate market a few years ago are now generally better off than those who dutifully decided to save up for a larger down payment. With that "larger down payment" they can now buy two double-thick rib lambchops and a partridge in a pear tree.

5 But inflation isn't the only thing that leaves the planners feeling betrayed. There are other issues that find them actively pitched against the nonplanners.

6 We all know families who saved for a decade to send their kids to college. A college diploma these days costs about the same amount as a Mercedes-Benz. Of course, the Mercedes lasts longer and has a higher trade-in value. But the most devoted parent can be infuriated to discover that a neighboring couple who spent its

income instead of saving is now eligible for college financial aid, while they are not. To the profligate go the spoils.

This can happen anywhere on the economic spectrum. There 7 is probably only one mother in the annals of the New York welfare rolls to save up a few thousand dollars in hopes of getting off aid. But she would have been better off spending it. When she was discovered this year, the welfare department took the money back. She, too, was penalized for planning.

In these crimped times, the Planned Parents of the Purse are 8 increasingly annoyed at other parents—whether they are unwed or on welfare or just prolific. For the first time in my own town, you can hear families with few children complaining out loud at the tax bill for the public schooling of families with many children.

One man I heard even suggesting charging tuition for the 9 third child. He admitted, "It's not a very generous attitude, I know. But I'm not feeling very generous these days." He is suffering from planner's warts.

At the same time I've talked with friends whose parents pre- 10 pared, often with financial difficulty, for their "old age" and illness. They feel sad when this money goes down a nursing home drain, but furious when other people who didn't save get this same care for free.

Now we are all aware that if many people don't plan their eco- 11 nomic lives, it may be because they can't. It does no one any good to keep the cashless out of college, to stash the old and poor into elderly warehouses, to leave the "extra" children illiterate. We do want to help others, but we also want our own efforts to make a difference.

There is nothing that grates a planner more than seeing a non- 12 planner profit. It's as if the ant had to watch the grasshopper get the goodies.

Our two notions about what's fair end up on opposite sides. 13 It isn't fair if the poor get treated badly, and it isn't fair if those who work and save, plan and postpone aren't given a better shake. We want the winners to be the deserving. Only there is no divining rod for the deserving.

The hard part is to create policies that are neither unkind nor 14 insane. It is, after all, madness not to reward the kind of behavior we want to encourage. If we want the ranks of the planners to increase in this massive behavior-modification program called society, we have to give them the rewards, instead of the outrage.

1981

White Guilt

Shelby Steele

1   I don't remember hearing the phrase "white guilt" very much before the mid-1960s. Growing up black in the 1950s, I never had the impression that whites were much disturbed by guilt when it came to blacks. When I would stray into the wrong restaurant in pursuit of a hamburger, it didn't occur to me that the waitress was unduly troubled by guilt when she asked me to leave. I can see now that possibly she was, but then all I saw was her irritability at having to carry out so unpleasant a task. If there was guilt, it was mine for having made an imposition of myself. I can remember feeling a certain sympathy for such people, as if I was victimizing them by drawing them out of an innocent anonymity into the unasked-for role of racial policemen. Occasionally they came right out and asked me to feel sorry for them. A caddymaster at a country club told my brother and me that he was doing us a favor by not letting us caddy at this white club and that we should try to understand his position, "put yourselves in my shoes." Our color had brought this man anguish and, if a part of that anguish was guilt, it was not as immediate to me as my own guilt. I smiled at the man to let him know he shouldn't feel bad and then began my long walk home. Certainly I also judge him a coward, but in that era his cowardice was something I had to absorb.

2   In the 1960s, particularly the black-is-beautiful late 1960s, this absorption of another's cowardice was no longer necessary. The lines of moral power, like plates in the earth, had shifted. White guilt became so palpable you could see it on people. At the time

what it looked like to my eyes was a remarkable loss of authority. And what whites lost in authority, blacks gained. You cannot feel guilty about anyone without giving away power to them. Suddenly, this huge vulnerability had opened up in whites and, as a black, you had the power to step right into it. In fact, black power all but demanded that you do so. What shocked me in the late 1960s, after the helplessness I had felt in the fifties, was that guilt had changed the nature of the white man's burden from the administration of inferiors to the uplift of equals—from the obligations of dominance to the urgencies of repentance.

I think what made the difference between the fifties and six- 3 ties, at least as far as white guilt was concerned, was that whites underwent an archetypal Fall. Because of the immense turmoil of the civil rights movement, and later the blackpower movement, whites were confronted for more than a decade with their willingness to participate in, or comply with, the oppression of blacks, their indifference to human suffering and denigration, their capacity to abide evil for their own benefit and in the defiance of their own sacred principles. The 1964 Civil Rights Bill that bestowed equality under the law on blacks was also, in a certain sense, an admission of white guilt. Had white society not been wrong, there would have been no need for such a bill. In this bill the nation acknowledged its fallenness, its lack of racial innocence, and confronted the incriminating self-knowledge that it had rationalized for many years a flagrant injustice. Denial is a common way of handling guilt, but in the 1960s there was little will left for denial except in the most recalcitrant whites. With this defense lost there was really only one road back to innocence— through actions and policies that would bring redemption.

In the 1960s the need for white redemption from racial guilt 4 became the most powerful, yet unspoken, element in America's social-policy-making process, first giving rise to the Great Society and then to a series of programs, policies, and laws that sought to make black equality and restitution a national mission. Once America could no longer deny its guilt, it went after redemption, or at least the look of redemption, and did so with a vengeance. Yet today, some twenty years later, study after study tells us that by many measures the gap between blacks and

whites is widening rather than narrowing. A University of
Chicago study indicates that segregation is more entrenched in
American cities today than ever imagined. A National Research
Council study notes the "status of blacks relative to whites (in
housing and education) has stagnated or regressed since the
early seventies." A follow-up to the famous Kerner Commission
Report warns that blacks are as much at risk today of becoming
a "nation within a nation" as we were twenty years ago, when
the original report was made.

5   I think the white need for redemption has contributed to this
tragic situation by shaping our policies regarding blacks in ways
that may deliver the look of innocence to society and its institutions but that do very little actually to uplift blacks. The specific effect of this hidden need has been to bend social policy more toward reparation for black oppression than toward the much
harder and more mundane work of black uplift and development.
Rather than facilitate the development of blacks to achieve parity
with whites, these programs and policies—affirmative action is a
good example—have tended to give blacks special entitlements
that in many cases are of no use because blacks lack the development that would put us in a position to take advantage of them. I
think the reason there has been more entitlement than development is (along with black power) the unacknowledged white need
for redemption—not true redemption, which would have concen-
trated policy on black development, but the appearance of redemption, which requires only that society, in the name of development, seem to be paying back its former victims with
preferences. One of the effects of entitlements, I believe, has been
to encourage in blacks a dependency both on entitlements and on
the white guilt that generates them. Even when it serves ideal justice, bounty from another man's guilt weakens. While this is not
the only factor in black "stagnation" and "regression," I believe it
is one very potent factor.

6   It is easy enough to say that white guilt too often has the effect
of bending social policies in the wrong direction. But what exactly
is this guilt, and how does it work in American life?

7   I think white guilt, in its broad sense, springs from a knowledge of ill-gotten advantage. More precisely, it comes from the jux-

taposition of this knowledge with the inevitable gratitude one feels for being white rather than black in America. Given the moral instincts of human beings, it is all but impossible to enjoy an ill-gotten advantage, much less to feel at least secretly grateful for it, without consciously or unconsciously experiencing guilt. If, as Kierkegaard writes, "innocence is ignorance," then guilt must always involve knowledge. White Americans *know* that their historical advantage comes from the subjugation of an entire people. So, even for whites today for whom racism is anathema, there is no escape from the knowledge that makes for guilt. Racial guilt simply accompanies the condition of being white in America.

I do not believe that this guilt is a crushing anguish for most 8 whites, but I do believe it constitutes a continuing racial vulnerability—an openness to racial culpability—that is a thread in white life, sometimes felt, sometimes not, but ever present as a potential feeling. In the late 1960s almost any black could charge this vulnerability with enough current for a white person to feel it. I had a friend who had developed this activity into a sort of specialty. I don't think he meant to be mean, though certainly he was mean. I think he was, in that hyperbolic era, exhilarated by the discovery that his race, which had long been a liability, now gave him a certain edge—that white guilt was the true force behind black power. To feel this power he would sometimes set up what he called "race experiments." Once I watched him stop a white businessman in the men's room of a large hotel and convince him to increase his tip to the black attendant from one to twenty dollars.

My friend's tactic was very simple, even corny. Out of the at- 9 tendant's earshot he asked the man simply to look at the attendant, a frail, elderly, and very dark man in a starched white smock that made the skin on his neck and face look as leathery as a turtle's. He sat listlessly, pathetically, on a straight-backed chair next to a small table on which sat a stack of hand towels and a silver plate for tips. Since the attendant offered no service whatever beyond the handing out of towels, one could only conclude the hotel management offered his lowly presence as flattery to their patrons, as an opportunity for that easy noblesse oblige that could reassure even the harried and weary traveling salesman of his superior station. My friend was quick to make this point to the businessman and to say that no white man would do in this job. But when the businessman put the single back in his wallet and took out a five, my friend only sneered. Did he understand the tragedy of a life spent this way, of what it must be like to earn one's paltry living as a symbol of inferiority? And did he realize that his privilege as an affluent white businessman (ironically he had just spent the day trying to sell a printing press to the Black Muslims for their newspaper *Mohammed Speaks*) was connected to the deprivation of this man and others like him?

10   But then my friend made a mistake that ended the game. In the heat of argument, which until then had only been playfully challenging, he inadvertently mentioned his father. This stopped the victim cold and his eyes turned inward. "What about your father?" the businessman asked. My friend replied, "He had a hard life, that's all." "How did he have a hard life?" the businessman asked. Now my friend was on the defensive. I knew he did not get along with his father, a bitter man who worked nights in a factory and demanded that the house be dark and silent all day. My friend blamed his father's bitterness on racism, but I knew he had not meant to exploit his own pain in this silly "experiment." Things had gotten too close to home, but he didn't know how to get out of the situation without losing face. Now, caught in his own trap, he did what he least wanted to do. He gave forth the rage he truly felt to a white stranger in a public men's room. "My father never had a chance," he said with the kind of anger that could easily turn to tears. "He never had a freakin' chance. Your father had all the goddamn chances, and you know he did. You sell printing presses to black people and make thousands and your father probably lives down in Fat City, Florida, all because you're white." On and on he went in this vein, using—against all that was honorable in him—his own profound racial pain to extract a flash of guilt from a white man he didn't even know.

11   He got more than a flash. The businessman was touched. His eyes became mournful, and finally he simply said, "You're right. Your people got a raw deal." He took a twenty dollar bill from his wallet and walked over and dropped it in the old man's tip plate.

When he was gone my friend and I could not look at the old man, nor could we look at each other.

It is obvious that this was a rather shameful encounter for all   12 concerned—my friend and I, as his silent accomplice, trading on our racial pain, tampering with a stranger for no reason, and the stranger then buying his way out of the situation for twenty dollars, a sum that was generous by one count and cheap by another. It was not an encounter of people but of historical grudges and guilts. Yet, when I think about it now twenty years later, I see that it had all the elements of a paradigm that I believe has been very much at the heart of racial policy-making in America since the 1960s.

My friend did two things that made this businessman vulner-   13 able to his guilt—that brought his guilt into the situation as a force. First he put this man in touch with his own knowledge of his ill-gotten advantage as a white. The effect of this was to disallow the man any pretense of racial innocence, to let him know that, even if he was not the sort of white who used the word *nigger* around the dinner table, he still had reason to feel racial guilt. But, as disarming as this might have been, it was too abstract to do much more than crack open this man's vulnerability, to expose him to the logic of white guilt. This was the five-dollar, intellectual sort of guilt. The twenty dollars required something more visceral. In achieving this, the second thing my friend did was something he had not intended to do, something that ultimately brought him as much shame as he was doling out: He made a display of his own racial pain and anger. (What brought him shame was not the pain and anger, but his trading on them for what turned out to be a mere twenty bucks.) The effect of this display was to reinforce the man's knowledge of ill-gotten advantage, to give credibility and solidity to it by putting a face on it. Here was human testimony, a young black beside himself at the thought of his father's racially constricted life. The pain of one man evidenced the knowledge of the other. When the businessman listened to my friend's pain, his racial guilt—normally only one source of guilt lying dormant among others—was called out like a neglected debt he would finally have to settle. An ill-gotten advantage is not hard to bear—it can be marked up to fate—until it touches the genuine human pain it has brought into the world. This is the pain that hardens guilty knowledge.

14   Such knowledge is a powerful influence when it becomes conscious. What makes it so powerful is the element of fear that guilt always carries, the fear of what the guilty knowledge says about us. Guilt makes us afraid for ourselves, and thus generates as much self-preoccupation as concern for others. The nature of this preoccupation is always the redemption of innocence, the reestablishment of good feeling about oneself.

15   In this sense, the fear for the self that is buried in all guilt is a pressure toward selfishness. It can lead us to put our own need for innocence above our concern for the problem that made us feel guilt in the first place. But this fear for the self does not only inspire selfishness; it also becomes a pressure to *escape* the guilt-inducing situation. When selfishness and escapism are at work, we are no longer interested in the source of our guilt and, therefore, no longer concerned with an authentic redemption from it. Then we only want the look of redemption, the gesture of concern that will give us the appearance of innocence and escape from the situation. Obviously the businessman did not put twenty dollars in the tip plate because he thought it would uplift black Americans. He did it selfishly for the appearance of concern and for the escape it afforded him.

16   This is not to say that guilt is never the right motive for doing good works or showing concern, only that it is a very dangerous one because of its tendency to draw us into self-preoccupation and escapism. Guilt is a civilizing emotion when the fear for the self that it carries is contained—a containment that allows guilt to be more selfless and that makes genuine concern possible. I think this was the kind of guilt that, along with the other forces, made the 1964 Civil Rights Bill possible. But since then I believe too many of our social policies related to race have been shaped by the fearful underside of guilt.

17   Black power evoked white guilt and made it a force in American institutions, very much in the same way as my friend brought it to life in the businessman. Few people volunteer for guilt. Usually others make us feel it. It was the expression of black

anger and pain that hardened the guilty knowledge of white ill-gotten advantage. And black power—whether from militant fringe groups, the civil rights establishment, or big city political campaigns—knew exactly the kind of white guilt it was after. It wanted to trigger the kind of white guilt in which whites fear for their own decency and innocence; it wanted the guilt of white self-preoccupation and escapism. Always at the heart of black power, in whatever form, has been a profound anger at what was done to blacks and an equally profound feeling that there should be reparations. But a sober white guilt (in which fear for the self is still contained) seeks a strict fairness—the 1964 Civil Rights Bill that guaranteed equality under the law. It is of little value when one is after more than fairness. So black power made its mission to have whites fear for their innocence, to feel a visceral guilt from which they would have to seek a more profound redemption. In such redemption was the possibility of black reparation. Black power upped the ante on white guilt.

With black power, all of the elements of the hidden paradigm 18 that shape America's race-related social policy were in place. Knowledge of ill-gotten advantage could now be shown and deepened by black power into the sort of guilt from which institutions could only redeem themselves by offering more than fairness—by offering forms of reparation and compensation for past injustice. I believe this bent our policies toward racial entitlements at the expense of racial development. In 1964, one of the assurances Senator Hubert Humphrey and others had to give Congress to get the landmark Civil Rights Bill passed was that the bill would not in any way require employers to use racial preferences to rectify racial imbalances. But this was before the explosion of black power in the late 1960s, before the hidden paradigm was set in motion. After black power, racial preferences became the order of the day.

If this paradigm brought blacks entitlements, it also brought 19 the continuation of the most profound problem in American society, the invisibility of blacks as a people. The white guilt that this paradigm elicits is the kind of guilt that preoccupies whites with their own innocence and pressures them toward escapism—

twenty dollars in the plate and out the door. With this guilt, as opposed to the contained guilt of genuine concern, whites tend to see
only their own need for quick redemption. Blacks then become a
means to this redemption and, as such, they must be seen as generally "less than" others. Their needs are "special," "unique," "different." They are seen exclusively along the dimension of their victimization, so that they become "different" people with whom
whites can negotiate entitlements but never fully see as people
like themselves. Guilt that preoccupies people with their own innocence blinds them to those who make them feel guilty. This, of
course, is not racism, and yet it has the same effect as racism since
it makes blacks something of a separate species for whom normal
standards and values do not automatically apply.

20   Nowhere is this more evident today than in American universities. At some of America's most elite universities administrators
have granted concessions in response to black student demands
(black power) that all but sanction racial separatism on campus—
black "theme" dorms, black student unions, black yearbooks,
homecoming dances, and so forth. I don't believe administrators
sincerely believe in these separatist concessions. Most of them are
liberals who see racial separatism as wrong. But black student demands pull administrators into the paradigm of self-preoccupied
white guilt, whereby they seek a quick redemption by offering
special entitlements that go beyond fairness. As a result, black students become all but invisible to them. Though blacks have the
lowest grade point average of any racial group in American universities, administrators never sit down with them and "demand"
in kind that black students bring their grades up to par. The paradigm of white guilt makes the real problems of black students secondary to the need for white redemption. It also cuts administrators off from their own values, which would most certainly
discourage racial separatism and encourage higher academic performance for black students. Lastly, it makes for escapist policies.
There is no difference between giving black students a separate
lounge and leaving twenty dollars in the tip plate on the way out
the door.

1990

Where Have All the Parents Gone?

Barbara Dafoe Whitehead

"Invest in kids," George Bush mused during his 1988 presidential   1
campaign, "I like it." Apparently so do others. A growing number
of corporate CEOs and educators, elected officials and child-wel-
fare advocates have embraced the same language. "Invest in kids"
is the bumper-sticker for an important new cause, aptly tagged the
kids as capital argument. It runs as follows:

America's human capital comes in two forms: The active   2
work force and the prospective work force. The bulk of tomorrow's workers are today's children, of course. So children make up
much of the stockpile of America's potential human capital.

If we look at them as tomorrow's workers, we begin to appre-   3
ciate our stake in today's children. They will determine when we
can retire, how well we can live in retirement, how generous our
health insurance will be, how strong our social safety net, how orderly our society. What's more, today's children will determine
how successfully we compete in the global economy. They will be
going head-to-head against Japanese, Korean, and West German
children.

Unfortunately, American children aren't prepared to run the   4
race, let alone win it. Many are illiterate, undernourished, impaired, unskilled, poor. Consider the children who started first
grade in 1986: 14 percent were illegitimate; 15 percent were physically or emotionally handicapped; 15 percent spoke another language other than English; 28 percent were poor; and fully 40 percent could be expected to live in a single-parent home before they
reached eighteen. Given falling birth rates, this future work force
is small—all the more reason to worry about its poor quality. So
"invest in kids" is not the cry of the soft-hearted altruist but the
call of the hardheaded realist.

Kids as capital has caught on because it responds to a broad set   5
of national concerns. Whether one is worried about the rise of the
underclass, the decline of the family, our standing in the global

economy, the nation's level of educational performance, or inter-generational conflict, kids as capital seems to offer an answer.

6   Further, *kids as capital* offers the rationale for a new coalition for child welfare programs. The argument reaches beyond the community of traditional children's advocates and draws business into the child-saving fold. American corporations clearly have a stake in tomorrow's work force as they don't have in today's children. *Kids as capital* gives the toughminded, fifty-five-year-old CEO a reason to "care" about the eight-year-old, Hispanic school girl.

7   Nevertheless, the argument left unchallenged could easily become yet another "feel-good" formula that doesn't work. Worse, it could end up betraying those it seeks to save—the nation's children.

8   First, *kids as capital* departs from a classic American vision of the future. Most often, our history has been popularly viewed as progressive, with each generation breaking with and improving on the past. As an immigrant nation, we have always measured our progress through the progress of our children; they have been the bearers of the dream.

9   *Kids as capital* turns this optimistic view on its head. It conjures up a picture of a dark and disorderly future. Essentially, kids as capital is dystopic—closer to the spirit of *Blade Runner* and *Black Rain* than *Wizard of Oz* or *It's a Wonderful Life*. Children, in this view, do not bear the dream. They carry the seeds of our destruction. In short, *kids as capital* plays on our fears, rather than our hopes. It holds out the vision of a troubled future in order to secure a safer and more orderly present.

10   There is something troubling, too, in such an instrumental view of children. To define them narrowly as tomorrow's wonders is to strip them of their full status as humans, as children: Kids can't be kids; they can only be embryonic workers. And treating *kids as capital* makes it easier to measure them solely through IQ tests, class standing, SAT scores, drop-out ratios, physical fitness tests. This leaves no place in the society for the slow starter, the handicapped, the quirky, and the nonconforming.

11   Yet kids-as-capital has an even more serious flaw. It evades the central fact of life for American children: They have parents.

As we all know, virtually every child in America grows up in 12 a family with one or more parents. Parents house children. Parents feed children. Parents clothe children. Parents nurture and protect children. Parents instruct children in everything from using a fork to driving a car. To be sure, there have been vast changes in family life, and, increasingly, parents must depend on teachers, doctors, day-care workers, and technology to help care for and educate their children. Even so, these changes haven't altered one fundamental fact: In American society, parents still bear the primary responsibility for the material and spiritual welfare of children. As our teachers and counselors and politicians keep reminding us, everything begins at home. So, if today's children are in trouble, it's because today's parents are in trouble.

As recently as a dozen years ago, it was the central argument 13 of an ambitious report by the Carnegie Council on Children. The Council put it plainly: "The best way to help children tomorrow is to support parents today." Yet, that view has been lost. The *kids as capital* argument suppresses the connection between parents and children. It imagines that we can improve the standing of children without improving the standing of the parents. In the new rhetoric, it is hard even to find the word "parent." Increasingly, kids are portrayed as standing alone out there somewhere, cosmically parent-free.

As a result, *kids as capital* ignores rather than addresses one of 14 the most important changes in American life: The decline in the power and standing of the nation's parents.

Only a generation ago, parents stood at the center of society. 15 First of all, there were so many of them—fully half the nation's households in 1960 were parent households with one or more children under eighteen. Moreover, parents looked alike—Dad worked and Mom stayed at home. And parents marched through the stages of childbearing and child rearing in virtual lockstep: Most couples who married in the 1940s and 1950s finished having their 3.2 children by the time they were in their late twenties.

Their demographic dominance meant two things: First, it made 16 for broad common ground in child rearing. Parents could do a great deal to support each other in raising the new generation. They could, and did, create a culture hospitable to children. Secondly, it made for political clout. When so many adults were parents and so many parents were part of an expanding consumer economy, private and public interests converged. The concerns of parents— housing, health, education—easily found their way into the national agenda. Locally, too, parents were dominant. In some postwar suburbs like Levittown, Pennsylvania, three-quarters of all residents were either parents or children under ten. Not surprisingly, there was little dissent when it came to building a new junior high or establishing a summer recreation program or installing a new playground. What's more, parents and kids drove the consumer economy. Every time they bought a pair of sneakers or a new bike, they were acting in the nation's best interest.

17   Behind this, of course, lurked a powerful pronatal ideology. Parenthood was the definitive credential of adulthood. More than being married, more than getting a job, it was having a child that baptized you as an adult in postwar America. In survey after survey, postwar parents rated children above marriage itself as the greatest reward of private life. For a generation forced to make personal sacrifices during the Depression and the war, having children and pursuing a private life represented a new kind of freedom.

18   By the 1970s, parents no longer enjoyed so central a place in the society. To baby boom children, postwar family life seemed suffocating and narrow. Women, in particular, wanted room to breathe. The rights movements of the sixties and seventies overturned the pronatal ideology, replacing it with an ideology of choice. Adults were free to choose among many options: Single, married, or divorced; career-primary or career-secondary; parent, stepparent, or child-free.

19   Thus, parenthood lost its singular status. It no longer served as the definitive credential of maturity and adult achievement. In fact, as careers and personal fulfillment beckoned, parenthood seemed just the opposite: A serious limitation on personal growth and success. As Gloria Steinem put it, "I either gave birth to someone else or I gave birth to myself."

20   As the pronatal ideology vanished, so did the close connection between private families and the public interest. Raising children

was no longer viewed as a valuable contribution to the society, an activity that boosted the economy, built citizen participation, and increased the nation's confidence in the future. Instead, it became one option among many. No longer a moral imperative, child rearing was just another "lifestyle choice."

Viewed this way, raising children looked like an economic disaster. Starting out, parents had to shell out $3,000 for basic prenatal care and maternity costs; $3,000–$5,000 per child for day care; and $2,500 for the basic baby basket of goods and services. Crib-to-college costs for middle-class Americans could run as high as $135,000 per child. And, increasingly, the period of economic dependency for children stretched well beyond age eighteen. College tuitions and start-up subsidies for the new college graduate became part of the economic burden of parenthood. In an ad campaign, Manufacturers Hanover Trust gave prospective parents fair warning: "If you want a bundle of joy; you'll need a bundle of money." 21

Hard-pressed younger Americans responded to these new realities in several ways. Some simply chose not to have children. Others decided to have one or two, but only after they had a good job and solid prospects. Gradually, the number of parent households in the nation declined from one-half to one-third, and America faced a birth dearth. 22

For those who chose the parent option, there was only one way to face up to the new economic pressures of child rearing: Work longer and harder outside the home. For all but the extremely well-off, a second income became essential. But in struggling to pay the bills, parents seemed to be short-changing their children in another way. They weren't taking their moral responsibilities seriously enough. They weren't spending enough time with their kids. They weren't reading to the children or playing with the kids or supervising homework. And, most important, they weren't teaching good values. 23

This emerging critique marked a dramatic change in the way society viewed parents. In the postwar period, the stereotypical parent was self-sacrificing, responsible, caring, attentive—an impossible standard, to be sure, but one that lent enormous popular 24

support and approval to adults engaged in the messy and difficult
work of raising children. Cruel, abusive, self-absorbed parents
might exist, but the popular culture failed to acknowledge them.
It was not until parents began to lose their central place in the society that this flattering image faded. Then, quite rapidly, the dominant image of The Good Parent gave way to a new and equally
powerful image—the image of The Bad Parent.

25   The shift occurred in two stages. The first-stage critique
emerged in the seventies and focused on an important new figure:
The working mother. Working mothers were destroying their children and the family, conservative critics charged. They weren't
feeding kids wholesome meals, they weren't taking the kids to
church, they weren't serving as moral exemplars. Liberals sided
with working mothers, but conceded that they were struggling
with some new and difficult issues: Was day care as good as
mother care? Was quality time good enough? Were the rewards of
twelve-hour workdays great enough to make up for the loss of
sleep and leisure-time? Where did the mother of a feverish child
belong—at the crib or at her desk?

26   On the whole, the first-stage critique was a sympathetic critique. In its view, parents might be affected by stress and guilt,
but they weren't yet afflicted by serious pathology. After all, in
the seventies, the nation's most suspect drug was laetrile, not
crack or ice. Divorce was still viewed as a healthy alternative to
an unhappy family life. But as the eighties began, a darker image
of parents appeared. In the second-stage critique, . . . parents became toxic.

27   Day after day, throughout the eighties, Americans confronted
an ugly new reality. Parents were hurting and murdering their
children. Day after day, the newspapers brought yet another story
of a child abandoned or battered. Day after day, the local news
told of a child sexually abused by a father or a stepfather or a
mother's boyfriend. Week by week, the national media brought us
into courtrooms where photographs of battered children were
held up to the camera. The sheer volume of stories suggested an
epidemic of historic proportion. In even the most staid publications, the news was sensational. The *New York Times* carried

bizarre stories usually found only in tabloids: A father who tortured his children for years; a mother who left her baby in a suitcase in a building she then set on fire; parents who abandoned babies dead or alive, in toilets, dumpsters, and alleyways.

Drug use among parents was one clear cause of abuse. And,   28
increasingly child abuse and drug abuse were linked in the most direct way possible. Pregnant women were battering their children in the womb, delivering drugs through their umbilical cords. Nightly images of crack-addicted babies in neonatal units destroyed any lingering public sympathy for mothers of the underclass. And as the highly publicized Joel Steinberg case made clear, middle-class parents, too, took drugs and killed babies. Even those parents who occasionally indulged were causing their children harm. The Partnership for Drug-Free America ran ads asking: "With millions of parents doing drugs, is it any wonder their kids are too?"

More than drugs, it was divorce that lay at the heart of mid-   29
dle-class parental failure. It wasn't the crackhouse but the courthouse that was the scene of their collapse. Parents engaged in bitter custody battles. Parents kidnapped their own children. Parents used children as weapons against each other or simply walked away from their responsibilities. In an important new study on the long-term effects of divorce, Judith Wallerstein challenged the earlier notion that divorce is healthy for kids. She studied middle-class families for fifteen years after divorce and came up with some startling findings: Almost half of the children in the study entered adulthood as worried, underachieving, self-deprecating, and sometimes angry young men and women; one in four experienced a severe and enduring drop in their standard of living; three in five felt rejected by at least one parent. Her study concluded: "Divorce is almost always more devastating for children than for their parents. . . . [W]hile divorce can rescue a parent from an intolerable situation, it can fail to rescue the children."

As a group, today's parents have been portrayed as selfish and   30
uncaring: Yuppie parents abandon the children to the au pair; working parents turn their kids over to the mall and the video arcade;

single parents hang a key around their kids' necks and a list of emergency numbers on the refrigerator. Even in the healthiest families, parents fail to put their children first.

31   The indictment of parents is pervasive. In a survey by the Carnegie Foundation, 90 percent of a national sample of public school teachers say a lack of parental support is a problem in their classrooms. Librarians gathered at a national convention to draft a new policy to deal with the problem of parents who send unattended children to the library after school. Daycare workers complain to Ann Landers that all too often parents hand over children with empty stomachs and full diapers. Everywhere, parents are flunking the most basic tests.

32   Declining demographically, hard-pressed economically, and disarrayed politically, parents have become part of the problem. For proponents of the *kids as capital* argument, the logic is clear: Why try to help parents—an increasingly marginal and unsympathetic bunch—when you can rescue their children?

33   To blame parents for larger social changes is nothing new. In the past, child-saving movements have depended on building a public consensus that certain parents have failed. Child reformers in the Progressive Era, for example, were able to expand the scope of public sector responsibility for the welfare of children by exploiting mainstream fears about immigrant parents and their child-rearing practices. But what is new is the sense that the majority of parents—up and down the social ladder—are failing. Even middle-class parents, once solid, dependable caretakers of the next generation, don't seem to be up to the job.

34   By leaving parents out of the picture, *kids as capital* conjures up the image of our little workers struggling against the little workers of Germany and the little workers of Japan. But this picture is obviously false. For the little workers of Germany and Japan have parents too. The difference is that their parents are strongly valued and supported by the society for their contributions *as parents*. We won't be facing up to reality until we are ready to pit our parents against their parents, and thus our family policy against theirs.

1990

If Hitler Asked You to Electrocute a Stranger, Would You? Probably

Philip Meyer

In the beginning, Stanley Milgram was worried about the Nazi 1
problem. He doesn't worry much about the Nazis anymore. He
worries about you and me, and, perhaps, himself a little bit too.

Stanley Milgram is a social psychologist, and when he began 2
his career at Yale University in 1960 he had a plan to prove, scien-
tifically, that Germans are different. The Germans-are-different hypothesis has been used by historians, such as William L. Shirer, to
explain the systematic destruction of the Jews by the Third Reich.

The appealing thing about this theory is that it makes those of 3
us who are not Germans feel better about the whole business. Obviously, you and I are not Hitler, and it seems equally obvious that
we would never do Hitler's dirty work for him. But now, because
of Stanley Milgram, we are compelled to wonder. Milgram developed a laboratory experiment which provided a systematic way to
measure obedience. His plan was to try it out in New Haven on
Americans and then go to Germany and try it out on Germans. He
was strongly motivated by scientific curiosity, but there was also
some moral content in his decision to pursue this line of research,
which was, in turn, colored by his own Jewish background. If he
could show that Germans are more obedient than Americans, he
could then vary the conditions of the experiment and try to find
out just what it is that makes some people more obedient than others. With this understanding, the world might, conceivably, be just
a little bit better.

But he never took his experiment to Germany. He never took 4
it any farther than Bridgeport. The first finding, also the most
unexpected and disturbing finding, was that we Americans are
an obedient people: Not blindly obedient, and not blissfully

obedient, just obedient. "I found so much obedience," says Milgram softly, a little sadly, "I hardly saw the need for taking the experiment to Germany."

5   There is something of the theatre director in Milgram, and his technique, which he learned from one of the old masters in experimental psychology, Solomon Asch, is to stage a play with every line rehearsed, every prop carefully selected, and everybody an actor except one person. That one person is the subject of the experiment. The subject, of course, does not know he is in a play. He thinks he is in real life.

6   The experiment worked like this: If you were an innocent subject in Milgram's melodrama, you read an ad in the newspaper or received one in the mail asking for volunteers for an educational experiment. The job would take about an hour and pay $4.50. So you make an appointment and go to an old Romanesque stone structure on High Street with the imposing name of The Yale Interaction Laboratory. It looks something like a broadcasting studio. Inside, you meet a young, crew-cut man in a laboratory coat who says he is Jack Williams, the experimenter. There is another citizen, fiftyish, Irish face, an accountant, a little overweight, and very mild and harmless-looking. This other citizen seems nervous and plays with his hat while the two of you sit in chairs side by side and are told that the $4.50 checks are yours no matter what happens. Then you listen to Jack Williams explain the experiment.

7   It is about learning, says Jack Williams in a quiet, knowledgeable way. Science does not know much about the conditions under which people learn and this experiment is to find out about negative reinforcement. Negative reinforcement is getting punished when you do something wrong, as opposed to positive reinforcement which is getting rewarded when you do something right. The negative reinforcement in this case is electric shock.

8   Then Jack Williams takes two pieces of paper, puts them in a hat, and shakes them up. One piece of paper is supposed to say, "Teacher" and the other, "Learner." Draw one and you will see which you will be. The mild-looking accountant draws one, holds it close to his vest like a poker player, looks at it, and says,

"Learner." You look at yours. It says, "Teacher." You do not know that the drawing is rigged, and both slips say "Teacher." The experimenter beckons to the mild-mannered "learner."

"Want to step right in here and have a seat, please?" he says. 9 "You can leave your coat on the back of that chair . . . roll up your right sleeve, please. Now what I want to do is strap down your arms to avoid excessive movement on your part during the experiment. This electrode is connected to the shock generator in the next room.

"And this electrode paste," he says, squeezing some stuff out 10 of a plastic bottle and putting it on the man's arm, "is to provide a good contact and to avoid a blister or burn. Are there any questions now before we go into the next room?"

You don't have any, but the strapped-in "learner" does. 11

"I do think I should say this," says the learner. "About two 12 years ago, I was at the veterans' hospital . . . they detected a heart condition. Nothing serious, but as long as I'm having these shocks, how strong are they—how dangerous are they?"

Williams, the experimenter, shakes his head casually. "Oh, 13 no," he says. "Although they may be painful, they're not dangerous. Anything else?"

Nothing else. And so you play the game. The game is for you 14 to read a series of word pairs: For example, blue-girl, nice-day, fat-neck. When you finish the list, you read just the first word in each pair and then a multiple-choice list of four other words, including the second word of the pair. The learner, from his remote, strapped-in position, pushes one of four switches to indicate which of the four answers he thinks is the right one. If he gets it right, nothing happens and you go on to the next one. If he gets it wrong, you push a switch that buzzes and gives him an electric shock. And then you go to the next word. You start with 15 volts and increase the number of volts by 15 for each wrong answer. The control board goes from 15 volts on one end to 450 volts on the other. So that you know what you are doing, you get a test shock yourself, at 45 volts. It hurts. To further keep you aware of what you are doing to that man in there, the board has verbal descriptions of the shock levels, ranging from "Slight Shock" at the left-hand side, through "Intense Shock" in the middle, to "Danger: Severe Shock" toward the far right. Finally, at the very end, under 435- and 450-volt switches, there are three ambiguous X's. If, at any point, you hesitate, Mr. Williams calmly tells you to go on. If you still hesitate, he tells you again.

15   Except for some terrifying details, which will be explained in a moment, this is the experiment. The object is to find the shock level at which you disobey the experimenter and refuse to pull the switch.

16   When Stanley Milgram first wrote this script, he took it to fourteen Yale psychology majors and asked them what they thought would happen. He put it this way: Out of one hundred persons in the teacher's predicament, how would their breakoff points be distributed along the 15-to-450-volt scale? They thought a few would break off very early, most would quit someplace in the middle and a few would go all the way to the end. The highest estimate of the number out of one hundred who would go all the way to the end was three. Milgram then informally polled some of his fellow scholars in the psychology department. They agreed that very few would go to the end. Milgram thought so too.

17   "I'll tell you quite frankly," he says, "before I began this experiment, before any shock generator was built, I thought that most people would break off at 'Strong Shock' or 'Very Strong Shock.' You would get only a very, very small proportion of people going out to the end of the shock generator, and they would constitute a pathological fringe."

18   In his pilot experiments, Milgram used Yale students as subjects. Each of them pushed the shock switches, one by one, all the way to the end of the board.

19   So he rewrote the script to include some protests from the learner. At first, they were mild, gentlemanly, Yalie protests, but, "it didn't seem to have as much effect as I thought it would or should," Milgram recalls. "So we had more violent protestation on the part of the person getting the shock. All of the time, of course, what we were trying to do was not to create a macabre situation, but simply to generate disobedience. And that was one of the first findings. This was not only a technical deficiency of the experiment, that we didn't get disobedience. It really was the first find-

ing: That obedience would be much greater than we had assumed it would be and disobedience would be much more difficult than we had assumed."

As it turned out, the situation did become rather macabre. The 20 only meaningful way to generate disobedience was to have the victim protest with great anguish, noise, and vehemence. The protests were tape-recorded so that all the teachers ordinarily would hear the same sounds and nuances, and they started with a grunt at 75 volts, proceeded through a "Hey, that really hurts," at 125 volts, got desperate with, "I can't stand the pain, don't do that," at 180 volts, reached complaints of heart trouble at 195, an agonized scream at 285, a refusal to answer at 315, and only heart-rending, ominous silence after that.

Still, sixty-five percent of the subjects, twenty- to fifty-year- 21 old American males, everyday, ordinary people, like you and me, obediently kept pushing those levers in the belief that they were shocking the mild-mannered learner, whose name was Mr. Wallace, and who was chosen for the role because of his innocent appearance, all the way up to 450 volts.

Milgram was now getting enough disobedience so that he had 22 something he could measure. The next step was to vary the circumstances to see what would encourage or discourage obedience.

He put the learner in the same room with the teacher. He 23 stopped strapping the learner's hand down. He rewrote the script so that at 150 volts the learner took his hand off the shock plate and declared that he wanted out of the experiment. He rewrote the script some more so that the experimenter then told the teacher to grasp the learner's hand and physically force it down on the plate to give Mr. Wallace his unwanted electric shock.

"I had the feeling that very few people would go on at that 24 point, if any," Milgram says. "I thought that would be the limit of obedience that you would find in the laboratory."

It wasn't.
25

Although seven years have now gone by, Milgram still re- 26 members the first person to walk into the laboratory in the newly rewritten script. He was a construction worker, a very short man. "He was so small," says Milgram, "that when he sat on the chair in front of the shock generator, his feet didn't reach the floor. When the experimenter told him to push the victim's hand down and give the shock, he turned to the experimenter, and he turned to the victim, his elbow went up, he fell down on the hand of the victim, his feet kind of tugged to one side, and he said, 'Like this, boss?' ZZUMPH!"

27   The experiment was played out to its bitter end. Milgram tried it with forty different subjects. And thirty percent of them obeyed the experimenter and kept on obeying.

28   "The protests of the victim were strong and vehement, he was screaming his guts out, he refused to participate, and you had to physically struggle with him in order to get his hand down on the shock generator," Milgram remembers. But twelve out of forty did it.

29   Milgram took his experiment out of New Haven. Not to Germany, just twenty miles down the road to Bridgeport. Maybe, he reasoned, the people obeyed because of the prestigious setting of Yale University.

30   The new setting was a suite of three rooms in a run-down office building in Bridgeport. The only identification was a sign with a fictitious name: "Research Associates of Bridgeport." Questions about professional connections got only vague answers about "research for industry."

31   Obedience was less in Bridgeport. Forty-eight percent of the subjects stayed for the maximum shock, compared to sixty-five percent at Yale. But this was enough to prove that far more than Yale's prestige was behind the obedient behavior.

32   For more than seven years now, Stanley Milgram has been trying to figure out what makes ordinary American citizens so obedient. The most obvious answer—that people are mean, nasty, brutish and sadistic—won't do. The subjects who gave the shocks to Mr. Wallace to the end of the board did not enjoy it. They groaned, protested, fidgeted, argued, and in some cases, were seized by fits of nervous, agitated giggling.

33   "They even try to get out of it," says Milgram, "but they are somehow engaged in something from which they cannot liberate themselves. They are locked into a structure, and they do not have the skills or inner resources to disengage themselves."

Milgram's theory assumes that people behave in two different 34
operating modes as different as ice and water. He does not rely on
Freud or sex or toilet-training hang-ups for this theory. All he says
is that ordinarily we operate in a state of autonomy, which means
we pretty much have and assert control over what we do. But in
certain circumstances, we operate under what Milgram calls a
state of agency (after agent, n . . . one who acts for or in the place
of another by authority from him; a substitute; a deputy—*Web-
ster's Collegiate Dictionary*). A state of agency, to Milgram, is nothing more than a frame of mind.

"There's nothing bad about it, there's nothing good about it," 35
he says. "It's a natural circumstance of living with other people.
. . . I think of a state of agency as a real transformation of a person;
if a person has different properties when he's in that state, just as
water can turn to ice under certain conditions of temperature, a
person can move to the state of mind that I call agency . . . the critical thing is that you see yourself as the instrument of the execu-
tion of another person's wishes. You do not see yourself as acting
on your own. And there's a real transformation, a real change of
properties of the person."

So, for most subjects in Milgram's laboratory experiments, the 36
act of giving Mr. Wallace his painful shock was necessary, even
though unpleasant, and besides they were doing it on behalf of
somebody else and it was for science.

Stanley Milgram has his problems, too. He believes that in the 37
laboratory situation, he would not have shocked Mr. Wallace. His
professional critics reply that in his real-life situation he has done
the equivalent. He has placed innocent and naïve subjects under
great emotional strain and pressure in selfish obedience to his
quest for knowledge. When you raise this issue with Milgram, he
has an answer ready. There is, he explains patiently, a critical difference between his naïve subjects and the man in the electric chair.
The man in the electric chair (in the mind of the naïve subject) is
helpless, strapped in. But the naïve subject is free to go at any time.

Immediately after he offers this distinction, Milgram antici- 38
pates the objection.

"It's quite true," he says, "that this is almost a philosophic posi- 39
tion, because we have learned that some people are psychologically

incapable of disengaging themselves. But that doesn't relieve them of the moral responsibility."

40   The parallel is exquisite. "The tension problem was unexpected," says Milgram in his defense. But he went on anyway. The naïve subjects didn't expect the screaming protests from the strapped-in learner. But they went on.

41   "I had to make a judgment," says Milgram. "I had to ask myself, was this harming the person or not? My judgment is that it was not. Even in the extreme cases, I wouldn't say that permanent damage results."

42   Sound familiar? "The shocks may be painful," the experimenter kept saying, "but they're not dangerous."

43   After the series of experiments was completed, Milgram sent a report of the results to his subjects and a questionnaire, asking whether they were glad or sorry to have been in the experiment. Eighty-three and seven-tenths percent said they were glad and only 1.3 percent were sorry; 15 percent were neither sorry nor glad. However, Milgram could not be sure at the time of the experiment that only 1.3 percent would be sorry.

44   Kurt Vonnegut Jr. put one paragraph in the preface to *Mother Night*, in 1966, which pretty much says it for the people with their fingers on the shock-generator switches, for you and me, and maybe even for Milgram. "If I'd been born in Germany," Vonnegut said, "I suppose I would have *been* a Nazi, bopping Jews and gypsies and Poles around, leaving boots sticking out of snowbanks, warming myself with my sweetly virtuous insides. So it goes."

45   Just so. One thing that happened to Milgram back in New Haven during the days of the experiment was that he kept running into people he'd watched from behind the one-way glass. It gave him a funny feeling, seeing those people going about their everyday business in New Haven and knowing what they would do to Mr. Wallace if ordered to. Now that his research results are in and you've thought about it, you can get this funny feeling too. You don't need one-way glass. A glance in your own mirror may serve just as well.

1970

Nubian Diet
Revealed at Last

Kathy A. Svitil

The Nubians were kings once: They built pyramids and temples; 1
carved delicate statues and jewelry; controlled trade along the
Nile; and for a century or so, beginning in the eighth century BC,
even ruled Egypt, their neighbor to the north.

Mostly, though, the Nubians have been pawns, invaded by 2
the Persians and Assyrians, dominated by the Egyptians—and finally flooded.

When the Aswan High Dam was completed in 1970, the reser- 3
voir it created inundated thousands of square miles of land along
the banks of the Nile, from Egypt south into the Sudan.

Nearly all of what was once the Lower Nubian heartland is 4
now Lake Nasser.

Before the flood, however, teams of archaeologists from 5
around the world flocked to the region, hurriedly salvaging what
they could of the Nubian past.

They recovered tons of ancient artifacts—including the entire 6
Temple of Dendur—and, even more remarkably, hundreds of ancient Nubians.

Most of these mummies were ordinary folk, buried in the 7
desert and accidentally preserved by the blistering heat and dry
sands.

Their bodies dried out so fast that not only the bones but also 8
the skin, hair and muscle were saved from decomposition.

And preserved along with the mummies, says Christine 9
White, a physical anthropologist at the University of Western Ontario, is a record of what the ancient Nubians ate—even in the last
weeks of their lives.

White gleaned that particular bit of information from the 10
mummies' hair.

Researchers already knew that the ancient Nubians' diet was 11
inadequate. Besides evidence of arthritis, tumors and parasites,

the mummies show clear signs of malnutrition, iron-deficiency anemia and osteoporosis.

12   Yet what that diet consisted of has been something of a mystery.

13   Despite the intensive excavation, no physical evidence—plant or animal remains—was ever recovered.

14   White has now extracted that physical evidence from the mummies themselves by looking at the isotope signatures of their tissue: The distinctive ratios of heavy nitrogen atoms to light ones and of heavy to light carbon that humans acquire from the plants and animals they eat.

15   White studied 167 mummies from a site along the west bank of the Nile in the Wadi Halfa region of northern Sudan.

16   The oldest mummies dated from the period between 350 BC and AD 350, when Lower Nubia was ruled by the Meroitic Empire of Upper Nubia.

17   White first looked at the mummies' nitrogen signature to find out their source of protein (which is rich in nitrogen).

18   Grasses and the cows that eat them have a relatively low ratio of heavy nitrogen 15 to nitrogen 14; scrubs and bushes and the goats and sheep that browse on them in the Nubian Desert have a higher ratio. Most of the mummies, White found, had eaten these desert animals rather than cattle.

19   Some had partaken more than others: Male mummies contained more nitrogen 15 relative to their body weight than did females. Apparently, the men of ancient Nubia got more than their fair share of the meat.

20   The ancient Nubians did not just ranch in the desert. They also made it bloom—and with crops that aren't easy to grow in hot, arid conditions.

21   The ratio of carbon 13 to carbon 12 in the mummies from the Meroitic period, White says, shows that fully 84 percent of the Nubians' plant intake consisted of "C3" foods such as wheat, barley and fruit—all of which require more water than is normally available in the Nubian Desert.

22   The Nubians, White figures, must therefore have been irrigating their crops, probably using the ox-driven waterwheel—a sort of Ferris wheel with buckets that dumped water from the Nile into irrigation channels. It was invented in Mesopotamia and brought to Lower Nubia by Meroitic settlers.

Lower Nubia, White speculates, may have been an agricul- 23
tural hinterland that produced wheat and barley for Meroe. That
might explain why mummies dating from after the fall of the
Meroitic Empire around 350 AD ate about 9 percent fewer C3
plants than their forebears.

"When the Meroitic Empire fell," White says, "the Nubians, 24
who no longer had to grow so much wheat and barley, may have
reverted to a more traditional diet of C4 plants, like sorghum and
millet."

Such grains are much easier to grow in the desert than C3 25
crops, even with irrigation.

Today in the Wadi Halfa, wheat and barley are grown in the 26
fall and winter, with the aid of irrigation and the annual flooding
of the Nile, while sorghum and millet are planted in the spring
and harvested beginning in early June.

Could the same crop rotation, White wondered, have been oc- 27
curring over a thousand years ago?

The mummies' hair said yes. 28

Until White's work, only bone had been used in isotopic analy- 29
ses, and bone takes between 25 and 30 years to replace its store of
isotopes—making its isotope signature "just a homogenized version of what was consumed over a lifetime," as White puts it.

But isotopes show up in hair two weeks after they're con- 30
sumed. Thus isotope signatures from a hair shaft can reveal any
changes in diet that occurred while the hair was growing.

White cut hair from 14 post-Meroe mummies into 3.25-inch- 31
long segments, each segment representing about two months'
growth.

She found that the isotopic signature fluctuated dramatically 32
between segments, indicating that the person had alternated between periods of eating mostly C3 plants and ones of relying on
C4 plants.

Furthermore, by looking at the hair closest to the scalp, White 33
could tell what the future mummies had eaten just weeks before
they died.

Nearly two-thirds of them had been eating C4 plants. That 34
suggested they died after the sorghum and millet harvest in June,
but before the wheat and barley harvest in the winter.

35   Why would more Nubians have died during summer?

36   Because of heat and malnutrition, White says.

37   C4 plants aren't as nutritious as C3 plants; sorghum is low in vitamin B, for instance, and vitamin B deficiency increases the incidence of pellagra, a disease that causes gastrointestinal and neurological problems.

38   Moreover, by the end of summer in Nubia, even C4 crops are scarce.

39   Today more residents of the Nubian Desert die in summer than during any other time of year. One thousand years ago, their ancestors may have faced the same hardships.

1995

9

Analogy

The Myth of the Cave

Plato

And now, I said, let me show in a figure how far our nature is en- 1
lightened or unenlightened:—Behold! human beings living in an
underground den, which has a mouth open toward the light and
reaching all along the den; here they have been from their childhood, and have their legs and necks chained so that they cannot
move, and can only see before them, being prevented by the
chains from turning round their heads. Above and behind them a
fire is blazing at a distance, and between the fire and the prisoners
there is a raised way; and you will see, if you look, a low wall built
along the way, like the screen which marionette players have in
front of them, over which they show the puppets.

I see. 2

And do you see, I said, men passing along the wall carrying 3
all sorts of vessels, and statues and figures of animals made of
wood and stone and various materials, which appear over the
wall? Some of them are talking, others silent.

You have shown me a strange image, and they are strange 4
prisoners.

Like ourselves, I replied; and they see only their own shad- 5
ows, or the shadows of one another, which the fire throws on the
opposite wall of the cave?

True, he said; how could they see anything but the shadows if 6
they were never allowed to move their heads?

321

7   And of the objects which are being carried in like manner they would only see the shadows?

8   Yes, he said.

9   And if they were able to converse with one another, would they not suppose that they were naming what was actually before them?

10   Very true.

11   And suppose further that the prison had an echo which came from the other side, would they not be sure to fancy when one of the passers-by spoke that the voice which they heard came from the passing shadow?

12   No question, he replied.

13   To them, I said, the truth would be literally nothing but the shadows of the images.

14   That is certain.

15   And now look again, and see what will naturally follow if the prisoners are released and disabused of their error. At first, when any of them is liberated and compelled suddenly to stand up and turn his neck round and walk and look toward the light, he will suffer sharp pains; the glare will distress him, and he will be unable to see the realities of which in his former state he had seen the shadows; and then conceive some one saying to him, that what he saw before was an illusion, but that now, when he is approaching nearer to being and his eye is turned toward more real existence, he has a clearer vision—what will be his reply? And you may further imagine that his instructor is pointing to the objects as they pass and requiring him to name them—will he not be perplexed? Will he not fancy that the shadows which he formerly saw are truer than the objects which are now shown to him?

16   Far truer.

17   And if he is compelled to look straight at the light, will he not have a pain in his eyes which will make him turn away to take refuge in the objects of vision which he can see, and which he will conceive to be in reality clearer than the things which are now being shown to him?

18   True, he said.

19   And suppose once more, that he is reluctantly dragged up a steep and rugged ascent, and held fast until he is forced into the pres-

ence of the sun himself, is he not likely to be pained and irritated?
When he approaches the light his eyes will be dazzled, and he will
not be able to see anything at all of what are now called realities.

Not all in a moment, he said.   20

He will require to grow accustomed to the sight of the upper   21
world. And first he will see the shadows best, next the reflections
of men and other objects in the water, and then the objects themselves; then he will gaze upon the light of the moon and the stars
and the spangled heaven; and he will see the sky and the stars by
night better than the sun or the light of the sun by day?

Certainly.   22

Last of all he will be able to see the sun, and not mere reflec-   23
tions of him in the water, but he will see him in his own proper
place, and not in another; and he will contemplate him as he is.

Certainly.   24

He will then proceed to argue that this is he who gives the sea-   25
son and the years, and is the guardian of all that is in the visible
world, and in a certain way the cause of all things which he and
his fellows have been accustomed to behold?

Clearly, he said, he would first see the sun and then reason   26
about him.

And when he remembered his old habitation, and the wisdom   27
of the den and his fellow-prisoners, do you not suppose that he
would felicitate himself on the change, and pity them?

Certainly, he would.   28

And if they were in the habit of conferring honors among   29
themselves on those who were quickest to observe the passing
shadows and to remark which of them went before, and which followed after, and which were together; and who were therefore
best able to draw conclusions as to the future, do you think that he
would care for such honors and glories, or envy the possessors of
them? Would he not say with Homer,

> Better to be the poor servant of a poor master,

and to endure anything, rather than think as they do and live after their manner?

Yes, he said, I think that he would rather suffer anything than   30
entertain these false notions and live in this miserable manner.

31   Imagine once more, I said, such a one coming suddenly out of the sun to be replaced in his old situation; would he not be certain to have his eyes full of darkness?

32   To be sure, he said.

33   And if there were a contest, and he had to compete in measuring the shadows with the prisoners who had never moved out of the den, while his sight was still weak, and before his eyes had become steady (and the time which would be needed to acquire this new habit of sight might be very considerable), would he not be ridiculous? Men would say of him that up he went and down he came without his eyes; and that it was better not even to think of ascending and if any one tried to loose another and lead him up to the light, let them only catch the offender, and they would put him to death.

34   No question, he said.

35   This entire allegory, I said, you may now append, dear Glaucon, to the previous argument; the prison-house is the world of sight, the light of the fire is the sun, and you will not misapprehend me if you interpret the journey upwards to be the ascent of the soul into the intellectual world according to my poor belief, which, at your desire, I have expressed—whether rightly or wrongly God knows. But, whether true or false, my opinion is that in the world of knowledge the idea of good appears last of all, and is seen only with an effort; and, when seen, is also inferred to be the universal author of all things beautiful and right, parent of light and of the lord of light in this visible world, and the immediate source of reason and truth in the intellectual; and that this is the power upon which he who would act rationally either in public or private life must have his eye fixed.

36   I agree, he said, as far as I am able to understand you.

37   Moreover, I said, you must not wonder that those who attain to this beatific vision are unwilling to descend to human affairs; for their souls are ever hastening into the upper world where they desire to dwell; which desire of theirs is very natural, if our allegory may be trusted.

38   Yes, very natural.

39   And is there anything surprising in one who passes from divine contemplations to the evil state of man, misbehaving him-

self in a ridiculous manner; if, while his eyes are blinking and before he has become accustomed to the surrounding darkness, he
is compelled to fight in courts of law, or in other places, about the
images or the shadows of images of justice, and is endeavoring
to meet the conceptions of those who have never yet seen absolute justice?

Anything but surprising, he replied.   40

Anyone who has common sense will remember that the be-   41
wilderments of the eyes are of two kinds, and arise from two
causes, either from coming out of the light or from going into the
light, which is true of the mind's eye, quite as much as of the bodily eye; and he who remembers this when he sees any one whose
vision is perplexed and weak, will not be too ready to laugh; he
will first ask whether that soul of man has come out of the brighter
life, and is unable to see because unaccustomed to the dark, or
having turned from darkness to the day is dazzled by excess of
light. And he will count the one happy in his condition and state
of being, and he will pity the other; or, if he have a mind to laugh
at the soul which comes from below into the light, there will be
more reason in this than in the laugh which greets him who returns from above out of the light into the den.

That, he said, is a very just distinction.   42

ca. 373 BC

The Myth
of Sisyphus

Albert Camus

The gods had condemned Sisyphus to ceaselessly rolling a rock to   1
the top of a mountain, whence the stone would fall back of its own
weight. They had thought with some reason that there is no more
dreadful punishment than futile and hopeless labor.

2   If one believes Homer, Sisyphus was the wisest and most prudent of mortals. According to another tradition, however, he was
disposed to practice the profession of highwayman. I see no contradiction in this. Opinions differ as to the reasons why he became
the futile laborer of the underworld. To begin with, he is accused
of a certain levity in regard to the gods. He stole their secrets.
Aegina, the daughter of Aesopus, was carried off by Jupiter. The
father was shocked by that disappearance and complained to
Sisyphus. He, who knew of the abduction, offered to tell about it
on condition that Aesopus would give water to the citadel of
Corinth. To the celestial thunderbolts he preferred the benediction
of water. He was punished for this in the underworld. Homer tells
us also that Sisyphus had put Death in chains. Pluto could not endure the sight of his deserted, silent empire. He dispatched the
god of war, who liberated Death from the hands of her conqueror.

3   It is said also that Sisyphus, being near to death, rashly
wanted to test his wife's love. He ordered her to cast his unburied
body into the middle of the public square. Sisyphus woke up in
the underworld. And there, annoyed by an obedience so contrary
to human love, he obtained from Pluto permission to return to
earth in order to chastise his wife. But when he had seen again the
face of this world, enjoyed water and sun, warm stones and the
sea, he no longer wanted to go back to the infernal darkness. Recalls, signs of anger, warnings were of no avail. Many years more
he lived facing the curve of the gulf, the sparkling sea, and the
smiles of earth. A decree of the gods was necessary. Mercury came
and seized the impudent man by the collar and, snatching him
from his joys, led him forcibly back to the underworld, where his
rock was ready for him.

4   You have already grasped that Sisyphus is the absurd hero.
He is, as much through his passions as through his torture. His
scorn of the gods, his hatred of death, and his passion for life won
him that unspeakable penalty in which the whole being is exerted
toward accomplishing nothing. This is the price that must be paid
for the passions of this earth. Nothing is told us about Sisyphus in
the underworld. Myths are made for the imagination to breathe
life into them. As for this myth, one sees merely the whole effort
of a body straining to raise the huge stone, to roll it and push it up

a slope a hundred times over; one sees the face screwed up, the cheek tight against the stone, the shoulder bracing the clay-covered mass, the foot wedging it, the fresh start with arms outstretched, the wholly human security of two earth-clotted hands. At the very end of his long effort measured by skyless space and time without depth, the purpose is achieved. Then Sisyphus watches the stone rush down in a few moments toward that lower world whence he will have to push it up again toward the summit. He goes back down to the plain.

It is during that return, that pause, that Sisyphus interests me. 5 A face that toils so close to stones is already stone itself! I see that man going back down with a heavy yet measured step toward the torment of which he will never know the end. That hour like a breathing-space which returns as surely as his suffering, that is the hour of consciousness. At each of those moments when he leaves the heights and gradually sinks toward the lairs of the gods, he is superior to his fate. He is stronger than his rock.

If this myth is tragic, that is because its hero is conscious. 6 Where would his torture be, indeed, if at every step the hope of succeeding upheld him? The workman of today works every day in his life at the same tasks, and this fate is no less absurd. But it is tragic only at the rare moments when it becomes conscious. Sisyphus, proletarian of the gods, powerless and rebellious, knows the whole extent of his wretched condition: it is what he thinks of during his descent. The lucidity that was to constitute his torture at the same time crowns his victory. There is no fate that cannot be surmounted by scorn.

If the descent is thus sometimes performed in sorrow, it can 7 also take place in joy. This word is not too much. Again I fancy Sisyphus returning toward his rock, and the sorrow was in the beginning. When the images of earth cling too tightly to memory, when the call of happiness becomes too insistent, it happens that melancholy rises in man's heart: this is the rock's
rock itself. The boundless grief is too heavy to b
nights of Gethsemane. But crushing truths per
knowledged. Thus, Oedipus at the outset o
knowing it. But from the moment he knows, I

Yet at the same moment, blind and desperate, he realizes that the only bond linking him to the world is the cool hand of a girl. Then a tremendous remark rings out: "Despite so many ordeals, my advanced age and the nobility of my soul make me conclude that all is well." Sophocles' Oedipus, like Dostoevsky's Kirilov, thus gives the recipe for the absurd victory. Ancient wisdom confirms modern heroism.

8   One does not discover the absurd without being tempted to write a manual of happiness. "What! by such narrow ways—?" There is but one world, however. Happiness and the absurd are two sons of the same earth. They are inseparable. It would be a mistake to say that happiness necessarily springs from the absurd discovery. It happens as well that the feeling of the absurd springs from happiness. "I conclude that all is well," says Oedipus, and that remark is sacred. It echoes in the wild and limited universe of man. It teaches that all is not, has not been, exhausted. It drives out of this world a god who had come into it with dissatisfaction and a preference for futile sufferings. It makes of fate a human matter, which must be settled among men.

9   All Sisyphus' silent joy is contained therein. His fate belongs to him. His rock is his thing. Likewise, the absurd man, when he contemplates his torment, silences all the idols. In the universe suddenly restored to its silence, the myriad wondering little voices of the earth rise up. Unconscious, secret calls, invitations from all the faces, they are the necessary reverse and price of victory. There is no sun without shadow, and it is essential to know the night. The absurd man says yes and his effort will henceforth be unceasing. If there is a personal fate, there is no higher destiny, or at least there is but one which he concludes is inevitable and despicable. For the rest, he knows himself to be the master of his days. At that subtle moment when man glances backward over his life, Sisyphus returning toward his rock, in that slight pivoting he contemplates that series of unrelated actions which becomes his fate, created by him, combined under his memory's eye and soon sealed by his death. Thus, convinced of the wholly human origin of all that is human, a blind man eager to see who knows that the night has no end, he is still on the go. The rock is rolling.

I leave Sisyphus at the foot of the mountain! One always finds 10
one's burden again. But Sisyphus teaches the higher fidelity that
negates the gods and raises rocks. He too concludes that all is well.
This universe henceforth without a master seems to him neither
sterile nor futile. Each atom of that stone, each mineral flake of that
night-filled mountain, in itself forms a world. The struggle itself
toward the heights is enough to fill a man's heart. One must imagine Sisyphus happy.

1955

"But a Watch in the Night": A Scientific Fable

James C. Rettie

Out beyond our solar system there is a planet called Copernicus. 1
It came into existence some four or five billion years before the
birth of our Earth. In due course of time it became inhabited by a
race of intelligent men.

About 750 million years ago the Copernicans had developed 2
the motion picture machine to a point well in advance of the stage
that we have reached. Most of the cameras that we now use in motion picture work are geared to take twenty-four pictures per second on a continuous strip of film. When such film is run through a
projector, it throws a series of images on the screen and these change
with a rapidity that gives the visual impression of normal movement. If a motion is too swift for the human eye to see it in detail, it
can be captured and artificially slowed down by means of the slow-
motion camera. This one is geared to take many more shots per second—ninety-six or even more than that. When the slow motion film
is projected at the normal speed of twenty-four pictures per second,
we can see just how the jumping horse goes over a hurdle.

3   What about motion that is too slow to be seen by the human eye? That problem has been solved by the use of the time-lapse camera. In this one, the shutter is geared to take only one shot per second, or one per minute, or even one per hour—depending upon the kind of movement that is being photographed. When the time-lapse film is projected at the normal speed of twenty-four pictures per second, it is possible to see a bean sprout growing up out of the ground. Time-lapse films are useful in the study of many types of motion too slow to be observed by the unaided, human eye.

4   The Copernicans, it seems, had time-lapse cameras some 757 million years ago and they also had superpowered telescopes that gave them a clear view of what was happening upon this Earth. They decided to make a film record of the life history of Earth and to make it on the scale of one picture per year. The photography has been in progress during the last 757 million years.

5   In the near future, a Copernican interstellar expedition will arrive upon our Earth and bring with it a copy of the time-lapse film. Arrangements will be made for showing the entire film in one continuous run. This will begin at midnight of New Year's Eve and continue day and night without a single stop until midnight of December 31. The rate of projection will be twenty-four pictures per second. Time on the screen will thus seem to move at the rate of twenty-four years per second; 1440 years per minute; 86,400 years per hour; approximately two million years per day; and sixty-two million years per month. The normal life-span of individual man will occupy about three seconds. The full period of earth history that will be unfolded on the screen (some 757 million years) will extend from what the geologists call Pre-Cambrian times up to the present. This will, by no means, cover the full time-span of the earth's geological history but it will embrace the period since the advent of living organisms.

6   During the months of January, February, and March the picture will be desolate and dreary. The shape of the land masses and the oceans will bear little or no resemblance to those that we know. The violence of geological erosion will be much in evidence. Rains will pour down on the land and promptly go booming down to the seas. There will be no clear streams anywhere except where the

rains fall upon hard rock. Everywhere on the steeper ground the stream channels will be filled with boulders hurled down by rushing waters. Raging torrents and dry stream beds will keep alternating in quick succession. High mountains will seem to melt like so much butter in the sun. The shifting of land into the seas, later to be thrust up as new mountains, will be going on at a grand scale.

Early in April there will be some indication of the presence of single-celled living organisms in some of the warmer and sheltered coastal waters. By the end of the month it will be noticed that some of these organisms have become multicellular. A few of them, including the Trilobites, will be encased in hard shells. 7

Toward the end of May, the first vertebrates will appear, but they will still be aquatic creatures. In June about 60 per cent of the land area that we know as North America will be under water. One broad channel will occupy the space where the Rocky Mountains now stand. Great deposits of limestone will be forming under some of the shallower seas. Oil and gas deposits will be in process of formation—also under shallow seas. On land there will still be no sign of vegetation. Erosion will be rampant, tearing loose particles and chunks of rock and grinding them into sand and silt to be sped out by the streams into bays and estuaries. 8

About the middle of July the first land plants will appear and take up the tremendous job of soil building. Slowly, very slowly, the mat of vegetation will spread, always battling for its life against the power of erosion. Almost foot by foot, the plant life will advance, lacing down with its root structures whatever pulverized rock material it can find. Leaves and stems will be giving added protection against the loss of the soil foothold. The increasing vegetation will pave the way for the land animals that will live upon it. 9

Early in August the seas will be teeming with fish. This will be what geologists call the Devonian period. Some of the races of these fish will be breathing by means of lung tissue instead of through gill tissues. Before the month is over, some of the lung fish will go ashore and take on a crude lizard-like appearance. Here are the first amphibians. 10

In early September the insects will put in their appearance. Some will look like huge dragonflies and will have a wing spread 11 of 24 inches. Large portions of the land masses will now be covered with heavy vegetation that will include the primitive spore-propagating trees. Layer upon layer of this plant growth will build up, later to appear as the coal deposits. About the middle of this month, there will be evidence of the first seed-bearing plants and the first reptiles. Heretofore, the land animals will have been amphibians that could reproduce their kind only by depositing a soft egg mass in quiet waters. The reptiles will be shown to be freed from the aquatic bond because they can reproduce by means of a shelled egg in which the embryo and its nurturing liquids are sealed and thus protected from destructive evaporation. Before September is over, the first dinosaurs will be seen—creatures destined to dominate the animal realm for about 140 million years and then to disappear.

12   In October there will be series of mountain uplifts along what is now the eastern coast of the United States. A creature with feathered limbs—half bird and half reptile in appearance—will take itself into the air. Some small and rather unpretentious animals will be seen to bring forth their young in a form that is a miniature replica of the parents and to feed these young on milk secreted by mammary glands in the female parent. The emergence of this mammalian form of animal life will be recognized as one of the great events in geologic time. October will also witness the high water mark of the dinosaurs—creatures ranging in size from that of the modern goat to monsters like Brontosaurus that weighed some 40 tons. Most of them will be placid vegetarians, but a few will be hideous-looking carnivores, like Allosaurus and Tyrannosaurus. Some of the herbivorous dinosaurs will be clad in bony armor for protection against their flesh-eating comrades.

13   November will bring pictures of a sea extending from the Gulf of Mexico to the Arctic in space now occupied by the Rocky Mountains. A few of the reptiles will take to the air on bat-like wings. One of these, called Pteranodon, will have a wingspread of 15 feet. There will be a rapid development of the modern flowering plants, modern trees, and modern insects. The dinosaurs will disappear. Toward the end of the month there will be a tremendous land disturbance in which the Rocky Mountains will rise out of the sea to assume a dominating place in the North American landscape.

As the picture runs on into December it will show the mam- 14
mals in command of the animal life. Seed-bearing trees and
grasses will have covered most of the land with a heavy mantle of
vegetation. Only the areas newly thrust up from the sea will be
barren. Most of the streams will be crystal clear. The turmoil of geologic erosion will be confined to localized areas. About December 25 will begin the cutting of the Grand Canyon of the Colorado
River. Grinding down through layer after layer of sedimentary
strata, this stream will finally expose deposits laid down in Pre-
Cambrian times. Thus in the walls of that canyon will appear geological formations dating from recent times to the period when
the Earth had no living organisms upon it.

The picture will run on through the latter days of December 15
and even up to its final day with still no sign of mankind. The
spectators will become alarmed in the fear that man has somehow
been left out. But not so; sometime about noon on December 31
(one million years ago) will appear a stooped, massive creature of
man-like proportions. This will be Pithecanthropus, the Java ape
man. For tools and weapons he will have nothing but crude stone
and wooden clubs. His children will live a precarious existence
threatened on the one side by hostile animals and on the other by
tremendous climatic changes. Ice sheets—in places 4,000 feet
deep—will form in the northern parts of North America and Eura-
sia. Four times this glacial ice will push southward to cover half
the continents. With each advance the plant and animal life will be
swept under or pushed southward. With each recession of the ice,
life will struggle to reestablish itself in the wake of the retreating
glaciers. The woolly mammoth, the musk ox, and the caribou all
will fight to maintain themselves near the ice line. Sometimes they
will be caught and put into cold storage—skin, flesh, blood, bones
and all.

The picture will run on through supper time with still very lit- 16
tle evidence of man's presence on the earth. It will be about 11
o'clock when Neanderthal man appears. Another half hour will go
by before the appearance of Cro-Magnon man living in caves and
painting crude animal pictures on the walls of his dwelling. Fifteen minutes more will bring Neolithic man, knowing how to chip
stone and thus produce sharp cutting edges for spears and tools.

In a few minutes more it will appear that man has domesticated the dog, the sheep and, possibly, other animals. He will then begin the use of milk. He will also learn the arts of basket weaving and the making of pottery and dugout canoes.

17   The dawn of civilization will not come until about five or six minutes before the end of the picture. The story of the Egyptians, the Babylonians, the Greeks, and the Romans will unroll during the fourth, the third, and the second minute before the end. At 58 minutes and 43 seconds past 11:00 PM (just 1 minute and 17 seconds before the end) will come the beginning of the Christian era. Columbus will discover the new world 20 seconds before the end. The Declaration of Independence will be signed just 7 seconds before the final curtain comes down.

18   In those few moments of geologic time will be the story of all that has happened since we became a nation. And what a story it will be! A human swarm will sweep across the face of the continent and take it away from the . . . red men. They will change it far more radically than it has ever been changed before in a comparable time. The great virgin forests will be seen going down before ax and fire. The soil, covered for eons by its protective mantle of trees and grasses, will be laid bare to the ravages of water and wind erosion. Streams that had been flowing clear will, once again, take up a load of silt and push it toward the seas. Humus and mineral salts, both vital elements of productive soil, will be seen to vanish at a terrifying rate. The railroads and highways and cities that will spring up may divert attention, but they cannot cover up the blight of man's recent activities. In great sections of Asia, it will be seen that man must utilize cow dung and every scrap of available straw or grass for fuel to cook his food. The forests that once provided wood for this purpose will be gone without a trace. The use of these agricultural wastes for fuel, in place of returning them to the land, will be leading to increasing soil impoverishment. Here and there will be seen a dust storm darkening the landscape over an area a thousand miles across. Man-creatures will be shown counting their wealth in terms of bits of printed paper representing other bits of a scarce but comparatively useless yellow metal that is kept buried in strong vaults. Meanwhile, the soil,

the only real wealth that can keep mankind alive on the face of this earth is savagely being cut loose from its ancient moorings and washed into the seven seas.

We have just arrived upon this earth. How long will we stay? 19

1950

The Cosmic Prison

Loren Eiseley

"A name is a prison, God is free," once observed the Greek poet 1 Nikos Kazantzakis. He meant, I think, that valuable though language is to man, it is by very necessity limiting, and creates for man an invisible prison. Language implies boundaries. A word spoken creates a dog, a rabbit, a man. It fixes their nature before our eyes; henceforth their shapes are, in a sense, our own creation. They are no longer part of the unnamed shifting architecture of the universe. They have been transfixed as if by sorcery, frozen into a concept, a word. Powerful though the spell of human language has proven itself to be, it has laid boundaries upon the cosmos.

No matter how far-ranging some of the mental probes that 2 man has philosophically devised, by his own created nature he is forced to hold the specious and emerging present and transform it into words. The words are startling in their immediate effectiveness, but at the same time they are always finally imprisoning because man has constituted himself a prison keeper. He does so out of no conscious intention, but because for immediate purposes he has created an unnatural world of his own, which he calls the cultural world, and in which he feels at home. It defines his needs and allows him to lay a small immobilizing spell upon the nearer portions of his universe. Nevertheless, it transforms that universe into a cosmic prison house which is no sooner mapped than man feels its inadequacy and his own.

3   He seeks then to escape, and the theory of escape involves bodily flight. Scarcely had the first moon landing been achieved before one U.S. senator boldly announced: "We are the masters of the universe. We can go anywhere we choose." This statement was widely and editorially acclaimed. It is a striking example of the comfort of words, also of the covert substitutions and mental projections to which they are subject. The cosmic prison is not made less so by a successful journey of some two hundred and forty thousand miles in a cramped and primitive vehicle.

4   To escape the cosmic prison man is poorly equipped. He has to drag portions of his environment with him, and his life span is that of a mayfly in terms of the distances he seeks to penetrate. There is no possible way to master such a universe by flight alone. Indeed such a dream is a dangerous illusion. This may seem a heretical statement, but its truth is self-evident if we try seriously to comprehend the nature of time and space that I sought to grasp when held up to view the fiery messenger that flared across the zenith in 1910. "Seventy-five years," my father had whispered in my ear, "seventy-five years and it will be racing homeward. Perhaps you will live to see it again. Try to remember."

5   And so I remembered. I had gained a faint glimpse of the size of our prison house. Somewhere out there beyond a billion miles in space, an entity known as a comet had rounded on its track in the black darkness of the void. It was surging homeward toward the sun because it was an eccentric satellite of this solar system. If I lived to see it it would be but barely, and with the dimmed eyes of age. Yet it, too, in its long traverse, was but a flitting mayfly in terms of the universe the night sky revealed.

6   So relative is the cosmos we inhabit that, as we gaze upon the outer galaxies available to the reach of our telescopes, we are placed in about the position that a single white blood cell in our bodies would occupy, if it were intelligently capable of seeking to understand the nature of its own universe, the body it inhabits. The cell would encounter rivers ramifying into miles of distance seemingly leading nowhere. It would pass through gigantic structures whose meaning it could never grasp—the brain, for example. It could never know there was an outside, a vast being on a

scale it could not conceive of and of which it formed an infinitesi-
mal part. It would know only the pouring tumult of the creation it
inhabited, but of the nature of that great beast, or even indeed that
it was a beast, it could have no conception whatever. It might examine the liquid in which it floated and decide, as in the case of
the fall of Lucretius's atoms, that the pouring of obscure torrents
had created its world.

It might discover that creatures other than itself swam in the 7
torrent. But that its universe was alive, had been born and was
destined to perish, its own ephemeral existence would never allow it to perceive. It would never know the sun; it would explore
only through dim tactile sensations and react to chemical stimuli
that were borne to it along the mysterious conduits of the arteries
and veins. Its universe would be centered upon a great arbores-
cent tree of spouting blood. This, at best, generations of white
blood cells by enormous labor and continuity might succeed, like
astronomers, in charting.

They could never, by any conceivable stretch of the imagina- 8
tion, be aware that their so-called universe was, in actuality, the
prowling body of a cat or the more time-enduring body of a
philosopher, himself engaged upon the same quest in a more gigantic world and perhaps deceived proportionately by greater
vistas. What if, for example, the far galaxies man observes make
up, across void spaces of which even we are atomically composed,
some kind of enormous creature or cosmic snowflake whose exte-
rior we will never see? We will know more than the phagocyte in
our bodies, but no more than that limited creature can we climb
out of our universe, or successfully enhance our size or longevity
sufficiently to thrust our heads through the confines of the universe that terminates our vision.

Some further "outside" will hover elusively in our thought, 9
but upon its nature, or even its reality, we can do no more than
speculate. The phagocyte might observe the salty turbulence of an
eternal river system, Lucretius the fall of atoms creating momen-
tary living shapes. We suspiciously sense, in the concept of the expanding universe derived from the primordial atom—the
monobloc—some kind of oscillating universal heart. At the instant

of its contraction we will vanish. It is not given us, nor can our science recapture, the state beyond the monobloc, nor whether we exist in the diastole of some inconceivable being. We know only a little more extended reality than the hypothetical creature below us. Above us may lie realms it is beyond our power to grasp.

1970

Shouting "Fire!"

Alan M. Dershowitz

1   When the Reverend Jerry Falwell learned that the Supreme Court had reversed his $200,000 judgment against Hustler magazine for the emotional distress that he had suffered from an outrageous parody, his response was typical of those who seek to censor speech: "Just as no person may scream 'Fire!' in a crowded theater when there is no fire, and find cover under the First Amendment, likewise, no sleazy merchant like Larry Flynt should be able to use the First Amendment as an excuse for maliciously and dishonestly attacking public figures, as he has so often done."

2   Justice Oliver Wendell Holmes's classic example of unprotected speech—falsely shouting "Fire!" in a crowded theater—has been invoked so often, by so many people, in such diverse contexts, that it has become part of our national folk language. It has even appeared—most appropriately—in the theater: In Tom Stoppard's play *Rosencrantz and Guildenstern Are Dead* a character shouts at the audience, "Fire!" He then quickly explains: "It's all right—I'm demonstrating the misuse of free speech." Shouting "Fire!" in the theater may well be the only jurisprudential analogy that has assumed the status of a folk argument. A prominent historian recently characterized it as "the most brilliantly persuasive expression that ever came from Holmes's pen." But in spite of its hallowed position in both the jurisprudence of the First Amendment and the arsenal of political discourse, it is and was an inapt

analogy, even in the context in which it was originally offered. It has lately become—despite, perhaps even because of, the frequency and promiscuousness of its invocation—little more than a caricature of logical argumentation.

The case that gave rise to the "Fire!"-in-a-crowded-theater   3 analogy, *Schenck v. United States*, involved the prosecution of Charles Schenck, who was the general secretary of the Socialist party in Philadelphia, and Elizabeth Baer, who was its recording secretary. In 1917 a jury found Schenck and Baer guilty of attempting to cause insubordination among soldiers who had been drafted to fight in the First World War. They and other party members had circulated leaflets urging draftees not to "submit to intimidation" by fighting in a war being conducted on behalf of "Wall Street's chosen few."

Schenck admitted, and the Court found, that the intent of the   4 pamphlets' "impassioned language" was to "influence" draftees to resist the draft. Interestingly, however, Justice Holmes noted that nothing in the pamphlet suggested that the draftees should use unlawful or violent means to oppose conscription: "In form at least [the pamphlet] confined itself to peaceful measures, such as a petition for the repeal of the act" and an exhortation to exercise "your right to assert your opposition to the draft." Many of its most impassioned words were quoted directly from the Constitution.

Justice Holmes acknowledged that "in many places and in or-   5 dinary times the defendants, in saying all that was said in the circular, would have been within their constitutional rights." "But," he added, "the character of every act depends upon the circumstances in which it is done." And to illustrate that truism he went on to say:

> The most stringent protection of free speech would not protect a man in falsely shouting fire in a theater, and causing a panic. It does not even protect a man from an injunction against uttering words that may have all the effect of force.

Justice Holmes then upheld the convictions in the context of a   6 wartime draft, holding that the pamphlet created "a clear and present danger" of hindering the war effort while our soldiers were fighting for their lives and our liberty.

7   The example of shouting "Fire!" obviously bore little relationship to the facts of the Schenck case. The Schenck pamphlet contained a substantive political message. It urged its draftee readers to *think* about the message and then—if they so chose—to act on it in a lawful and nonviolent way. The man who shouts "Fire!" in a crowded theater is neither sending a political message nor inviting his listener to think about what he has said and decide what to do in a rational, calculated manner. On the contrary, the message is designed to force action *without* contemplation. The message "Fire!" is directed not to the mind and the conscience of the listener but, rather, to his adrenaline and his feet. It is a stimulus to immediate *action*, not thoughtful reflection. It is—as Justice Holmes recognized in his follow-up sentence—the functional equivalent of "uttering words that may have all the effect of force."

8   Indeed, in that respect the shout of "Fire!" is not even speech, in any meaningful sense of that term. It is a *clang* sound, the equivalent of setting off a nonverbal alarm. Had Justice Holmes been more honest about his example, he would have said that freedom of speech does not protect a kid who pulls a fire alarm in the absence of a fire. But that obviously would have been irrelevant to the case at hand. The proposition that pulling an alarm is not protected speech certainly leads to the conclusion that shouting the word "fire" is also not protected. But the core analogy is the nonverbal alarm, and the derivative example is the verbal shout. By cleverly substituting the derivative shout for the core alarm, Holmes made it possible to analogize one set of words to another—as he could not have done if he had begun with the self-evident proposition that setting off an alarm bell is not free speech.

9   The analogy is thus not only inapt but also insulting. Most Americans do not respond to political rhetoric with the same kind of automatic acceptance expected of schoolchildren responding to a fire drill. Not a single recipient of the Schenck pamphlet is known to have changed his mind after reading it. Indeed, one draftee, who appeared as a prosecution witness, was asked whether reading a pamphlet asserting that the draft law was unjust would make him "immediately decide that you must erase that law." Not surprisingly, he replied, "I do my own thinking." A

theatergoer would probably not respond similarly if asked how he would react to a shout of "Fire!"

Another important reason why the analogy is inapt is that Holmes emphasizes the factual falsity of the shout "Fire!" The Schenck pamphlet, however, was not factually false. It contained political opinions and ideas about the causes of the war and about appropriate and lawful responses to the draft. As the Supreme Court recently reaffirmed (in *Falwell v. Hustler*), "The First Amendment recognizes no such thing as a 'false' idea." Nor does it recognize false opinions about the causes of or cures for war.

A closer analogy to the facts of the Schenck case might have been provided by a person's standing outside a theater, offering the patrons a leaflet advising them that in his opinion the theater was structurally unsafe, and urging them not to enter but to complain to the building inspectors. That analogy, however, would not have served Holmes's argument for punishing Schenck. Holmes needed an analogy that would appear relevant to Schenck's political speech but that would invite the conclusion that censorship was appropriate.

Unsurprisingly, a war-weary nation—in the throes of a know-nothing hysteria over immigrant anarchists and socialists—welcomed the comparison between what was regarded as a seditious political pamphlet and a malicious shout of "Fire!" Ironically, the "Fire!" analogy is nearly all that survives from the Schenck case; the ruling itself is almost certainly not good law. Pamphlets of the kind that resulted in Schenck's imprisonment have been circulated with impunity during subsequent wars.

Over the past several years I have assembled a collection of instances—cases, speeches, arguments—in which proponents of censorship have maintained that the expression at issue is "just like" or "equivalent to" falsely shouting "Fire!" in a crowded theater and ought to be banned, "just as" shouting "Fire!" ought to be banned. The analogy is generally invoked, often with self-satisfaction, as an absolute argument-stopper. It does, after all, claim the high authority of the great Justice Oliver Wendell Holmes. I have rarely heard it invoked in a convincing, or even particularly relevant, way. But that, too, can claim lineage from the great Holmes.

14   Not unlike Falwell, with his silly comparison between shouting "Fire!" and publishing an offensive parody, courts and commentators have frequently invoked "Fire!" as an analogy to expression that is not an automatic stimulus to panic. A state
supreme court held that "Holmes's aphorism . . . applies with
equal force to pornography"—in particular to the exhibition of the
movie *Carmen Baby* in a drive-in theater in close proximity to highways and homes. Another court analogized "picketing . . . in support of a secondary boycott" to shouting "Fire!" because in both
instances "speech and conduct are brigaded." In the famous
Skokie case one of the judges argued that allowing Nazis to march
through a city where a large number of Holocaust survivors live
"just might fall into the same category as one's 'right' to cry fire in
a crowded theater."

15   Outside court the analogies become even more badly
stretched. A spokesperson for the New Jersey Sports and Exposi-
tion Authority complained that newspaper reports to the effect
that a large number of football players had contracted cancer after
playing in the Meadowlands—a stadium atop a landfill—were the
"journalistic equivalent of shouting fire in a crowded theater." An
insect researcher acknowledged that his prediction that a certain
amusement park might become roach-infested "may be tanta-
mount to shouting fire in a crowded theater." The philosopher
Sidney Hook, in a letter to the New York Times bemoaning a
Supreme Court decision that required a plaintiff in a defamation
action to prove that the offending statement was actually false, argued that the First Amendment does not give the press carte
blanche to accuse innocent persons "any more than the First
Amendment protects the right of someone falsely to shout fire in
a crowded theater."

16   Some close analogies to shouting "Fire!" or setting off an
alarm are, of course, available: Calling in a false bomb threat;
dialing 911 and falsely describing an emergency; making a loud,
gun-like sound in the presence of the President; setting off a voice-
activated sprinkler system by falsely shouting "Fire!" In one case
in which the "Fire!" analogy was directly to the point, a creative
defendant tried to get around it. The case involved a man who
calmly advised an airline clerk that he was "only here to hijack the
plane." He was charged, in effect, with shouting "Fire!" in a

crowded theater, and his rejected defense—as quoted by the court—was as follows: "If we built fire-proof theaters and let people know about this, then the shouting of 'Fire!' would not cause panic."

Here are some more-distant but still related examples: The recent incident of the police slaying in which some members of an onlooking crowd urged a mentally ill vagrant who had taken an officer's gun to shoot the officer; the screaming of racial epithets during a tense confrontation; shouting down a speaker and preventing him from continuing his speech. 17

Analogies are, by their nature, matters of degree. Some are closer to the core example than others. But any attempt to analogize political ideas in a pamphlet, ugly parody in a magazine, offensive movies in a theater, controversial newspaper articles, or any of the other expressions and actions catalogued above to the very different act of shouting "Fire!" in a crowded theater is either self-deceptive or self-serving. 18

The government does, of course, have some arguably legitimate bases for suppressing speech which bear no relationship to shouting "Fire!" It may ban the publication of nuclear-weapon codes, of information about troop movements, and of the identity of undercover agents. It may criminalize extortion threats and conspiratorial agreements. These expressions may lead directly to serious harm, but the mechanisms of causation are very different from that at work when an alarm is sounded. One may also argue—less persuasively, in my view—against protecting certain forms of public obscenity and defamatory statements. Here, too, the mechanisms of causation are very different. None of these exceptions to the First Amendment's exhortation that the government "shall make no law . . . abridging the freedom of speech, or of the press" is anything like falsely shouting "Fire!" in a crowded theater; they all must be justified on other grounds. 19

A comedian once told his audience, during a stand-up routine, about the time he was standing around a fire with a crowd of people and got in trouble for yelling "Theater, theater!" That, I think, is about as clever and productive a use as anyone has ever made of Holmes's flawed analogy. 20

1989

Blue = Sad
White — freedom

Am I Blue?

Alice Walker

Imprisonment of the horse

1 For about three years my companion and I rented a small house in the country that stood on the edge of a large meadow that appeared to run from the end of our deck straight into the mountains. The mountains, however, were quite far away, and between us and them there was, in fact, a town. It was one of the many pleasant aspects of the house that you never really were aware of this.

2 It was a house of many windows, low, wide, nearly floor to ceiling in the living room, which faced the meadow, and it was from one of these that I first saw our closest neighbor, a large white horse, cropping grass, flipping its mane, and ambling about—not over the entire meadow, which stretched well out of sight of the house, but over the five or so fenced-in acres that were next to the twenty-odd that we had rented. I soon learned that the horse, whose name was Blue, belonged to a man who lived in another town, but was boarded by our neighbors next door. Occasionally, one of the children, usually a stocky teenager, but sometimes a much younger girl or boy, could be seen riding Blue. They would appear in the meadow, climb up on his back, ride furiously for ten or fifteen minutes, then get off, slap Blue on the flanks, and not be seen again for a month or more.

3 There were many apple trees in our yard, and one by the fence that Blue could almost reach. We were soon in the habit of feeding him apples, which he relished, especially because by the middle of summer the meadow grasses—so green and succulent since January—had dried out from lack of rain, and Blue stumbled about munching the dried stalks half-heartedly. Sometimes he would stand very still just by the apple tree, and when one of us came out he would whinny, snort loudly, or stamp the ground. This meant, of course: I want an apple.

4 It was quite wonderful to pick a few apples, or collect those that had fallen to the ground overnight, and patiently hold them, one by one, up to his large, toothy mouth. I remained as thrilled as a child by his flexible dark lips, huge, cubelike teeth that crunched

the apples, core and all, with such finality, and his high, broad-breasted *enormity;* beside which, I felt small indeed. When I was a child, I used to ride horses, and was especially friendly with one named Nan until the day I was riding and my brother deliberately spooked her and I was thrown, head first, against the trunk of a tree. When I came to, I was in bed and my mother was bending worriedly over me; we silently agreed that perhaps horseback riding was not the safest sport for me. Since then I have walked, and prefer walking to horseback riding—but I had forgotten the depth of feeling one could see in horses' eyes.

I was therefore unprepared for the expression in Blue's. Blue was lonely. Blue was horribly lonely and bored. I was not shocked that this should be the case; five acres to tramp by yourself, endlessly, even in the most beautiful of meadows—and his was—cannot provide many interesting events, and once rainy season turned to dry that was about it. No, I was shocked that I had forgotten that human animals and nonhuman animals can communicate quite well; if we are brought up around animals as children we take this for granted. By the time we are adults we no longer remember. However, the animals have not changed. They are in fact *completed* creations (at least they seem to be, so much more than we) who are not likely to change; it is their nature to express themselves. What else are they going to express? And they do. And, generally speaking, they are ignored.

After giving Blue the apples, I would wander back to the house, aware that he was observing me. Were more apples not forthcoming then? Was that to be his sole entertainment for the day? My partner's small son had decided he wanted to learn how to piece a quilt; we worked in silence on our respective squares as I thought . . .

Well, about slavery: About white children, who were raised by black people, who knew their first all-accepting love from black women, and then, when they were twelve or so, were told they must "forget" the deep levels of communication between themselves and "mammy" that they knew. Later they would be able to relate quite calmly, "My old mammy was sold to another good family." "My old mammy was ———— ————." Fill in the blank. Many more years later a white woman would say:"I can't understand these Negroes, these blacks. What do they want? They're so different from us."

8   And about the Indians, considered to be <u>"like animals"</u> by the "settlers" (a very benign euphemism for what they actually were), who did not understand their description as a compliment.

9   And about the thousands of American men who marry Japanese, Korean, Filipina, and other non-English-speaking women and of how happy they report they are, *"blissfully,"* until their brides learn to speak English, at which point the marriages tend to fall apart. What then did the men see, when they looked into the eyes of the women they married, before they could speak English? Apparently only their own reflections.

10   I thought of society's impatience with the young. "Why are they playing the music so loud?" Perhaps the children have listened to much of the music of oppressed people their parents danced to before they were born, with its <u>passionate</u> but <u>soft cries</u> <u>for acceptance and love,</u> and they have wondered why their parents failed to hear.

11   I do not know how long Blue had inhabited his five beautiful, boring acres before we moved into our house; a year after we had arrived—and had also traveled to other valleys, other cities, other worlds—he was still there.

12   But then, in our second year at the house, something happened in Blue's life. One morning, looking out the window at the fog that lay like a ribbon over the meadow, I saw another horse, a brown one, at the other end of Blue's field. Blue appeared to be afraid of it, and for several days made no attempt to go near. We went away for a week. When we returned, Blue had decided to make friends and the two horses ambled or galloped along together, and Blue did not come nearly as often to the fence underneath the apple tree.

13   When he did, bringing his new friend with him, there was a different look in his eyes. A look of <u>independence,</u> of <u>self-posses-</u> sion, of inalienable *horse*ness. His friend eventually became pregnant. For months and months there was, it seemed to me, <u>a mu-</u> <u>tual feeling</u> between me and the horses <u>of justice, of</u> peace. I fed apples to them both. The look in Blue's eyes was one of unabashed "this is *it*ness."

It did not, however, last forever. One day, after a visit to the   14
city, I went out to give Blue some apples. He stood waiting, or so
I thought, though not beneath the tree. When I shook the tree and
jumped back from the shower of apples, he made no move. I carried some over to him. He managed to half-crunch one. The rest
he let fall to the ground. I dreaded looking into his eyes—because
I had of course noticed that Brown, his partner, had gone—but I
did look. If I had been born into slavery, and my partner had been
sold or killed, my eyes would have looked like that. The children
next door explained that Blue's partner had been "put with him"
(the same expression that old people used, I had noticed, when
speaking of an ancestor during slavery who had been impreg-
nated by her owner) so that they could mate and she conceive.
Since that was accomplished, she had been taken back by her
owner, who lived somewhere else.

Will she be back? I asked.   15

They didn't know.   16

Blue was like a crazed person. Blue *was*, to me, a crazed per-   17
son. He galloped furiously, as if he were being ridden, around and
around his five beautiful acres. He whinnied until he couldn't. He
tore at the ground with his hooves. He butted himself against his
single shade tree. He looked always and always toward the road
down which his partner had gone. And then, occasionally, when
he came up for apples, or I took apples to him, he looked at me. It
was a look so piercing, so full of grief, a look so *human*, I almost
laughed (I felt too sad to cry) to think there are people who do not
know that animals suffer. People like me who have forgotten, and
daily forget, all that animals try to tell us. "Everything you do to
us will happen to you; we are your teachers, as you are ours. We
are one lesson" is essentially it, I think. There are those who never
once have even considered animals' rights: Those who have been
taught that animals actually want to be used and abused by us, as
small children "love" to be frightened, or women "love" to be mutilated and raped. . . . They are the great-grandchildren of those
who honestly thought, because someone taught them this:
"Women can't think," and "niggers can't faint." But most disturbing of all, in Blue's large brown eyes was a new look more painful
than the look of despair: The look of disgust with human beings,

with life; the look of hatred. And it was odd what the look of hatred did. It gave him, for the first time, the look of a beast. And what that meant was that he had put up a barrier within to protect himself from further violence; all the apples in the world wouldn't change that fact.

18   And so Blue remained, a beautiful part of our landscape, very peaceful to look at from the window, white against the grass. Once a friend came to visit and said, looking out on the soothing view: "And it *would* have to be a *white* horse; the very image of freedom." And I thought, yes, the animals are forced to become for us merely "images" of what they once so beautifully expressed. And we are used to drinking milk from containers showing "contented" cows, whose real lives we want to hear nothing about, eating eggs and drumsticks from "happy" hens, and munching hamburgers advertised by bulls of integrity who seem to command their fate.

19   As we talked of freedom and justice one day for all, we sat down to steaks. I am eating misery, I thought, as I took the first bite. And spit it out.

1986

Gawk Shows

Nicols Fox

1   I remember the dusty heat of late summer, the yellow and white tent, and the barker strutting on the platform. His voice rose above the sounds of the carnival, hinting of the wonders within the tent, wonders painted in cheap colors on the cracked backdrop: The two-headed baby, the world's fattest man, the bearded woman. I remember the sideshows. I thought they were long behind us.

2   I turn on the television and see an astonishing sight: A woman. Her soul is beautiful. It penetrates the atmosphere, even across airwaves. Her body is not. It is covered with the lumps and

bumps of Elephant Man disease. Sally Jessy Raphael, wearing her trademark red spectacles, cocks her blond head and asks what the woman's life is like. A window is opened into pain. There are more victims of the disease sitting in the audience. We are treated to its various manifestations. We are horrified and amazed: We gawk.

Phil Donahue interviews tiny, wizened children. They have ₃ progeria, "the aging disease." With their outsize, hairless heads and huge eyes imparting solemnity and even wisdom, they offer us themselves as a sacrifice to our curiosity. We are compelled into silence, fascinated. We are back in the tent.

While I was living in Europe in the late sixties and early sev- ₄ enties, friends often asked me to tell them what to expect when they visited America. "Think of America as a carnival," I would tell them. "An unending carnival." This was the only way I knew to explain my country. Not just the quality of light and landscape but the excess, the enthusiasm, the love of excitement. We want no limitations on what we can have, on what we can do. We deny ourselves nothing—no objects, no sensations. "The pursuit of happiness": What other nation has made it an absolute right?

The carnival plays on, and we have returned to the ₅ sideshows—minus the honesty that made no pretense about what lay behind the curtain, the honesty that divided the world into those who were able to resist satisfying their curiosity at the expense of others and those who were not. Gawking is painted in shades of solicitude now. We justify much in the name of compassion, but we are in fact being entertained in the same ancient tradition. Gawk shows sell.

"I offer no apology," says Donahue. "These children have ₆ been unmercifully pressured by their very distinctive appearance." The purpose of the show? "To humanize people who have suffered. It becomes a vehicle for examining our prejudices. Just because it may be true that this kind of show draws a crowd does not condemn it," he says.

For Sally Jessy Raphael the rationale is the same: "Teaching ₇ the lessons of compassion. Man's triumph over adversity."

These are noble thoughts, and not entirely hypocritical. Com- ₈ passion and understanding are always in short supply. There is an outside chance that some of each might be spread around in this exercise. We may also be witnessing exploitation. "These children are risking their lives to be here," says Sally, introducing children who will die if exposed to light. What may *she* be risking if they don't appear? As Donahue says, "If I don't draw a crowd, I could be parking cars for a living."

9   Donahue is open about the dilemma: "Americans are more interested in Madonna than Managua. The country suffers, in my opinion, from the diminished interest in serious news. Whichever way you look at it we have a culture of decay." It's tricky playing two sides at once. "It's like walking on eggs. I don't want to be a dead hero," he says.

10   We watch our cultural demise in living color.

11   Do you find yourself addicted to sex with prostitutes? Tell Oprah Winfrey and her audience all about it. Did you engage in an affair with your priest? Have your breast implants started slipping? Geraldo Rivera wants to know. Do you wish you could reverse your sex-change operation? Are you a celebrity subject to diarrhea at odd moments? Does your mother keep stealing your boyfriends? We care, we are interested. Whatever your problem, there's a television talk show that will accommodate you.

12   Donahue, Oprah, Sally, Geraldo: They are the virtuosos of voyeurism, lifting the skirts of our culture, peering into the closets, airing the national soiled linen. Sally thinks of her program as a kind of updated town meeting—the modern version of something we no longer have. Electronic gossip, in other words—the national back fence. Wishful thinking.

13   As Americans we've been indulging in an orgy of self-analysis and self-revelation—coupled with a natural curiosity now totally unbridled. We've become a society hooked on the bizarre and the astonishing—living in a perpetual state of "Can you top this?" Transvestite men marry women on Sally's show, thus proving an important point, one we all needed to know: Sixty-five percent of all transvestites are not homosexual.

14   Nothing is sacred. There are no memories, no mysteries too precious to reveal. A woman discusses her husband's sexual addiction. Geraldo asks the husband for details—and gets them. There is nothing we won't share, or watch someone else share, with a million strangers.

We have invented a new social contract on the talk shows: 15
Lay bare your body, your bed, your soul, your emotions, your
worst fears, your innermost secrets, and we will give you a moment or two of fame. Every sacrifice can and should be made to
the video god.

Are there topics too hot to talk about?   16

"How to blow up your local post office," says Donahue. He'd 17
draw the line there.

There is no topic Sally wouldn't consider if it "concerns the 18
human condition." She draws the line only at being boring. We
have to want to watch it. So we set the agenda.

Donahue, a man obviously in conflict between his natural 19
honesty and better instincts and his ambition, admits that his audience calls the shots. Devoting a recent show to strippers—both
male and female—he says, "It must be ratings week. I don't want
to do these shows . . . they make me." Sure they do. But who is
making us watch?

Freedom of expression is not the issue here. Nobody's sug- 20
gesting censorship or even paternalistic decisions based on what
someone else thinks is good for us. The issue is honesty—honesty
about why we watch. The talk shows are merely giving us what
we want. The question is, Why do we want it?

In some cultures it was thought that illness or bad luck could 21
be transferred from one person to another by magic. James G.
Frazer, in his classic work *The Golden Bough,* told of one example:
"To get rid of warts, take a string and make as many knots in it as
you have warts. Then lay the string under a stone. Whoever treads
upon the stone will get the warts, and you will be rid of them."
Something like that draws us to the tent. We confirm our own nor-
malcy because our worst fears have been manifested in someone
else—the visual equivalent of burying the string. Or, if we see ourselves in someone who has survived our common plight, we are
reassured; we are not alone.

There is no slouching into the tent today. We walk in shame- 22
lessly, casting off inhibitions in the name of openness.

The new openness has, in fact, turned out to be an empty 23
promise. Are things any better than they were two decades ago?
Has drug abuse or wife abuse or child abuse declined as we have

learned more? Are we any happier thinking that a friend who takes a drink is a potential alcoholic, that every stranger is a child-snatcher?

24   How has this new compassion we are teaching been made evident? Ask the parents who have three HIV-positive sons and found their house burned down because of it. Ask the people who cluster over the grates of subways in our largest cities. If you were a trapped whale or a little girl down a well, solicitude would flow your way in great waves. It still helps to be cute or little or white or furry or totally nonthreatening when you're looking for compassion—or pretty, when you want a bone marrow transplant.

25   The potential is there on the TV talk shows for real entertainment—and for service. Oprah scored with a terrific show on female comics. Programs on health matters or economic questions are valuable. During the first days of the war in the Persian Gulf, Donahue aired shows that were serious and important contributions to our understanding of the conflict. "I do have a conscience," he says.

26   Geraldo, however, ever subject to the temptations of the flesh, spoiled what could have been a serious discussion of breast implants by having Jessica Hahn as the honored guest and by fondling examples of the implants interminably. Does he have it right? Are we a people who need to watch breast implants being fondled?

27   What happens when we set aside our last taboo? What happens when we've finally been titillated to a terminal numbness, incapable of shock, on the prowl for a new high? What manner of stimulation will we need next? Are we addicted? Talk show codependent?

28   Which topic affects us more: the discussion of the S & L crisis Donahue did last summer or the interviews with the strippers? Which do you think got the better ratings?

29   In a free society we get what we want. We shouldn't be surprised when we end up with what we deserve. But we can't transfer blame. It's not the hosts' fault—it's the viewers'.

1991

Chapter

Argument and Persuasion
Argument

10

Should This Student Have Been Expelled?

Nat Hentoff

> *The day that Brown denies any student freedom of speech is the day I give up my presidency of the university.*

—Vartan Gregorian, president of Brown University,
February 20, 1991

Doug Hann, a varsity football player at Brown, was also concen- 1
trating on organizational behavior and management and business
economics. On the night of October 18, 1990, Hann, a junior, was
celebrating his twenty-first birthday, and in the process had im-
bibed a considerable amount of spirits.

At one point, Hann shouted into the air, "Fuck you, niggers!" 2
It was aimed at no one in particular but apparently at all black students at Brown. Or in the world. A freshman leaned out a dormitory window and asked him to stop being so loud and offensive.

Hann, according to reporters on the *Brown Daily Herald*, 3
looked up and yelled, "What are you, a faggot?" Hann then noticed an Israeli flag in the dorm. "What are you, a Jew?" he
shouted. "Fucking Jew!"

Hann had achieved the hat trick of bigotry. (In hockey, the hat 4
trick is scoring three goals in a game.) In less than a minute, Hann
had engaged in racist, anti-Semitic, and homophobic insults.

353

5   He wasn't through. As reported by Smita Nerula in the *Brown Daily Herald*, the freshman who had asked Hann to cool it recruited a few people from his dorm "and followed Hann and his friends."

6   "This resulted in a verbal confrontation outside of Wayland Arch. At this time, [Hann] was said to have turned to one of the freshman's friends, a black woman, and shouted, 'My parents own your people.'"

7   To the Jewish student, or the student he thought was Jewish, Hann said, "Happy Hanukkah."

8   There are reports that at this juncture Hann tried to fight some of the students who had been following him. But, the *Brown Daily Herald* reports, he "was held back by one of his friends, while [another] friend stretched his arm across the Wayland Gates to keep the students from following Hann."

9   John Howard Crouch—a student and Brown chapter secretary of the American Civil Liberties Union there—tells me that because Hann had friends restraining him, "nobody seriously expected fighting, regardless of anyone's words."

10   Anyway, there was no physical combat. Just words. Awful words, but nothing more than speech. (Nor were there any threats.)

11   This was not the first time Hann's disgraceful drunken language had surfaced at Brown. Two years before, in an argument with a black student at a fraternity bar, Hann had called the student a "nigger." Thereupon he had been ordered to attend a race relations workshop and to get counseling for possible alcohol abuse. Obviously, he has not been rehabilitated.

12   Months went by after Hann's notorious birthday celebration as Brown's internal disciplinary procedures cranked away. (To steal a phrase from Robert Sherrill, Brown's way of reaching decisions in these matters is to due process as military music is to music. But that's true of any college or university I know anything about.)

13   At last, the Undergraduate Disciplinary Council (five faculty or administration members and five students) ruled that Doug Hann was to leave the university forevermore. Until two years ago, it was possible for a Brown student to be dismissed, which meant that he or she could reapply after a decent period of

penance. But now, Brown has enshrined the sentence of expulsion. You may go on to assist Mother Teresa in caring for the dying or you may teach a course in feminism to 2 Live Crew, but no accomplishments, no matter how noble, will get you back into Brown once you have been expelled.

Doug Hann will wander the earth without a Brown degree for 14 the rest of his days.

The president of Brown, Vartan Gregorian—formerly the ge- 15 nial head of the New York Public Library—had the power to commute or even reverse the sentence. But the speech code under which Hann was thrown out had been proposed by Gregorian himself shortly after he was inaugurated in 1989, so he was hardly a detached magistrate.

On January 25, 1991, Vartan Gregorian affirmed, with vigor, 16 the expulsion decision by the Undergraduate Disciplinary Council.

Hann became a historic figure. Under all the "hate speech" 17 codes enacted around the country in recent years, he is the first student to actually be expelled for violating one of the codes.

The *New York Times* (February 12) reported that "Howard 18 Ehrlich, the research director of the National Institute Against Prejudice and Violence, said that he did not know of any other such expulsions, but that he was familiar with cases in which students who had harassed others were moved to other dormitories or ordered to undergo counseling."

But that takes place in *educational* institutions, whose presi- 19 dents recognize that there are students who need help, not exile.

At first, there didn't seem to be much protest among the stu- 20 dent body at Brown on free speech grounds—except for members of the Brown chapter of the ACLU and some free thinkers on the student paper, as well as some unaffiliated objectors to expelling students for what they say, not for what they do. The number of these dissenters is increasing, as we shall see.

At the student paper, however, the official tone has changed 21 from the libertarian approach of Vernon Silver, who was editor-in-chief last semester. A February 13 *Brown Daily Herald* editorial was headed: "*Good Riddance.*"

It began: "Doug Hann is gone, and the university is well to be 22 rid of him."

23   But President Gregorian has been getting a certain amount of flack and so, <u>smiting</u> his critics hip and thigh, he wrote a letter to the *New York Times*. Well, that letter (printed on February 21) was actually a press release, distributed by the Brown University News Bureau to all sorts of people, including me, on February 12. There were a few changes—and that *Brown Daily Herald* editorial was attached to it—but Gregorian's declaration was clearly not written exclusively for the *Times*.

24   Is this a new policy at the *Times*—taking public relations hand-outs for the letters page?

25   Next week I shall include a <u>relentlessly</u> accurate analysis of President Gregorian's letter by the executive director of the Rhode Island ACLU. But first, an account of what Gregorian said in that letter to the *Times*.

26   President Gregorian indignantly denies that Brown has ever expelled "anyone for the exercise of free speech, nor will it ever do so." Cross his heart.

27   He then goes into self-celebration: "My commitment to free speech and condemnation of racism and homophobia are well known . . . ."

28   "The university's code of conduct does not prohibit speech; it prohibits *actions*."

29   Now watch this pitiable curve ball:

30   "Offense III [of the Brown code]—which deals with harassment—prohibits inappropriate, abusive, threatening, or demeaning actions based on race, religion, gender, handicap, ethnicity, national origin, or sexual orientation."

31   In the original press release, Gregorian underlined the word *actions*. There, and in the letter to the *Times*—lest a dozing reader miss the point—Gregorian emphasizes that "The rules do not proscribe words, epithets, or slanders, they proscribe behavior." Behavior that "shows flagrant disrespect for the well-being of others or is unreasonably disruptive of the University community."

32   Consider the overbreadth and vagueness of these penalty-bearing provisions. What are the definitions of "harassment," "inappropriate," "demeaning," "flagrant," "disrespect," "well-being," "unreasonably"?

Furthermore, with regard to Brown's termination of Doug   33
Hann with extreme prejudice, Gregorian is engaging in the crud-
est form of Orwellian newspeak. Hann was kicked out for *speech,*
and only speech—not for *actions,* as Gregorian huffily insists. As
for behavior, the prickly folks whose burning of the American flag
was upheld by the Supreme Court were indeed engaged in behavior, but that behavior was based entirely on symbolic speech.
So was Hann's. He didn't punch anybody or vandalize any property. He brayed.

Art Spitzer, legal director of the ACLU's National Capital   34
Area affiliate, wrote a personal letter to Gregorian:

"There is a very simple test for determining whether a person   35
is being punished for his actions or his speech. You just ask
whether he would have received the same punishment if he had
spoken different words while engaging in the same conduct."

"Thus, would your student have been expelled if he had got-   36
ten drunk and stood in the same courtyard at the same hour of the
night, shouting at the same decibel level, 'Black is Beautiful!' 'Gay
is Good!' or 'Go Brown! Beat Yale!' or even 'Nuke Baghdad! Kill
Saddam!'?

"I am confident," Spitzer said, that "he would not have been   37
expelled for such 'actions.' If that is correct, it follows that *he was
expelled for the unsavory content of his speech,* and not for his actions.
I have no doubt that you can understand this distinction. (Emphasis added.)

"Now, you are certainly entitled to believe that it is appropri-   38
ate to expel a student for the content of his speech when that content is sufficiently offensive to the 'university community.' . . .

"If that is your position, why can't you deliver it forthrightly?   39
Then the university community can have an open debate about
which opinions it finds offensive, and ban them. Perhaps this can
be done once a year, so that the university's rules can keep pace
with the tenor of the times—after all, it wouldn't do to have out-
moded rules banning procommunist or blasphemous speech still
on the books, now that it's 1991. Then students and teachers applying for admission or employment at Brown will know what
they are getting into.

40   "Your recent statements, denying the obvious, are just hypocritical . . . ."

41   And what did the *New York Times*—in a stunningly fatuous
February 21 editorial—say of Vartan Gregorian's sending Doug
Hann into permanent exile? "A noble attempt both to govern and
teach."

42   The *Times* editorials should really be signed, so that the rest of
the editorial board isn't blamed for such embarrassments.

1991

How Much Hate to Tolerate
New York Times editorial, (February 21, 1991)

1   Free speech and human relations seemed to collide last month at
Brown University when it expelled a student for racial and religious harassment. In fact, however, to judge by all that is publicly
known, the school walked a fine line with sensitivity toward its
complex mission.

2   One mission of a university is to send into the world gradu-
ates who are tolerant of many races, faiths and cultures. Another
mission is to teach the value of free expression and tolerance even
for hateful ideas. But should such tolerance cover racist, sexist or
homophobic speech that makes the learning environment intolerable for racial and religious minorities, women and other targets
of abuse? Brown found a reasonable basis for saying, clearly, no.

3   Douglas Hann, white, a junior and a varsity football player,
had previously been disciplined for alcohol abuse and for racial
insults against a black fellow student. Then, one evening last fall,
he shouted racial insults in a university courtyard. A Jewish student who opened a dormitory window and called for quiet was
answered with a religious insult. Later that evening Mr. Hann directed a racial insult at a black undergraduate.

4   The student-faculty discipline committee found him guilty of
three violations of student rules, including another count of alcohol abuse. Vartan Gregorian, the university's president, upheld

the student's expulsion last month. He had a sound basis for doing so. If the facts are reported correctly, Mr. Hann crossed the line between merely hateful speech and hateful speech that directly confronted and insulted other undergraduates.

Some courts have found that public universities are bound by 5 the First Amendment's ban on state censorship and thus may not punish students for expressing politically incorrect or socially distasteful ideas. Brown, like other private schools, is less directly bound by the Constitution but committed to its precepts. It is trying to avoid censorship but draws a line between strong language and what the courts often call "fighting words."

In the adjacent Letters column today, Mr. Gregorian insists that 6 Brown does not punish unruly speech as such but will decide case-by-case whether a student has passed "the point at which speech becomes behavior" that flagrantly disregards the well-being of others or "subjects someone to abusive or demeaning actions."

That formula is a noble attempt both to govern and teach. It 7 offers a principled basis for disciplinary action against Mr. Hann for his direct, confrontational conduct.

The lines may not be so clearly drawn in other cases. There 8 may also be more of them in the present climate of evidently increasing student intolerance. But when bigots attack other students with ugly invective, universities, whether public or private, need not remain silent. Their presidents, like Mr. Gregorian, may denounce indecency and, in so doing, protect tolerance.

Brown Expulsion Not About Free Speech
New York Times letter to the editor, (February 21, 1991)

To the Editor:
"Student at Brown Is Expelled Under a Rule Barring 'Hate 1 Speech' " (news article, Feb. 12) suggests I have instituted "hate-speech" prohibitions at Brown University and that the expulsion of a student who shouted racial and homophobic epithets on campus last October is the first such in the nation based on restrictions of free speech. Brown University has never expelled anyone for free speech, nor will it ever do so.

2   My commitment to free speech and condemnation of racism and homophobia are well known. In April 1989, several students were subjected to a cowardly attack of racial and homophobic graffiti. The words and slogans scrawled anonymously on doors in one of our dormitories were vicious attacks threatening the well-being and security of Brown students.

3   I condemned that anonymous poisoning of our community and said I would prosecute vigorously and seek the expulsion of those who incite hatred or perpetuate such acts of vandalism. Nothing I said then or have done since should be construed as limiting anyone's freedom of speech, nor have I revised the university's code of conduct to that effect.

4   The university's code of conduct does not prohibit speech; it prohibits actions, and these include behavior that "shows flagrant disrespect for the well-being of others or is unreasonably disruptive of the university community."

5   Offense III, which deals with harassment, prohibits inappropriate, abusive, threatening or demeaning actions based on race, religion, gender, handicap, ethnicity, national origin or sexual orientation.

6   "The Tenets of Community Behavior," which outline community standards for acceptable behavior at Brown, have been read for more than 10 years by entering students, who agree in writing to abide by them.

7   The rules do not proscribe words, epithets or slanders; they proscribe behavior. The point at which speech becomes behavior and the degree to which that behavior shows flagrant disrespect for the well-being of others (Offense II), subjects someone to abusive or demeaning actions (Offense III) or is related to drug or alcohol use (Offense IV) is determined by a hearing to consider the circumstances of each case. The student is entitled to an appeal, which includes review by a senior officer and a decision by the president.

8   I cannot and will not comment about any specific case. I regret the release of any student's name in connection with a disciplinary hearing and the exposure any case may receive in *The Brown Herald*.

9   Freedom-of-speech questions lie at the heart of any academic community. The very nature of the academic enterprise necessi-

tates that universities remain partisans of heterodoxy, of a rich and full range of opinions, ideas and expression. Imposed orthodoxies of all sorts, including what is called "politically correct" speech, are anathema to our enterprise.

The university's most compelling challenge is to achieve a bal- 10 ance between the right of its individual members to operate and speak freely, and fostering respect for and adherence to community values and standards of conduct.

VARTAN GREGORIAN
President, Brown University
Providence, R.I., Feb. 21, 1991

A Step Back to the Workhouse?

Barbara Ehrenreich

The commentators are calling it a "remarkable consensus." Work- 1 fare, as programs to force welfare recipients to work are known, was once abhorred by liberals as a step back toward the 17th-century workhouse or—worse—slavery. But today no political candidate dares step outdoors without some plan for curing "welfare dependency" by putting its hapless victims to work—if necessary, at the nearest Burger King. It is as if the men who run things, or who aspire to run things (and we are, unfortunately, talking mostly about men when we talk about candidates), had gone off and caucused for a while and decided on the one constituency that could be safely sacrificed in the name of political expediency and "new ideas," and that constituency is poor women.

Most of the arguments for workfare are simply the same in- 2 destructible stereotypes that have been around, in one form or another, since the first public relief program in England 400 years ago: That the poor are poor because they are lazy and dissolute, and that they are lazy and dissolute because they are suffering from "welfare dependency." Add a touch of modern race and gender stereotypes and you have the image that haunts the workfare advocates: A slovenly, over-weight, black woman who produces a baby a year in order to augment her welfare checks.

3   But there is a new twist to this season's spurt of welfare-bashing: Workfare is being presented as a kind of *feminist* alternative to welfare. As Senator Daniel Patrick Moynihan (D.–N.Y.) has put it, "A program that was designed to pay mothers to stay at home with their children [i.e., welfare, or Aid to Families with Dependent Children] cannot succeed when we now observe most mothers going out to work." Never mind the startling illogic of this argument, which is on a par with saying that no woman should stay home with her children because other women do not, or that a laid-off male worker should not receive unemployment compensation because most men have been observed holding jobs. We are being asked to believe that pushing destitute mothers into the work force (in some versions of workfare, for no other compensation than the welfare payments they would have received anyway) is consistent with women's strivings toward self-determination.

4   Now I will acknowledge that most women on welfare—like most unemployed women in general—would rather have jobs. And I will further acknowledge that many of the proponents of workfare, possibly including Senator Moynihan and the Democratic Presidential candidates, have mounted the bandwagon with the best of intentions. Welfare surely needs reform. But workfare is not the solution, because "dependency"—with all its implications of laziness and depravity—is not the problem. The problem is poverty, which most women enter in a uniquely devastating way—with their children in tow.

5   Let me introduce a real person, if only because real people, as opposed to imaginative stereotypes, never seem to make an appearance in the current rhetoric on welfare. "Lynn," as I will call her, is a friend and onetime neighbor who has been on welfare for two years. She is also about as unlike the stereotypical "welfare mother" as one can get—which is to say that she is a fairly typical welfare recipient. She has only one child, which puts her among

the 74 percent of welfare recipients who have only one or two children. She is white (not that that should matter), as are almost half of welfare recipients. Like most welfare recipients, she is not herself the daughter of a welfare recipient, and hence not part of anything that could be called an "intergenerational cycle of dependency." And like every woman on welfare I have ever talked to, she resents the bureaucratic hassles that are the psychic price of welfare. But, for now, there are no alternatives.

When I first met Lynn, she seemed withdrawn and disoriented. She had just taken the biggest step of her 25 years; she had left an abusive husband and she was scared: Scared about whether she could survive on her own and scared of her estranged husband. He owned a small restaurant; she was a high school dropout who had been a waitress when she met him. During their three years of marriage he had beaten her repeatedly. Only after he threw her down a flight of stairs had she realized that her life was in danger and moved out. I don't think I fully grasped the terror she had lived in until one summer day when he chased Lynn to the door of my house with a drawn gun.

Gradually Lynn began to put her life together. She got a divorce and went on welfare; she found a pediatrician who would accept Medicaid and a supermarket that would take food stamps. She fixed up her apartment with secondhand furniture and flea market curtains. She was, by my admittedly low standards, a compulsive housekeeper and an overprotective mother; and when she wasn't waxing her floors or ironing her two-year-old's playsuits, she was studying the help-wanted ads. She spent a lot of her time struggling with details that most of us barely notice—the price of cigarettes, mittens, or of a bus ticket to the welfare office—yet, somehow, she regained her sense of humor. In fact, most of the time we spent together was probably spent laughing—over the foibles of the neighbors, the conceits of men, and the snares of welfare and the rest of "the system."

Yet for all its inadequacies, Lynn was grateful for welfare. Maybe if she had been more intellectually inclined she would have found out that she was suffering from "welfare dependency," a condition that is supposed to sap the will and demolish the work ethic. But "dependency" is not an issue when it is a choice between an abusive husband and an impersonal government. Welfare had given Lynn a brief shelter in a hostile world, and as far as she was concerned, it was her ticket to *independence.*

9   Suppose there had been no welfare at the time when Lynn finally summoned the courage to leave her husband. Suppose she had gone for help and been told she would have to "work off" her benefits in some menial government job (restocking the toilet paper in rest rooms is one such "job" assigned to New York women in a current workfare program). Or suppose, as in some versions of workfare, she had been told she would have to take the first available private sector job, which (for a non-high school graduate like Lynn) would have paid near the minimum wage, or $3.35 an hour. How would she have been able to afford child care? What would she have done for health insurance (as a welfare recipient she had Medicaid, but most low-paying jobs offer little or no coverage)? Would she have ever made the decision to leave her husband in the first place?

10   As Ruth Sidel points out in *Women and Children Last* (Viking), most women who are or have been on welfare have stories like Lynn's. They go onto welfare in response to a crisis—divorce, illness, loss of a job, the birth of an additional child to feed—and they remain on welfare for two years or less. They are not victims of any "welfare culture," but of a society that increasingly expects women to both raise and support children—and often on wages that would barely support a woman alone. In fact, even some of the most vociferous advocates of replacing welfare with workfare admit that, in their own estimation, only about 15 percent of welfare recipients fit the stereotype associated with "welfare dependency": Demoralization, long-term welfare use, lack of drive, and so on.

11   But workfare will not help anyone, not even the presumed 15 percent of "bad apples" for whose sake the majority will be penalized. First, it will not help because it does not solve the problem that drives most women into poverty in the first place: How to hold a job *and* care for children. Child care in a licensed, professionally run center can easily cost as much as $100 a week per child—more than most states now pay in welfare benefits (for two

children) and more than most welfare recipients could expect to earn in the work force. Any serious effort to get welfare recipients into the work force would require childcare provisions at a price that would probably end up higher than the current budget for AFDC. But none of the workfare advocates are proposing that sort of massive public commitment to child care.

Then there is the problem of jobs. So far, studies show that existing state workfare programs have had virtually no success in improving their participants' incomes or employment rates. Small wonder: Nearly half the new jobs generated in recent years pay poverty-level wages; and most welfare recipients will enter jobs that pay near the minimum wage, which is $6,900 a year—26 percent less than the poverty level for a family of three. A menial, low-wage job may be character-building (from a middle-class vantage point), but it will not lift anyone out of poverty. 12

Some of my feminist activist friends argue that it is too late to stop the workfare juggernaut. The best we can do, they say, is to try to defeat the more pernicious proposals: Those that are over-coercive, that do not offer funds for child care, or that would relegate work clients to a "subemployee" status unprotected by federal labor and civil rights legislation. Our goal, the pragmatists argue, should be to harness the current enthusiasm for workfare to push for services welfare recipients genuinely need, such as child care and job training and counseling. 13

I wish the pragmatists well, but for me, it would be a betrayal of women like Lynn to encourage the workfare bandwagon in any way. Most women, like Lynn, do not take up welfare as a career, but as an emergency measure in a time of personal trauma and dire need. At such times, the last thing they need is to be hustled into a low-wage job, and left to piece together child care, health insurance, transportation, and all the other ingredients of survival. In fact, the main effect of workfare may be to discourage needy women from seeking any help at all—a disastrous result in a nation already suffering from a child poverty rate of nearly 25 percent. Public policy should be aimed at giving impoverished mothers (and, I would add, fathers) the help they so urgently need—not only in the form of job opportunities, but sufficient income support to live on until a job worth taking comes along. 14

15   Besides, there is an ancient feminist principle at stake. The premise of all the workfare proposals—the more humane as well as the nasty—is that single mothers on welfare are not *working*. But, to quote the old feminist bumper sticker, EVERY MOTHER IS A WORKING MOTHER. And those who labor to raise their children in poverty—to feed and clothe them on meager budgets and to nurture them in an uncaring world—are working the hardest. The feminist position has never been that all women must pack off their children and enter the work force, but that all women's work—in the home or on the job—should be valued and respected.

Barbara Ehrenreich's essay stimulated a lively response from Ms. *readers. The following letters were published in the February 1988 issue.*

16   I was absolutely thrilled when I read Barbara Ehrenreich's article on workfare ("A Step Back to the Workhouse?" November 1987). As a single mother who received welfare for several years (with no child support) I'm against everything that workfare stands for. I belong to an organization called Women, Work, and Welfare, a group of current and former welfare recipients trying to empower ourselves and become a part of the decisions that affect our lives as poor women. It seems as if everybody but the welfare recipient herself has a hand in the decisions that are made.

CHERI HONKALA
Minneapolis, Minn.

17   I arrived in Chicago in 1952 with a husband and two children from a camp in Europe. I had another child in 1953, lost a newborn in 1954, had a miscarriage, a hysterectomy, and a divorce in 1955. I never received child support. My ex-husband was remarried within two months.

18   I *never* received welfare. I worked in another culture, while in very bad health. I found a two-room flat, had no furniture and slept for years on the floor. I even went back to school at night and had to contend with companies like Gulf Oil Corp., which did not believe in promoting women. But I just slugged on.

By the end of the sixties, I had two daughters in college, and I   19
had bought a house. My total earnings for 1970 from three jobs
came to a whopping $8,000.

A full-time minimum wage job *can* support one adult and one   20
child. One just has to learn how to do it.

URRSULA SCHRAMM
Hurley, Wis.

I found myself agreeing with the problems that Barbara   21
Ehrenreich outlines in the present workfare program.

Yet deep inside a protesting rumbling exploded when I read   22
that impoverished mothers should receive sufficient income support to live on "until a job worth taking comes along." *Bullshit!*
Sure, we all should have the right to only work a job we love, but
how many of us can afford to wait for it? That we are often forced
to work at jobs that are not fulfilling says a lot about our society in
which more needs to be changed than just the welfare system!

My mother was forced to go to work when I was nine years   23
old. Our family was in dire financial straits and at the age of 50 she
took a job in a factory. Was that job "worth taking"? Did it utilize
her unique talents? *No!* Did it bring her personal fulfillment? *No!*
Did it prevent the bank from foreclosing on our home? *Yes!* Did it
give my mother the power to overcome our financial crisis and
maintain her autonomy? *Yes!* You tell me if it was "worth taking."
That depends on what your self-respect is worth to you.

GAIL FREI
Newtown Square, Pa.

Barbara Ehrenreich omitted a major element in her discussion   24
of the victimization of welfare families: The inability or unwill-
ingness of the legal system to award *and enforce* realistic child support. Until it stops being easier to abandon your children than to
default on that car loan, women and those who depend on them
will be welfare/workfare victims.

SUSAN MARTIN RYNARD
Durham, N.C.

25   I went on welfare when my daughter was three, when I left my husband. I had a high school education, but had always wanted to go to college. I was 25.

26   So, with the help of the government, I got my B.S. in nursing. I worked for several years as an R.N. and then returned to school for my master's degree. For graduate school, I lived on savings, loans, and grants. The loans ($19,000 for undergrad and graduate in all) will be paid off in less than a year, in time for my daughter to begin college!

KATHRYN REID
Silverado, Calif.

27   Although I share Barbara Ehrenreich's concerns about work-fare and the plight of her friend Lynn, the conclusions she draws strike me as misguided. We live in a society where the myths of the work ethic and self-help are deeply embedded in the popular culture; where resort to the dole is frowned upon unless the need is temporary or arises from disability; where the middle-class majority feels inequitably taxed, as compared to the wealthy, to support a system that directly benefits few of its members.

28   Feminists and other liberals should acknowledge the swelling demand for welfare reform. Our support should be conditional upon the incorporation in any welfare reform plan of provision for *quality* childcare facilities; upon the minimization of coercion; and upon further efforts to compel ex-spouses to pay their fair share of support. Nothing in this approach rules out our going ahead simultaneously with other, parallel efforts to question the mystique of work or to expose the links between welfare and poverty, on the one hand, and capitalism and the subordination of women, on the other.

DAVID G. BECKER
Hanover, N.H.

29   California is serious about workfare, but we call it GAIN (Greater Avenues for Independence). It offers welfare recipients vocational counseling, up to two years of vocational training, and workshops in how to get and hold a job.

GAIN also pays for child care and transportation. No job need 30
be accepted by the recipient unless she/he will *net* at least as much
as their AFDC grant, *including* child care, transportation, and medical insurance. And even then, they will receive funds to cover
these costs for three months after they begin working to help them
make the transition to the work force.

JANE KIRCHMAN
Guerneville, Calif.

Lifeboat Ethics: The Case Against Helping the Poor

Garrett Hardin

Environmentalists use the metaphor of the earth as a "spaceship" 1
in trying to persuade countries, industries and people to stop wasting and polluting our natural resources. Since we all share life on
this planet, they argue, no single person or institution has the right
to destroy, waste, or use more than a fair share of its resources.

But does everyone on earth have an equal right to an equal 2
share of its resources? The spaceship metaphor can be dangerous
when used by misguided idealists to justify suicidal policies for
sharing our resources through uncontrolled immigration and foreign aid. In their enthusiastic but unrealistic generosity, they confuse the ethics of a spaceship with those of a lifeboat.

A true spaceship would have to be under the control of a cap- 3
tain, since no ship could possibly survive if its course were determined by committee. Spaceship Earth certainly has no captain; the
United Nations is merely a toothless tiger, with little power to enforce any policy upon its bickering members.

If we divide the world crudely into rich nations and poor na- 4
tions, two thirds of them are desperately poor, and only one third

comparatively rich, with the United States the wealthiest of all. Metaphorically each rich nation can be seen as a lifeboat full of comparatively rich people. In the ocean outside each lifeboat swim the poor of the world, who would like to get in, or at least to share some of the wealth. What should the lifeboat passengers do?

5   First, we must recognize the limited capacity of any lifeboat. For example, a nation's land has a limited capacity to support a population and as the current energy crisis has shown us, in some ways we have already exceeded the carrying capacity of our land. So here we sit, say 50 people in our lifeboat. To be generous, let us assume it has room for 10 more, making a total capacity of 60. Suppose the 50 of us in the lifeboat see 100 others swimming in the water outside, begging for admission to our boat or for handouts. We have several options: We may be tempted to try to live by the Christian ideal of being "our brother's keeper," or by the Marxist ideal of "to each according to his needs." Since the needs of all in the water are the same, and since they can all be seen as our "brothers," we could take them all into our boat, making a total of 150 in a boat designed for 60. The boat swamps; everyone drowns. Complete justice, complete catastrophe.

6   Since the boat has an unused excess capacity of 10 more passengers, we could admit just 10 more to it. But which 10 do we let in? How do we choose? Do we pick the best 10, the neediest 10, "first come, first served"? And what do we say to the 90 we exclude? If we do let an extra 10 into our lifeboat, we will have lost our "safety factor," an engineering principle of critical importance. For example, if we don't leave room for excess capacity as a safety factor in our country's agriculture, a new plant disease or a bad change in the weather could have disastrous consequences.

7   Suppose we decide to preserve our small safety factor and admit no more to the lifeboat. Our survival is then possible, although we shall have to be constantly on guard against boarding parties.

8   While this last solution clearly offers the only means of our survival, it is morally abhorrent to many people. Some say they feel guilty about their good luck. My reply is simple: "Get out and yield your place to others." This may solve the problem of the guilt-ridden person's conscience, but it does not change the ethics of the lifeboat. The needy person to whom the guilt-ridden person

yields his place will not himself feel guilty about his good luck. If he did, he would not climb aboard. The net result of conscience-stricken people giving up their unjustly held seats is the elimination of that sort of conscience from the lifeboat.

This is the basic metaphor within which we must work out 9 our solutions. Let us now enrich the image, step by step, with substantive additions from the real world, a world that must solve real and pressing problems of overpopulation and hunger.

The harsh ethics of the lifeboat become even harsher when we 10 consider the reproductive differences between the rich nations and the poor nations. The people inside the lifeboats are doubling in numbers every 87 years; those swimming around outside are doubling, on the average, every 35 years, more than twice as fast as the rich. And since the world's resources are dwindling, the difference in prosperity between the rich and the poor can only increase.

As of 1973, the United States had a population of 210 million 11 people, who were increasing by 0.8 percent per year. Outside our lifeboat, let us imagine another 210 million people (say the combined populations of Colombia, Ecuador, Venezuela, Morocco, Pakistan, Thailand, and the Philippines), increasing at a rate of 3.3 percent per year. Put differently, the doubling time for this aggregate population was 21 years, compared to 87 years for the United States.

Now suppose the United States agreed to pool its resources 12 with those seven countries, with everyone receiving an equal share. Initially the ratio of Americans to non-Americans in this model would be one-to-one. But consider what the ratio would be after 87 years, by which time the Americans would have doubled to a population of 420 million. By then, doubling every 21 years, the other group would have swollen to 3.54 billion. Each American would have to share the available resources with more than eight people.

But, one could argue, this discussion assumes that current population trends will continue, and they may not. Quite so. Most likely the rate of population increase will decline much faster in the United States than it will in the other countries, and there does not seem to be much we can do about it. In sharing with "each according to his needs," we must recognize that needs are determined by population size, which is determined by the rate of reproduction, which at present is regarded as a sovereign right of every nation, poor or not. This being so, the philanthropic load created by the sharing ethic of the spaceship can only increase.

14   The fundamental error of spaceship ethics, and the sharing it requires, is that it leads to what I call "the tragedy of the commons." Under a system of private property, people who own property recognize their responsibility to care for it, for if they don't they will eventually suffer. A farmer, for instance, will allow no more cattle in a pasture than its carrying capacity justifies. If he overloads it, erosion sets in, weeds take over, and he loses the use of the pasture.

15   If a pasture becomes a commons open to all, the right of each to use it may not be matched by a corresponding responsibility to protect it. Asking everyone to use it with discretion will hardly do, for the considerate herdsman who refrains from overloading the commons suffers more than a selfish one who says his needs are greater. If everyone would restrain himself, all would be well; but it takes only one less than everyone to ruin a system of voluntary restraint. In a crowded world of less than perfect human beings, mutual ruin is inevitable if there are no controls. This is the tragedy of the commons.

16   One of the major tasks of education today should be the creation of such an acute awareness of the dangers of the commons that people will recognize its many varieties. For example, the air and water have become polluted because they are treated as commons. Further growth in the population or per-capita conversion of natural resources into pollutants will only make the problem worse. The same holds true for the fish of the oceans. Fishing fleets have nearly disappeared in many parts of the world; technological improvements in the art of fishing are hastening the day of complete ruin. Only the replacement of the system of the commons with a responsible system of control will save the land, air, water and oceanic fisheries.

17   In recent years there has been a push to create a new commons called a World Food Bank, an international depository of food reserves to which nations would contribute according to their abilities

and from which they would draw according to their needs. This humanitarian proposal received support from many liberal international groups, and from such prominent citizens as Margaret Mead, the U.N. Secretary General, and Senator Edward Kennedy.

A world food bank appeals powerfully to our humanitarian 18 impulses. But before we rush ahead with such a plan, let us ask if such a program would actually do more good than harm, not only momentarily but also in the long run. Those who propose a food bank usually refer to a current "emergency" or "crisis" in terms of world food supply. But what is an emergency? Although they may be infrequent and sudden, everyone knows that emergencies will occur from time to time. A well-run family, company, organization or country prepares for the likelihood of accidents and emergencies. It expects them, it budgets for them, it saves for them.

What happens if some organizations or countries budget for 19 accidents and others do not? If each country is solely responsible for its own well-being, poorly managed ones will suffer. But they can learn from experience. They may mend their ways, and learn to budget for infrequent but certain emergencies. For example, the weather varies from year to year, and periodic crop failures are certain. A wise and competent government saves out of the production of the good years in anticipation of bad years to come. Joseph taught this policy to Pharaoh in Egypt more than 2,000 years ago. Yet the great majority of the governments in the world today do not follow such a policy. They lack either the wisdom or the competence, or both. Should those nations that do manage to put something aside be forced to come to the rescue each time an emergency occurs among the poor nations?

"But it isn't their fault!" some kind-hearted liberals argue. 20 "How can we blame the poor people who are caught in an emergency? Why must they suffer for the sins of their governments?" The concept of blame is simply not relevant here. The real question is, what are the operational consequences of establishing a world food bank? If it is open to every country every time a need develops, slovenly rulers will not be motivated to take Joseph's advice. Someone will always come to their aid. Some countries will deposit food in the world food bank, and others will withdraw it. There will be almost no overlap. As a result of such solutions to food shortage emergencies, the poor countries will not learn to mend their ways, and will suffer progressively greater emergencies as their populations grow.

21   On the average, poor countries undergo a 2.5 percent increase in population each year; rich countries, about 0.6 percent. Only rich countries have anything in the way of food reserves set aside, and even they do not have as much as they should. Poor countries have none. If poor countries received no food from the outside, the rate of their population growth would be periodically checked by crop failures and famines. But if they can always draw on a world food bank in time of need, their population can continue to grow unchecked, and so will their "need" for aid. In the short run, a world food bank may diminish that need, but in the long run it actually increases the need without limit.

22   Without some system of worldwide food sharing, the proportion of people in the rich and poor nations might eventually stabilize. The overpopulated poor countries would decrease in numbers while the rich countries that had room for more people would increase. But with a well-meaning system of sharing, such as a world food bank, the growth differential between the rich and the poor countries will not only persist, it will increase. Because of the higher rate of population growth in the poor countries of the world, 88 percent of today's children are born poor, and only 12 percent rich. Year by year the ratio becomes worse as the fast-reproducing poor outnumber the slow-reproducing rich.

23   A world food bank is thus a commons in disguise. People will have more motivation to draw from it than to add to any common store. The less provident and less able will multiply at the expense of the abler and more provident, bringing eventual ruin upon all who share in the commons. Besides, any system of "sharing" that amounts to foreign aid from the rich nations to the poor nations will carry the taint of charity, which will contribute little to the world peace so devoutly desired by those who support the idea of a world food bank.

24   As past U.S. foreign-aid programs have amply and depressingly demonstrated, international charity frequently inspires mistrust and antagonism rather than gratitude on the part of the recipient nation.

The modern approach to foreign aid stresses the export of technology and advice, rather than money and food. As an ancient Chinese proverb goes: "Give a man a fish and he will eat for a day; teach him how to fish and he will eat for the rest of his days." Acting on this advice, the Rockefeller and Ford Foundations have financed a number of programs for improving agriculture in the hungry nations. Known as the "Green Revolution," these programs have led to the development of "miracle rice" and "miracle wheat," new strains that offer bigger harvests and greater resistance to crop damage. 25

Whether or not the Green Revolution can increase food production as much as its champions claim is a debatable but possibly irrelevant point. Those who support this well-intended humanitarian effort should first consider some of the fundamentals of human ecology. Ironically, one man who did was the late Alan Gregg, a vice president of the Rockefeller Foundation. Two decades ago he expressed strong doubts about the wisdom of such attempts to increase food production. He likened the growth and spread of humanity over the surface of the earth to the spread of cancer in the human body, remarking that "cancerous growths demand food, but, as far as I know, they have never been cured by getting it." 26

Every human born constitutes a draft on all aspects of the environment: Food, air, water, forests, beaches, wildlife, scenery and solitude. Food can, perhaps, be significantly increased to meet a growing demand. But what about clean beaches, unspoiled forests, and solitude? If we satisfy a growing population's need for food, we necessarily decrease its per capita supply of the other resources needed by people. 27

India, for example, now has a population of 600 million, which increases by 15 million each year. This population already puts a huge load on a relatively impoverished environment. The country's forests are now only a small fraction of what they were three centuries ago, and floods and erosion continually destroy the insufficient farmland that remains. Every one of the 15 million new lives added to India's population puts an additional burden on the environment, and increases the economic and social costs of crowding. However humanitarian our intent, every Indian life 28 saved through medical or nutritional assistance from abroad diminishes the quality of life for those who remain, and for subsequent generations. If rich countries make it possible, through foreign aid, for 600 million Indians to swell to 1.2 billion in a mere 28 years, as their current growth rate threatens, will future generations of Indians thank us for hastening the destruction of their environment? Will our good intentions be sufficient excuse for the consequences of our actions?

29   Without a true world government to control reproduction and the use of available resources, the sharing ethic of the spaceship is impossible. For the foreseeable future, our survival demands that we govern our actions by the ethics of a lifeboat, harsh though they may be. Posterity will be satisfied with nothing less.

1974

Sex, Drugs, Disasters, and the Extinction of Dinosaurs

Stephen Jay Gould

1   Science, in its most fundamental definition, is a fruitful mode of inquiry, not a list of enticing conclusions. The conclusions are the consequence, not the essence.

2   My greatest unhappiness with most popular presentations of science concerns their failure to separate fascinating claims from the methods that scientists use to establish the facts of nature. Journalists, and the public, thrive on controversial and stunning statements. But science is, basically, a way of knowing—in P. B. Medawar's apt words, "the art of the soluble." If the growing corps of popular science writers would focus on *how* scientists de-

velop and defend those fascinating claims, they would make their greatest possible contribution to public understanding.

Consider three ideas, proposed in perfect seriousness to ex-   3
plain that greatest of all titillating puzzles—the extinction of dinosaurs. Since these three notions invoke the primally fascinating themes of our culture—sex, drugs, and violence—they surely reside in the category of fascinating claims. I want to show why two of them rank as silly speculation, while the other represents science at its grandest and most useful.

Science works with testable proposals. If, after much compila-   4
tion and scrutiny of data, new information continues to affirm a hypothesis, we may accept it provisionally and gain confidence as further evidence mounts. We can never be completely sure that a hypothesis is right, though we may be able to show with confidence that it is wrong. The best scientific hypotheses are also generous and expansive: They suggest extensions and implications that enlighten related, and even far distant, subjects. Simply consider how the idea of evolution has influenced virtually every intellectual field.

Useless speculation, on the other hand, is restrictive. It gener-   5
ates no testable hypothesis, and offers no way to obtain potentially refuting evidence. Please note that I am not speaking of truth or falsity. The speculation may well be true; still, if it provides, in principle, no material for affirmation or rejection, we can make nothing of it. It must simply stand forever as an intriguing idea. Useless speculation turns in on itself and leads nowhere; good science, containing both seeds for its potential refutation and implications for more and different testable knowledge, reaches out. But, enough preaching. Let's move on to dinosaurs, and the three proposals for their extinction.

1. *Sex:* Testes function only in a narrow range of temperature (those of mammals hang externally in a scrotal sac because internal body temperatures are too high for their proper function). A worldwide rise in temperature at the close of the Cretaceous period caused the testes of dinosaurs to stop functioning and led to their extinction by sterilization of males.

2. *Drugs:* Angiosperms (flowering plants) first evolved toward the end of the dinosaurs' reign. Many of these plants contain

psychoactive agents, avoided by mammals today as a result of their bitter taste. Dinosaurs had neither means to taste the bitterness nor livers effective enough to detoxify the substances. They died of massive overdoses.

3. *Disasters:* A large comet or asteroid struck the earth some 65 million years ago, lofting a cloud of dust into the sky and blocking sunlight, thereby suppressing photosynthesis and so drastically lowering world temperatures that dinosaurs and hosts of other creatures became extinct.

6 Before analyzing these three tantalizing statements, we must establish a basic ground rule often violated in proposals for the dinosaurs' demise. *There is no separate problem of the extinction of dinosaurs.* Too often we divorce specific events from their wider contexts and systems of cause and effect. The fundamental fact of dinosaur extinction is its synchrony with the demise of so many other groups across a wide range of habitats, from terrestrial to marine.

7 The history of life has been punctuated by brief episodes of mass extinction. A recent analysis by University of Chicago paleontologists Jack Sepkoski and Dave Raup, based on the best and most exhaustive tabulation of data ever assembled, shows clearly that five episodes of mass dying stand well above the "background" extinctions of normal times (when we consider all mass extinctions, large and small, they seem to fall in a regular 26-million-year cycle). The Cretaceous debacle, occurring 65 million years ago and separating the Mesozoic and Cenozoic eras of our geological time scale, ranks prominently among the five. Nearly all the marine plankton (single-celled floating creatures) died with geological suddenness; among marine invertebrates, nearly 15 percent of all families perished, including many previously dominant groups, especially the ammonites (relatives of squids in coiled shells). On land, the dinosaurs disappeared after more than 100 million years of unchallenged domination.

8 In this context, speculations limited to dinosaurs alone ignore the larger phenomenon. We need a coordinated explanation for a system of events that includes the extinction of dinosaurs as one component. Thus it makes little sense, though it may fuel our de-

sire to view mammals as inevitable inheritors of the earth, to guess that dinosaurs died because small mammals ate their eggs (a perennial favorite among untestable speculations). It seems most unlikely that some disaster peculiar to dinosaurs befell these massive beasts—and that the debacle happened to strike just when one of history's five great dyings had enveloped the earth for completely different reasons.

The testicular theory, an old favorite from the 1940s, had its root in an interesting and thoroughly respectable study of temperature tolerances in the American alligator, published in the staid *Bulletin of the American Museum of Natural History* in 1946 by three experts on living and fossil reptiles—E. H. Colbert, my own first teacher in paleontology; R. B. Cowles; and C. M. Bogert.

The first sentence of their summary reveals a purpose beyond alligators: "This report describes an attempt to infer the reactions of extinct reptiles, especially the dinosaurs, to high temperatures as based upon reactions observed in the modern alligator." They studied, by rectal thermometry, the body temperatures of alligators under changing conditions of heating and cooling. (Well, let's face it, you wouldn't want to try sticking a thermometer under a 'gator's tongue.) The predictions under test go way back to an old theory first stated by Galileo in the 1630s—the unequal scaling of surfaces and volumes. As an animal, or any object, grows (provided its shape doesn't change), surface areas must increase more slowly than volumes—since surfaces get larger as length squared, while volumes increase much more rapidly, as length cubed. Therefore, small animals have high ratios of surface to volume, while large animals cover themselves with relatively little surface.

Among cold-blooded animals lacking any physiological mechanism for keeping their temperatures constant, small creatures have a hell of a time keeping warm—because they lose so much heat through their relatively large surfaces. On the other hand, large animals, with their relatively small surfaces, may lose heat so slowly that, once warm, they may maintain effectively constant temperatures against ordinary fluctuations of climate. (In fact, the resolution of the "hot-blooded dinosaur" controversy that burned so brightly a few years back may simply be that, while large dinosaurs possessed no physiological mechanism for constant temperature, and were not therefore warm-blooded in the technical sense, their large size and relatively small surface area kept them warm.)

12   Colbert, Cowles, and Bogert compared the warming rates of small and large alligators. As predicted, the small fellows heated up (and cooled down) more quickly. When exposed to a warm sun, a tiny 50-gram (1.76-ounce) alligator heated up one degree Celsius every minute and a half, while a large alligator, 260 times bigger at 13,000 grams (28.7 pounds), took seven and a half minutes to gain a degree. Extrapolating up to an adult 10-ton dinosaur, they concluded that a one-degree rise in body temperature would take eighty-six hours. If large animals absorb heat so slowly (through their relatively small surfaces), they will also be unable to shed any excess heat gained when temperatures rise above a favorable level.

13   The authors then guessed that large dinosaurs lived at or near their optimum temperatures; Cowles suggested that a rise in global temperatures just before the Cretaceous extinction caused the dinosaurs to heat up beyond their optimal tolerance—and, being so large, they couldn't shed the unwanted heat. (In a most unusual statement within a scientific paper, Colbert and Bogert then explicitly disavowed this speculative extension of their empirical work on alligators.) Cowles conceded that this excess heat probably wasn't enough to kill or even to enervate the great beasts, but since testes often function only within a narrow range of temperature, he proposed that this global rise might have sterilized all the males, causing extinction by natural contraception.

14   The overdose theory has recently been supported by UCLA psychiatrist Ronald K. Siegel. Siegel has gathered, he claims, more than 2,000 records of animals who, when given access, administer various drugs to themselves—from a mere swig of alcohol to massive doses of the big H. Elephants will swill the equivalent of twenty beers at a time, but do not like alcohol in concentrations greater than 7 percent. In a silly bit of anthropocentric speculation, Siegel states that "elephants drink, perhaps, to forget . . . the anxiety produced by shrinking rangeland and the competition for food."

15   Since fertile imaginations can apply almost any hot idea to the extinction of dinosaurs, Siegel found a way. Flowering plants did

not evolve until late in the dinosaurs' reign. These plants also produced an array of aromatic, amino-acid-based alkaloids—the major group of psychoactive agents. Most mammals are "smart" enough to avoid these potential poisons. The alkaloids simply don't taste good (they are bitter); in any case, we mammals have livers happily supplied with the capacity to detoxify them. But, Siegel speculates, perhaps dinosaurs could neither taste the bitterness nor detoxify the substances once ingested. He recently told members of the American Psychological Association: "I'm not suggesting that all dinosaurs OD'd on plant drugs, but it certainly was a factor." He also argued that death by overdose may help explain why so many dinosaur fossils are found in contorted positions. (Do not go gentle into that good night.)

Extraterrestrial catastrophes have long pedigrees in the popular literature of extinction, but the subject exploded again in 1979, after a long lull, when the father-son, physicist-geologist team of Luis and Walter Alvarez proposed that an asteroid, some 10 km in diameter, struck the earth 65 million years ago (comets, rather than asteroids, have since gained favor. Good science is self-corrective).

The force of such a collision would be immense, greater by far than the megatonnage of all the world's nuclear weapons. In trying to reconstruct a scenario that would explain the simultaneous dying of dinosaurs on land and so many creatures in the sea, the Alvarezes proposed that a gigantic dust cloud, generated by particles blown aloft in the impact, would so darken the earth that photosynthesis would cease and temperatures drop precipitously. (Rage, rage against the dying of the light.) The single-celled photosynthetic oceanic plankton, with life cycles measured in weeks, would perish outright, but land plants might survive through the dormancy of their seeds (land plants were not much affected by the Cretaceous extinction, and any adequate theory must account for the curious pattern of differential survival). Dinosaurs would die by starvation and freezing; small, warm-blooded mammals, with more modest requirements for food and better regulation of body temperature, would squeak through. "Let the bastards freeze in the dark," as bumper stickers of our chauvinistic neighbors in sunbelt states proclaimed several years ago during the Northeast's winter oil crisis.

18   All three theories, testicular malfunction, psychoactive overdosing, and asteroidal zapping, grab our attention mightily. As
pure phenomenology, they rank about equally high on any hit parade of primal fascination. Yet one represents expansive science,
the others restrictive and untestable speculation. The proper criterion lies in evidence and methodology; we must probe behind the
superficial fascination of particular claims.

19   How could we possibly decide whether the hypothesis of testicular frying is right or wrong? We would have to know things
that the fossil record cannot provide. What temperatures were optimal for dinosaurs? Could they avoid the absorption of excess heat
by staying in the shade, or in caves? At what temperatures did their
testicles cease to function? Were late Cretaceous climates ever
warm enough to drive the internal temperatures of dinosaurs close
to this ceiling? Testicles simply don't fossilize, and how could we
infer their temperature tolerances even if they did? In short,
Cowles's hypothesis is only an intriguing speculation leading
nowhere. The most damning statement against it appeared right in
the conclusion of Colbert, Cowles, and Bogert's paper, when they
admitted: "It is difficult to advance any definite arguments against
the hypothesis." My statement may seem paradoxical—isn't a hypothesis really good if you can't devise any arguments against it?
Quite the contrary. It is simply untestable and unusable.

20   Siegel's overdosing has even less going for it. At least Cowles
extrapolated his conclusion from some good data on alligators.
And he didn't completely violate the primary guideline of siting
dinosaur extinction in the context of a general mass dying—for
rise in temperature could be the root cause of a general catastrophe, zapping dinosaurs by testicular malfunction and different
groups for other reasons. But Siegel's speculation cannot touch
the extinction of ammonites or oceanic plankton (diatoms make
their own food with good sweet sunlight; they don't OD on the
chemicals of terrestrial plants). It is simply a gratuitous, attention-
grabbing guess. It cannot be tested, for how can we know what
dinosaurs tasted and what their livers could do? Livers don't fossilize any better than testicles.

21   The hypothesis doesn't even make any sense in its own context. Angiosperms were in full flower ten million years before di-

nosaurs went the way of all flesh. Why did it take so long? As for the pains of a chemical death recorded in contortions of fossils, I regret to say (or rather I'm pleased to note for the dinosaurs' sake) that Siegel's knowledge of geology must be a bit deficient: Muscles contract after death and geological strata rise and fall with motions of the earth's crust after burial—more than enough reason to distort a fossil's pristine appearance.

The impact story, on the other hand, has a sound basis in evidence. It can be tested, extended, refined, and, if wrong, disproved. The Alvarezes did not just construct an arresting guess for public consumption. They proposed their hypothesis after laborious geochemical studies with Frank Asaro and Helen Michael had revealed a massive increase of iridium in rocks deposited right at the time of extinction. Iridium, a rare metal of the platinum group, is virtually absent from indigenous rocks of the earth's crust; most of our iridium arrives on extraterrestrial objects that strike the earth.   22

The Alvarez hypothesis bore immediate fruit. Based originally on evidence from two European localities, it led geochemists throughout the world to examine other sediments of the same age. They found abnormally high amounts of iridium everywhere—from continental rocks of the western United States to deep sea cores from the South Atlantic.   23

Cowles proposed his testicular hypothesis in the mid-1940s. Where has it gone since then? Absolutely nowhere, because scientists can do nothing with it. The hypothesis must stand as a curious appendage to a solid study of alligators. Siegel's overdose scenario will also win a few press notices and fade into oblivion. The Alvarezes' asteroid falls into a different category altogether, and much of the popular commentary has missed this essential distinction by focusing on the impact and its attendant results, and forgetting what really matters to a scientist—the iridium. If you talk just about asteroids, dust, and darkness, you tell stories no better and no more entertaining than fried testicles or terminal trips. It is the iridium—the source of testable evidence—that counts and forges the crucial distinction between speculation and science.   24

The proof, to twist a phrase, lies in the doing. Cowles's hypothesis has generated nothing in thirty-five years. Since its   25 proposal in 1979, the Alvarez hypothesis has spawned hundreds of studies, a major conference, and attendant publications. Geologists are fired up. They are looking for iridium at all other extinction boundaries. Every week exposes a new wrinkle in the scientific press. Further evidence that the Cretaceous iridium represents extraterrestrial impact and not indigenous volcanism continues to accumulate. As I revise this essay in November 1984 (this paragraph will be out of date when the book is published), new data include chemical "signatures" of other isotopes indicating unearthly provenance, glass spherules of a size and sort produced by impact and not by volcanic eruptions, and high-pressure varieties of silica formed (so far as we know) only under the tremendous shock of impact.

26   My point is simply this: Whatever the eventual outcome (I suspect it will be positive), the Alvarez hypothesis is exciting, fruitful science because it generates tests, provides us with things to do, and expands outward. We are having fun, battling back and forth, moving toward a resolution, and extending the hypothesis beyond its original scope.

27   As just one example of the unexpected, distant cross-fertilization that good science engenders, the Alvarez hypothesis made a major contribution to a theme that has riveted public attention in the past few months—so-called nuclear winter. In a speech delivered in April 1982, Luis Alvarez calculated the energy that a ten-kilometer asteroid would release on impact. He compared such an explosion with a full nuclear exchange and implied that all-out atomic war might unleash similar consequences.

28   This theme of impact leading to massive dust clouds and falling temperatures formed an important input to the decision of Carl Sagan and a group of colleagues to model the climatic consequences of nuclear holocaust. Full nuclear exchange would probably generate the same kind of dust cloud and darkening that may have wiped out the dinosaurs. Temperatures would drop precipitously and agriculture might become impossible. Avoidance of nuclear war is fundamentally an ethical and political imperative, but we must know the factual consequences to make firm judgments. I am heartened by a final link across disciplines and deep concerns—another criterion, by the way, of science at its best. A

recognition of the very phenomenon that made our evolution possible by exterminating the previously dominant dinosaurs and
clearing a way for the evolution of large mammals, including us,
might actually help to save us from joining those magnificent
beasts in contorted poses among the strata of the earth.

1984

The Press Needs a National Monitor

Mike Wallace

"You arrogant journalists, you spend your lives looking down our   1
throats and holding us up to public obloquy, but you cry foul (or
First Amendment) when we want to look down yours!"

That's the plaint of hundreds of thousands of businessmen,   2
doctors, lawyers, politicians and other public figures who have
lost confidence in what we report and in our professed journalistic objectivity.

And how do we respond? Too often too many of us shrug our   3
shoulders and dismiss the criticism as an occupational hazard,
one that comes with the territory, or we suggest a letter to the editor. And if someone really feels his ox has been unfairly gored, his
attorney may remind him that he can file a libel suit.

Is there no better way?   4

As we reported recently on "60 Minutes," for the past 26 years   5
an organization called the Minnesota News Council has been taking on these complaints and resolving them with some success.

Any individual, business or public institution in the state that   6
feels its integrity or reputation has been traduced in a news report
may file a complaint with the council. If the council decides the
complaint is worth its attention, it'll study the news report, hear
from both sides in private and in public, and come to a decision.

Either the council's members vote that the complaint is valid, or that the news report in question told its story fairly.

7   The Minnesota News Council consists of 24 members, half of them journalists and half of them public members—businessmen, lawyers, teachers, other interested citizens. A state Supreme Court justice presides over their public hearings. These 24, chosen over the years by previous council members, study the article or broadcast in question. Then they read written arguments prepared by the news organization and the complainant and sit for a public session, amply covered by all the media, at which each side argues its case. Questions are asked and answered, opinions and rebuttals aired, and finally a vote is taken.

8   And what happens if the journalists are found wanting? No one goes to jail, no one is put out of business, no money is awarded. Instead, the journalists suffer the same kind of humiliation the objects of our scrutiny are bound to feel when our searching spotlight uncovers their flaws or malfeasances.

9   Over the past quarter-century, about half the cases filed with the Minnesota News Council have been decided in favor of the journalists. The Minnesota group is not the only such news council currently operating. There is one more, just one, the Honolulu Community Media Council. But there are suggestions that perhaps several regional councils or a national news council should be established.

10   Back in the 1970s and into the early 1980s, there was just such a national body, spawned by a group of journalists led by Richard Salant, who was president of CBS News. He believed the public should have some means to bring their complaints to someone with the competence and authority to give a public "thumbs up" or "thumbs down" as to the accuracy and the fairness of certain troubling news reports. Something, he felt, more defining than a letter to the editor and less onerous than a libel suit, with its attendant huge legal fees and interminable court procedures.

11   That early effort to establish a national news council was hampered by a struggle for funding, and by catcalls from inside the hypersensitive journalistic community. It sputtered after a few years and eventually it died, killed off mainly because two heavy hitters, Abe Rosenthal, then the executive editor of the *New York Times*,

and Walter Cronkite, then the trusted anchor of "The CBS Evening News," were dead set against it—as was my colleague Don Hewitt, who heads up "60 Minutes." All three felt they didn't need anyone looking over their editorial shoulders; they were professionals, they said, and if not infallible surely they needed no help from unqualified outsiders.

Today Abe Rosenthal, no longer the man who runs the *Times* 12 but whose columns appear regularly on the paper's op-ed page, hasn't changed his mind one whit. And Walter Cronkite? At a memorial service for Dick Salant a couple of years ago, this was Walter's take: "In the 1970s, I thought it was the worst idea I ever heard in my life, that we should put judgment as to the kind of job we do in the hands of another, somewhere outside our profession, outside our immediate workplace. But I think now, as I look back at it, that Dick was probably right."

At a time when the public trust in us may be even lower than 13 it was in Dick Salant's time, I've come to the reluctant conclusion that Walter's change of mind is right.

1996

Mea Culpa? Not Mea!

Don Hewitt

As I've said to my close friend and esteemed colleague Mike Wallace, bias, like beauty, is in the eye of the beholder. And while I behold bias from time to time in news coverage, I would rather leave it to a good editor to weed it out than to a news council made up of a bunch of guys named Joe (as in Kennedy, who wanted to ride Mike out of town on a rail for giving his son Jack a hard time). Or Henry (as in Kissinger, who wanted to tar and feather Mike because the story he aired about him wasn't as flattering as he thought it should be). Or Alfonse (as in D'Amato, who wanted to take Mike to the woodshed because he didn't like what Mike said about him). Or L. Ron (as in Hubbard, whose Church of Scientology disciples threatened to "get" Mike for what he reported about them). Or Howard (as in Squadron, of the Council of Presidents of Jewish Organizations, who wanted Mike drawn and quartered for reporting that the Jerusalem police were not as innocent as they said they were in the recent temple mount massacre). Or Reed (as in Irvine, of Accuracy in Media, who is convinced to this day that Mike is conspiring with the Clintons to cover up the murder of Vince Foster).

2   And that doesn't even include what a news council sitting in judgment of my esteemed colleague would have said about him if some old soldiers who refused to die or fade away showed up at a news council to join in the fun after Mike's famous Westmoreland broadcast.

3   Are journalists as good as they think they are at avoiding bias? No, nobody is. But at least journalists are trained to report fairly—unlike corporate executives, academics, PR types and assorted members of the citizenry who have the time and the inclination to sit on a news council. If anyone thinks certain journalists are unfair, he or she can always complain to, or boycott, the advertisers who pay the reporters' salaries. Or turn them off or tune them out or go buy or watch another news magazine.

4   It has been my experience that what viewers and readers are most unhappy about is not that journalists slant the news, but that we don't slant it their way. And it's those readers and viewers who would sit on the news councils in Mike's brave new world.

5   On paper, it may not be a bad idea. But in practice? Whoa there, Mikey, slow down. Where in the world are you going to find the saints to sit in judgment of us sinners? Mea culpa? Not mea.

1996

A Modest Proposal

Jonathan Swift

It is a <u>melancholy object</u> to those who walk through this great 1
town or travel in the country, when they see the streets, the roads,
and cabin doors, crowded with beggars of the female sex, followed by three, four, or six children, all in rags and importuning
every passenger for an alms. These mothers, instead of being able
to work for their honest livelihood, are forced to employ all their
time in strolling to beg sustenance for their helpless infants: Who
as they grow up either turn thieves for want of work, or leave their
dear native country to fight for the Pretender in Spain, or sell
themselves to the Barbadoes.

I think it is agreed by all parties that this prodigious number 2
of children in the arms, or on the backs, or at the heels of their
mothers, and frequently of their fathers, is in the present de-
plorable state of the kingdom a very great additional grievance;
and, therefore, whoever could <u>find out a fair, cheap, and easy</u>
<u>method of making these children sound</u>, useful members of the
<u>commonwealth, would deserve so well of the public as to have his</u>   ✳
<u>statue set up for a preserver of the nation.</u>

But my intention is very far from being confined to provide 3
only for the children of professed beggars; it is of a much greater
extent, and shall take in the whole number of infants at a certain
age who are born of parents in effect as little able to support them
as those who demand our charity in the streets.

As to my own part, having turned my thoughts for many 4
years upon this important subject, and maturely weighed the several schemes of our projectors, I have always found them grossly
mistaken in their computation. It is true, a child just dropped from
its dam may be supported by her milk for a solar year, with little
other nourishment; at most not above the value of 2s., which the
mother may certainly get, or the value in scraps, by her lawful occupation of begging; and it is exactly at one year old that I propose
to provide for them in such a manner as instead of being a charge
upon their parents or the parish, or wanting food and raiment for

the rest of their lives, they shall on the contrary contribute to the feeding, and partly to the clothing, of many thousands.

5 .   There is likewise another great advantage in my scheme, that it will prevent those voluntary abortions, and that horrid practice of women murdering their bastard children, alas! too frequent among us! sacrificing the poor innocent babes I doubt more to avoid the expense than the shame, which would move tears and pity in the most savage and inhuman breast.

6   The number of souls in this kingdom being usually reckoned one million and a half, of these I calculate there may be about 200,000 couples whose wives are breeders; from which number I subtract 30,000 couples who are able to maintain their own children (although I apprehend there cannot be so many, under the present distress of the kingdom); but this being granted, there will remain 170,000 breeders. I again subtract 50,000 for those women who miscarry, or whose children die by accident or disease within the year. There only remain 120,000 children of poor parents annually born. The question therefore is, how this number shall be reared and provided for? which, as I have already said, under the present situation of affairs, is utterly impossible by all the methods hitherto proposed. For we can neither employ them in handicraft or agriculture; we neither build houses (I mean live in the country) nor cultivate land; they can very seldom pick up a livelihood by stealing, till they arrive at six years old, except where they are of towardly parts; although I confess they learn the rudiments much earlier; during which time they can, however, be properly looked upon only as probationers; as I have been informed by a principal gentleman in the county of Cavan, who protested to me that he never knew above one or two instances under the age of six, even in a part of the kingdom so renowned for the quickest proficiency in that art.

7   I am assured by our merchants, that a boy or a girl before twelve years old is no saleable commodity; and even when they come to this age they will not yield above 31. or 31.2s. 6d. at most on the exchange; which cannot turn to account either to the parents or kingdom, the charge of nutriment and rags having been at least four times that value.

8   I shall now therefore humbly propose my own thoughts, which I hope will not be liable to the least objection.

I have been assured by a very knowing American of my ac-   9
quaintance in London, that a young healthy child well nursed is at
a year old a most delicious, nourishing, and wholesome food,
whether stewed, roasted, baked, or broiled; and I make no doubt
that it will equally serve in a fricassee or a ragout.

I do therefore humbly offer it to public consideration that of   10
the 120,000 children already computed, 20,000 may be reserved for
breed, whereof only one-fourth part to be males; which is more
than we allow to sheep, black cattle, or swine; and my reason is,
that these children are seldom the fruits of marriage, a circumstance not much regarded by our savages; therefore one male will
be sufficient to serve four females. That the remaining 100,000
may, at a year old, be offered in sale to the persons of quality and
fortune through the kingdom; always advising the mother to let
them suck plentifully in the last month, so as to render them
plump and fat for a good table. A child will make two dishes at an
entertainment for friends; and when the family dines alone, the
fore or hind quarter will make a reasonable dish, and seasoned
with a little pepper or salt will be very good boiled on the fourth
day, especially in winter.

I have reckoned upon a medium that a child just born will   11
weigh 12 pounds, and in a solar year, if tolerably nursed, will increase to 28 pounds.

I grant this food will be somewhat dear, and therefore very   12
proper for landlords, who, as they have already devoured most of
the parents, seem to have the best title to the children.

Infant's flesh will be in season throughout the year, but more   13
plentiful in March, and a little before and after; for we are told by
a grave author, an eminent French physician, that fish being a prolific diet, there are more children born in Roman Catholic countries about nine months after Lent than at any other season; therefore, reckoning a year after Lent, the markets will be more glutted
than usual, because the number of popish infants is at least three
to one in this kingdom: and therefore it will have one other collat-
eral advantage, by lessening the number of papists among us.

I have already computed the charge of nursing a beggar's child   14
(in which list I reckon all cottagers, laborers, and four-fifths of the
farmers) to be about 2s. per annum, rags included; and I believe no

gentleman would repine to give 10s. for the carcass of a good fat child, which, as I have said, will make four dishes of excellent nutritive meat, when he has only some particular friend or his own family to dine with him. Thus the squire will learn to be a good landlord, and grow popular among the tenants; the mother will have 8s. net profit, and be fit for work till she produces another child.

15   Those who are more thrifty (as I must confess the times require) may flay the carcass; the skin of which artificially dressed will make admirable gloves for ladies, and summer boots for fine gentlemen.

16   As to our city of Dublin, shambles may be appointed for this purpose in the most convenient parts of it, and butchers we may be assured will not be wanting: although I rather recommend buying the children alive, and dressing them hot from the knife as we do roasting pigs.

17   A very worthy person, a true lover of his country, and whose virtues I highly esteem, was lately pleased in discoursing on this matter to offer a refinement upon my scheme. He said that many gentlemen of this kingdom, having of late destroyed their deer, he conceived that the want of venison might be well supplied by the bodies of young lads and maidens, not exceeding fourteen years of age nor under twelve; so great a number of both sexes in every country being now ready to starve for want of work and service; and these to be disposed of by their parents, if alive, or otherwise by their nearest relations. But with due deference to so excellent a friend and so deserving a patriot, I cannot be altogether in his sentiments; for as to the males, my American acquaintance assured me from frequent experience that their flesh was generally tough and lean, like that of our schoolboys by continual exercise, and their taste disagreeable; and to fatten them would not answer the charge. Then as to the females, it would, I think, with humble submission be a loss to the public, because they soon would become breeders themselves; and besides, it is not improbable that some scrupulous people might be apt to censure such a practice (although indeed very unjustly), as a little bordering upon cruelty; which, I confess, has always been with me the strongest objection against any project, how well so-ever intended.

But in order to justify my friend, he confessed that this expe- 18
dient was put into his head by the famous Psalmanazar, a native
of the island Formosa, who came from thence to London about
twenty years ago: And in conversation told my friend, that in his
country when any young person happened to be put to death, the
executioner sold the carcass to persons of quality as a prime
dainty; and that in his time the body of a plump girl of fifteen, who
was crucified for an attempt to poison the emperor, was sold to his
imperial majesty's prime minister of state, and other great man-
darins of the court, in joints from the gibbet, at 400 crowns. Neither indeed can I deny, that if the same use were made of several
plump young girls in this town, who without one single groat to
their fortunes cannot stir without a chair, and appear at the play-
house and assemblies in foreign fineries which they never will pay
for, the kingdom would not be the worse.

Some persons of a desponding spirit are in great concern 19
about that vast number of poor people, who are aged, diseased, or
maimed, and I have been desired to employ my thoughts what
course may be taken to ease the nation of so grievous an encum-
brance. But I am not in the least pain upon that matter, because it
is very well known that they are every day dying and rotting by
cold and famine, and filth and vermin, as fast as can be reasonably
expected. And as to the young laborers, they are now in as hope-
ful a condition: they cannot get work, and consequently pine away
for want of nourishment, to a degree that if at any time they are accidentally hired to common labor, they have not strength to perform it; and thus the country and themselves are happily delivered from the evils to come.

I have too long digressed, and therefore shall return to my 20
subject. I think the advantages by the proposal which I have made
are obvious and many, as well as of the highest importance.

For first, as I have already observed, it would greatly lessen 21
the number of papists, with whom we are yearly overrun, being
the principal breeders of the nation as well as our most dangerous
enemies; and who stay at home on purpose to deliver the kingdom to the Pretender, hoping to take their advantage by the absence of so many good Protestants, who have chosen rather to

leave their country than stay at home and pay tithes against their conscience to an Episcopal curate.

22   Secondly, the poor tenants will have something valuable of their own, which by law may be made liable to distress and help to pay their landlord's rent, their corn and cattle being already seized, and money a thing unknown.

23   Thirdly, whereas the maintenance of 100,000 children from two years old and upward, cannot be computed at less than 10s. apiece per annum, the nation's stock will be thereby increased £50,000 per annum, beside the profit of a new dish introduced to the tables of all gentlemen of fortune in the kingdom who have any refinement in taste. And the money will circulate among ourselves, the goods being entirely of our own growth and manufacture.

24   Fourthly, the constant breeders beside the gain of 8s. sterling per annum by the sale of their children, will be rid of the charge of maintaining them after the first year.

25   Fifthly, this food would likewise bring great custom to taverns, where the vintners will certainly be so prudent as to procure the best receipts for dressing it to perfection, and consequently have their houses frequented by all the fine gentlemen, who justly value themselves upon their knowledge in good eating; and a skilful cook who understands how to oblige his guests, will contrive to make it as expensive as they please.

26   Sixthly, this would be a great inducement to marriage, which all wise nations have either encouraged by rewards or enforced by laws and penalties. It would increase the care and tenderness of mothers toward their children, when they were sure of a settlement for life to the poor babes, provided in some sort by the public, to their annual profit instead of expense. We should see an honest emulation among the married women, which of them would bring the fattest child to the market. Men would become as fond of their wives during the time of their pregnancy as they are now of their mares in foal, their cows in calf, their sows when they are ready to farrow; nor offer to beat or kick them (as is too frequent a practice) for fear of a miscarriage.

27   Many other advantages might be enumerated. For instance, the addition of some thousand carcasses in our exportation of barreled beef, the propagation of swine's flesh, and improvement in

the art of making good bacon, so much wanted among us by the great destruction of pigs, too frequent at our table; which are no way comparable in taste or magnificence to a well-grown, fat, yearling child, which roasted whole will make a considerable figure at a lord mayor's feast or any other public entertainment. But this and many others I omit, being studious of brevity.

Supposing that 1,000 families in this city would be constant customers for infants' flesh, besides others who might have it at merry-meetings, particularly at weddings and christenings, I compute that Dublin would take off annually about 20,000 carcasses; and the rest of the kingdom (where probably they will be sold somewhat cheaper) the remaining 80,000. 28

I can think of no one objection that will possibly be raised against this proposal, unless it should be urged that the number of people will be thereby much lessened in the kingdom. This I freely own, and it was indeed one principal design in offering it to the world. I desire the reader will observe, that I calculate my remedy for this one individual kingdom of Ireland and for no other than ever was, is, or I think ever can be upon earth. Therefore let no man talk to me of other expedients: Of taxing our absentees at 5s. a pound: Of using neither clothes nor household furniture except what is of our own growth and manufacture: Of utterly rejecting the materials and instruments that promote foreign luxury: Of curing the expensiveness of pride, vanity, idleness, and gaming in our women: Of introducing a vein of parsimony, prudence, and temperance: Of learning to love our country, in the want of which we differ even from Laplander and the inhabitants of Topinamboo: Of quitting our animosities and factions, nor acting any longer like the Jews, who were murdering one another at the very moment their city was taken: Of being a little cautious not to sell our country and conscience for nothing: Of teaching landlords to have at least one degree of mercy toward their tenants: Lastly, of putting a spirit of honesty, industry, and skill into our shopkeepers; who, if a resolution could now be taken to buy only our native goods, would immediately unite to cheat and exact upon us in the price, the measure, and the goodness, nor could ever yet be brought to make one fair proposal of just dealing, though often and earnestly invited to it. 29

30   Therefore I repeat, let no man talk to me of these and the like expedients, till he has at least some glimpse of hope that there will be ever some hearty and sincere attempt to put them in practice.

31   But as to myself, having been wearied out for many years with offering vain, idle, visionary thoughts, and at length utterly despairing of success, I fortunately fell upon this proposal; which, as it is wholly new, so it has something solid and real, of no expense and little trouble, full in our own power, and whereby we can incur no danger in disobliging England. For this kind of commodity will not bear exportation, the flesh being of too tender a consistence to admit a long continuance in salt, although perhaps I could name a country which would be glad to eat up our whole nation without it.

32   After all, I am not so violently bent upon my own opinion as to reject any offer proposed by wise men, which shall be found equally innocent, cheap, easy, and effectual. But before something of that kind shall be advanced in contradiction to my scheme, and offering a better, I desire the author or authors will be pleased maturely to consider two points. First, as things now stand, how they will be able to find food and raiment for 100,000 useless mouths and backs. And secondly, there being a round million of creatures in human figure throughout this kingdom, whose subsistence put into a common stock would leave them in debt 2,000,000*l.* sterling, adding those who are beggars by profession to the bulk of farmers, cottagers, and laborers, with the wives and children who are beggars in effect; I desire those politicians who dislike my overture, and may perhaps be so bold as to attempt an answer, that they will first ask the parents of these mortals, whether they would not at this day think it a great happiness to have been sold for food at a year old in the manner I prescribe, and thereby have avoided such a perpetual scene of misfortunes as they have since gone through by the oppression of landlords, the impossibility of paying rent without money or trade, the want of common sustenance, with neither house nor clothes to cover them from the inclemencies of the weather, and the most inevitable prospect of entailing the like or greater miseries upon their breed for ever.

33   I profess, in the sincerity of my heart, that I have not the least personal interest in endeavoring to promote this necessary work,

having no other motive than the public good of my country, by advancing our trade, providing for infants, relieving the poor, and giving some pleasure to the rich. I have no children by which I can propose to get a single penny; the youngest being nine years old, and my wife past childbearing.

1714

Persuasion

I Have a Dream

Martin Luther King, Jr.

Five score years ago, a great American, in whose symbolic shadow 1
we stand, signed the Emancipation Proclamation. This momentous decree came as a great beacon light of hope to millions of Negro slaves who had been seared in the flames of withering injustice. It came as a joyous daybreak to end the long night of captivity.

But one hundred years later, we must face the tragic fact that 2
the Negro is still not free. One hundred years later, the life of the Negro is still sadly crippled by the manacles of segregation and the chains of discrimination. One hundred years later, the Negro lives on a lonely island of poverty in the midst of a vast ocean of material prosperity. One hundred years later, the Negro is still languishing in the corners of American society and finds himself an exile in his own land. So we have come here today to dramatize an appalling condition.

In a sense we have come to our nation's capital to cash a 3
check. When the architects of our republic wrote the magnificent words of the Constitution and the Declaration of Independence, they were signing a promissory note to which every American

was to fall heir. This note was a promise that all men would be guaranteed the unalienable rights of life, liberty, and the pursuit of happiness.

4   It is obvious today that America has defaulted on this promissory note insofar as her citizens of color are concerned. Instead of honoring this sacred obligation, America has given the Negro people a bad check; a check which has come back marked "insufficient funds." But we refuse to believe that the bank of justice is bankrupt. We refuse to believe that there are insufficient funds in the great vaults of opportunity of this nation. So we have come to cash this check—a check that will give us upon demand the riches of freedom and the security of justice. We have also come to this hallowed spot to remind America of the fierce urgency of *now*. This is no time to engage in the luxury of cooling off or to take the tranquilizing drugs of gradualism. *Now* is the time to make real the promises of Democracy. *Now* is the time to rise from the dark and desolate valley of segregation to the sunlit path of racial justice. *Now* is the time to open the doors of opportunity to all of God's children. *Now* is the time to lift our nation from the quicksands of racial injustice to the solid rock of brotherhood.

5   It would be fatal for the nation to overlook the urgency of the moment and to underestimate the determination of the Negro. This sweltering summer of the Negro's legitimate discontent will not pass until there is an invigorating autumn of freedom and equality. 1963 is not an end, but a beginning. Those who hope that the Negro needed to blow off steam and will now be content will have a rude awakening if the nation returns to business as usual. There will be neither rest nor tranquillity in America until the Negro is granted his citizenship rights. The whirlwinds of revolt will continue to shake the foundations of our nation until the bright day of justice emerges.

6   But there is something that I must say to my people who stand on the warm threshold which leads into the palace of justice. In the process of gaining our rightful place we must not be guilty of wrongful deeds. Let us not seek to satisfy our thirst for freedom by drinking from the cup of bitterness and hatred. We must forever conduct our struggle on the high plane of dignity and discipline. We must not allow our creative protest to degenerate into physi-

cal violence. Again and again we must rise to the majestic heights of meeting physical force with soul force. The marvelous new militancy which has engulfed the Negro community must not lead us to a distrust of all white people, for many of our white brothers, as evidenced by their presence here today, have come to realize that their destiny is tied up with our destiny and their freedom is inextricably bound to our freedom. We cannot walk alone.

And as we walk, we must make the pledge that we shall 7 march ahead. We cannot turn back. There are those who are asking the devotees of civil rights, "When will you be satisfied?" We can never be satisfied as long as the Negro is the victim of the unspeakable horrors of police brutality. We can never be satisfied as long as our bodies, heavy with the fatigue of travel, cannot gain lodging in the motels of the highways and the hotels of the cities. We cannot be satisfied as long as the Negro's basic mobility is from a smaller ghetto to a larger one. We can never be satisfied as long as a Negro in Mississippi cannot vote and a Negro in New York believes he has nothing for which to vote. No, no, we are not satisfied, and we will not be satisfied until justice rolls down like waters and righteousness like a mighty stream.

I am not unmindful that some of you have come here out of 8 great trials and tribulations. Some of you have come fresh from narrow jail cells. Some of you have come from areas where your quest for freedom left you battered by the storms of persecution and staggered by the winds of police brutality. You have been the veterans of creative suffering. Continue to work with the faith that unearned suffering is redemptive.

Go back to Mississippi, go back to Alabama, go back to South 9 Carolina, go back to Georgia, go back to Louisiana, go back to the slums and ghettos of our northern cities, knowing that somehow this situation can and will be changed. Let us not wallow in the valley of despair.

I say to you today, my friends, that in spite of the difficulties 10 and frustrations of the moment I still have a dream. It is a dream deeply rooted in the American dream.

I have a dream that one day this nation will rise up and live 11 out the true meaning of its creed: "We hold these truths to be self-evident; that all men are created equal."

12   I have a dream that one day on the red hills of Georgia the sons of former slaves and the sons of former slaveowners will be able to sit down together at the table of brotherhood.

13   I have a dream that one day even the state of Mississippi, a desert state sweltering with the heat of injustice and oppression, will be transformed into an oasis of freedom and justice.

14   I have a dream that my four little children will one day live in a nation where they will not be judged by the color of their skin but by the content of their character.

15   I have a dream today.

16   I have a dream that one day the state of Alabama, whose governor's lips are presently dripping with the words of interposition and nullification, will be transformed into a situation where little black boys and black girls will be able to join hands with little white boys and white girls and walk together as sisters and brothers.

17   I have a dream today.

18   I have a dream that one day every valley shall be exalted, every hill and mountain shall be made low, the rough places will be made plain, and the crooked places will be made straight, and the glory of the Lord shall be revealed, and all flesh shall see it together.

19   This is our hope. This is the faith with which I return to the South. With this faith we will be able to hew out of the mountain of despair a stone of hope. With this faith we will be able to transform the jangling discords of our nation into a beautiful symphony of brotherhood. With this faith we will be able to work together, to pray together, to struggle together, to go to jail together, to stand up for freedom together, knowing that we will be free one day.

20   This will be the day when all of God's children will be able to sing with new meaning

> My country, 'tis of thee,
> Sweet land of liberty,
>   Of thee I sing:
> Land where my fathers died,
> Land of the pilgrims' pride,
> From every mountain-side
>   Let freedom ring.

And if America is to be a great nation this must become true. So   21
let freedom ring from the prodigious hilltops of New Hampshire.
Let freedom ring from the mighty mountains of New York. Let freedom ring from the heightening Alleghenies of Pennsylvania!

Let freedom ring from the snowcapped Rockies of Colorado!   22
Let freedom ring from the curvaceous peaks of California!   23
But not only that; let freedom ring from Stone   24
    Mountain of Georgia!
Let freedom ring from Lookout Mountain of Tennessee!   25
Let freedom ring from every hill and molehill of Mississippi.   26
    From every mountainside, let freedom ring.

When we let freedom ring, when we let it ring from every vil-   27
lage and every hamlet, from every state and every city, we will be
able to speed up that day when all of God's children, black men and
white men, Jews and Gentiles, Protestants and Catholics, will be
able to join hands and sing in the words of the old Negro spiritual,
"Free at last! free at last! thank God almighty, we are free at last!"

1963

Who Shot Johnny?

Debra Dickerson

Given my level of political awareness, it was inevitable that I   1
would come to view the everyday events of my life through the
prism of politics and the national discourse. I read *The Washington
Post, The New Republic, The New Yorker, Harper's, The Atlantic
Monthly, The Nation, National Review, Black Enterprise,* and *Essence*
and wrote a weekly column for the Harvard Law School *Record*
during my three years just ended there. I do this because I know
that those of us who are not well-fed white guys in suits must not
yield the debate to them, however well-intentioned or well-informed they may be. Accordingly, I am unrepentant and vocal

about having gained admittance to Harvard through affirmative action; I am a feminist, stoic about my marriage chances as a well-educated, thirty-six-year-old black woman who won't pretend to need help taking care of herself. My strength flags, though, in the face of the latest role assigned to my family in the national drama. On July 27, 1995, my sixteen-year-old nephew was shot and paralyzed.

2   Talking with friends in front of his house, Johnny saw a car he thought he recognized. He waved boisterously—his trademark—throwing both arms in the air in a full-bodied, hip-hop Y. When he got no response, he and his friends sauntered down the walk to join a group loitering in front of an apartment building. The car followed. The driver got out, brandished a revolver, and fired into the air. Everyone scattered. Then he took aim and shot my running nephew in the back.

3   Johnny never lost consciousness. He lay in the road, trying to understand what had happened to him, why he couldn't get up. Emotionlessly, he told the story again and again on demand, remaining apologetically firm against all demands to divulge the missing details that would make sense of the shooting but obviously cast him in a bad light. Being black, male, and shot, he must apparently be involved with gangs or drugs. Probably both. Witnesses corroborate his version of events.

4   Nearly six months have passed since that phone call in the night and my nightmarish headlong drive from Boston to Charlotte. After twenty hours behind the wheel, I arrived haggard enough to reduce my mother to fresh tears and to find my nephew reassuring well-wishers with an eerie sang-froid.

5   I take the day shift in his hospital room; his mother and grandmother, a clerk and cafeteria worker, respectively, alternate nights there on a cot. They don their uniforms the next day, gaunt after hours spent listening to Johnny moan in his sleep. How often must his subconscious replay those events and curse its host for saying hello without permission, for being carefree and young while a would-be murderer hefted the weight of his uselessness and failure like Jacob Marley's chains? How often must he watch himself lying stubbornly immobile on the pavement of his nightmares while the sound of running feet syncopate his attacker's taunts?

6   I spend these days beating him at gin rummy and Scrabble, holding a basin while he coughs up phlegm and crying in the cor-

ridor while he catheterizes himself. There are children here much
worse off than he. I should be grateful. The doctors can't, or won't,
say whether he'll walk again.

I am at once repulsed and fascinated by the bullet, which re- 7
mains lodged in his spine (having done all the damage it can do,
the doctors say). The wound is undramatic—small, neat, and perfectly centered—an impossibly pink pit surrounded by an otherwise undisturbed expanse of mahogany. Johnny has asked me
several times to describe it but politely declines to look in the mirror I hold for him.

Here on the pediatric rehab ward, Johnny speaks little, never 8
cries, never complains, works diligently to become independent.
He does whatever he is told; if two hours remain until the next
pain pill, he waits quietly. Eyes bloodshot, hands gripping the bed
rails. During the week of his intravenous feeding, when he was
tormented by the primal need to masticate, he never asked for
food. He just listened while we counted down the days for him
and planned his favorite meals. Now required to dress himself
unassisted, he does so without demur, rolling himself back and
forth valiantly on the bed and shivering afterward, exhausted. He
"ma'am"s and "sir"s everyone politely. Before his "accident," a
simple request to take out the trash could provoke a firestorm of
teenage attitude. We, the women who have raised him, have
changed as well; we've finally come to appreciate those boxer-bar-
ing, oversized pants we used to hate—it would be much more difficult to fit properly sized pants over his diaper.

He spends a lot of time tethered to rap music still loud enough 9
to break my concentration as I read my many magazines. I hear
him try to soundlessly mouth the obligatory "mothafuckers"
overlaying the funereal dirge of the music tracks. I do not normally tolerate disrespectful music in my or my mother's presence,
but if it distracts him now . . .

"Johnny," I ask later, "do you still like gangster rap?" During 10
the long pause I hear him think loudly, I'm paralyzed, Auntie, not
stupid. "I mostly just listen to hip-hop," he says evasively into his
Sports Illustrated.

Miserable though it is, time passes quickly here. We always 11
seem to be jerking awake in our chairs just in time for the next pill,

his every-other-night bowel program, the doctor's rounds. Harvard feels a galaxy away—the world revolves around Family Members Living with Spinal Cord Injury class, Johnny's urine output, and strategizing with my sister to find affordable, accessible housing. There is always another long-distance uncle in need of an update, another church member wanting to pray with us, or Johnny's little brother in need of some attention.

12   We Dickerson women are so constant a presence the ward nurses and cleaning staff call us by name and join us for cafeteria meals and cigarette breaks. At Johnny's birthday pizza party, they crack jokes and make fun of each other's husbands (there are no men here). I pass slices around and try not to think, Seventeen with a bullet.

13   Oddly, we feel little curiosity or specific anger toward the man who shot him. We have to remind ourselves to check in with the police. Even so, it feels pro forma, like sending in those $2 rebate forms that come with new pantyhose: You know your request will fall into a deep, dark hole somewhere, but still, it's your duty to try. We push for an arrest because we owe it to Johnny and to ourselves as citizens. We don't think about it otherwise—our low expectations are too ingrained. A Harvard aunt notwithstanding, for people like Johnny, Marvin Gaye was right that only three things are sure: Taxes, death, and trouble. At least it wasn't the second.

14   We rarely wonder about or discuss the brother who shot him because we already know everything about him. When the call came, my first thought was the same one I'd had when I'd heard about Rosa Parks's beating: A brother did it. A non-job-having, middle-of-the-day malt-liquor-drinking, crotch-clutching, loud-talking brother with many neglected children born of many forgotten women. He lives in his mother's basement with furniture rented at an astronomical interest rate, the exact amount of which he does not know. He has a car phone, an $80 monthly cable bill, and every possible phone feature but no savings. He steals Social Security numbers from unsuspecting relatives and assumes their identities to acquire large TV sets for which he will never pay. On the slim chance that he is brought to justice, he will have a colorful criminal history and no coherent explanation to offer for his

act. His family will raucously defend him and cry cover-up. Some liberal lawyer just like me will help him plea-bargain his way to yet another short stay in a prison pesthouse that will serve only to add another layer to the brother's sociopathology and formless, mindless nihilism. We know him. We've known and feared him all our lives.

As a teenager, he called, "Hey, baby, gimme somma that boodie!" at us from car windows. Indignant at our lack of response, he followed up with, "Fuck you, then, 'ho!" He called me a "white-boy-lovin' nigger bitch oreo" for being in the gifted program and loving it. At twenty-seven, he got my seventeen-year-old sister pregnant with Johnny and lost interest without ever informing her that he was married. He snatched my widowed mother's purse as she waited in predawn darkness for the bus to work and then broke into our house while she soldered on an assembly line. He chased all the small entrepreneurs from our neighborhood with his violent thievery and put bars on our windows. He kept us from sitting on our own front porch after dark and laid the foundation for our periodic bouts of self-hating anger and racial embarrassment. He made our neighborhood a ghetto. He is the poster fool behind the maddening community knowledge that there are still some black mothers who raise their daughters but merely love their sons. He and his cancerous carbon copies eclipse the vast majority of us who are not sociopaths and render us invisible. He is the Siamese twin who has died but cannot be separated from his living, vibrant sibling; which of us must attract more notice? We despise and disown this anomalous loser, but for many he *is* black America. We know him, we know that he is outside the fold, and we know that he will only get worse. What we didn't know is that, because of him, my little sister would one day be the latest hysterical black mother wailing over a fallen child on TV.

Alone, lying in the road bleeding and paralyzed but hideously conscious, Johnny had lain helpless as he watched his would-be murderer come to stand over him and offer this prophecy: "Betch'ou won't be doin' nomo' wavin', mothafucker."

Fuck you, asshole. He's fine from the waist up. You just can't do anything right, can you?

Bilingual Education: Outdated and Unrealistic

Richard Rodriguez

1 How shall we teach the dark-eyed child *ingles?* The debate continues much as it did two decades ago.

2 Bilingual education belongs to the 1960s, the years of the black civil rights movement. Bilingual education became the official Hispanic demand; as a symbol, the English-only classroom was intended to be analogous to the segregated lunch counter; the locked school door. Bilingual education was endorsed by judges and, of course, by politicians well before anyone knew the answer to the question: Does bilingual education work?

3 Who knows? *Quien sabe?*

4 The official drone over bilingual education is conducted by educationalists with numbers and charts. Because bilingual education was never simply a matter of pedagogy, it is too much to expect educators to resolve the matter. Proclamations concerning bilingual education are weighted at bottom with Hispanic political grievances and, too, with middle-class romanticism.

5 No one will say it in public; in private, Hispanics argue with me about bilingual education and every time it comes down to memory. Everyone remembers going to that grammar school where students were slapped for speaking Spanish. Childhood memory is offered as parable; the memory is meant to compress the gringo's long history of offenses against Spanish, Hispanic culture, Hispanics.

6 It is no coincidence that, although all of America's ethnic groups are implicated in the policy of bilingual education, Hispanics, particularly Mexican-Americans, have been its chief advocates. The English words used by Hispanics in support of bilingual education are words such as "dignity," "heritage," "culture." Bilingualism becomes a way of exacting from gringos

a grudging admission of contrition—for the 19th-century theft of the Southwest, the relegation of Spanish to a foreign tongue, the injustice of history. At the extreme, Hispanic bilingual enthusiasts demand that public schools "maintain" a student's sense of separateness.

Hispanics may be among the last groups of Americans who 7 still believe in the 1960's. Bilingual-education proposals still serve the romance of that decade, especially of the late 60s, when the heroic black civil rights movement grew paradoxically wedded to its opposite—the ethnic revival movement. Integration and separatism merged into twin, possible goals.

With integration, the black movement inspired middle-class 8 Americans to imitations—the Hispanic movement; the Gray Panthers; feminism; gay rights. Then there was withdrawal, with black glamour leading a romantic retreat from the anonymous crowd.

Americans came to want it both ways. They wanted in and 9 they wanted out. Hispanics took to celebrating their diversity, joined other Americans in dancing rings around the melting pot.

MYTHIC METAPHORS

More intently than most, Hispanics wanted the romance of their 10 dual cultural allegiance backed up by law. Bilingualism became proof that one could have it both ways, could be a full member of public America and yet also separate, privately Hispanic. "Spanish" and "English" became mythic metaphors like country and city, describing separate islands of private and public life.

Ballots, billboards, and, of course, classrooms in Spanish. For 11 nearly two decades now, middle-class Hispanics have had it their way. They have foisted a neat ideological scheme on working-class children. What they want to believe about themselves, they wait for the child to prove, that it is possible to be two, that one can assume the public language (the public life) of America, even while remaining what one was, existentially separate.

Adulthood is not so neatly balanced. The tension between pub- 12 lic and private life is intrinsic to adulthood—certainly middle-class adulthood. Usually the city wins because the city pays. We are mass people for more of the day than we are with our intimates. No Congressional mandate or Supreme Court decision can diminish the loss.

13   I was talking the other day to a carpenter from Riga, in the Soviet Republic of Latvia. He has been here six years. He told me of his having to force himself to relinquish the "luxury" of reading books in Russian or Latvian so he could begin to read books in English. And the books he was able to read in English were not of a complexity to satisfy him. But he was not going back to Riga.

14   Beyond any question of pedagogy there is the simple fact that a language gets learned as it gets used, fills one's mouth, one's mind, with the new names for things.

15   The civil rights movement of the 1960s taught Americans to deal with forms of discrimination other than economic—racial, sexual. We forget class. We talk about bilingual education as an ethnic issue; we forget to notice that the program mainly touches the lives of working-class immigrant children. Foreign-language acquisition is one thing for the upper-class child in a convent school learning to curtsy. Language acquisition can only seem a loss for the ghetto child, for the new language is psychologically awesome, being, as it is, the language of the bus driver and Papa's employer. The child's difficulty will turn out to be psychological more than linguistic because what he gives up are symbols of home.

PAIN AND GUILT

16   I was that child! I faced the stranger's English with pain and guilt and fear. Baptized to English in school, at first I felt myself drowning—the ugly sounds forced down my throat—until slowly, slowly (held in the tender grip of my teachers), suddenly the conviction took; English was my language to use.

17   What I yearn for is some candor from those who speak about bilingual education. Which of its supporters dares speak of the price a child pays—the price of adulthood—to make the journey from a working-class home into a middle-class schoolroom? The

real story, the silent story of the immigrant child's journey is one of embarrassments in public; betrayal of all that is private; silence at home; and at school the hand tentatively raised.

Bilingual enthusiasts bespeak an easier world. They seek a linguistic solution to a social dilemma. They seem to want to believe that there is an easy way for the child to balance private and public, in order to believe that there is some easy way for themselves. 18

Ten years ago, I started writing about the ideological implications of bilingual education. Ten years from now some newspaper may well invite me to contribute another Sunday supplement essay on the subject. The debate is going to continue. The bilingual establishment is now inside the door. Jobs are at stake. Politicians can only count heads; growing numbers of Hispanics will insure the compliance of politicians. 19

Publicly, we will continue the fiction. We will solemnly address this issue as an educational question, a matter of pedagogy. But privately, Hispanics will still seek from bilingual education an admission from the gringo that Spanish has value and presence. Hispanics of middle class will continue to seek the romantic assurance of separateness. Experts will argue. Dark-eyed children will sit in the classroom. Mute. 20

Food Pets Die For

Ann N. Martin

Pets in pet food? No, you say? Be assured that this is happening. Rendered companion animals are just another source of protein used in both pet foods and livestock feeds. 1

Rendering is a cheap, viable means of disposal. Pets are mixed with other material from slaughterhouse facilities that has been condemned for human consumption—rotten meat from supermarket shelves, restaurant grease and garbage, "4-D" (dead, 2

Rejected

diseased, dying and disabled) animals, roadkill and even zoo animals [Summer '96 *EIJ*].

3   In 1990, *San Francisco Chronicle*, reporter John Eckhouse wrote a two-part exposé on the rendering of companion animals in California. While the pet food companies vehemently denied that this was happening, a rendering plant employee told Eckhouse that "it was common practice for his company to process dead pets into products sold to pet food manufacturers."

4   Eckhouse's informant, upset that some of the most disturbing information was left out of the *Chronicle* article, subsequently brought his story to *Earth Island Journal*. (After the *Journal* published this insider's extensive report ["The Dark Side of Recycling," Fall 1990], the author placed a frantic call to the *Journal* to say that he was "going underground" because he feared for his safety.)

A SEARCH FOR THE TRUTH

5   I had always assumed that deceased pets were either buried or cremated. I had never heard of rendering. In early 1992, I decided to find out what was happening to the euthanized pets in London, Ontario.

6   Veterinary clinics advised me that dead pets were incinerated by a local disposal company. After hearing U.S. horror stories, I was skeptical. I obtained the name of the company that was picking up the pets, a dead-stock removal operation. Classified as "recollectors," these companies—along with "receiving plants," "brokers," and "rendering plants"—are licensed by Canada's Ministry of Agriculture.

7   I asked the ministry how the recollector disposed of the dogs and cats that it picked up. Two months later, I received a letter along with a document from the dead-stock removal company. This document, addressed to the investigator, was stamped with the warning that the information in the document was "not to be made known to any other agency or person without the written permission of the Chief Investigator."

8   Small wonder. The document confirmed that dead pets were, in fact, disposed of by rendering (unless cremation was "specially

requested" and "paid [for] . . . by their owners or by the veterinary
clinic").

The dead animals were shipped to a broker located about 300 ₉
miles away who sold the bodies to a rendering plant in Quebec.
When I contacted the rendering plant, the owner admitted that
cats and dogs were rendered along with livestock and roadkill."Do pet food companies purchase this rendered material?" I
asked. Again, his reply was, "Yes."

I was numb. How had this barbaric practice gone undetected ₁₀
all these years?

When I advised the veterinarians in my city about what was ₁₁
happening, most of them immediately ceased using the dead-
stock company and began using the local humane society where
the animals are cremated.

In the United States and Canada, the rendering of companion ₁₂
animals is not illegal. Millions of pets are disposed of by rendering each year. According to the Eckhouse article, an employee and
ex-employee of Sacramento Rendering, a plant in California,
stated that their company "rendered somewhere between 10,000
and 30,000 pounds of dogs and cats a day out of a total of 250,000
to 500,000 pounds of cattle, poultry, butcher shop scraps and other
material." The rendering plant in Quebec was rendering 11 tons of
dogs and cats per week—from one province alone.

THE SITUATION IN THE U.S.

If this was the case in Canada, I wondered if the U.S. government ₁₃
was aware of what was happening?

The Food and Drug Administration's Center for Veterinary ₁₄
Medicine (CVM) responded to my query regarding the disposal of
pets, stating: "In recognizing the need for disposal of a large number of unwanted pets in this country, CVM has not acted to specifically prohibit the rendering of pets. However, that is not to say that
the practice of using this material in pet food is condoned by CVM."

The U.S. Department of Agriculture's (USDA) Food Safety and ₁₅
Inspection Services (FSIS) informed me that dog and cat cadavers
are excluded as an ingredient in pet foods under FSIS regulations.

forgiven.

But, when I asked the USDA if it could provide me with a list of the companies that were using this inspection service, I was told that only two small facilities were licensed for this service and neither had subscribed to the service for four years.

16   Pet food companies advertise that only quality meats are being used in their products. As of 1996, however, not one of the major pet food companies was using the USDA's inspection service.

WHAT'S IN THE CAN?

17   Television commercials and magazine advertisements for pet food would have us believe that the meats, grains, and fats used in these foods could grace our dining tables. Over seven long years, I have been able to unearth information about what actually is contained in most commercial pet food. My initial shock has turned to anger as I've realized how little consumers are told about the actual contents of pet food.

18   Animal slaughterhouses strip the flesh and send the remains—heads, feet, skin, toenails, hair, feathers, carpal and tarsal joints, and mammary glands—to rendering plants. Also judged suitable for rendering: Animals who have died on their way to slaughter; cancerous tissue or tumors and worm-infested organs; injection sites, blood clots, bone splinters or extraneous matter; contaminated blood; stomach and bowels.

19   At the rendering plant, slaughterhouse material, restaurant and supermarket refuse (including Styrofoam trays and Shrink-wrap), dead-stock, roadkill, and euthanized companion animals are dumped into huge containers. A grinding machine slowly pulverizes the entire mess. After it is chipped or shredded, it is cooked at temperatures between 220 F and 270 F (104.4 to 132.2 C) for 20 minutes to one hour. The grease or tallow that rises to the top is used as a source of animal fat in pet foods. The remaining material is put into a press where the moisture is squeezed out to produce meat and bone meal.

20   The Association of American Feed Control Officials describes "meat meal" as the rendered product from mammal tissue exclusive of blood, hair, hoof, hide, trimmings, manure, stomach, and

rumen (the first stomach of a cud-chewing animal) contents—except in such amounts as may occur unavoidably in "good processing" practices. In his article, "Animal Disposal: Fact and Fiction," David C. Cooke asks, "Can you imagine trying to remove the hair and stomach contents from 600,000 tons of dogs and cats prior to cooking them?"

DRUGS, METAL, PESTICIDES

Pet food labels only provide half the story. Labels do not indicate   21
the hidden hazards that lurk in most pet food. Hormones, pesticides, pathogens, heavy metals, and drugs are just a few of the hidden contaminants.

Sodium pentobarbital and Fatal Plus™ are barbiturates used   22
to euthanize companion animals. When animals eat pet food that has gone through the rendering process, it is likely that they are ingesting one of these euthanizing drugs.

Almost 50 percent of the antibiotics manufactured in the United   23
States are dumped into animal feed, according to the 1996 Consumer Alert brochure, "The Dangers of Factory Farming." Pigs, cows, veal calves, turkeys, and chickens are continually fed antibiotics (primarily penicillin and tetracycline) in an attempt to eradicate the many ills that befall factory-farmed animals—pneumonia, intestinal disease, stress, rhinitis, e-coli infections and mastitis.

While this high-level application of antibiotics means millions   24
of dollars for the pharmaceutical companies, the U.S. Centers for Disease Control, National Resources Defense Council and the U.S. Food and Drug Administration (FDA) all warn that these "levels of antibiotics and other contaminants in commercially raised meat constitute a serious threat to the health of the consumer."

Zinc, copper, and iron are listed on most pet food labels. But   25
the metals in pet foods that do *not* need to be listed on the label include: Silver, beryllium, cadmium, bismuth, cobalt, manganese, barium, molybdenum, nickel, lead, strontium, vanadium, phosphorus, titanium, chromium, aluminum, selenium, and tungsten.

The U.S. FDA and Health and Welfare Canada would be very   26
concerned if the level of lead found in pet food were found in the

human food chain. For the dog food I had tested, for example, a dog ingesting 15 ounces would receive .43 to 2.4 mg of lead per day. Three mg per day is considered hazardous for a child. But when it comes to pet food, no testing is undertaken by state officials for heavy metals, pathogens, pesticides or drugs.

27   Although the pet food industry is not regulated in the United States and Canada, we as consumers have been lulled into believing that government and voluntary organizations are overseeing every ingredient stuffed into a container of pet food. What is required is government-enforced regulation of the industry. Only state legislatures can turn the tide, but it will be a long and difficult battle to persuade our representatives to take up the fight.

28   In the meantime, let the buyer beware!

1997

Next Time You Are Sick, You'd Better Go to the Vet . . .

The Nature of Wellness

The following selection appeared originally as the text of a full-page ad paid for by The Nature of Wellness, a not-for-profit organization.

Crazy, isn't it?

1   If you are reading this, it is because you found the headline totally ridiculous, absurd or both. And you are absolutely right. It is absurd. How can anyone possibly believe that a veterinarian who

2   treats dogs and cats can cure *human* diseases? Ridiculous.

        But, unfortunately, millions of Americans have been misled into believing that cures for *human* diseases can be found by conducting experiments on different species of healthy *animals*—ani-

3   mals that are totally different not only from humans *but also from each other*. Equally ridiculous and totally illogical.

Written by Javier B. Burgos of The Nature of Wellness, copyright 1996, *www. animalresearch.org*.

If it were true that cures for human diseases could be found by 4 experimenting on animals, your going to the vet when feeling sick wouldn't be such a bad idea. In fact, it would be a darn good idea. And our headline wouldn't be so crazy after all.

But, you see, it has to be one or the other. Either human 5 medicine *cannot* be based on veterinary medicine—in which case animal experimentation is an obvious medical and scientific impossibility—or else, you'd better make an appointment with your local vet next time you need glasses or your appendix taken out.

This madness is costing us plenty. Our health is in a state of 6 collapse because no cures can be found by biomedical research and pharmaceutical testing that base human medicine on veterinary medicine. Little wonder that the "miracle cures" and "medical breakthroughs" that are always "just around the corner" never materialize. Our environment is being systematically destroyed by thousands of pesticides and toxicants that, no matter how destructive, are routinely and conveniently found "safe" based on invalid animal tests.

Consequently, our economic survival is also at stake. In 1995 7 alone, the United States spent over 1.4 trillion dollars—a figure that is growing exponentially—on what is euphemistically called "health care."

It is time to bury the decaying remains of a medicine based on 8 the medieval ritual of animal experimentation. It is time to stop the latest mind-boggling absurdities such as animal-to-human bone marrow and organ transplantation and genetic manipulation. It's time to usher in the medicine of the 21st century. A medicine based on *prevention, clinical research* and, above all, logic and common sense.

We offer true hope. After all, our way, you won't have to get 9 distemper shots.

We invite all Americans to join in a most constructive campaign, 10 aimed at ending animal experimentation—the most horrifying crime ever committed against both human and nonhuman animals. Your tax-deductible donation is urgently needed. Thank you for caring.

1997

Permissions Acknowledgments

Angelou, Maya, "Grandmother's Victory" from *I Know Why The Caged Bird Sings* by Maya Angelou. Copyright © 1969 and renewed 1997 by Maya Angelou. Reprinted by permission of Random House, Inc.

Baldwin, James, Excerpted from "Fifth Avenue, Uptown" by James Baldwin. Collected in *Nobody Knows My Name*, © 1960, copyright renewed. Reprinted by arrangement with the James Baldwin Estate.

Bloom, Alice, "On a Greek Holiday" by Alice Bloom. Reprinted by permission from *The Hudson Review*, Vol. XXXVI, No. 3 (Autumn 1983). Copyright © 1983 by Alice Bloom.

Britt, Suzanne, "Neat People vs. Sloppy People" from *Show and Tell* by Suzanne Britt. Copyright © 1982 by Suzanne Britt. Reprinted by permission of the author.

Buckley, William F., Jr., "Why Don't We Complain?" by William F. Buckley, Jr. Copyright 1960 by Esquire. Renewed. Reprinted by permission of The Wallace Literary Agency, Inc.

Burgos, Javier B., text from ad, "Next Time You Are Sick, You'd Better Go to the Vet . . ." by Javier B. Burgos of The Nature of Wellness, as appeared in *The Washington Post*, March 14, 1996, p. 5. Reprinted by permission of the author.

Camus, Albert, "The Myth of Sisyphus" from *The Myth of Sisyphus and Other Essays* by Albert Camus, trans., J. O'Brien. Copyright © 1955 by Alfred A. Knopf, Inc. Reprinted by permission of the publisher.

Catton, Bruce, "Grant and Lee: A Study in Contrasts" from *The American Story* by Bruce Catton. Copyright U.S. Capitol Historical Society, all rights reserved. Reprinted by permission.

Cousins, Norman, From *Anatomy of an Illness as Perceived by the Patient: Reflections on Healing and Regeneration* by Norman Cousins. Copyright © 1979 by W. W. Norton & Company, Inc. Reprinted by permission of W. W. Norton & Company, Inc.

Dabney, Virginia Bell, "The Day the Fire Came" from *Once There Was A Farm* by Virginia Bell Dabney. Copyright © 1990 by Virginia Bell Dabney. Reprinted by permission of Random House, Inc.

Simeti, Mary Taylor, From *On Persephone's Island* by Mary Taylor Simeti. Copyright © 1986 by Mary Taylor Simeti. Reprinted by permission of Alfred A. Knopf, Inc.

Sontag, Susan, "Women's Beauty: Put Down or Power Source?" by Susan Sontag. Copyright © 1975 by Susan Sontag. Reprinted by permission of Farrar, Straus & Giroux, Inc.

Steele, Shelby, "White Guilt" by Shelby Steele, first published in *The American Scholar*, Autumn 1990. Copyright © 1990 by Shelby Steele. Reprinted by permission of Carol Mann Agency.

Steinem, Gloria, "Erotica and Pornography" by Gloria Steinem, *Ms.* magazine, November 1978. © 1978 by Gloria Steinem. Reprinted by permission of the author.

Svitil, Kathy A., "Nubian Diet Revealed At Last" by Kathy A. Svitil/ © 1995. Reprinted with permission of *Discover Magazine*.

Tannen, Deborah. "Talk in the Intimate Relationship, His and Hers" from *That's Not What I Meant* by Deborah Tannen, Ph.D. Copyright © 1986 by Deborah Tannen, Ph.D. Reprinted by permission of William Morrow & Company, Inc.

Toth, Susan Allen, "Cinematypes" by Susan Allen Toth. Reprinted by permission of the author.

Viorst, Judith, "The Truth About Lying" by Judith Viorst originally appeared in *Redbook*. Copyright © 1981 by Judith Viorst. Reprinted by permission of Lescher & Lescher, Ltd.

Walker, Alice. "Am I Blue?" from *Living By the Word: Selected Writings 1973–1987*, copyright © 1986 by Alice Walker, reprinted by permission of Harcourt Brace & Company.

Wallace, Mike, "The Press Needs a National Monitor" by Mike Wallace from *The Wall Street Journal*, December 18, 1996. Reprinted with permission of *The Wall Street Journal* and Mike Wallace, Senior Correspondent, CBS News, 60 Minutes. © 1996 Dow Jones & Company, Inc. All rights reserved.

Whitehead, Barbara Defoe, "Where Have All the Parents Gone" by Barbara Defoe Whitehead from *New Perspectives Quarterly*, Vol. 7, Winter 1990. © by The Center for the Study of Democratic Institutions. Reprinted by permission of The Center and Blackwell Publishers, Inc.

Woolf, Virginia, "The Death of the Moth" from *The Death of the Moth and Other Essays* by Virginia Woolf. Copyright 1942 by Harcourt Brace & Company and renewed 1970 by Marjorie T. Parsons, Executrix, reprinted by permission of the publisher.

Index

422